PRAISE FOR *TRAUMA-INFORMED JUSTICE IN CANADA*

"As an Indigenous scholar, I was engaged from the onset and value the accurate inclusion of Indigenous peoples' history and correlating problems in justice. The chapters are comprehensively sequenced, thought-provoking, and innovative. By problematizing a punitive approach and casting a critical gaze on structural violence, colonization, and patriarchal violence, the author creates an ethical space for affirming the principles and values of trauma-informed justice with the goal of restoration and holistic healing. In this manner, this book becomes an educational catalyst for anyone interested in informative critical reading, dialogue, and creating change."

—Kathy Absolon, MSW, PhD,
Coordinator of the Aboriginal Field of Study Program,
Faculty of Social Work,
Wilfrid Laurier University

"The author offers a compelling argument that challenges the reader to consider that community healing comes from unveiling the trauma and distress created by the very systems meant to support and protect our youth. This is a challenge to all members of our communities—but especially to the justice community—to build resiliency, foster healing, support accountability, and tear down the walls of injustice. This text reveals a refreshing and pivotal perspective of youth justice that offers a practical approach to reaching youth and addressing the limitations of our system."

—Cynthia Booth, MA,
Coordinator of the Community and Justice Services Program,
Cambrian College

Trauma-Informed Youth Justice in Canada

Trauma-Informed Youth Justice in Canada

A New Framework toward a Kinder Future

Judah Oudshoorn

Foreword by Howard Zehr

Canadian Scholars' Press
Toronto

Trauma-Informed Youth Justice in Canada: A New Framework toward a Kinder Future
by Judah Oudshoorn

First published in 2015 by
Canadian Scholars' Press Inc.
425 Adelaide Street West, Suite 200
Toronto, Ontario
M5V 3C1
www.cspi.org

Copyright © 2015 Judah Oudshoorn and Canadian Scholars' Press Inc. All rights reserved. No part of this publication may be photocopied, reproduced, stored in a retrieval system, or transmitted, in any form or by any means, electronic, mechanical, or otherwise, without the written permission of Canadian Scholars' Press Inc., except for brief passages quoted for review purposes. In the case of photocopying, a licence may be obtained from Access Copyright: One Yonge Street, Suite 1900, Toronto, Ontario, M5E 1E5, (416) 868-1620, fax (416) 868-1621, toll-free 1-800-893-5777, www.accesscopyright.ca.

Every reasonable effort has been made to identify copyright holders. CSPI would be pleased to have any errors or omissions brought to its attention.

Author royalties will be donated to the Sexual Assault Support Centre of Waterloo Region and Aboriginal Services at Conestoga College

Library and Archives Canada Cataloguing in Publication

Oudshoorn, Judah, 1977-, author
    Trauma-informed youth justice in Canada : a new framework toward a kinder future / Judah Oudshoorn ; foreword by Howard Zehr.

Includes bibliographical references and index.
Issued in print and electronic formats.
ISBN 978-1-55130-885-2 (bound). — ISBN 978-1-55130-887-6 (epub). — ISBN 978-1-55130-886-9 (pdf)

    1. Juvenile justice, Administration of—Canada. 2. Juvenile delinquents—Mental health--Canada. 3. Psychic trauma in adolescence. I. Title.

HV9108.O93 2015   364.360971   C2015-904674-2   C2015-904675-0

Text design by Brad Horning
Cover design by Gordon Robertson

Printed and bound in Canada by Marquis

Canada

To my partner, Cheryl J. Oudshoorn:

> *May your heart always be joyful;*
> *And may your song always be sung.*

To my children, Emery Peace and Selah Rain:

> *May you build a ladder to the stars,*
> *And climb on every rung.*[1]

Table of Contents

Acknowledgements — xi

Foreword *by Howard Zehr* — xiii

Introduction
Youth Justice that Heals — xvii

Chapter 1
A Framework for Trauma-Informed Youth Justice — 1

Chapter 2
A History of Youth Justice in Canada—1867 to 1984 — 21

Chapter 3
Youth Justice Today—1984 to the Present — 41

Chapter 4
Theory of Trauma-Informed Youth Justice—
   Why Do Young People Commit Crimes? — 65

Chapter 5
Understanding Individual Trauma — 85

Chapter 6
Collective Trauma, Colonialism, and Patriarchy — 107

Chapter 7
Prison, Risk, and Punishment—A Trauma-Inducing Justice System — 129

Chapter 8
Restorative Justice—The Worldview of Trauma-Informed Youth Justice — 155

Chapter 9
Youth Justice as Trauma-Informed Care — 181

Chapter 10
Trauma-Informed Prevention—Ending Cycles of Violence 205

Chapter 11
Victim-Centred Justice 227

Conclusion
Principles of Trauma-Informed Youth Justice 249

Notes 261

Selected References 297

Copyright Acknowledgements 319

Index 323

Acknowledgements

Thank you to Canadian Scholars' Press Inc. for partnering on this project. Thank you to Acquisitions Editor Laura Godsoe for believing in the idea of the book. Right from the get-go it was a pleasure to work with you. Thank you to editorial staff Andrea Gill, Natalie Garriga, Emma Johnson, and Martha Hunter for helping make the idea a reality. A special thank you to the peer reviewers for the incredibly useful feedback.

Thank you, Anna Humphrey for the stylistic edits: I imagine the work of an editor like that of a gardener who pulls weeds, but you helped the text bloom.

Thank you, Ruth Neustifter for the inspiration to share royalties.

Thank you to the contributors who have written valuable pieces: Kao Saechao, Josiah Thorogood, Julie Lalonde, Marion Evans, Joan Tuchlinsky, Arley Irvine, Myeengun Henry, Jennifer Robinson, and Abe Oudshoorn.

Thank you to Howard Zehr for writing a foreword. You inspire me. Your way of living—kind, generous, creative, hard working, and compassionate—is worthwhile to aspire to. Your work in the field of restorative justice has provided a framework for this book.

Thank you to Andrea Arthur-Brown at the Waterloo Region Sexual Assault Centre for coordinating a focus group of survivors to explore some elements of this work. I am indebted to this group for trusting me with their stories, and sharing their perspectives. Especially, thank you to Dianne Piluk who has also courageously shared her story with many of my students.

I am forever grateful to many family, friends, and colleagues who have taught me so much about life and justice. These relationships have really given shape to this book. My brothers, Joshua Jones, Daniel Oudshoorn, and Abe Oudshoorn have consistently been rocks in my life. My friends, Eric Noordam and Jennifer Davies make me smile. Jennifer Davies has taught me so much about restorative justice, and about being myself. Lowell Ewert and Wayne Morris: thank you for giving me an opportunity to teach. Tania Petrellis (Restorative Justice Division of the Correctional Service of Canada) and Eileen Henderson (Mennonite Central Committee, Circles of Support and Accountability): thank you for giving me a chance at doing restorative justice—both of you are true leaders. Marion Evans and Jennifer Robinson, my fun, intelligent, passionate, and compassionate colleagues in the Bachelor of Community and Criminal Justice program at Conestoga College, thanks for being so great! Other colleagues deserve a "shout out": Christine Lecompte, Renee Laframboise, and Veronica Mineyko, you're all awesome. It is a pleasure to work with you in the restorative justice field. To the many victims (survivors—especially Heather White) and offenders who have trusted me with their stories: I hope this book does you justice. To Myeengun Henry, and others in Indigenous communities across Turtle Island: I hope for an end to colonization, a renewed, mutually beneficial relationship between our peoples. Thank you to my mom, Cheryl O, and my mother-in-law, Joyce Smiley, for sharing and role-modelling strength through kindness to my girls. Thank you, most of all, to my children, Emery and Selah, and my partner, Cheryl, for making life meaningful and fun.

Foreword[1]
Howard Zehr

A warning: this is not the usual book foreword. Instead, I am offering you a brief exercise, a puzzle.

Below are photographic portraits of two people. I encourage you to gaze at the photos, interact with these people, and ask yourself three questions that I sometimes ask of my photo students, in this order: (1) What do you see? (2) What do you feel? (3) What do you think?

Next, imagine who each of these people is. When you have done that, turn to the next page.

Gaye Morley

Conrad Moore

"A life sentence is a vacuum. Everything is sucked out of me, leaving me with nothing. I know I have to fight that. I have to create a whole world within myself and hopefully be able to spread that to those around me." —Gaye	"We've talked to the man who murdered Gerald and have had an opportunity to extend forgiveness to him, directly, in the face. We're forgiving the frightened young girl, the only witness. She came forward and said she had lied. But we're having a problem forgiving the judge and the system." —Conrad

Gaye Morley once worked in the mental health field. She attended the same upscale gardening school that my wife did. Now Gaye is serving a life sentence for murder. In Pennsylvania, unlike Canada, a life sentence is actually for life—with little chance of release.

Conrad Moore's stepson, like many young Black men in the United States, was wrongly convicted and imprisoned. His sentence was overturned and while waiting for the prosecutor ("Crown" in Canada) to decide whether he would be retried, he was murdered.

Gaye is an "offender." Conrad is a "victim" or "survivor." Do these facts surprise you? In what ways are they different than what you imaged? I would guess that they are in fact different than you expected. Also, as you might imagine, there is much more to both of them than the terms victim or offender suggest.

I share these portraits and stories for two reasons. First, as the author of this book suggests later, it is important for those considering work in the justice field to be aware of our own biases, assumptions, and stereotypes. And second, it is important for us to engage with real people and real stories, not simply categories of people and stereotypes, and not simply academic abstractions. Unfortunately, much of what we hear in the news and from politicians is the latter. In this book, you will encounter not only theories and research but also stories—including Judah's, the author's, own story. I applaud Judah's willingness to share and to speak in first person unlike so much academic writing that seeks to give the impression of objectivity by hiding behind the third person.

Both of the two individuals introduced here have experienced substantial trauma, an area that is fortunately receiving increasing attention, and a theme of this book: trauma that gives rise to wrongdoing, trauma that results from wrongdoing, trauma that results from punishment, trauma that, once experienced in prison, may result in more wrongdoing. For Gaye, the sudden immersion from a middle class life into the culture of prison was itself highly traumatic.

On that theme, I would like to introduce another person. Marie Scott ("Mechie") entered prison at a very young age, the result of a murder in which she was an accessory. Not surprisingly, she experienced significant trauma as a child. In her words, "I had nightmares when I was a child, because I was sexually and physically abused. Sometimes I'd wake up and couldn't tell the nightmares from reality."

Foreword

Mechie and daughter Hope in 1993

Marie's parents spent time in prison, and her son was in prison for a time. Working from her prison cell—she too has a life sentence—her passion is educating parents and the public about the situation of children who have parents in prison. As she observes,

> I was serving time with a woman who had only 10 years to do. Twenty years later, some kid comes up to me and says, "Aren't you Ms. Mechie? My mom told me to look you up when I got here." At first I was glad to see someone else's child, like they dropped by my home to visit. Then it occurred to me just how tragic a scene this is. Now it happens all the time—I'm forever looking out for somebody's kid here in prison.
>
> I see three generations of mothers, all in prison at once. For those who lack clear evidence of intergenerational incarceration—here we all are.

A focus on trauma is only one of many reasons this book is so important. Rarely has a textbook on youth crime and justice presented as holistic an approach to understanding the causes and healthy responses to wrongdoing as this one does. In fact, it may be the most comprehensive and yet accessible book you will read on youth justice.

There is much I could say in support of the themes of this book, but I'll get out of the way and let Judah—my friend and former student—take you on this journey. If we can listen to what he has to say and implement what he suggests, I believe we will live in much healthier and more just communities.

Howard Zehr, PhD
Distinguished Professor of Restorative Justice
Co-Director, Zehr Institute for Restorative Justice
Center for Justice and Peacebuilding
Eastern Mennonite University
Harrisonburg, Virginia USA

Introduction: Youth Justice that Heals

"Do your little bit of good where you are; it's those little bits of good put together that overwhelm the world."

—Desmond Tutu

Research consistently shows that as many as 90 percent of young offenders have experienced some sort of trauma in their childhood.[1] From domestic violence, to neglect, to poverty, to sexual abuse, to colonization (in the case of Indigenous peoples), these youth are struggling to cope with overwhelming experiences. The impacts of trauma on young people often include mental health, substance abuse, and relational challenges, which at times bring them into conflict with the law. Enter the youth justice system, focused on punishing criminal behaviours. What happens when we punish with minimal regard for the context that influences crime? Evidence suggests that contact with the justice system contributes toward youth reoffending in the future more than it discourages crime.[2] A youth justice system premised on punishment doesn't work. Instead, it adds more trauma.

It's easy enough to be a critic of a flawed, if not broken, youth justice system. After all, it's not difficult to be against what isn't working. In this book, I'll write about some important critiques of the current youth justice system. However, this book is also *for* something—a sensible alternative: a trauma-informed approach to youth justice. If trauma is the primary underlying cause for why young offenders commit crime, then youth justice must take a different approach. We need a system of youth justice that *heals*.

Trauma-informed youth justice doesn't mean that we eliminate consequences for harmful behaviours, nor that we stop holding young offenders accountable. It means that we carefully ask what has contributed to the choices these young people have made. In *Trauma-Informed Youth Justice in Canada*, meaningful consequences for young offenders mean:

- Acknowledging harms they have committed, while
- Supporting them through their own challenges.

Howard Zehr, an innovator in the field of restorative justice, says that crime is something that hurts people and relationships.[3] From a restorative justice perspective a person doesn't face consequences because they broke the law, but because they have caused harm to people and relationships. This moves offenders toward taking responsibility for their actions, rather than simply "doing time." Notice, though, that the second bullet point is about support. Accountability happens best when we help offenders to heal from their own trauma. Trauma-informed youth justice works toward *healing* offenders.

Some might be skeptical that a shift from punishment toward restorative justice will lose sight of victims. However, with its focus on addressing harms, restorative justice actually puts victims' needs at the forefront of youth justice processes. In his *Little Book of Restorative Justice*, Zehr cites the following as key questions to ask after a crime has been committed:

- Who has been hurt?
- What do victims need?
- Whose obligation is it to meet these needs?[4]

The machinery of current youth justice practices is dramatically skewed toward offenders. Billions of dollars are spent on policing, courts, and corrections—often at the expense of victims.

Whether the crime was a property crime or an assault, victims often experience crime as traumatic. For this reason, a new orientation in youth justice is needed. Victims need to heal. Trauma-informed youth justice works toward *healing* victims.

Interventions are only one side of a trauma-informed youth justice story. The other side is prevention. Two significant causes of trauma in the lives of young offenders are patriarchal male violence and the colonization of Indigenous peoples. Patriarchy must be dismantled. Canada must be decolonized. Trauma-informed youth justice works toward *healing* communities.

OUTLINE OF *TRAUMA-INFORMED YOUTH JUSTICE IN CANADA*

Chapter 1 sets the stage for the book by outlining my thesis: a trauma-informed approach to youth justice will make communities safer and more livable for all. In this opening chapter, I establish a set of values (critical thinking, human dignity, participation, peace, a holistic approach to addressing crime, and social change) for trauma-informed youth justice. I also argue that a restorative justice framework is the best way to put these values into practice.

Chapter 2 describes the history of youth justice in Canada from pre-Confederation until 1984, told in parallel with a history of the "Indian" residential school (IRS) system. (I put Indian in quotations here because this label was imposed on Indigenous peoples.) The two histories—of youth justice and the IRS system—cannot be separated. One speaks to the historical rationale for a youth justice system generally, while the other provides context for why Indigenous youth are overrepresented in the youth justice system today.

Chapter 3 tells a story of the youth justice system from 1984 to the present day. The focus is on legislation, the ongoing politicization of youth crime, as well as on how those in power tend to criminalize those on the margins of society.

Chapter 4 offers a number of theoretical explanations for why youth commit crime. A history of explanations—from criminological to biological, from sociological to psychological—is given. Ultimately, this text puts forward a trauma-informed theory: Young people mostly commit crimes because they have experienced trauma. A cycle of violence theory explains this further.

Chapter 5 defines trauma and discusses how it affects individuals emotionally, cognitively, behaviourally, physiologically (the brain and mental health), relationally (attachment), and in their ability to cope (addictions).

Chapter 6 shines a spotlight on two root causes of young people committing crimes: colonialism and patriarchal male violence. The focus is on better understanding how collective trauma affects entire communities and trickles down to influence the behaviour of individuals.

Chapter 7 puts a critical lens on current youth justice practices. Why is it that they tend to make things worse? Prison, risk assessments, and punishment are all problematized.

Chapter 8 functions as the turning point of the text, from analysis and critique toward finding a way forward. It describes restorative justice as a framework and describes a set of practices for trauma-informed youth justice.

Chapter 9 talks about trauma-informed care for victims, offenders, and communities. The focus of trauma-informed care is on increasing individual and community resilience, while also establishing safe, healthy relationships for trauma survivors.

Chapter 10 is about trauma-informed prevention. The first half argues in favour of decolonization: the responsibility of settlers to honour treaties, implement youth justice practices that are pluralistic, and to learn from Indigenous peoples. The second half looks at ways to dismantle patriarchy and put an end to male violence.

Chapter 11 is about victims. The central question is, "How can we make criminal justice more victim-centred?" I describe how victims are traditionally sidelined in justice processes and how the victim movement in Canada has counteracted this. The chapter ends with words from survivors of sexual abuse, who were generous enough to provide input for this book.

The conclusion establishes five principles for trauma-informed youth justice. I suggest that we are working toward trauma-informed youth justice when:

- Principle 1: A set of shared values gives shape to practices.
- Principle 2: Indigenous peoples and women are in leadership roles in order to decolonize and dismantle patriarchy.
- Principle 3: Restorative justice is the framework.
- Principle 4: Trauma-informed care and prevention guides practices.
- Principle 5: Justice processes are victim-centred.

PURPOSES FOR WRITING: MY RESPONSIBILITY AND INTENT

> "If you want to make peace with your enemy, you have to work with your enemy. Then he becomes your partner."
>
> —Nelson Mandela

> "Feminist education for critical consciousness is rooted in the assumption that knowledge and critical thought done in the classroom should inform our habits of being and ways of living outside the classroom."
>
> —bell hooks[5]

Some traditional academics might criticize this work because I choose sides. I try to identify what is wrong and argue for it to be replaced by what is right. I do this purposefully. I want to be clear about where I stand. Many traditional academics take a position of (assumed) neutrality, or objectivity. They present multiple sides of data or debates without adopting a position. From my perspective, however, neutrality is impossible. This traditional way of doing research does in fact choose a side. Neutrality in the face of oppression, including in academia, is to choose the side of the oppressor. Youth justice in Canada is not neutral. It is oppressive. Therefore, I choose to stand against oppression and for something better.

My purposes for writing this book are fairly straightforward: I want the youth justice system to be more humane. I want victims to be given proper spaces to heal. I want offenders to be accountable and to, likewise, be given proper spaces to heal. I want communities to live more peacefully, devoid of violence and injustice. I'm increasingly convinced that as a white, heterosexual male, and as a settler on Indigenous lands, I have an obligation because of my privileges to work toward justice and fairness for all. My intended audience for this book includes those like me—people who come from positions of power and privilege. We must do better. It is also my hope that this book will inspire practicing and aspiring justice professionals, child and youth workers, social service workers, and criminologists to adopt a trauma-informed approach to youth justice.

I hope this work can function as a conduit to improving youth justice. I hope that, as you read it, you'll ask yourself: Who am I in relation to my community? How does a trauma-informed approach to youth justice fit (or not fit) with my value system? How can I use this book to make my community better?

I'm interested in developing character among my students and readers, perhaps even more than in developing intelligence. What youth justice really needs is people of integrity who are willing to take responsibility for their actions, and who are willing to treat all people with dignity and respect. Ultimately, my hope is for critical and creative action in youth justice. Trauma-informed youth justice is a new framework that can move us toward a kinder future.

1 | A Framework for Trauma-Informed Youth Justice

"... all writers, including writers of dictionaries, are propagandists."
—Derrick Jensen[1]

THE CANADIAN JUSTICE SYSTEM IS FAILING OUR YOUTH

Youth justice in Canada isn't working very well. In fact, I'd go so far as to say that it's broken. The net of criminal justice tends to catch poor, mentally challenged, and Indigenous youth more often than anyone else—essentially, those who are on the margins of society and who have experienced some sort of trauma or victimization themselves. Subsequently, the system ensnares these young people so tightly that they often become further damaged, making them more likely to reoffend. Victims, meanwhile, are dissatisfied; their needs often ignored. Communities, too, are in need of repair in the aftermath of crime.

There are many reasons behind the failure of the current youth justice system. (We'll explore these in detail in the chapters that follow.) These include the punitive nature of the criminal justice system, an overemphasis on risk assessment, and broader social problems like the colonization of Indigenous peoples and patriarchal male violence. By becoming trauma-informed, youth justice can counter what isn't working and instead provide a system of justice that's focused on healing, resilience, and hope. The purpose of this book is to tell a story of the youth justice system's flaws and to propose ways we can mend it.

But, reader beware: As American author Derrick Jensen writes in *Endgame* (a book about the destructive nature of the so-called progress of civilization on communities and the environment), all writers are propagandists—even the writers of textbooks who often falsely claim to be objective. In other words, I have an agenda. It is based on the values, worldviews, and theories that have shaped my work as a restorative justice mediator and as a professor of criminal justice. This book is my propaganda, and in many ways, my story.

It's a story that lies between the way the justice system currently stands and my vision for how it could be improved. It's also a story that runs counter to some predominant myths: that punishment resolves crime; that victims are entirely vengeful and a tough-on-crime approach is the best way to meet their needs; and that offenders alone (apart from the society that created them) are responsible for their crimes. Each of these powerful myths influences the current state of youth justice in Canada and serves a powerful, white, male majority over other people—especially those who are on the margins of society. This book will explain why this is and will challenge you to see crime, young offenders, and victims in a different way.

I will also propose that the punitive culture of the youth justice system does a disservice to youth. To punish is to inflict pain. When we punish, we're simply adding more hurt to young people who often behave as they do because they're already hurting. Furthermore, punishment gets in the way of accountability, and can prevent offenders from coming to truly understand the impacts of their actions. It also fails to meet the needs of victims, who are sidelined and made witnesses to their own experiences. In essence, punishment gets in the way of creating resilient, inclusive, and hopeful communities. What is needed instead is a movement of social responsibility, a society that recognizes that crime and violence can be prevented. But, in order to achieve this, we must first address issues of structural violence, such as the colonization of Indigenous peoples, who are dramatically overrepresented in the youth justice system, and patriarchal violence, which is at the root of so many young offenders' actions.

In this chapter, I will introduce what I believe are the core values of trauma-informed youth justice: critical thinking, human dignity, participation, peace, a holistic approach to addressing crime, and social change. Arising from these values is the worldview of **restorative justice**—an approach that takes a broad view of complex issues while creating a vision for a kinder future.

TRAUMA-INFORMED JUSTICE CAN CREATE SAFER, MORE LIVABLE COMMUNITIES

The main argument of this book is that a trauma-informed approach to youth justice will make communities safer and more livable for all. There are five cascading premises upon which this thesis stands: First, the majority of young people who commit crimes do so because of trauma they have experienced in their own lives. Second, in explaining why traumatized youth are at risk of coming into conflict with the law, it's important to understand how trauma affects people—specifically the brain, attachment, shame, and identity. Third, many of these traumas are collective (or intergenerational) traumas, like the colonization of Indigenous peoples by settler society, male violence, and domestic and sexual abuse. Also at play are traumas related to exposure to the justice system itself. That is, many young offenders are traumatized by their experiences in the criminal justice system, which can lead them to reoffend. Fourth, victims of crime are, at best, largely left unsatisfied by the justice system and, at worst, retraumatized by it. The fifth and final premise offers hope, however. It is that, by attending to youth justice through a trauma-informed lens, we can be more likely to hold offenders meaningfully accountable, allow offenders to heal, support victims in ways that help them to recover, prevent future harms from happening, and dismantle structures of violence. The sum total will be safer, more livable communities where everyone can belong.

A FEW DEFINITIONS

Trauma is any out-of-the-ordinary event that is experienced as overwhelming. There are two parts to trauma: first an incident (or ongoing incidents), second, an individual's experience of it. The latter will determine whether a person is traumatized or not. Trauma is different from stress. In the words of trauma expert Christine Courtois, it is "shocking, terrifying, and devastating to the victim, resulting in profoundly upsetting feelings of terror, shame, helplessness, and powerlessness."[2] Stress is often about growth, while trauma is a limiting experience. I'll comment further about the effects of trauma in later chapters, but for now it's important to understand that people who have been traumatized often live in fear and develop maladaptive coping mechanisms. Furthermore, trauma isn't limited to individuals; it can also be a collective experience. Poverty, colonialism, natural disasters, gender-based violence, and war can traumatize entire populations. This is important to remember when considering that many people who come into conflict with the law come from marginalized groups, with shared—or similar—experiences of trauma.

A **trauma-informed** approach means that we bring an awareness of the impacts of trauma to our work in youth justice. It also means that we shape interventions on principles of trauma-healing and restorative justice rather than on punishment. This requires justice processes to foster resilience in young people. The approach doesn't diminish accountability. Instead, it nests accountability within a context of support.

When people are traumatized, they are often disempowered and feel out of control. A trauma-informed approach creates safe spaces for young people to make healthy choices. Following a trauma, people typically feel alienated. A trauma-informed response considers how to decrease isolation and promote connections. Trauma often shatters meaning—how a person sees the world and how safe they feel in it. A trauma-informed approach establishes safety and provides opportunities for a young person to make sense of their reality.

A Vision for a Trauma-Informed Youth Justice System

- From ineffective punishments, toward meaningful accountability
- From powerlessness, toward choice and autonomy
- From isolation, toward connection and belonging
- From disorientation, toward meaning and hope
- From fear, toward safety and healing

A trauma-informed youth justice system prioritizes meaningful accountability, choice, autonomy, connection, belonging, hope, safety, and healing. It means reconsidering current justice practices. Are they adding to the trauma of young people, or are they moving youth toward resilience? What are the effects of an arrest on a young person? What about an emphasis on risk assessment? What about the court process? Incarceration? *Trauma-Informed Youth Justice in Canada* argues that many of these practices retraumatize youth, reinforce maladaptive coping strategies, and exacerbate how isolated youth already feel. What are the consequences of our justice consequences? What is the effect on community safety when justice means punishment? What is the effect on **recidivism**, the act of reoffending, when rehabilitation is individualized? A trauma-informed youth justice system takes responsibility for its interventions.

THE VALUES OF TRAUMA-INFORMED YOUTH JUSTICE

A 75-year-old silver maple stood in my old front yard. It was majestic, with a trunk too big to hug and branches and leaves that filled the street. Imagine trauma-informed youth justice as that kind of tree. The leaves are the ways to practise it—to put it into action. Each of these leaves (or practices) is connected to various branches (or theories), which in turn grow from a trunk—which represents a particular worldview. Every part of the tree is essential; however, a tree cannot stand without roots. In a trauma-informed approach, the roots represent values. Values give shape to a way of seeing the world, which in turn sprouts theoretical branches and practical leaves.

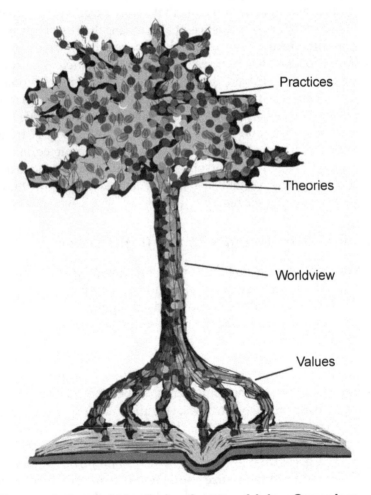

Figure 1.1: Trauma-Informed Youth Justice as a Living Organism

Often in academia, the starting point for many conversations is theory—an explanation for why something is the way it is. Theories are more than guesses; they're hypotheses that have been tested. However, when talking about trauma-informed justice, it's better to begin at the roots, with values. After all, every theory grows from a particular way of seeing the world, which encompasses a set of values or core beliefs about what is most important. I'm not trying to articulate a trauma-informed approach as a metatheory—an explanation of everything—in criminal justice. Rather, I see it as one tree in a forest of possibility. The core values of a trauma-informed framework are critical thinking, human dignity, participation, peace, a holistic approach to addressing crime, and social change.

The First Core Value: Critical Thinking

The first value—and the starting place for effective justice—is critical thinking. Trauma-informed youth justice should be reasoned and well thought out. Although logic is part of this, our thinking should be more holistic. We come to know things as much through our emotions, senses, and relationships as through our intellects. Opaskwayk Cree researcher Shawn Wilson highlights this in *Research Is Ceremony: Indigenous Research Methods*. He states that the intent of his work in academia is to be relationally accountable.[3] Ideas cannot be separate from the people or communities from which they come.[4] Thus, neither can the researcher.[5] Anishinaabe/English Indigenous researcher Kathleen E. Absolon affirms this perspective in *Kaandossiwin: How We Come to Know*. From her perspective, knowledge is relational. It means being accountable to others in a web of relationship.[6] This is why I feel that the true test of whether or not my book is successful will be whether or not it improves the lives of victims, offenders, and communities.

The Second Core Value: Human Dignity

The second value of trauma-informed youth justice is human dignity. I've learned a lot from the people I've worked with. A few years ago, I counselled men who had been violent toward their partners and children. My goal was to help them learn how to make healthy, respectful choices. One young man in particular stands out in my mind. He was homeless. He was particularly brutal to the women in his life—controlling them through violence and psychological torture. Part of his probation order required that he see me for counselling. Our sessions were always a little late in starting because he would have to remove his five jackets (it was winter) and he would want to show me his latest dumpster dive finds. His eyes gleamed whenever he thought he had something of value, and he always believed he had something of value.

Halfway through one of our first sessions he fell asleep. (My counselling sessions must have been riveting!) He'd told me earlier that, the night before, he had been removed from the lobby of a bank where he was sleeping, attempting to escape the cold. The police had given him a ticket. He'd shown it to me with no glint in his eyes. The money in the vault of that bank had rested peacefully, but he had not. As he took long, laboured sleeping breaths, I remember wondering what I should do. Should I wake him or let him sleep? Wasn't my responsibility to counsel him? What if someone knocked on the door and noticed that he was sleeping? In the end, I let him sleep, waking him up just before my next client arrived.

It's a tough story for me to tell. There are no heroes and no clear resolutions. This client scared me. He never threatened me personally, but I worried for the women in his life. His possessiveness and objectification were deeply troubling and his violent behaviour was ugly. At times, the things he'd told me kept me awake at night. During his few months in counselling, his girlfriend left him, sneaking away. I took my task of talking him through this very seriously. I knew from previous work experience and research that women are most at risk of violence when they leave a violent relationship.

The work of justice is complicated—very complicated. It's not enough to look at someone's own hurts, for example, whether they are homeless or living in poverty. We must also hold people accountable; helping them to face what they've done. We cannot always support people into changing. In spite of his circumstances, my client never missed a session. He claimed to have little regard for the justice system, yet he always came to see me, as he was required to do. I treated him with dignity, but I never put up with any of his excuses or justifications. When he'd try to get me to side with him against his girlfriend or when he'd attempt to justify his violent behaviour, I would challenge him. Over time, his excuses transformed into acknowledgement about what he called his "dark side." His rants changed into questions. "What would you do?" he would ask.

I've learned that if a young homeless man can show up on a bike, in the dead of winter, with five jackets and a backpack of treasures, to acknowledge his "dark side" to a relative stranger in a sterile counselling office, then society should consider going to similar lengths to acknowledge its dark side. I'm referring to the dark side of capitalism that allows some people to live in big, luxurious houses while others live on the street—the dark side that dehumanizes. A social movement promoting human dignity is needed. The challenge of trauma-informed youth justice is how to treat everyone—even those who have caused great harm—as we would want to be treated ourselves.

The Third Core Value: Participation

The third value of a trauma-informed framework is that justice must be participatory. How do we engage all voices in justice—especially the voices of those on the margins of society? In her work and research with homeless youth, Professor Jennifer Robinson has explored this question at length. In this case study, she explores her research approach: "methods from the margins."

Studying Youth Homelessness: Methods from the Margins
By Jennifer Robinson, Coordinator & Professor, Community and Criminal Justice, Conestoga College

Common understandings of "the homeless" often reflect negative stereotypes. Some people assume that homelessness is a personal choice, or the result of "bad" choices of an individual. Societal understanding of homelessness is further confounded when the person experiencing it is young. As Karabanow observes, youth who are homeless are understood as "public nuisances, or worse, criminals that warrant increased control and punishment."[7] These perceptions, he charges, evince a lack of "understanding of the root causes of homelessness,"[8] which often include abuse (physical and sexual) and neglect; family violence; substance abuse; mental health issues; poverty; bullying; homophobia; learning disabilities and school failure; and residency in foster care settings and institutional care facilities. These social stereotypes, Schissel charges, operate as an "oppressive mechanism" and further entrench the social exclusion of an already marginalized group.[9] Youth who experience homelessness often lack voice, or input, into policies and projects that focus on, or impact them. This is, I argue, because of two main factors: their marginal social locations and the traditional authority of positivism in social science research. In this overview, I suggest an alternative methodological approach to working with youth who experience homelessness. The aim of this alternative approach is to democratize the production of knowledge based on the lived experiences of marginal groups, such as youth who experience homelessness.

According to Karabanow, much of the current academic literature on youth who experience homelessness presents this diverse population as a stigmatized, exploited group that is in need of care and assistance. However, he reports that many studies frame their discussion of aid for youth within correctional or "law-and-order" approaches. Few opportunities are granted to youth to include their voices within such discussions. Certainly, youth are seldom consulted on what sorts of themes or topics researchers should examine, or what they regard as appropriate solutions to the intertwined problems of homelessness and poverty they face. This is a concern as it hampers youths' opportunity to express their ideas and have their concerns heard about the policies and mechanisms that directly impact them. Research to address homelessness should empower and provide a space for voice to a group of people "who otherwise might be silent."[10]

The social sciences have long been dominated by logical positivism—approaches that emphasize the importance of "objectivity" and favour methods that retain the maintenance of clear distance between researchers and "subjects," "establishing mastery over subjects demanding the absence of feelings, and enforcing the separateness of the knower from the known."[11] Kirby, Greaves, and Reid explain that positivism focuses on controlling physical/social environments and suggests that "truth" in the social world is available only through the pursuit of "objectivity" in structured research.[12] Further, these approaches to social research are "sanctioned on the established power relationship between the researcher and the researched."[13]

Such positivistic approaches quiet the voices of marginalized groups and order the structure of knowledge production. Lyon-Callo (2004) suggests that if researchers wish to eradicate social inequities, they should begin by trying to reduce hierarchical conditions and power dimensions in the research process.[14] Youth who have lived as "homeless" persons experience marginal social positions and are often subject to oppression, subordination, and powerlessness. They can be included in the research process in meaningful ways including, but not limited to, participatory approaches.

The aim of participatory research (PR) is to work "with" rather than "for" marginal groups. It seeks to legitimize the voice, experiences, and knowledge of those who have traditionally been cast as the "objects" or "subjects" of research. PR emphasizes the importance of researchers working in tandem with those who are impacted by a particular social issue and jointly striving for social action and social change.[15] A specific PR approach developed by Kirby and McKenna, "Methods from the Margins" (MFM), encourages the researcher to forge relationships with those they study; promotes the voice of participants as key founders of concepts, ideas, and project direction; and requires researchers to identify their own position and "conceptual baggage" in the research process.[16] All of these strategies are believed useful in the quest to incorporate the insights of marginalized groups in the production of knowledge on youth homelessness.

According to Kirby and McKenna, the ways in which knowledge and information are used are determined by privileged groups, such as academics and policy makers, whose claims to expertise are "credited" or who maintain positions that hold them as "credible" adjudicators/compilers of "truth."[17] Many individuals and groups are remote from the process of knowledge production; their views are neither solicited nor credited as authoritative. Youth who experience homelessness and share information about their social realities with researchers may be viewed as less "knowledgeable" about their experiences than those who study them. MFM emphasizes reciprocity, intersubjectivity and reflexivity, and seeks to redress this situation by encouraging those who are a focal inclusion in the research to share insights derived from lived experience and crediting them as experts.

Decades ago, Becker challenged social researchers to identify "whose side are we on?" Becker described a "hierarchy of credibility" in the production of knowledge.[18] He noted that in ranked groups, those who are positioned at the top, who possess power, such as academics, are believed capable of founding truths; those who occupy lower rankings, such as youth who experience homelessness, are seen as having incomplete or fragmented notions of the truth. Becker maintains that the ability to establish "truth" and "knowledge" are defined by such hierarchies, as is the right to speak and the right to be heard.[19]

Researchers possess tremendous power in the production of knowledge about those who are socially marginal. When researchers make the private worlds of marginalized people public through their writings, the researcher is the one who retains the power of representation.[20] Kirby et al. claim that voice and representation are pivotal in addressing power differentials in research.[21] They observe that "voice focuses more on the representing and writing than upon the process of problem formulation and data gathering. Voice is the struggle to determine how to present the author's self while simultaneously writing the respondents' accounts and representing their selves."[22] By critically assessing the positionality and social locations of researchers as well as those that they seek to investigate, the construction of voice and representation can be better

> contextualized in discussions of power relations. This also requires an open exchange of ideas and checking back with participants throughout the research process. This approach works to include and extend the voices of the marginal by deliberately enhancing their involvement in all stages of the research project, beginning with its design. Working within an empowerment framework can allow researchers to develop a more nuanced understanding of power and difference.[23] MFM offers an alternative approach to research. It presents opportunities to include the voices of youth who have experienced homelessness in meaningful ways, crediting their voices in the production of knowledge and "truth."

The Fourth Core Value: Peace

The fourth value of trauma-informed justice is peace. Peace is not just the absence of conflict. Rather, it is expressed in communities that are working to end violence in all its forms. My children have a book called *The Peace Book* written by Todd Parr. It's a collection of colourful pictures with different definitions of peace on each page. One picture shows a caterpillar wearing many pairs of shoes. The caption reads: "Peace is giving shoes to someone who needs them."[24] As a father of young children, my favourite is: "Peace is taking a nap," but the definition of peace Parr gives us that's most relevant to this textbook is this: "Peace is being who you are."[25] Imagine a world where all young people belong; where they can all be who they are.

One of the central ideas I'll present in this book is that crime is actually an issue of peace. That is, the most meaningful way to approach crime is by thinking about intervention and prevention as acts of peacebuilding. After all, criminal acts represent only a limited range of legally defined harms in society. There are other harms that don't fall into the category of criminal acts but that are arguably just as destructive to society. For example, consider the story of my homeless client above, which highlights the growing inequality of wealth in Canada. This too is harm. Increasingly, wealth is being concentrated in the hands of very few. Why isn't this considered criminal? By discussing crime as an issue of peace, we can look deeper at root causes and be sure that our interventions aren't simply exacerbating the problems we're trying to solve.

The United Nations describes the following four objectives for peacebuilding:

1. Address drivers and root causes (of conflict and violence).
2. Build institutions and capacities of individuals, communities and authorities to manage conflict and deliver services (e.g., political, security, justice, and government institutions that deliver social services).
3. Enhance social cohesion and build trust among social groups (society-society relations).
4. Build trust and legitimacy of governments (state-society relations).[26]

Using peace as a value to shape youth justice allows for two things. First, it allows us to move beyond the individualization of responsibility. Yes, youth are responsible for their harmful choices; however, at the same time society has a responsibility to them. This includes a responsibility for the circumstances that influenced their poor choices in the first place. Second, it allows us to take a holistic approach. It moves us beyond black-and-white thinking. Society isn't divided into the "good" and the "bad." It isn't "us" and "them." In reality, within all of us there's potential to cause harm, and an even greater potential to do good.

By moving the work of youth justice in the direction of peacebuilding, practitioners can more clearly define and build a safer, more livable society. And those who are interested in change can more clearly articulate what needs to be changed. Some aspects of peacebuilding are about social justice and some are about politics. It's important to note that there's already a rich theoretical history in the work of peacemaking criminology. This school of thought began to emerge in criminology in the late 1970s. Instead of framing issues around crime and criminals, peacemaking criminologists like Hal Pepinksy suggested that bigger picture issues like violence and its antithesis (peacemaking) are more helpful and should be the starting points for creating healthy societies.[27] The concern of peacemaking criminologists is unequal power—how the use of power can be violent. Their aim is for a synergistic sharing of power in ways that eliminate violence.[28] In essence, this focus is about what hurts people and societies, and what helps. It's about grounding youth justice in the values of love and compassion, rather than the typical fear-based stance of crime control models. In the words of Pepinsky: "Violence is driven by fear, peacemaking by love and compassion…. Responding to violence with violence is like trying to hold the same pole of two magnets together; peacemaking is an attractive force that happens as that expressive pole in some actors is attracted by the listening pole of other actors in an alternating current."[29] Peacemaking is a move away from the status quo, toward radical social change. It's about improving the lives of everyone in society, not simply protecting the interests of an elite few.

This is complex work. Peacebuilder John Paul Lederach in his book *The Moral Imagination: The Art and Soul of Building Peace* asks a fundamental question: "How do we transcend the cycles of violence that bewitch our human community while still living in them?"[30] He suggests that doing so requires the capacity to generate and mobilize the moral imagination:

1. The capacity to imagine ourselves in a web of relationships that includes our enemies: "The mystery of peace is located in the nature and quality of relationships developed with those most feared."[31]
2. The ability to sustain the curiosity necessary to find complex solutions.
3. A belief in the value of the creative act in building peace: art provides the conduit for giving "birth to something new that in its birthing changes our world and the way we see things … art makes moral reasoning possible."[32]
4. The acceptance of the risk necessary to step into the unknown.

Fundamentally, peacebuilding is about building relationships, or bridges, across divided groups of people—between rich and poor, young and old, inmate and guard, victim and offender, Indigenous and settler, criminal and society.

It acknowledges that we exist within a web of relationships and that we have responsibilities to each other. It proposes that we must all take responsibility for our choices, mistakes, and privileges and do our utmost to resolve our problems. M. Scott Peck in *The Road Less Traveled* explains that "… we must accept responsibility for a problem before we can solve it…. I can solve a problem only when I say 'This is my problem and it's up to me to solve it.'"[33] Peace is working together to resolve complex problems.

The Fifth Core Value: A Holistic Approach to Addressing Crime

The fifth value of trauma-informed justice is that it takes a holistic approach to addressing crime. In recent decades, some people have started to call for violence to be considered a public health issue. There's something to be said for this idea. After all, violence has far-reaching, often long-term, effects on the health of individuals and communities. Next to the criminal justice system, the health system bears the brunt of this. Making violence a public health issue would (a) allow for a more holistic understanding of its causes, and (b) help us to place a greater focus on prevention.

Over time, public health has become less focused on the individual and more focused on the population. Public health has been defined as, "collective action for sustained population-wide health improvement."[34] As a result, organizations like the World Health Organization (WHO) have noted that violence issues require public health attention. Thus, the WHO named rape and violence against women as a public health as well as a human rights issue.[35] In 1996, the World Health Assembly adopted resolution 49.25, "Prevention of Violence: A Public Health Priority," which "broke a barrier of silence, recognizing violence, including gender-based violence, as a public health issue requiring urgent action."[36] Psychiatrist James Gilligan, who has treated violent offenders for many years, agrees that violence should be treated as a public health issue. In an article "Violence in Public Health and Preventative Medicine," he states: "We can prevent violence if, and only if, we replace the moral and legal approach with the approaches of public health and preventative medicine. This is a matter of vital importance to the future of humanity, in which the medical professionals can serve an invaluable role as educators and leaders."[37] He goes on to quote the physician Rudolph Virchow, a founder of public health and preventative medicine: "Medicine is a social science, and politics is simply medicine on a larger scale."[38]

Over the last decade, one focus of public health has been looking at the social determinants of health. Nursing Professor Abe Oudshoorn uses this perspective in his work and research with homeless populations in Ontario, Canada. He describes this in the following box.

Social Determinants of Health
By Abe Oudshoorn, PhD, RN, Assistant Professor, Arthur Labatt Family School of Nursing, Western University

I use a social determinants of health lens to do research on the health and social outcomes of ending homelessness. This perspective is grounded in my work as a street nurse. I started at a health clinic for people experiencing homelessness fresh out of Nursing School. I had a sense that I would be doing walk-in clinic kind of care, dealing with wounds, injuries, intoxication, immunization, and infection. And I guess I did a lot of that, but it became very clear very quickly that no amount of Band-Aids would fix the issues my patients were dealing with. Until our patients could obtain safe, affordable, and permanent housing, they would fall victim to the health challenges of living homeless. And their experiences of poverty made it hard to meet necessities for food, clothing, and shelter. I was very much dependent on an interdisciplinary team, with social workers who could address income, education, and housing; mental health workers who could address illness and addictions; and friendly, non-judgmental receptionists who could provide consistent social support.

My comments capture the importance of the social determinants of health, which are:

- Income and social status
- Social support networks
- Education and literacy
- Employment/working conditions
- Social environments
- Physical environments
- Personal health practices and coping skills
- Healthy child development
- Biology and genetic endowment
- Health services
- Gender
- Culture

It might be a bit uncomfortable to say as a health professional, but medical care actually plays only a fairly small role in life expectancy. If you tell me what neighbourhood a child grew up in, and what their parents did for a living, I can more accurately guess their life expectancy than if you tell me who their family doctor is. If you presented me with a person experiencing poverty and poor health and gave me $50,000 to assist them, rather than hiring a private nurse to manage their care, I would just give them the cash. Of all the social determinants, income is the most predictive of well-being. Which is tricky, because as soon as you start talking about income and social assistance things become political, values come into play. What I think we can do though is continue to highlight the holistic nature of health, and that all of the determinants are health issues.

This underlying holistic perspective and use of the determinants of health as a guiding theory can be seen playing out in some of my research. Although often bringing the focus back to health outcomes, I have explored issues as far reaching as municipal zoning of methadone maintenance treatment clinics, structural violence in the lives of homeless youth, providing stable housing for the chronically homeless, what makes a health centre a safe space for people experiencing homelessness, and how to provide home care for people who have no home. Much of this is rooted in health equity, or the idea that for everyone to achieve the same health outcomes, some people actually need more resources and support than others. So, although you, I, and a person experiencing homelessness all have access to free health care in Canada, without additional support, we know that the person experiencing homelessness will encounter worse health outcomes over time. This is the foundation of a welfare state like Canada; because of different opportunities around the social determinants of health that people encounter by lottery of birth, more equal outcomes are obtained by an unequal distribution of public resources.

As a final note on the social determinants of health, we must realize how inextricably intertwined they are. Take for example education, employment, and income. These are listed as three separate determinants of health. Imagine for a moment a child of a sole-parenting mother, who moves schools 12 times in eight years. What might this mean for their education, employment, and income? What will be the long-term impact of low income on housing quality, or who may be in their social sphere? Without a time machine to go back and provide more support for the child's mother, and therefore more stability, what resources might the child now need as she hits adulthood with the deck already stacked against her? With this social history, she is more likely to smoke, but perhaps an intervention to address education and poverty is likely to be more effective in the long term than a simple smoking cessation program. Health is determined by far more than genes and personal health behaviours.

The Sixth Core Value: Social Change

The purpose of trauma-informed youth justice is to create positive social change. An important element of social change is creating healthy dialogue. Listening and talking, reading and writing can be starting points.

In his classic work on social change, *Pedagogy of the Oppressed*, Paulo Freire identifies six components of healthy dialogue—or dialogue that leads to change. First, he says that dialogue must be an act of love. Love, he says, is an act of courage, a commitment to the cause of the oppressed. Second, dialogue must be approached with a spirit of humility. Dialogue, Freire says, must not come about from a place of superiority, casting judgment on the ignorance of the other while remaining blind to one's own ignorance. Third, dialogue requires an intense faith in humanity: a belief that people can, and want to, live more fully. Fourth, dialogue is an act of trust. He describes this as integrity. Parties must act according to their word, not say one thing while doing another. Fifth, dialogue is an act of hope. Freire says, "Hopelessness is a form of silence, of denying the world and fleeing from it. The dehumanization resulting from an unjust order is not a cause for despair but for hope, leading to the incessant pursuit of the humanity denied by injustice. Hope, however, does not consist in crossing one's arms and waiting. As long as I fight, I am moved by hope; and if I fight with hope, then I can wait."[39] Finally, dialogue according to Freire is an act of critical thinking. It is about constantly transforming, rather than remaining static.[40]

A RESTORATIVE JUSTICE WORLDVIEW FOR TRAUMA-INFORMED YOUTH JUSTICE

> "If he who employs coercion against me could mold me to his purposes by argument, no doubt he would. He pretends to punish me because his argument is strong; but he really punishes me because he is weak."
> —William Godwin, 18th-century philosopher

The values cited above give shape to the worldview of trauma-informed youth justice. The lens through which this book views youth justice is a lens of restorative justice. Many people know of restorative justice as a form of practice—perhaps as victim-offender mediation, where victims and offenders meet face-to-face to discuss the impacts of harm and to create meaningful resolutions. However, restorative justice is more than one type of practice. In fact, it is better understood as a worldview through which to view harm, crime, and justice.

For thousands of years, many Indigenous communities all over the world have dealt with justice matters in more restorative ways. Of course, the term *Indigenous* does not refer to a homogenous group of people. There are many groups of people who are original inhabitants of regions of land. In Canada alone, there are hundreds of diverse clans, or tribes. For example, Gitxsan and Tlingit in the Pacific region; Blackfoot in the Plains; the Anishinaabe and Algonquin beside the Great Lakes; the Mi'kmaq along the Atlantic coast; and the Innu and Dene in the North are but a small sampling. That being said, there are some significant similarities in how many of these Indigenous groups understand justice, at least between original inhabitants. This text focuses on the Indigenous peoples of Turtle Island (North America) and the Maori in New Zealand.

For many generations, these Indigenous communities have met in circles to determine how best to resolve harm. The focus is on healing for the whole group. Relationships and interconnections—both between humans and with the land—are valued above all else. When harm occurs, justice is about restoring what has been disrupted. One of the most significant components of this approach is that power is not individualized or professionalized. The community as a whole "owns" it. As such, justice is more a part of everyday life. Métis Scholar Craig Proulx describes it like this: "Justice and law for many Aboriginal people in the past were never separated from everyday life. They were integral parts of life…. Justice and law, on the most basic level, are about relationships."[41] In *Returning to the Teachings: Exploring Aboriginal Justice*, Crown Attorney Rupert Ross shares what he learned from working with Indigenous communities in Northern Canada. He describes the disconnection between his own Western ways of knowing and Indigenous ways. Ross explains this by quoting a report from the Oji-Cree Sandy Lake First Nation: "In the non-Indian community, committing a crime seems to mean that the individual is a bad person and therefore must be punished.... The Indian communities view a wrongdoing as a misbehavior which requires teaching or an illness which requires healing."[42] This significant shift in understanding about justice has also started to influence Western criminal justice. It's an ethic of justice that gives people obligations to each other. Yellowknives Dene professor Glen Sean Coulthard describes the interdependency of relationships in his community: "This relational conception of identity ... stressed, among other things, the importance of sharing, egalitarianism, respecting the freedom and autonomy of both individuals and groups, and recognizing the obligations that one has not only to other people, but to the natural world as a whole."[43]

In the late 1970s and early 1980s, some settlers (i.e., people not originally from Turtle Island) in Canada and the United States started to talk about justice in similar terms. One of these people was Howard Zehr. Although more influenced by his Mennonite faith tradition, as well as by experiences he had during the civil rights era in the United States (including being the first white graduate of Morehouse College), Zehr argued for criminal justice to adopt a new paradigm. His foundational work *Changing Lenses: A New Focus for Crime and Justice*, published in 1990, was the first detailed account of this "new" form of justice. Zehr's work has received acclaim because he listens to—even invites—critique, and puts victims', offenders', and communities' stories and needs at the forefront. Furthermore, my own experience of him—as a professor, mentor, and person—is that he is kind, generous, creative, and humble. His body of work reflects these qualities. Alongside what I've learned from Indigenous communities, I will use his teachings as a starting point to describe the worldview of trauma-informed youth justice. Zehr explains restorative justice by contrasting it with criminal justice.

Traditional criminal justice asks:

1. What law has been broken?
2. Who did it?
3. Are they guilty?
4. What punishment fits the crime?

Alternatively, restorative justice asks:

1. Who has been hurt?
2. What are their needs?
3. Whose obligation is it to meet those needs?
4. What are the root causes?
5. Who needs to be involved in a justice process?
6. What is the best process for making things as right as possible?[44]

Notice the different starting places of each perspective. The first approach begins with law and focuses on the offender. The second approach is focused on resolving harm. According to Zehr, crime is something that damages people and relationships.[45] Thus, he suggests the starting place should be finding out who has been hurt and determining how they can be helped. Although victims are given some supports in the criminal justice system, law is not primarily about meeting their needs. In reality, in the courts, victims become witnesses. The primary victim is the state. This is why court cases are titled *R. v. "last name of offender."* R stands for Regina (Latin for a female monarch), which in Canada means the Queen of England. Prosecutors are called Crown attorneys, indicating whom they represent. This can create a safety buffer for victims, but usually the fancy footwork of criminal justice shifts victims to the sidelines. Power moves into the hands of professionals who are charged with resolving the victim's case. The focus of resolution is the determination of guilt followed by, where appropriate, a punishment. Criminal justice values giving offenders what they deserve.

By contrast, restorative justice puts victims' needs at the forefront and seeks to hold offenders meaningfully accountable by helping them understand the harms they have caused. As well, there is more community involvement—both in decision-making and in outcomes. Restorative justice stands on a foundation of respect, grassroots ownership, accountability, and healing. Zehr defines restorative justice as "a process to involve to the extent possible, those who have a stake in a specific offense and to collectively identify and address harms, needs, and obligations, in order to heal and put things as right as possible."[46]

In order to be trauma-informed, youth justice needs to shift its focus from punishment toward more meaningful accountability and needs to stand on a foundation that honours the interconnections of human relationships. Sociologist Michelle Brown has exhaustively studied the topic of punishment, how inflicting pain on those who we feel deserve it is deeply embedded in many aspects of Western culture. In *The Culture of Punishment: Prison, Society, and Spectacle,* she suggests that restorative justice offers a transformative framework. It implicates the community's role in injustices, as well as in reconstructing social relationships.[47] Another researcher, Jennifer J. Llewellyn, a law professor at Dalhousie University, argues that restorative justice is a relational theory of justice. The primary question of relational theory, as articulated by Llewellyn, "is not so much 'what is X in relationship to or with?' but, rather, 'what is the effect of being in relation?'"[48] The fundamental claim of relational theory is that the self exists only because of relationships and connections with others. As the human self is not individualistic, or solely defined on its own, justice processes must also adopt a more community-minded stance. As Llewellyn explains, this is not the outlook in our current justice system:

> Justice is our response to the powerful moral intuition that something is wrong and begs redress. In its service, we have created processes, institutions, and systems tasked with recognizing and responding to wrong. Prevailing conceptions of justice that underlie and animate contemporary [Western] justice systems ... are rooted in a particular set of assumptions about selves and ideal social conditions drawn from the liberal tradition. As a result, these theories privilege the protection of individual independence through separation as the animating ideal of justice.[49]

A shift is in order; one that pushes justice to start from a place of connection and interdependence.[50] This is about establishing equity in relationships. It is concerned with respect, care, and dignity. Relational theory understands crime as a tear in the fabric of human relationships. In *Security With Care: Restorative Justice and Healthy Societies*, criminologist Elizabeth M. Elliott suggests that restorative justice holds deeper meanings about building peaceful communities because, when they are broken, it attends to the health of relationships.[51]

In later chapters, I will also describe this from a biological perspective. Attachment theory, an explanation of the impact of relationships on people, articulates a basic, fundamental human need for safe, healthy relationships, especially with caregivers when children are young, but also with others into adulthood. When the biology of attachment is disrupted by traumatic experiences, it can be very difficult to form healthy relationships. A lot of violent criminal behaviour can be traced back to this. Criminal justice responses often exacerbate what is already damaged by isolating offenders—causing further harm through incarceration and other punitive practices. Conversely, restorative justice approaches have shown some promising results in repairing attachment. Researchers Lori Haskell and Melanie Randall have this to say on the subject:

> If one of the core harms of trauma is disruption to attachments, then restoration of secure and healthy attachments and relationships is the context for resolving traumatic damage…. The resolution of trauma for an individual and for traumatized communities requires restoration of connection, to self and to others. One of the important and innovative components of restorative justice approaches to justice is the insistence on active community involvement, on identifying the community as a stakeholder in the process.[52]

Ultimately, a restorative justice worldview works toward restoring relationships. Of course, in many situations victims and offenders will not want, or need, a relationship. In those cases restoration means victims being able to heal, offenders being given proper support so they can be accountable, and communities having their needs met. At other times, however, there is a need for restoring relationships between victims and offenders. Violent crimes are more likely to happen within families than among strangers. Oftentimes, these families need support to be able to move forward.

Meanwhile, society needs to find a better way of living with justice; one that works to create kinder communities. Elliott suggests that restorative justice can help to achieve this. With regard to offenders, she suggests that the relational form of restorative justice accountability works better: "it is primarily relationships—not laws or sanctions—that deter criminal or harmful activity."[53] Her argument is that restorative justice is principally about healing harms. To be trauma-informed, youth justice requires a restorative justice worldview. This perspective broadens the limited, individualized definitions of crime that the criminal justice system operates with by widening the focus to consider violent social structures as well. By thinking about justice as healing, restorative justice allows for multiple levels of focus: harms done to victims, harms perpetrated by offenders, harms done to victims and offenders by communities, and social structures. It takes the view that both the individual harms and the root causes of these harms must be addressed.

The notion that justice should be about healing is not a new one. I am convinced that our justice processes and systems in North America would look very different if we had but learned from Indigenous communities, rather than devastating them. Settler relations toward Indigenous peoples have been about colonization and assimilation, while dispossessing them of their land and forcing a Western, "civilized" way of life upon them. It is significant that Indigenous youth are overrepresented in the youth justice system. A restorative justice framework puts obligations on settler society—Canada as a nation—to decolonize, while also working toward the healing of victims, offenders, and communities.

CONCLUSION: HEALING RELATIONSHIPS AND FINDING HOPE

In the early 2000s, I was invited by an Indigenous Elder to participate in the Toronto Pine Tree Healing Circle. The purpose of this healing circle was to begin to heal relationships between Indigenous peoples of the Six Nations (Mohawk, Cayuga, Onondaga, Seneca, Tuscarora, and Oneida peoples), and the Anglican and United Churches. Over the course of 100 years, the churches had forced Indigenous children to attend residential schools where they were not allowed to speak their own languages, or practice their cultures or spirituality. Instead, they had the English language and Western ways forced upon them. There were other forms of abuse, too.

I will go into greater detail on the topic of "Indian" residential schools in the next few chapters, but for now, let me just say that my time in the circle was life changing. I heard church leaders taking responsibility for abuses and Indigenous peoples speaking about their traumas. I also heard Indigenous peoples taking responsibility for the traumas that they subsequently passed on to their partners and children later in life. This opened my eyes to the horrors of settler colonialism, to individual and collective trauma, and also to hopeful ways of living justice. In this context, the worldview of restorative justice seemed to embrace the complexity of the situation while providing space for hope and healing.

In writing this book, I have held the life-altering lessons I learned in the Pine Tree Healing Circle at heart, and have also done my best to honour the six core values of trauma-informed youth justice: critical thinking, human dignity, participation, peace, a holistic approach to addressing crime, and social change.

In my work and in my personal life, I have witnessed tremendous good rise from tremendous despair—and while I know firsthand about human beings' unfortunate capacity to do great harm, I also believe in our even greater abilities for kindness. As such, my messages come from a place of concern for the victims and for the offenders who have trusted me with their stories, and my hope is that this text will contribute in some small way to making this world a better place for all.

We will explore topics such as a history of youth justice in Canada, the impacts of trauma, and hopeful, trauma-informed, restorative justice–based models of justice; however, at its core, this book is an invitation to dialogue and a plea for a gentler approach to youth justice, because while I still have much to learn and experience, one thing I know to be true is this: violence ripples, but kindness makes waves.

GLOSSARY OF TERMS

Recidivism is the act of reoffending, or for an offender to relapse into crime.

Restorative justice as defined by Howard Zehr is "a process to involve to the extent possible, those who have a stake in a specific offense and to collectively identify and address harms, needs, and obligations, in order to heal and put things as right as possible."

Trauma is an incident or event experienced in a way that causes so much stress that it overwhelms a person's ability to cope. Trauma can also refer to an injury or wound, but in this text we will mostly talk about trauma in the psychological sense.

Trauma-informed is a term that refers to bringing an awareness of the impacts of trauma to our work in youth justice. It also means that we shape interventions upon principles of trauma healing and restorative justice, instead of focusing on punishment. Fundamentally, this requires justice processes to foster resilience in young people.

QUESTIONS FOR REFLECTION

1. This book encourages the values of critical thinking, human dignity, participation, peace, a holistic approach to addressing crime, and social change. Which values are most important to your life and work/studies? Are there others that you would include as central to the work of youth justice?
2. Why do you think academic books seldom talk about values, instead choosing to focus on theoretical frameworks?
3. One of the main contentions of *Trauma-Informed Youth Justice in Canada* is that youth justice processes need to focus on healing rather than on punishment. What do you think about this approach? Are there times, crimes, or places where you think punishment should be central? Why do you think society places so much emphasis on punishment within the criminal justice system?

RECOMMENDED READING

Absolon, Kathleen E. *Kaandossiwin: How We Come to Know*. Halifax: Fernwood Publishing, 2011.

In this important work, Indigenous researcher Kathleen Absolon critiques Western academia for ignoring and silencing Indigenous ways of knowing. She writes about her research with 14 Indigenous scholars to highlight the fundamentally holistic nature of Indigenous theories and methods.

Ross, Rupert. *Returning to the Teachings: Exploring Aboriginal Justice.* Toronto: Penguin Canada, 1996.

Having worked for many years with Indigenous communities in Northern Canada, Crown attorney Ross shares some of the fundamental differences he has become aware of between settler and Indigenous justice.

Zehr, Howard. *The Little Book of Restorative Justice.* Intercourse: Good Books, 2002.

This book gives readers a strong foundation for understanding the worldview of restorative justice. In it, Zehr articulates restorative justice as a framework for responding to crime and harm, highlighting its usefulness for victims, offenders, and communities.

2 | A History of Youth Justice in Canada— 1867 to 1984

The history of youth justice in Canada is fascinating not only because of what's written, but also because of what isn't. The domain of criminology largely controls the narrative. Typically, the story goes that youth justice in Canada has gone back and forth between a tough-on-crime approach and a desire to address root causes. In other words, there's been an oscillation between punitive and rehabilitative agendas. Textbooks usually frame this discussion in four ways. The first is by describing legislation and corresponding dates of implementation; for example, 1908, the Juvenile Delinquents Act; 1984, the Young Offenders Act; and 2003, the Youth Criminal Justice Act. Second, by tracking crime statistics: Are youth committing more or fewer crimes over time? What types of crimes do young people most often commit? Which groups of young people are committing these crimes? Third, by including sociological discussion about the constructs of media and the changing definitions of childhood and adolescence, and how these affect youth justice. Fourth, by analyzing the criminological, psychological, biological, and sociological reasons that young people commit crime. However, there's much more to the story.

Winston Churchill once said that the victors are the ones who write history. In the same vein, anarchist Emma Golding once remarked: if "every society has the criminals they deserve," then what is to be written about those who find themselves vanquished by law? What if, instead of being told by the domain of criminology, the story of youth justice in Canada was told by young people themselves, specifically the ones behind bars? Unfortunately, a history from the point of view of young offenders has not yet been written. What this text aims to do, however, is to tell the story of youth justice using a critical perspective. An analysis of youth justice in Canada must cast a critical eye on those in power, while turning an ear in the direction of the voices of those on the margins of society. Otherwise, the telling will be at best incomplete, and at worst dramatically skewed.

This chapter will use a chronological format to tell the story of youth justice up until 1984, describing relevant legislation and some of the social context. With every piece of information—every change in direction in youth justice—ask yourself: Who is deciding this? Why are they doing so? Who do these decisions benefit? Who do they hurt? How are people impacted?

Also, keep in mind that implicit to this discussion is the variable of power. By power, I don't mean the ability to act, which is the more neutral sense of the word, but rather the ability to control others. Once power enters the narrative of youth justice, other variables also become important: specifically race, socio-economic status, and gender.

A history of youth justice in Canada cannot be divorced from an analysis of race, and it especially cannot be separated from Canada's settler relationship with **Indigenous peoples**, for example, the forced removal of Indigenous children and youth from their homes and their placement in "Indian" residential schools. This treatment was akin to incarceration and it remains a primary root cause of the significant intergenerational trauma in Indigenous communities, which has led to the overrepresentation of Indigenous youth in the justice system. To tell this part of the story, I will draw largely on John S. Milloy's *A National Crime: The Canadian Government and the Residential School System, 1879 to 1986*. Milloy notes in the early part of chapter 3 that "it is not surprising that residential schools had their parallel in the industrial school and correctional schools of the same era for incorrigible white children."[1] This chapter will tell these stories side by side.

A history of youth justice must also include the stories of reformatories and industrial schools—full of impoverished children in the first half of the 20th century—which will be discussed alongside the stories of "Indian" residential schools. Next, an analysis of gender will also be essential. After all, the annals of history are rich with books (and laws) written by men. The first legislation that focused specifically on youth, the Juvenile Delinquents Act (JDA), dates back to 1908, a time when women were not allowed to vote in Canada. In fact, it wasn't until 1921 that women were given this right. How has this affected the course of youth justice?

We will also consider the intersection of variables such as race and gender, because I should have specified that all women except Asians and Aboriginals were granted the right to vote in 1921. Not until 1948 could all Asian Canadians vote, and not until 1960 could Indigenous peoples vote. It was even later that people with mental disabilities and those living in prison were included. The list of intersections could go on. We could also talk about socio-economic status, age, ability, sexual orientation, and other factors that affect where power resides. For our purposes, though, the consideration of race and gender will allow for a more in-depth discussion of the role of the state in young people's lives, as well as the state's response to behaviours defined as criminal.

RULE OF LAW

Why have I chosen to tell the story of youth justice in Canada by tracking the history of youth legislation? There are two reasons. First, and most importantly, Canada's government is structured under rule of law. Second, for this reason, how law is written affects how people treat each other. What does "rule of law" mean? It means that everyone is to be governed by the law.

Before the existence of rule of law, many nations, territories, or states were governed by a rule of man, or of some type of sovereign person like a king or queen. The monarch held most, if not all, of the power within a territory. They could arbitrarily decide what was allowed and what wasn't, usually to their own benefit and to the detriment of the least valued of their subjects. Of course, this raised issues of fairness and fundamental questions about justice. Rule of law was created to keep power in check. Nations that operate under rule of law claim that everyone—powerful or not—is bound by the restrictions of law.

In Canada, rule of law means that whether a person is street-involved, an investment banker, or a leader in government, they are to be treated equally under law. In his book *How Canadians Govern Themselves*, renowned governmental historian the Honourable Eugene E. Forsey explains rule of law as follows, "It means that everyone is subject to law; that no one, no matter how important or powerful, is above the law—not the government; not the prime minister, or any other minister; not the Queen or the Governor General or any lieutenant-governor; not the most powerful bureaucrat; not the armed forces; not Parliament itself, or any provincial legislature."[2] In Canada, the accountability of legislators is the responsibility of an independent judiciary, which means the courts are meant to be the counter-balancing mechanism if those in power act inappropriately. For example, if laws created by parliament don't meet the measure of the Charter of Rights and Freedoms, the courts are supposed to respond accordingly by making decisions that restore fairness.

You might guess that this structure would function like a great equalizer. For example, in crimes like domestic violence and sexual abuse—where perpetrators come from all religions and ethnicities, have varying socio-economic statuses, and hold varying amounts of power—you would expect to find an equal amount of each "type" of person behind bars in Canada. However, the troubling truth is that, even taking only these types of crimes into consideration, there's an overrepresentation of poor, Indigenous, Black, and other less powerful (or more marginalized) populations incarcerated in Canada. What does this tell us about rule of law?

At minimum, it means we must keep a critical eye on who is writing law, as well as on who is enforcing it. Furthermore, it begs the question of whether equality is the same thing as equity. It isn't. When people who aren't equals are treated equally, inequality is perpetuated. For example, not everyone who comes before the courts has the same resources for hiring a lawyer. When this is taken into consideration, it could be argued that Canada is ruled more by money than by law. In a compelling book, *Wealth by Stealth: Corporate Crime, Corporate Law, and the Perversion of Democracy*, legal scholar Harry Glassbeek carefully describes the ways in which corporations bend governments to their will. He argues that this is a major obstacle to democracy in Canada.[3] The rich are therefore powerful and able to sidestep, in some ways, rule of law.

Given the overrepresentation of Indigenous youth in the justice system, it seems clear that there are also racial overtones to power. Furthermore, the imbalance of power also has gendered (patriarchal) components. For example, Indigenous women are more likely to be victims of violence than women of other races, with hundreds having gone missing and been murdered in the past few decades.

Ultimately, when examining youth justice from a trauma-informed perspective, these "big picture" structural issues must be taken into serious consideration. As I tell the story of youth justice by following a timeline of legislation, you will start to better understand how issues of racism, classism, sexism, and other -isms are relevant to discussions of youth justice.

Therefore, in our examination of the history of youth justice in Canada, we'll keep two important variables at the forefront: power and privilege. Although power can be considered more neutrally, in this text we will understand it as a way that people control or dominate others. Likewise, privilege will be understood as one person having an advantage over another. Examining power and privilege in this way will allow for discussions about what kind of society we want to live in.

What follows is an examination of two periods in Canadian history: from Confederation to 1907, and from 1908 to 1984. Each represents a time period when a certain piece (or pieces) of legislation governed youth justice in the country. To give some context, each section begins with an article from the *Toronto Star* telling about an incident of youth crime, and the corresponding sentence given. Following the article, we'll examine how people understood youth crime at the time. Parallel to this, the story of "Indian" residential schools will also be told for the reasons previously explained.

YOUTH JUSTICE: FROM CONFEDERATION TO 1907

> **"Offenders Found Guilty To-day," from *The Evening Star*, January 4, 1899**
>
> Quite nonchalantly young Thomas McKillop gave the court several details of the operations of a band of young thieves. The boy was charged with sneaking a tray containing 19 watches from Ambrose Kent & Sons' store on Yonge street.
>
> "I didn't steal the watches," said McKillop. "I didn't go into the store. Charlie March and Tom Glassford and a couple of the rest went in. When he came out Glassford gave me two watches. Then we went up the street and the fellows stole some more, handkerchiefs and stuff. I didn't want to keep the watches, but the other boys said they had about 20 more, so I kept them."
>
> "Where are the rest of the watches now?" was asked.
>
> "March and Glassford took them to Buffalo."
>
> The youth had kept two detectives digging up cellars in the northwestern portion of the city, looking for the stolen "tickers."
>
> "If he didn't actually steal them, he received them after they were stolen, so it's all the same," said His Worship as he sent McKillop to jail for 60 days.
>
> McKillop was also convicted of stealing a suit of clothes from E. Boisseau & Co.'s wagon.

- **Explanation for youth crime:** Immorality
- **Purpose of punishment:** Reform
- **Age of youth:** Doli incapax (incapable of intending to commit a crime, and therefore not culpable to the courts) under the age of seven. Older children,

although given some lenience, were tried similarly to adults. A similar defence could be established or refuted for children up to the age of 13.[4]

The story of youth legislation in Canada starts before the adoption of the Juvenile Delinquents Act (JDA) in 1908. In fact, it predates Confederation. If one listens to the justice stories—or the ways of justice—of the Original peoples (the oral traditions of Indigenous peoples on Turtle Island), then the story of youth legislation begins with their creation stories. For our purposes, however, I will describe the history of (European) settler crime control. Although some activity related to this predates Confederation, I will focus on 1867 forward. This approach could be challenged from a critical perspective. Many pieces of legislation appeared prior to this date, such as the Gradual Civilization Act of 1857, which was about colonization—the dispossession of lands and the assimilation of Indigenous peoples.

The period prior to 1908 is characterized by three themes: one, a gradual separation of juveniles from adults in criminal justice proceedings; two, a movement introducing the use of the penitentiary as a means of reform; and three, humanitarian efforts to save children from "bad" environments, such as a life of poverty or a difficult family situation (or both).

An examination of the first theme (the separation in the criminal justice system of juveniles from adults) might lead us to consider the changing definitions of childhood, starting in the industrial revolution and moving into the modern era. For our purposes, however, we'll focus more on how courts have treated young people. In a chapter titled "From 'Misguided Children' to 'Criminal Youth,'" in *Youth at Risk and Youth Justice: A Canadian Overview*, sociologist Russell Smandych argues that differential treatment of young people in Canada predates the introduction of youth courts.[5] In fact, he suggests that the term *juvenile delinquency* goes back to the 1700s, with courts using a young person's age to mitigate the severity of punishment.[6] Citing the French criminologist Jean Trepenier, Smandych claims that it's more accurate to say that in Canadian history, as well as in the history of other Western countries, there was a "gradual separation of juveniles and adults in court proceedings and institutions of confinement."[7] In spite of some differentiation, children and adolescents were still often punished similarly to adults.

A History of the Penitentiary in Canada: Reform or Status Quo?

The history of the penitentiary in Canada provides some important context to the history of youth justice in Canada. It not only gives us clues about attitudes toward criminals at the time, but also about commonly held beliefs about what counted as justice or, more to the point, as punishment. Ultimately, it was in wrestling with the issue of whether or not children should be incarcerated with adults that a youth justice system came to be.

In the early colonial years, as well as at the time of Confederation, children were often incarcerated with adults. Canada's first prison, Kingston Penitentiary, which opened in 1835, housed some of these juvenile delinquents—as they were called. As an example, in 1848, an act put before the Legislative Assembly of Ontario accounts for those who entered and exited Kingston Penitentiary in that year. Six young people under the age of 18 are said to have been released, each after having served three-year sentences. Stephen Jacques, released at age 14, would have entered Kingston Penitentiary at age 11. His crime was larceny, which is known today as theft. Another youth, Paley Wheeler, stole a horse, and was sent to the prison for three years at the age of 15.[8]

These boys are indicative of the mixing of children with adults in the "new" penitentiary system of the time. However, children were not incarcerated without critique or concern. The first chaplain at the Kingston Penitentiary (Reverend W. M. Herchmer, Church of England) stated upon his resignation in June of 1843: "The admission of boys into our Penitentiary, to be subject to the same discipline as adults, is, the Chaplain fears, not calculated to reform, but to injure. Should not some respect be paid to the peculiarities of youth, even in a place of confinement? Would not the desired end be more effectually secured by a judicious admixture of school, labour, and recreation?"[9] His words reflected the thoughts of many at the time, but it would not be until much later that a truly distinct youth justice system would be created.

Of note is that the penitentiary as a form of punishment was still a relatively new idea at this time. Reformers thought it would be a better and more humane way to punish criminals. Time in a prison would allow for quiet reflection and would provide an opportunity to learn the importance of hard work. Prior to this, Canadian historian Simon Devereux suggests that many criminals were simply put to death (usually by public hanging) or, as a secondary option, were shipped to the American colonies for hard labour.[10] For more minor crimes, public punishments were used, including whipping or the pillory (a wooden device that bound a person's head and hands).

What's more, the punishments I've just described were often being used arbitrarily; that is, similar offences were not receiving similar punishments. Furthermore, reformers were concerned that too many crimes were leading to execution, while some were also worried about the callousness being created in the general population by the public spectacle of punishment.[11] The ideas of Italian philosopher Cesare Beccaria were prominent in discussions of reform (further discussion of Beccaria's ideas appear in chapter 4). He could find no justification for the way punishment was being carried out and believed it was being used as a tool of vengeance, instead of being proportional to the crime committed.[12] He argued for crime to be understood as harmful instead of sinful.[13] These principles—the idea of punishment being proportional to the offence committed, and being just enough to deter people from committing future offences—still hold sway today.

By the time Kingston Penitentiary was to be built, many other penitentiaries existed in the United States and prison as a mode of punishment was well established. Kingston Penitentiary's architects travelled south to learn more about methods of building prisons, and ultimately modelled the first Canadian penitentiary after Auburn Correctional Facility in New York, USA. The Auburn model of imprisonment is characterized by hard labour in groups during the day, solitary confinement at night, and complete inmate silence. The building was intended to be a foreboding place, as evidenced by its massive structure and intimidating design. However, the finished prison didn't meet the hopes of the reformers who had envisioned it, nor did it actually meet its objective of "changing" criminals into contributing members of society. In 1848—just 13 years after the Kingston Penitentiary opened—a report was commissioned by the Province of Canada. This report highlighted the prison's many shortcomings and flaws.[14] In fact, many people began to argue that prison was an outright failure as a means of reform. From 1848 to 1849, George Brown, one of the fathers of Confederation in Canada, investigated troubling forms of conduct that seemed inherently connected to the penitentiary model.

Of particular concern was the constant abuse of inmates by keepers and guards, alongside the use of corporal punishment (whipping), and torture (the box). As a case in point, one young boy named Alexis Lafleur, who was incarcerated from 1842 to 1845 and again from 1846 to 1850, was whipped on many occasions, mostly for talking, laughing, or singing. In the words of George Brown, "It is horrifying to think of a child of 11 to 14 years of age, being lacerated with the lash before 500 grown men; to say nothing of the cruelty, the effect of such a scene, so often repeated, must have been to the last degree brutalizing."[15] As if that were not shocking enough, another convict, Antoine Beauche, incarcerated from 1845 to 1848 received similar punishments throughout his term of incarceration. When he entered Kingston Penitentiary he was eight years old. About this case George Brown says, "This child received the lash within a week of his arrival, and that he had no fewer than 47 corporal punishments in nine months, and all for offences of the most childish character. We regard this as another case of revolting inhumanity."[16]

Needless to say, reforms were in the works. The child-savers movement of the early 1900s began to raise concerns both publicly and politically. Of primary concern to these activists was why certain children—typically impoverished children—were more often incarcerated than others. They were also concerned about the fact that children were being punished in the same ways as, and were being incarcerated together with, adults. They started to consider other ways that children might be punished—or might receive correction and training. A prominent figure in this movement was J. J. Kelso, the founder of the Toronto Humane Society, which was dedicated to protecting women and children as well as animals at the time.[17] According to Smandych, Kelso had been a newspaper reporter in Toronto in the 1880s and had witnessed firsthand the brutal effects of poverty, particularly on children. In fact, he noted that it was often poverty that was putting children into conflict with the law, through larceny or theft.[18] Along with another reformer, W. L. Scott, Kelso began to draft a new piece of criminal legislation: one that would focus on children and young people. This was the Juvenile Delinquents Act of 1908.[19] This legislation marked the creation of a separate justice system for young people.

Before describing this era of youth justice, however, it's important to understand what Aboriginal children and youth in Canada were experiencing at around the same time. These young people were being forcibly removed from homes and held against their will—not in prisons (although one might call them that too)—but in residential schools.

Residential Schools: 1879 to 1907

Beginning in 1879, many Indigenous children were sent to live in residential schools. Initially, going to these schools was voluntary, but eventually it became compulsory.

I tell this story as part of a chapter on the history of youth justice because (a) many Indigenous children and youth attended these schools, (b) the conditions at the schools and the experiences children had there were similar (if not worse) to the conditions and experiences of incarceration, (c) children were "confined"—or forced to attend, and (d) the effects of this practice are seen to this day in the ongoing overrepresentation of Indigenous youth in the Canadian justice system, including prisons. It is my hope that, by remembering and understanding this dark chapter in Canadian history, we can work toward a better future for today's youth.

Residential schools were primarily funded by the Canadian government, but were mostly operated by the Protestant and Catholic churches, among other Christian denominations. The government claimed that these schools were part of building a nation, but at their foundation lay racist beliefs that disregarded the value of Aboriginal culture, language, and traditions. The explicit message was that these schools were needed to make the "savage" civilized[20] and to "kill the Indian in the child."[21] White people, or European settlers, considered themselves superior in race and religion. The churches seemed intent on Christianizing Indigenous peoples while the government seemed determined to take their land. The churches' approach was racist, as well as religiously and culturally abusive. They provided education that ignored—and, in fact, disallowed—Indigenous culture and languages. Meanwhile, the government's focus was on assimilation. As Indigenous communities were decimated by residential schools, it provided the perfect cover for the government to dispossess them of their land. This is **settler colonialism**: controlling Indigenous peoples in order to steal their land.[22]

Over 150,000 Indigenous children and youth attended residential schools, and although these schools claimed to exist to give education and care to children in the name of Christ, in reality, very little education was involved. In the words of historian John S. Milloy: "Instead, the system's history is marked by the persistent neglect and abuse of children and through them of Aboriginal communities in general."[23] Upon entering the schools children were no longer called by their names. Instead, they were each given a number. Clothes were taken, hair was cut, and nearly everything from their Aboriginal identity was whitewashed.[24] Survivors who have been brave enough to share their stories have been fairly consistent on these facts. The following excerpt is from a 2005 Aboriginal Affairs Parliamentary Committee:

> My name is Flora Merrick, the daughter of the late Flora McKinney and Archie Myron. I am the widow of the former chief of Long Plain First Nation in Manitoba, Angus Merrick, who was awarded the Order of Canada by the Governor General of Canada for his long-time work on behalf of the Aboriginal people in Canada.
>
> I was born on Remembrance Day, November 11, 1916, and I've lived my whole life on Long Plain First Nation, approximately 120 kilometres west of Winnipeg, Manitoba.
>
> I thank everybody for inviting me and my stepdaughter, Grace Daniels, here today to say a few words about what we went through at residential school

and our experience with the Government of Canada's alternative dispute resolution....

I attended the Portage la Prairie residential school from 1921 until 1932. In all my 88 years, I have not forgotten the pain and suffering I went through while at residential school. Being separated from my loving parents and family at five years of age and enduring constant physical, emotional, psychological, and verbal abuse still haunts me. I was punished for speaking my own language and was always frightened and scared of what the teachers and principals would do to me. It was like being in prison.

During my stay at Portage la Prairie residential school, I witnessed the injustices of beatings and abuse of other children, some of whom were my siblings. We were treated worse than animals and lived in constant fear. I have carried the trauma of my experience and seeing what happened to other children all my life.

I cannot forget one painful memory. It occurred in 1932 when I was 15 years old. My father came to the Portage la Prairie residential school to tell my sister and I that our mother had died and to take us to the funeral. The principal of the school would not let us go with our father to the funeral. My little sister and I cried so much, we were taken away and locked in a dark room for about two weeks.

After I was released from the dark room and allowed to be with other residents, I tried to run away to my father and family. I was caught in the bush by teachers and taken back to the school and strapped so severely that my arms were black and blue for several weeks. After my father saw what they did to me, he would not allow me to go back to school after the school year ended.[25]

While Canada was beginning to consider what made other children unique for the purposes of creating a youth justice system, residential schools were destroying Indigenous young people. While seeking to accommodate and take special care of white children, Canada was beginning a process that ultimately decimated Indigenous communities. It wasn't supposed to be this way. Settler communities had committed to live side-by-side with the original inhabitants. Some background on treaties between these groups explains this.

Although—over the course of hundreds of years—there are dozens of treaties that were agreed to across Canada, I will focus this part of the text on one of the wampum belt treaties that predates Confederation. It speaks to why many—or most—Indigenous groups today claim the right to self-governance and self-determination. Those rights were never surrendered. Canada has overtly assimilated Indigenous peoples without their consent.

The premise of much of the relationship between the Haudenosaunee/Iroquois (Mohawk, Oneida, Onondaga, Cayuga, Seneca, and Tuscarora) peoples and settler (Dutch) peoples was the Two Row Wampum treaty of 1613. These Indigenous groups, at the time, occupied significant parts of what is now the North Eastern United

States, as well as significant parts of Central Canada. Symbolized by the two row wampum belt—a long, white, beaded belt with two rows of purple beads running parallel to each other—this treaty outlined that the Haudenosaunee and settlers were to live interdependent of each other. In Iroquoian terms this is described as Kaswentha. It meant that the two parties to the agreement would share the same space, while retaining their distinct political identities.[26] As other European nations came to dominate areas of North America other two row wampum treaties were made. Evidence of treaties with France, England, and the United States has been found.[27] Ultimately, in the words of historian Jon Parmenter, Kaswentha "may best be understood as a Haudenosaunee term embodying the ongoing negotiation of their relationship to European colonizers and their descendants; the underlying concept of kaswentha emphasizes the distinct identity of the two peoples and a mutual engagement to coexist in peace without the interference in the affairs of the other."[28] In essence, the groups were supposed to be like two ships travelling side by side, sharing some resources, but ultimately being steered separately.

How is it, then, that, even though colonial settlers agreed to a mutually beneficial relationship and Indigenous peoples never surrendered their rights to self-determination, Canada imposed residential schools on them? Fast-forward a few hundred years. Through treaties, settlers had agreed to provide Indigenous communities with some form of education—but this, from Indigenous perspectives, was never meant to come about in such an oppressive way. As John S. Milloy explains, the vision for residential schools was to separate Indigenous children from their parents in order to disrupt their parenting processes.[29] In fact, the Davin Report, completed in 1879, assumed that after graduating from residential schools—or industrial schools, as they were originally called—most Indigenous peoples would not return to their tribes. It was hoped that, in this way, communities would break apart.[30] As stated before, the primary objective was to save the man by killing the "Indian" in him.[31] The policy was one of "aggressive assimilation," with the hope that the young would be easier to mold than the old.[32] This assimilation was a process of disorienting Indigenous children from their culture, and reorienting "them in a place filled with European 'meaning.'"[33]

Clearly, there was an attitude of superiority at the time, and it continued to play out in Canada's treatment of Indigenous peoples. In March of 1920, the *Toronto Daily Star* published an article about the Haudenosaunee (Six Nations), commenting on how surprised most Canadians were that they did not wish to become citizens:

> Last week a bill to amend the Indian Act received its first reading at Ottawa, and was described as a measure for granting all qualified Indians full and complete rights as citizens of Canada ... most people ... feel some surprise when the Six Nations Indians object to the proposed action of the Government. They say their status is that of allies of the King of Great Britain and not subjects, and that the proposed legislation invades their legal and historic rights.... The main purpose of the amendments proposed to the Act, however, have to do with enfranchisement.... An official recommends who is fit, and rejects the unfit.... This plan means the disintegration of the Indian

communities, by the withdrawal of the foremost men and families from among them, together with the most highly improved property....[34]

The agreement with the King of Britain mentioned in the article was the Royal Proclamation of 1763, which stated that British subjects were not to take land from the Haudenosaunee without their consent. Indigenous scholars, like John Borrows, have argued that this proclamation was not unilaterally imposed by the British, but was negotiated with First Nations. As such, this legislation, in their view, is critical today for Indigenous self-government and self-determination.[35]

The imposition of residential schools failed to live up to treaty standards. At heart, this was because of racist attitudes and beliefs about Indigenous peoples. In an article from September 3, 1902, the *Toronto Daily Star* again puts an exclamation point on this:

> Closely connected in importance with the evangelizing of the Indian is the work of educating him.... Our industrial institutes ... must prove an important factor in the solution of the so-called "Indian problem". But to this end such provision should be made for the boys and girls after graduation as shall save them from the necessity of returning to the reservations, where, under the pressure of unfavorable surroundings, they are almost sure to suffer, more or less, a reversion to former conditions.[36]

By 1907, there were 77 residential schools in all with 2,000 children in attendance.[37] In that year, the Chief Medical Officer of the Department of Indian Affairs, Dr. P. H. Bryce, submitted *The Report on the Indian Schools of Manitoba and the North-West Territories*, describing the deplorable conditions of residential schools to the Government of Canada. According to his investigation, 24 percent of students who attended the schools had died either before leaving the school or just after. These numbers were even higher in particular schools. Most deaths were attributed to tuberculosis or to other diseases caused by unsanitary conditions. In his words: "... we have created a situation so dangerous to health that I was often surprised that the results were not even worse than they have been shown statistically to be."[38]

YOUTH JUSTICE: FROM 1908 TO 1984

"Juvenile Court Cases," from the *Toronto Daily Star*, September 11, 1913

Fred and Duncan, Clarence and Cecil backed their hand sleigh up in front of a new house on Greenwood avenue last winter, and went off with yards of things which are specified in the charges, such as electric bells, electric batteries, wires, insulators, in fact all the internal electric workin's of the house. They were charmed with their success and continued, entering between twelve and fourteen in all. Then one day they came to the little house used by the carpenter in charge of the erection of the houses, and drove off with his electric motor, which he valued at $78.

> This all happened between January and March of this year, and when the landlords had made sure it wasn't ghosts they turned the police force on the case. To-day they placed the four boys in front of the desk while the commissioner struggled with words with which to make them realize the seriousness of their offence. The boys go on probation, restitution having been made.
>
> Bill was walking thoughtfully up Kennedy road, and found a small revolver lying right in the middle of the sidewalk. On his way home he stopped off in the park with Alf and tried firing off the Lucifer matches in it. It made a noise like a midnight tragedy, which caught the ear of a constable. To-day's fine of $20 for carrying firearms was suspended.
>
> Mothers who wonder why their boys want to go to the racetracks and what kind of knowledge they glean when they do go should have been present in the court this morning, when nine big boys and one tiny, delicate chap of twelve were filed in. They were charged with gambling on Sunday. All were uncared for, badly dressed, and at least four of them in very bad health. Joe, who stood in the middle, had a receding chin and protruding teeth which indicated adenoids and a brain much interfered with. At the end stood little Jimmie, the mascot, and his face was yellow and thin. His eyes were all red and bloodshot, and at times leered forth with an uncanny knowingness that shot horrors through the pulses of those who were there to judge him.
>
> Then they called in what appeared to be the kind of creature Joe and Jimmie are growing up to be. This unhappy, degraded wreck of male humanity was found with the boys, holding the hat, which contained their gambling money. He was charged with causing boys to become juvenile delinquents, the fine for which is $500 or a year in prison.
>
> The boys were each fined $2, which they immediately paid, all except poor little Jimmie, who began to cry, and was allowed till Saturday to find it.

- **Explanation for youth crime:** Social causes
- **Purpose of punishment:** Parens patriae: welfare or rehabilitation-based
- **Age of youth:** 7–15 (except Manitoba and Quebec, 7–17). Provisions were in place for a judge to send anyone over the age of 14 to be tried in an adult court.

With the introduction of the Juvenile Delinquents Act in 1908 came a number of significant shifts. For the first time, justice legislation considered a special category of offenders based on age. Juvenile delinquents, as they were called, were young people between the ages of 7 and 15 (up to age 17 in Quebec and Manitoba) who were convicted of a crime. In a 1929 update to the act, juvenile delinquency was formally defined as:

> any child who violates any provision of the Criminal Code or of any Dominion or provincial statute, or of any by-law or ordinance of any municipality, or who is guilty of a sexual immorality or any similar form of vice, or who is liable

by reason of any other act to be committed to an industrial school or juvenile reformatory under the provisions of any Dominion or provincial statute.[39]

The legislation also established separate courts for young people and changed the focus of justice for them from punishment to rehabilitation.

Let's consider this last point first. Throughout the latter part of the 19th century, reformers called for a more humane system of justice. A precursor to the John Howard Society, the Prisoners' Aid Society held a series of conferences. A report from one of these conferences not only advocated for a separate law for young people, it even hoped for a separate prison system for young adults: "... that this Conference is fully alive to the frightful evils necessarily resulting from the association of youthful offenders with the most depraved and hardened criminals in the ... Kingston and other Penitentiaries in the Dominion ... necessity for the establishment of a special reformatory for young men between the age of 16 and 30...."[40] Furthermore, an examination of legislation prior to the JDA in 1908 shows that it did not come about overnight.

In Ontario, the Act for Establishing Prisons for Young Offenders (1857) and the Canada-wide Act Respecting Arrest, Trial and Imprisonment of Youthful Offenders (1894) were moving Canada toward a more rehabilitative approach to youth justice. According to criminologist Sandra J. Bell, the JDA of 1908 was a welfare-based juvenile justice system.[41] This meant that the purpose of the system was rehabilitation, focusing on the needs of the individual offender, with an eye to the best interests of the child and family.[42] The principle of parens patriae that guided the act meant that the state would function like a parent, becoming responsible for the well-being of young people who ended up in conflict with the law. Section 38 explains it as follows: "the care and custody of a juvenile delinquent shall approximate as nearly as may be that which should be given by its parents, and that as far as practicable every juvenile delinquent shall be treated, not as criminal, but as a misdirected and misguided child, and one needing of aid, encouragement, help and assistance."[43]

Fundamentally, these changes brought about a dedicated juvenile justice system. As mentioned, the JDA flowed from the principle of parens patriae, Latin for "parent of the nation," indicating the role of the state in caring for children where their own caregivers could not. Essentially, this also created the role of probation officers. Probation officers would play a central role—as they continue to do today—in the functioning of the youth justice system. Section 31 of the act defines their role as follows: to represent the interests of the child when a case is heard in court. Some might argue that the role of probation officers had competing objectives. They were responsible for conducting investigations, as well as for supervising children sentenced to probation. Thus, they worked for both the court and the juvenile.

The JDA was a fairly discretionary system geared toward treating children as misguided, rather than as criminals. However, throughout its lengthy history (1908–1984) both these pillars of discretion and rehabilitation came under attack. On one hand, opponents were concerned that the legislation was too open-ended and didn't do enough to safeguard the rights of children. On the other hand, some attacked the legislation for being too lenient or soft on crime and felt that young people needed to be punished as responsible agents.

In 1961, the Government of Canada commissioned a report to study the state of juvenile delinquency in Canada. It was published in 1965 as *The Report of the Department of Justice Committee on Juvenile Delinquency*, or more colloquially as the "McLeod Report," named after its commissioner. There was some concern at the time that juvenile crime was on the rise. The youth population was growing following the Second World War. It was generally believed that rates of youth crime were even outpacing this growth. Statistics cited in the report indicate an overall 9.5 percent increase in the Canadian youth population between 1957 and 1961, but a 17 percent increase in juvenile court appearances.[44] Furthermore, the report cited the tension between the two primary explanations for youth crime at the time: individual responsibility, like hereditary or character defects (psychological), vs. the influence of the social environment, like gang involvement or an impoverished family (sociological).[45]

Subtly, yet significantly, there was another noteworthy philosophical shift happening. In spite of supporting the need for a special justice system for youth, the narrative of the report articulates the problem somewhat differently than had previously been conceived. Section 62 states that youth legislation is simply a modification of ordinary, adult criminal legislation, but for young people.[46] However, this was not quite accurate. The authors of the JDA came at crime from a welfare model, while adult legislation was much more about crime control. Adult criminal legislation individualized responsibility for criminal behaviour, yet the JDA intentionally placed blame on the social context of the young person. This way of talking about crime control would become prominent in youth justice, and remains so today.

The McLeod Report identified three key problems with the JDA and its implementation. First, there was a blurring of federal and provincial responsibilities. Typically, child welfare is provincial, while criminal law is federal. The JDA skirted both. It was a response to juvenile crime, and at the same time it was about child welfare. This created some troubling discrepancies in implementation. Criminal law, or any law for that matter (as is the intent of rule of law), is to be applied equally across the country. However, as the McLeod Report cited, many provinces were treating young people more as child welfare cases, while others were focused on juvenile delinquency. The focus of the legislation wasn't clear. Second, the words "juvenile delinquent" were of concern to some. The fear was that the term stigmatized young people, regardless of their reasons for involvement with youth courts. The report recommended changing the language to "child offender" or "youth offender." Third, it was recommended that both the lower and upper age limits be changed. On the younger side, this was meant to account for the inability of children ages seven, eight, and nine to be fully responsible for delinquent actions. And, on the upper end, it was meant to accommodate for changes in youth development to recognize that teenagers as old as 16 and 17 were still very much dependent on parents, while also not yet being fully emotionally mature. The report recommended that the act apply to young people from the ages of either 10 to 17, or 12 to 17.

Overall, the report supported a more rehabilitative approach with young people. This might be surprising, given the unresolved tensions between the ideas of rehabilitation and punishment—or individual versus social responsibility—which have remained throughout the history of youth justice. The report reinforced the value of not punishing children and youth, instead treating them as people in need of treatment (as section 38 of the JDA described them): "In the case of the juvenile offender it is accepted that incapacitation should not be the primary objective in itself. The goal instead is to ensure, as the pre-eminent consideration, that the juvenile offender is assisted to become a law-abiding citizen."[47] It was believed, in spite of calls for harsher punishments, that a rehabilitative philosophy should remain the primary framework for dealing with juvenile delinquents. Much effort was put into this report and new legislation was crafted. However, it ultimately died at the legislative table, and significant proposals for change did not emerge again until the mid-1970s.

In an effort to clarify what was not working with the JDA, and to implement changes, the Solicitor General of Canada submitted a report in 1975 proposing that new legislation titled "Young Persons in Conflict with the Law Act" be introduced. Fundamentally, this proposal shared the premise that young people in trouble are really children in need.[48] It also proposed that any legislation regarding youth crime should improve the lives of the people who perpetrate it. Significantly, the Solicitor General identified that the state had not always been able to function as the "kindly parent," as had been intended, largely because resources were insufficiently allocated toward youth justice practices.[49] Furthermore, in spite of the stated and perceived intention of this kindliness, many youth courts were in fact focusing primarily on deterrence, punishment, and detention.[50] As the McLeod Report did before it, the Young Persons in Conflict with the Law Act also suggested that blurring between the goals of welfare and crime control was problematic. Legal scholar Jeffrey S. Leon summarized this when he asked in a research article: Is the legislation about protecting children, or protecting people from children?[51] In Victorian times it worked both ways; the neglected child *was* seen as a potential criminal. However, creating a distinction was important in the modern era. As such, in 1975, the Solicitor General of Canada put forward 108 recommendations for change, including redrafting the entire JDA. Here are a few highlights:

1. The legislation should only focus on criminal offences.
2. The age of a youth should be 14–18.
3. Diversion programs should be created and encoded.
4. The informal system of the JDA should be replaced by a formal, rights-based system.
5. There should be an adequate mechanism for review: the system itself should be accountable.
6. Children should not be detained where adults are detained.
7. Youth should be assisted by a lawyer.
8. Youth should be assisted by a youth worker who can stand by them and explain the process along the way.
9. Custody and probation comulatively should not be greater than 3 years.[52]

However, like the preceding report, the Solicitor General's recommendations also failed to be translated into law. It wasn't until 1982 that the Young Offenders Act was legislated, and it wasn't until 1984 that it was adopted. Before examining the act in the next chapter, I would like to once again return to the parallel—yet connected—discussion of residential schools.

Residential Schools: 1908 to 1983

> "The assault on Aboriginal identity began the moment the child took the first step across the school's threshold."
> —Truth & Reconciliation Commission[53]

I concluded the previous section on residential schools by discussing the grave concerns presented in the Bryce report in 1907 (i.e., that many Indigenous children were dying in the schools). Tragically, despite the report, nothing was done. In fact, the situation worsened. By 1920, it became compulsory for all status Indigenous children to attend residential schools. There are documented incidents of parents refusing. In these cases, the children were forcibly removed from their homes, and the parents were jailed for their opposition.[54] In 1922—after his forced retirement—Dr. Peter Bryce wrote another account of the failure of the government to care for the health of Indigenous peoples. This one, much more frank in its delivery and title, *The Story of a National Crime: Being an Appeal for Justice to the Indians of Canada*.

Bryce claimed that the Minister of Aboriginal Affairs at the time, Duncan Scott, opposed his previous recommendations for change. After the first report was published, Scott informed Dr. Bryce that his annual medical reports of "Indian" residential schools were no longer needed.[55] However, despite this, Bryce continued to examine some troubling trends—including the decline of the Indigenous population. After examining trends in the overall health of Indigenous peoples across the country, including those in residential schools, Bryce concluded that there had been an overall decline in the population due to early mortality, where there in fact should have been a 1.5 percent increase based on the growth trends of Indigenous peoples.[56] Bryce called this a "criminal disregard" for the Canadian government's treaty obligations.[57] He was ultimately forced to retire after continued government rebuttal and disregard for his concerns.[58] Other public figures of the day also characterized government conduct toward Indigenous peoples as criminal. In 1907, S. H. Blake, a lawyer who was examining the mission work of the Anglican Church, described the deaths of so many Indigenous children as preventable and near to deserving the charge of manslaughter.[59]

The threat of tuberculosis was constant in the early decades of the schools. It rampaged through the schools, a clear consequence of settler colonization. In the words of historian John S. Milloy,

> The tubercular epidemic, which had moved across the country with the tide of settlement, was the result of white presence coupled with the Aboriginal community's lack of immunity to infectious diseases. It was also, however, a consequence of the process of colonization, of the forces that marginalized communities, divorcing them from their traditional life ways. Confinement

to reserves and overcrowded European-style lodgings of the lowest quality provided the fertile ground with malnutrition, lack of sanitation, despair, alcoholism, and government parsimony, from which infection ran its mortal course through communities.[60]

In the early days of white settlement, observers noted that Indigenous children were strong and robust, but now many were withered and ragged. Poor health was a symptom of an assimilative process. The overall environment was radically different than what Aboriginal children were used to. Without being able to dress as they had dressed, without being able to speak their languages, without family and community support, poor physical, emotional, and mental health ensued.

The era through to the Second World War and beyond was similar, and health outcomes continued to be poor.[61] Indigenous children were not fed properly. In fact, the Mohawk Institute near Brantford, Ontario was known as the Mush Hole for the disgusting gruel that was the primary, sometimes only, source of nutrition for the children who attended.

Aside from the health issues already discussed, this era of residential school history was also characterized by insufficient funding and the continued mistreatment of Indigenous children.[62] In some cases there were instances of Indigenous parents trying to intervene, especially those who had experienced the abuses of the school environment as children themselves. However, the ongoing mantra of the Department of Indian Affairs was that the best way to change "Indians" was by educating the "Indian" out of the child, thus changing entire communities.[63] Despite this mantra, even the educational components of the system were found to be lacking. Milloy, citing a report by the Director of Educational Services, found that residential schools up until the 1950s "contained very little of instructional value but consisted mainly of the performance of repetitive, routine chores of little or no educational value."[64] In other words, residential schools were hardly schools.

Moreover, physical and sexual abuses were rampant. Many children were beaten for failing to comply with rules and some clergy and teachers perpetrated sexual abuse. The powerful Aboriginal Peoples' Television Network (2012) documentary *We Were Children* tells the stories of two survivors of residential school, Lyna and Glen. These stories involve children locked in cellars and children afraid to fall asleep at night for fear of sexual abuse. This pattern of abuse existed from the early days of residential schools until the time they closed: "All too often [children] were overworked, underfed, badly clothed, housed in unsanitary quarters, beaten with whips, rods and fists, chained and shackled, bound hand and foot, locked in closets, basements and bathrooms, and had their heads shaved or closely cropped."[65] Even before all the residential schools were closed, Phil Fontaine, the Grand Chief of the Assembly of Manitoba Chiefs was calling for a national inquiry. A truth and reconciliation commission was established in 2008. One of its reports, *They Came for the Children*, spoke about Fontaine's experiences of sexual abuse at the Fort Alexander school in Manitoba. When asked how extensive the abuse had been he replied, "If we took an example, my Grade 3 class, if there were twenty boys in this particular class, every single one of the twenty would have experienced what I experienced."[66]

Willful government ignorance of deplorable conditions in residential schools, patterns of physical, sexual, and cultural abuse, as well as the flawed and racist premises of the entire system, would set the tone for the next 80 years until the closure of the schools in the mid-1990s. Beginning in the 1960s, residential schools began to close. Some were taken out of the hands of the churches to be overseen by government, while others were handed over to Indigenous communities. By the mid-1980s most schools were closed, and the last one shut its doors in 1996. By that time, over 100 years of trauma had been imposed on generations of Indigenous young people, and residential schools had had devastating impacts on Indigenous families and communities. Taking this into account is it any wonder that, today, there's an overrepresentation of Indigenous youth in conflict with the law?

CONCLUSION: SOME CONSIDERATIONS OF POWER, RACE, GENDER, AND CLASS

Over the last 125 years, youth justice law in Canada has followed an oscillating pattern between tough on crime versus tough on root causes. At the core of this swinging pendulum three questions have remained. First, what is the culpability of a young person who commits a crime? Second, who counts as a youth? Third, do young people have diminished responsibility for their choices? Is it their social environment that is responsible for their behaviour or are they, as individuals, at fault for their criminal activity? What has remained consistent is that those in power have had control when it comes to answering these questions. It is not possible to talk about a history of youth justice in Canada without discussing this variable.

It is the powerful—those with privilege—who shape the lives of the less powerful. Throughout Canada's history, impoverished youth have been more likely to come into conflict with the law. Meanwhile, in the case of Aboriginal peoples, we have seen the creation of a destructive system of "education," which was really a system of incarceration. Residential schools saw children forcibly removed from communities and placed in institutions that took away their name and replaced it with a number. While the child-savers movement in the early 20th century was busy trying to make youth justice better for settler Canadians (especially those with lower socio-economic status) little attention was given to Indigenous children and youth confined in residential schools. While men were busy maintaining **patriarchy**, unilaterally writing laws and building prisons, women were second-class citizens. The system of youth justice reflects patriarchy. It is one of dominance, power, and control, of powerful white men ruling over those with less power. A careful analysis of youth justice must examine all of these layers.

As I have studied and documented some of this history, I have become increasingly convinced that, since Confederation—but especially so in the last 40 years—legislators have been less interested in understanding the *real* reasons behind criminal behaviour and more focused on controlling those who are different from them. The agenda has been political rather than social. If policies were indeed premised on social welfare, they would have to examine structural violence and the effects of settler colonialism on

Indigenous peoples. If policies were truly about rehabilitation, we would need to know more about the pain of young people who break the law, in order to help them heal. One of the main premises of this book is that youth justice law, and the corresponding criminal justice practices, must account for histories of trauma in youth who come in conflict with it. In the next chapter, I'll discuss a history of youth justice from 1984 to the present day—from the Young Offenders Act to the Youth Criminal Justice Act.

GLOSSARY OF TERMS

Indigenous peoples are the Original peoples in the area now known as Canada. Historically, these people were inappropriately called "Indians" by settlers and were lumped together as one group. However, Indigenous peoples represent more than one group. They include First Nations, Métis, and Inuit people—essentially the original inhabitants of Turtle Island (North America). There are thousands of Indigenous peoples across Canada, reflecting many languages, many cultures, and many communities.

Patriarchy is a system of domination that involves men using power to control women. This can be ideological, political, or religious, and can take place in the work environment, the home, or in any other social spheres. This text presumes that patriarchy is ingrained in most, if not all, Canadian social systems. As much as society has taken steps toward equality, there is still more work to do. In later chapters, when we specifically address the issue of male violence, this will become more evident.

Settler colonialism is about one group (landed) taking territory from another (current inhabitants).[67] In Canada, this has taken place through a variety of overt and covert practices, for example: settler people committing to but not honouring treaties; legislation (i.e., the Indian Act); the Canadian government forcing Indigenous children to attend residential schools; removing Indigenous children from their homes and placing them into foster care (i.e., the sixties scoop—the Canadian practice, beginning in the 1960s and continuing until the late 1980s, of apprehending Indigenous children and fostering or adopting them out, usually into non-Aboriginal families); removing Indigenous peoples from their lands and forcing them onto reserves; forcing capitalism and resource extraction on to a way of life that was formerly about sharing and preservation; and so on. Each of these practices represents an attempt to assimilate Indigenous peoples, destroying their cultures and ultimately their identities.

QUESTIONS FOR REFLECTION

Imagine the following scenario: In order to keep warm, a homeless Indigenous youth falls asleep in the lobby of a bank after it closes. Two university students discover him as they come in to use the bank machine. They phone the police because they are unable to step around him to get money out for cab fare. Police officers arrive. They forcibly remove the homeless boy and ticket him for trespassing.

1. Is this an example of rule of law being functional or dysfunctional? Why is it illegal for a street-involved person to seek shelter, particularly in a bank?
2. Do you think it should be illegal for some people in Canadian society to live in opulence while others suffer on the streets? Is this question beyond rule of law? Why might this question be important to consider for youth justice?
3. Under Canadian law, should it make a difference that the young person in this example is Indigenous? Why or why not?

RECOMMENDED READING

Milloy, John S. *A National Crime: The Canadian Government and the Residential School System, 1879 to 1986*. Winnipeg: University of Manitoba Press, 1999.

John S. Milloy provides an exhaustive account of the history of Indigenous residential schools. This book provides for an education not often taught in Canadian schools. It exposes a darker, yet very significant, side of Canada's treatment of Indigenous peoples.

Schissel, Bernard. *Still Blaming Children: Youth Conduct and the Politics of Child Hating*. Halifax: Fernwood Publishing, 2006.

In this book, sociologist Bernard Schissel demonstrates that getting tough on crime with young people is ineffective.

Truth and Reconciliation Commission of Canada. *They Came for the Children*. Winnipeg: Truth and Reconciliation Commission of Canada, 2012.

This book, a product of the Truth and Reconciliation Commission, describes the troubling history of "Indian" residential schools in Canada. It explains the racist rationale, as well as the colonial agenda of taking lands and assimilating Indigenous peoples, while also describing the pattern of horrific abuses prevalent in the schools.

3 | Youth Justice Today— 1984 to the Present

"It is difficult to punish people who are like us or our children, but much easier to punish those we do not understand or with whom we do not empathize."
—Bernard Schissel[1]

It's debatable whether or not Canada is tuning in to the unique needs of youth in relation to criminal justice. Since it came into effect in 2003, the Youth Criminal Justice Act (YCJA) has significantly decreased the number of young people behind bars. Canadian youth incarceration rates were particularly high—the highest in the world—during the 1980s and 1990s. Measures in the YCJA seek to more clearly separate serious from non-serious crimes and to deal with violent crimes differently than non-violent crimes. Alternatives to the criminal justice system have also been clearly written into the legislation. Restorative justice is more prominent, as is the role of the probation officer in community-based sanctions. What remains to be seen is whether there's political will to stay faithful to the original purposes of the 2003 YCJA. Some recent changes to the legislation indicate that politicians and the public quickly forget—conveniently for the first group and naively for the second—the greater risks of incarceration over more meaningful consequences.

In spite of important advances, the needs of Indigenous youth continue to be blatantly ignored. Close to 36 percent of inmate populations in youth justice facilities sentenced to custody are Indigenous young people—while they represent only 6 percent of the general population.[2] This crisis should be of concern and requires immediate attention. In the previous chapter, I identified some of the roots of this problem, such as settler colonialism and the harmful nature of residential school practices. As residential schools were all but closed by the 1980s we will not be discussing them in this chapter; however, in future chapters we will visit other aspects of settler colonialism and will explore what it could mean to act in just ways toward Aboriginal peoples.

As in chapter 2, this chapter will continue to follow a critical perspective, asking questions about power in the current youth justice system. In some ways, this is similar to a social justice stance. It moves criminology beyond a focus on individual crimes toward looking at society as a whole. It asks why some are marginalized while others are privileged. In a chapter titled "Critical Criminology and Youth Justice in the Risk Society" in *Youth at Risk and Youth Justice: A Canadian Overview*, Bryan Hogeveen and Joanne C. Minaker discuss the value of adopting a social justice approach in criminology: "While mainstream criminology does its part to examine root causes, consequences, and control of youth crime, critical criminology begins from a very different perspective. One strand of critical scholarship takes contemporary criminal justice processes to task for their part in contributing to structural inequalities that marginalize young people. Others presume that Canadian society is organized in hierarchies of age, gender, race, ethnicity, class, sexuality, and ability ... the most marginalized in society ... are thrown into a world that is discriminatory, racist, and sexist."[3] A trauma-informed youth justice perspective must somehow account for all of this, starting by putting the formation of youth legislation under a microscope, and continuing to look at enforcement and the incapacitation of young people. It must also take a wide-angled view to ask how we can get the system working better for all—in particular the most marginalized groups in our communities.

This chapter will tell the story of youth justice legislation from 1984 until the present day, and will provide a context for discussing (a) how we understand young people; (b) how we understand their culpability regarding criminal activity; and (c) what Canadian society has considered to be an appropriate response at each historical, legislative stage. A discussion of declining youth crime rates in recent years, as well as looking at the number of youth who are coming into conflict with the law, will set us up to consider questions about why rates of incarceration for Aboriginal youth continue to rise. A case study of recent amendments to the YCJA will further our critical agenda explaining (a) how media influences public perceptions about fear of youth crime, and (b) how government and political parties use this fear to change laws in ways that gain them political advantage even though the changes aren't shaped by evidence.

1984 TO 2003: YOUNG OFFENDERS ACT

> **"Teen Gets 20 Months for 7 Week Spree of Office Burglaries," from the *Toronto Star*, December 24, 1985**
>
> A teenager responsible for 24 burglaries in downtown offices during a seven-week "spree" has been sentenced to 20 months in a reformatory.
>
> Sean Massicotte and a co-accused obtained money and goods worth more than $4,000 and caused damages of more than $3,000 during the break-ins, prosecutor Ian Scott told District Court Judge H. Ward Allen yesterday.
>
> Massicotte, 18, of no fixed address, pleaded guilty to 19 charges of breaking, entering and theft and five of breaking and entering with intent to steal. The last five charges were laid in cases where the premises were illegally entered but nothing was taken.

> As well as being sent to a reformatory, Massicotte was placed on probation for two years.
> The co-accused, a young offender who can't be named, was earlier sentenced to nine months in custody. They got into a University Ave. office through an unsecured window and managed to steal more than $3,600 in cash, $900 of which was used to buy a motorcycle which has since been seized by police, Scott said.
> He added that in a couple of cases, the burglars found liquor on the premises and drank it. In one case they flung files and plants around an office and caused considerable damage.
> They stole radios, pen and pencil sets, calculators and recording devices and from a Richmond St. W. office managed to "score" a pair of tickets to a Blue Jays baseball game, the prosecutor told the judge.[4]

- **Explanation for youth crime:** Individual responsibility. A young person is to blame for their actions.
- **Purpose of punishment:** Protection of society while respecting the rights of offenders.
- **Age of youth:** 12–17

With the advent of the Young Offenders Act (YOA) in 1984, there was a marked shift in how Canada dealt with youth crime. Formerly, a social welfare model (the Juvenile Delinquents Act, or JDA) focused on the environment around the young person. With the YOA, a rights-based justice model came into being. The YOA introduced due process into the youth system. It was about procedural justice: trying to treat everyone equally. Before this, youth justice had largely been informal, but now the process was clearly defined. The belief was that the rights of young people needed to be better protected in the justice process by ensuring that youth were treated equally, and thus with fairness.

However, with these changes, responsibility for crime was shifted from society-at-large or from certain social environmental factors—like the family—onto the individual young person. Along with rights for the young person came the obligation that they take responsibility. In many ways, this mirrored the approach used with adult criminals, only with some accommodation for the (young) age of the person in question. Not surprisingly, this change led to skyrocketing rates of youth behind bars in Canada. Before discussing this, however, some analysis of the YOA legislation will be useful. Although the legislation continued to use terms like "rehabilitation" and talked about functioning in the best interests of the child, a drift toward the protection of society was articulated in its principles. For example, see Section 3(1):

> (a) crime prevention is essential to the long-term protection of society and requires addressing the underlying causes of crime by young persons and

developing multi-disciplinary approaches to identifying and effectively responding to children and young persons at risk of committing offending behaviour in the future;

(a.1) while young persons should not in all instances be held accountable in the same manner or suffer the same consequences for their behaviour as adults, young persons who commit offences should nonetheless bear responsibility for their contraventions;

(b) society must, although it has the responsibility to take reasonable measures to prevent criminal conduct by young persons, be afforded the necessary protection from illegal behaviour[5]

Canadian sociologist Bernard Schissel has taken a particularly strong stance in describing the change youth justice has undergone from protecting children to protecting society from children.[6] In *Still Blaming Children: Youth Conduct and the Politics of Child Hating* he calls Canada's war on crime a "war against youth."[7] When examining which young people were coming into conflict with the law in the era of the JDA, we saw impoverished youth and, in residential school settings, Aboriginal children. It shouldn't come as a great surprise that those in power would move in the direction of individualizing blame. Schissel says of government that "Crime control is essentially a political act; it involves domination by wealthy men over poor men, by men over women, by politically dominant racial groups over marginalized racial minorities, and by enfranchised adults over children."[8] In this way, it (falsely) releases society from its responsibility for disadvantaged children.

Schissel uses the metaphor of a theatre to describe various actors involved in the deflection of responsibility from society onto young people. He suggests that the theatrical nature of youth justice conversations convince the audience—the general public—that the hero is the person/actor who solves the problem. By taking on a tough-on-crime persona, the state casts itself in the role of hero. Another important actor is the media. Schissel argues that media has incredible power. That is, it is the main vehicle for shaping knowledge, or how the public comes to understand events. Articulating this along the same lines as Marshall McLuhan, Schissel says that media simply delivers messages that society wants to hear. In this case, society doesn't want to hear about its culpability, how it marginalizes and harms some young people.[9] Society doesn't want to hear that it creates criminals.

One of the tools of the media is the creation of "folk devils." Schissel describes the term coined by Stanley Cohen as follows, "those who are identified as threats to the moral and physical well-being of society."[10] Not surprisingly, one of the primary versions of the folk devil created by media, in partnership with government, is the criminal. The criminal as a folk devil is different than "us"—the rest of society, the law-abiding citizens. In examining the role of the media in the creation of the young offender as a folk devil, Swedish criminologist Felipe Estrada claims, "The juvenile offender has gone from being perceived as a victim of a poor upbringing and difficult environments, to being a 'super predator' who assaults other people out of choice."[11] Thus, when we consider the predominant place that "protecting society" has come to occupy in youth justice discourse and legislation, whom are we being "protected" against? Schissel shares a few ideas:

- People unlike "us"
- The street person
- The drug trafficker
- The violent
- The amoral[12]

The language used by the media is inflammatory. Contrary to media reports, youth violent crime during the era of the YOA did not increase. Instead, crime rates remained relatively steady over time.[13] Homicide rates (which criminologists believe to be the best way of measuring violent crime) also remained stable.[14] Similar language is used when media is reporting about youth gangs. Criminologist Julian Tanner calls it vitriolic: "According to newspaper sources, gangs are not only new, they are also widespread. This assertion does not, however, relate well to actual patterns of youthful behavior."[15] The role of the legislation then becomes about protection. Although the legislation suggests the best way to protect society is by rehabilitating young people, one cannot divorce rehabilitation from the punitive outcomes of the YOA. Within a few short years of the introduction of the YOA, Canada was incarcerating young people at a higher rate than any other country in the world.

This relates to a social constructionist perspective—that how people make sense of their world happens through language—of social problems. As Tanner states, "Constructionists interested in the problem of youth are more likely to pose questions about media representations of youth gangs than the cause of gang behaviour. They might also ask, 'Why do we care more about youth gangs than youth homelessness?'"[16] Crime is a problem because it is labelled as such. The casting of the young offender as a folk devil impacts communities' perceptions and, ultimately, increases their fear of crime.

Tracking legislation for these types of changes is relevant to understanding how society understands crime. Furthermore, legislation affects peoples' lives. Logically, it's important to ask why. Why make a shift toward individual responsibility? Some scholars, like the ones described above, argue that media fuelled a fear of a growing youth crime problem and that politicians capitalized on this. Presenting tough-on-crime policies was one way for people to get elected. In some ways this is true; however, the increasing politicization of crime in Canada emerged somewhat later than it did for its neighbour to the south, the United States. While President Ronald Reagan was mobilizing the War on Drugs in the early 1980s (a particularly tough-on-crime approach that has had grave consequences for marginalized communities, especially African-American and Latino people), Canada was still—in some ways— more progressive in its approach to crime. At the same time as the War on Drugs was taking place to the south, the emergence of the Canadian Charter of Rights and Freedoms provided the impetus for ensuring that young offenders were also granted the same rights as adults. Nonetheless, attitudes about young offenders were also changing—the rehabilitative approach was not necessarily looked at favourably. In some ways, the discussion of rights disguised the punitive nature of the YOA—because having the same rights as adults also meant being subjected to similar punishments.

In 1994, the *Canadian Journal of Criminology* did a special issue on the YOA, 10 years after its implementation. Some of the discussion and debate in the issue focused on the differences between the attitudes of the public and police on one side, and academics on the other. The former felt the YOA was still too soft on crime, while the latter were concerned with growing rates of incarcerated young people and the minimal impact this was having on youth crime rates. In his article "What's Wrong with YOA Bashing? What's Wrong with the YOA?—Recognizing the Limits of Law," criminologist Nicholas Bala detailed arguments on both sides. He suggested that critics who wanted to get tougher on crime—like most of the federal parties running in the 1993 election—failed to recognize the limits of punishment, which ignored the complexity of the social problems that give rise to youth crime.[17]

Paul Gendreau and Alan Leschied, two Canadian scholars, examined the YOA for its impacts on youth incarceration. Not only did they find a dramatic increase in imprisonment of young people, they also discovered that prison was itself a **criminogenic**—or crime-causing—factor.[18] That is, putting young people in prison increased their likelihood of committing a crime again. I'll return to this topic in future discussions (see chapter 7). Suffice it to say, it was at this point in Canadian history that criminologists began to name the harmful effects of incarceration and the iatrogenic nature of youth justice systems. The term **iatrogenic** is Greek, referring in this case to when harm (that is preventable) is brought on by the healer. Research during this era—as well as evidence today—indicated that the more a young person was involved with the youth criminal justice system, the more likely she or he was to do poorly in the future.[19] Of course, this begs the question of the purpose of youth justice. If the protection of society is supposed to be accomplished through the rehabilitation of young people, yet the justice system actually makes things worse, then whose needs is it serving? While academics have consistently raised these issues, politicians, media, and the general public largely ignore them. At the time, those in favour of punitive measures argued instead that the YOA legislation wasn't tough enough.

The critical reader needs to ask why. Does media sensationalize events to sell newspapers? Media is capitalistic, after all. Or does it also have to do with who newspapers are identifying as criminal? Is media racist, symptomatic of a racist society? Research findings certainly suggest that race is a factor in the tale of the folk devil. According to Tanner:

> Content analysis of the main Toronto daily newspapers, the *Star* and the *Sun*, reveals black people to be overrepresented ... particularly ... in news stories involving ... crime.... In crime stories they primarily appear as offenders, less often as victims. Whereas black offenders appear as predatory street criminals, white offenders show up in stories about (less threatening) white collar criminals.[20]

These racist portrayals of youth crime in the media are symptomatic of a growing divide in Canadian discourse between "us" and "them"—"the criminal" and the "law-abiding citizen." As Schissel says in the epigraph at the outset of this chapter, it is easier to punish when we cannot—or choose not to—empathize with a young offender.

Furthermore, the momentum often shifts toward favouring punitive measures as youth crimes—or particularly serious cases—become increasingly publicized by media and political parties. Thus, politicians and media have significant power. Many politicians will grab hold of a story and use it to advance an apparent tough-on-crime agenda. Really, this is an attempt to appeal to ignorant masses for votes. In this way, politicians put themselves in the position of rescuer, of hero. When I go on to discuss recent changes to the YCJA below, you'll see an example of this. Contrarily, a shift toward favouring a helping approach (e.g., rehabilitation, support, etc.) only seems to take place when people speak out about the impact of marginalization on young people. These advocates point toward mental health, poverty, family violence, and other social causes as the reasons for youth delinquency. Appropriate responses, they argue, should be geared toward social support. Movements away from a tough-on-crime approach have often started in more grassroots (e.g., nonprofits, community groups, etc.) or academic environments. This power struggle is real.

Ultimately, in 1995, politicians pandering to—or capitalizing on—the fear of the "criminal other" increased sentencing rates. Sentences changed from a maximum of three years of incarceration for second-degree murder to a maximum of five years, and went up to seven years for first-degree murder. This created a crisis in youth incarceration; the YOA, attitudes about youth crime, and the politicization of crime laid the groundwork for Canada having the highest rate of youth incarceration in the world. Something had to be done. Enter the Youth Criminal Justice Act.

CLOSURE OF "INDIAN" RESIDENTIAL SCHOOLS

During the era of the YOA, "Indian" residential schools were finally closing their doors for good. However, as residential schools began to close, the state dramatically increased the number of Indigenous children in the Child Welfare System. This practice, which mostly began in the 1960s, was known as the "sixties scoop." Patrick Johnston, in a 1983 report titled *Native Children and the Child Welfare System*, said the term came from a social worker during that era who said, "It was common practice in [British Columbia] in the mid-sixties to 'scoop' from their mothers on reserves almost all newly born children."[21] In British Columbia, the percentage of Aboriginal children in care prior to the 1960s was about 1 percent. By the end of the decade, it was closer to 35 percent.[22] This was one of the legacies of residential schools. Indigenous children were deeply hurt during their time in these schools and, as a result, as adults were unable to parent their own children properly. Rather than take responsibility for this harm, the state swooped in and removed children from homes, further adding to the intergenerational trauma in Indigenous communities. One survivor, Raymond Mason, explains it like this:

> For the longest time after I got married, I couldn't figure out why I was so distant, so cold to my own children. I thought the only way to show love to my children was to give them money and send them on their way. After going

through a healing process ... I found out that because of the fact that I went through the system for so long, not being able to be brought up by parents or have any parenting at all, I was never taught how to love as a parent, so how could I pass on love to my own children? This system has created a lot of dysfunctional situations, and not only with my family. You can look all over this system. I am having trouble to this day with my own son, with alcoholism, because I wasn't a good father. I didn't know how to be a good father. It was too late when I found out, and it's sad.[23]

In 2008, the Government of Canada issued a formal apology, in Parliament, to residential school survivors. In the opening words, Prime Minister Stephen Harper said:

The treatment of children in Indian Residential Schools is a sad chapter in our history. For more than a century, Indian Residential Schools separated over 150,000 Aboriginal children from their families and communities. In the 1870's, the federal government, partly in order to meet its obligation to educate Aboriginal children, began to play a role in the development and administration of these schools. Two primary objectives of the Residential Schools system were to remove and isolate children from the influence of their homes, families, traditions and cultures, and to assimilate them into the dominant culture. These objectives were based on the assumption Aboriginal cultures and spiritual beliefs were inferior and unequal. Indeed, some sought, as it was infamously said, "to kill the Indian in the child." Today, we recognize that this policy of assimilation was wrong, has caused great harm, and has no place in our country.[24]

Much has been written about the apology, some in praise, some in criticism. On one hand, some Indigenous peoples claim it doesn't go far enough; that it is words without action. How can the government apologize when it still colonially imposes itself on Indigenous lands, dishonours treaties, and assimilates through legislation? On the other hand, some of the Canadian public thought it was a waste of time and wondered why it was even necessary. In their belief, the schools were a thing of the past, and weren't something for those in the present to say "sorry" for. In spite of these polarized perspectives, there might be some small merit in an apology.

As part of a class action settlement for survivors, Canada established a five-year Truth and Reconciliation Commission (TRC) to document the experiences of survivors and to hold public events of reconciliation. In her analysis of the apology, a researcher for the TRC, Paulette Regan, says the following: "Official apologies by their nature may act as a catalyst in that they increase public understanding of the historical origins of Indigenous disadvantage."[25] Like a marker in the ground, Prime Minister Harper's statement is on record acknowledging wrongdoing. Of course, in and of itself, it doesn't change the nature of the relationship between Aboriginal peoples and settler Canadians. In fact, Regan suggests that apologies usually maintain the colonial status quo rather than precipitate change.[26] What most Canadians have failed to acknowledge, from her perspective, is that current attitudes and policies are similar to the ones being apologized for.[27] Without addressing this, an apology might simply be an exercise in alleviating the abuser's guilt, rather than addressing the abused person's pain. When we experience harm committed by another person against us, most of us want (a) the harm to stop, and (b) the person who did it to make changes so it doesn't happen again. As such, unless changed behaviour flows from an apology, the act of saying "sorry" simply becomes a part of the cycle of harmful behaviour.

To make the apology meaningful, there's more work for Canada to do to take responsibility. The trauma of colonialism has affected Indigenous peoples at individual, family, and community levels. As Melissa Walls et al. say in an article on high rates of Indigenous youth suicide: "For the Aboriginal peoples of North America, a unique and traumatic history of colonization contributes to intergenerational exposures to stressors and contemporary chronic strains."[28] In fact, suicide rates are five to six times higher among Indigenous youth than in the general population.[29] Furthermore, within Aboriginal communities in Canada, suicide rates are highest among youth whose parents attended residential schools.[30] This is but one impact of intergenerational trauma. Others include poverty, inadequate housing, loss of culture and language, high substance abuse rates coupled with poor health outcomes, and—significant for this text—conflict with the law.

2003 TO THE PRESENT: YOUTH CRIMINAL JUSTICE ACT

"Kids Who Hurt Can also Heal; Offenders, Victims Meet in Mediation Attempt to Reduce Courtroom Trials," from the *Toronto Star*, March 28, 2004

One year ago, when the new Youth Criminal Justice Act came into force, two 16-year-old boys were arrested and charged with an attack on a 14-year-old involving beer bottles and knives outside a Scarborough shopping mall. Instead of going to trial before a judge, the young offenders ... were sent to a program aimed at steering youths away from a life of crime, courts and custody.... A mediation conference like PACT can't proceed without a victim.... Sooner or later, then, it meant the 14-year-old would have a chance to speak. He tells the circle how "25 or 30 big guys" were chasing him, how his sister was threatened.... The victim's father, struggling with his emotions, says the family is still frightened a year after the incident, his daughter can't sleep and he won't let his kids take the bus. He installed a security alarm in the house, "but still we are scared." ... One of the most powerful aspects of a resolution conference is its emotional impact, says Lockett. "The offenders see the impact of their actions on others." ... There's a consensus on their restitution, a written letter of apology, a 1,000-word essay on how to deal with anger other than through violence, 50 hours of community service arranged by a probation officer, a course in anger management, and they must abide by their parents' rules and have no contact with the victim.[31]

- **Explanation for youth crime:** Individual responsibility
- **Purpose of Punishment:** Accountability, protection of the public, and rehabilitation
- **Age of youth:** 12–17

Currently, the Youth Criminal Justice Act (YCJA) primarily governs youth justice in Canada. Alongside the Criminal Code of Canada, the United Nations Convention on the Rights of the Child, and the Canadian Charter of Rights and Freedoms, the YCJA provides the shape for youth justice policy and interventions. It came into force in 2003. There were a number of reasons for its creation. It attempts to: (a) better separate serious from non-serious, or violent from non-violent offences, in order to more appropriately deal with both (under the YOA, many youth were being indiscriminately incarcerated even in situations of non-violent crime); (b) balance rehabilitation with punishment; (c) create more opportunities for restorative justice and other alternatives to incarceration; and (d) provide more meaningful opportunities for victims to have a say in their case. As the Department of Justice Canada says:

> The YCJA introduced significant reforms to address concerns about how the youth justice system had evolved under [previous legislation] ... the overuse of courts and incarceration in less serious cases, disparity and unfairness in sentencing, a lack of effective reintegration of young people released from custody, and the need to better take into account the interests of victims.[32]

Accordingly, the YCJA is thought by some to be a more middle of the road approach between the JDA and the YOA—returning some of the notions of youth justice to their social welfare roots. Criminologists John Winterdyk and Nicholas Jones suggest that the YCJA fits best within a community change model because it is interested in modifying, or getting at, the roots of youth crime.[33] As much as this might be true for some cases, one still has to wonder where the positive outcomes are for Indigenous youth.

The preamble to the legislation outlines the context and purpose of youth criminal justice. It states that society has a responsibility to young people to help guide them into adulthood, because of developmental and other needs.[34] The state also identifies its obligation, as well as the obligation of communities, to prevent crime from happening in the first place by getting at root causes. The YCJA states:

> Canadian society should have a youth criminal justice system that commands respect, takes into account the interests of victims, fosters responsibility and ensures accountability through meaningful consequences and effective rehabilitation and reintegration, and that reserves its most serious intervention for the most serious crimes and reduces the over-reliance on incarceration for non-violent young persons.[35]

For scholars and practitioners who want to take a more trauma-informed approach, it is significant to note that serious consequences are equated with incarceration.

Later in this book, an argument will be made that imprisonment fails the seriousness test; that is, it does not adequately address crime in a way that holds young people accountable, addresses victims' needs, or allow for appropriate reintegration. Ultimately, it fails in producing public safety. While some attention is paid in the YCJA to the developmental differences of young people in comparison to adults, none is given to trauma. In the next chapter, I'll describe young offenders as people who have more often than not experienced some form of victimization and trauma.

The YCJA starts with a Declaration of Principle. It describes the intention to protect the public, while also recognizing the uniqueness of age—that a young person has less blameworthiness than an adult—and the special needs of certain categories of youth, like Aboriginal peoples. The following principles in Section 3(1) guide this act: the protection of the public, through accountability, rehabilitation, and crime prevention; the idea that young people are less blameworthy than adults who commit crime; the belief that criminal justice responses should attend to the needs of diverse young people differently, with special attention to Indigenous persons; and, an increased emphasis on victims.[36]

Alternative measures are an important part of the YCJA, both for effectiveness and cost. It is four times more expensive to incarcerate youth than to supervise them in the community, and youth who go through alternative measures are less likely to reoffend than those who are incarcerated. Alternatives are mostly premised on the philosophy of restorative justice. Restorative justice is a philosophical orientation to crime, as well as a set of particular practices. As a philosophy, it focuses on justice as healing, rather than punishment. It puts victims' needs at the forefront and attempts to hold offenders directly accountable for their actions. As a practice, restorative justice often, although not always, involves some type of encounter between victims and offenders, such as victim-offender conferencing, family group conferencing, or some type of Peacemaking Circle. Options like extrajudicial measures (EJM) and extrajudicial sanctions (EJS) are legislatively available to police and courts to divert youth away from the formal system.

Police are given discretion to use EJM options prior to charging a young person. Under the legislation, they can:

- Take no further action
- Issue a warning
- Issue a formal caution
- Make a referral to a community program
- If the situation is more serious, refer the matter to the Crown for them to issue a formal caution.[37]

Police officers are encouraged to make use of these more informal practices in order to keep youth out of the criminal justice system.[38] Section 6(1) states:

> A police officer shall, before starting judicial proceedings or taking any other measures under this Act against a young person alleged to have committed

an offence, consider whether it would be sufficient, having regard to the principles set out in section 4, to take no further action, warn the young person, administer a caution, if a program has been established under section 7, or, with the consent of the young person, refer the young person to a program or agency in the community that may assist the young person not to commit offences.[39]

It is important to note that police officers are explicitly given permission to refer a young person to **extrajudicial** measures even where it is not their first offence. Some researchers, as well as the Canadian Department of Justice, recommend that this should be the approach used even for young people who breach probation orders, as long as their actions are non-violent. Research has shown this approach is working to keep young people out of the system. There has been a steady decline in charges brought against young people by police since the implementation of the YCJA, as well as an increase in less formal sanctions. EJS can also be used from pre-charge all the way to post-conviction. If EJS are applied the young person is expected to take responsibility for their behaviour, there is sufficient evidence for the Crown to proceed with a charge, and the parent/guardian must be notified.[40]

EJS and EJM are considered alternatives to the criminal justice system: a way to better meet the needs of victims, and a way to steer young offenders away from the criminal justice system. It should be noted, though, that restorative justice is more than an alternative to the traditional criminal justice system. It's also about re-envisioning what justice is and how best to meet the needs of communities. In the restorative justice model, power is shifted from the courts toward those most directly affected by crimes: victims, offenders, and communities. The PACT program described in the previous *Toronto Star* article is an example of restorative justice. Victims are given a voice and young offenders are made to understand the impacts of their actions. Together, a consensus is reached about a just outcome; in this case some form of restitution. The coordinator of the PACT program, Diane Sparling, describes how this fits into the grander story of youth justice in Canada:

> They're typically the sort of incidents that years ago might have been settled on the spot by a principal, storeowner or police officer under the old Juvenile Delinquents Act. But over the past two decades, a kind of demonization of youth under the Young Offenders Act (which replaced the Juvenile Delinquents Act in 1984), as one youth justice expert describes it, thrust these incidents into the court system.[41]

Legislation also includes support for conferencing, and youth justice committees. These are restorative justice processes whereby victims, offenders, and community members are brought together, where appropriate, to deal with an offence. Impacts of the crime are discussed, and agreements are written and returned to the courts. Outcomes include sanctions like restitution, community service, and other forms of taking responsibility. Overall, the YCJA has decreased youth incarceration.

Sentencing Principles of the Youth Criminal Justice Act, S.C. 2002, c. 1, s. 38(1) and (2)

38. (1) The purpose of sentencing under section 42 (youth sentences) is to hold a young person accountable for an offence through the imposition of just sanctions that have meaningful consequences for the young person and that promote his or her rehabilitation and reintegration into society, thereby contributing to the long-term protection of the public.

(2) A youth justice court that imposes a youth sentence on a young person shall determine the sentence in accordance with the principles set out in section 3 and the following principles:

(a) the sentence must not result in a punishment that is greater than the punishment that would be appropriate for an adult who has been convicted of the same offence committed in similar circumstances;

(b) the sentence must be similar to the sentences imposed in the region on similar young persons found guilty of the same offence committed in similar circumstances;

(c) the sentence must be proportionate to the seriousness of the offence and the degree of responsibility of the young person for that offence;

(d) all available sanctions other than custody that are reasonable in the circumstances should be considered for all young persons, with particular attention to the circumstances of aboriginal young persons;

(e) subject to paragraph (c), the sentence must

(i) be the least restrictive sentence that is capable of achieving the purpose set out in subsection (1),

(ii) be the one that is most likely to rehabilitate the young person and reintegrate him or her into society, and

(iii) promote a sense of responsibility in the young person, and an acknowledgement of the harm done to victims and the community; and

(f) subject to paragraph (c), the sentence may have the following objectives:

(i) to denounce unlawful conduct, and

(ii) to deter the young person from committing offences.

In addition to decreased rates of incarceration for youth, youth crime rates have also dropped. In fact, since 2009, there has been a decrease of almost 20 percent.[42] The majority of cases that do come before the courts are non-violent, theft under $5,000, mischief, offence against the administration of justice, and possession of cannabis being the most common.[43] Significantly, police formally charge less than 50 percent of accused youth. This, at least in part, indicates that the more informal mechanisms are being used.

Table 3.1: Youth in Custody in Canada, 2003 to 2009

Year	Remand to Custody	Sentence to Custody
2003/2004	845	1548
2004/2005	920	1298
2005/2006	853	1145
2006/2007	951	1040
2007/2008	1009	981
2008/2009	981	899

Source: Statistics Canada, *Youth Custody and Community Services, 2008/2009* (http://www.statcan.gc.ca/pub85-0002-x/2010001/article/11147-eng.htm#a9), accessed July 4, 2014.

Overall, the number of young people in custody continues to decline, although the proportion of Indigenous youth is rising. About Indigenous youth, Statistics Canada says, "According to the 2006 Census, 6% of all youth 12 to 17 years old in Canada self-identified as Aboriginal. In comparison, the representation of Aboriginal youth in custody and community services has traditionally been higher. In 2008/2009, Aboriginal youth accounted for 27% of youth admitted to remand, 36% of youth admitted to sentenced custody, and 24% of youth admitted to probation."[44] The proportion continued to increase in the 2011/2012 data:

> Aboriginal youth accounted for 7% of all youth in the provinces and territories providing data on youth admissions to the corrections system. However, they accounted for a much higher proportion (39%) of young people admitted to the corrections system in 2011/2012.... The over-representation of Aboriginal youth was more disproportionate among girls, where Aboriginal girls accounted for 49% of female youth admitted to the corrections system, compared to 36% of males.[45]

The Youth Probation Officer

One of the most important roles within youth justice in Canada is that of the probation officer. This public servant is responsible for the community supervision of sentenced (and some pre-sentence) youth. Almost 60 percent of youth sentencing involves probation.[46] And, outside of incarceration, youth justice funds are mostly spent on probation.[47] The Ministry of Children and Youth Services, which in Ontario oversees the youth justice file, states that probation case management is the cornerstone of youth justice: "The Ministry's objective in case management is to take maximum advantage of the time that a young person is in the youth justice system, using that time to change his or her mindset and other aspects of his or her situation that could reduce the likelihood of reoffending."[48] A probation officer meets regularly with a young person, as often as is deemed appropriate based on the youth's assessed level of risk. Each probation officer is expected to carry a caseload of 30–35. Probation officers carry out a variety of tasks including but not limited to:

- Writing pre-sentence reports
- Monitoring and supervising youth while they are under sentence in the community
- Building strong relational and network connections for a young person with schools, family, counselling centres, and so on

Pre-sentence reports tell a story of the young person and have become a primary tool used by the courts to determine sanctions. These reports are usually created by a youth probation officer who does the exhaustive work of connecting with the young person, their family, and a variety of other stakeholders (e.g., schools, counselling agencies, etc.). Records on the young person are also accessed, including educational records. The finished reports include information about the young person's background, their risk for reoffending, their needs, and more. Section 40 of the YCJA lays the legal foundation for pre-sentence reports.

Probation has a long history in youth justice in Canada. It was first enacted through legislation in 1903.[49] Early advocates of a full-scale probation system hoped that it would allow for an intervention that prevented future young offending. The following is an excerpt from a 1977 article by lawyer Jeffrey S. Leon tracking the history of juvenile justice in Canada back to the child-savers movement:

> The idea of a probation system, manned by both volunteers and professionals, to "help the children before they become criminally disposed" was increasingly discussed. In an address to the Sixth Canadian Conference of Charities and Corrections, Kelso gave this top priority: "Prevention work should begin when the children are small.... We want to bring about what is called the Probation System, following these children up from their first offence and never letting them get any further." The probation officer would "frequently visit the home and insist on school attendance and proper moral instruction ... [and], having a constant supervision of the child, would prevent his getting into trouble again." Consistent with the related goals of protection and prevention, the methods used by probation officers would be based on "kindly advice and practical aid."[50]

Proponents believed this approach would be softer and smarter than the punitive tactics often used by police and courts.[51]

Given the conflicting agendas of the YCJA (punishment versus rehabilitation, for example), the youth probation officer has an incredibly difficult job. How can a youth probation officer enforce the law while also being supportive? Some interesting research out of British Columbia and Ontario has examined this question. Findings suggest that in order to navigate this tension probation officers should focus on trust and relationship-building with young offenders by empathizing, being nonjudgmental, recognizing most young people have had difficult pasts, celebrating small victories, working collaboratively with other agencies that support youth, and pushing youth to hold themselves accountable.[52] Other research suggests that probation officers apply a mixed-model theoretical approach to their work; that is, combining care (welfare) with control (punishment), while trying to rely more heavily on the former.[53]

What Makes a Good Youth Probation Officer?
By Kao Saechao, Youth Probation Officer, Ontario

Some personal opinions on what traits probation officers should have, and the challenges that our young people have will be discussed below.

What makes a good probation officer? I believe a probation officer has to have the following traits: someone who is a people person; able to communicate and willing to help others; someone who can be fair, yet firm at the same time and not judgmental or biased. We cannot allow preconceived notions and personal biases to affect the work we do as a probation officer with our clients. Someone who can be flexible; the youth we serve are kids after all and they will make mistakes. We have to be able to be disappointed, but also to challenge, hold the youth accountable when they make mistakes, and celebrate the positives. Studies have shown that the brain may not fully develop until age 25. Another trait a probation officer should have is to be a good listener. Oftentimes young people just want to be heard, as people/adults are often talking at them instead of involving them or allowing them to speak. Being a positive role model is very important also, many youth don't have a positive role model in their life, and you could be the only one who they meet that can be that figure.

As probation officers, one of our prime goals is rehabilitation. To achieve this we have to find out what every youth's story is. There are a number of factors to a young person's story, and how they have got to where they are. It's up to us to help them find that story, challenge them, motivate them, and empower them to change their story. How do we do this? We use a cognitive, behavioural, and strengths-based approach. It's about building each youth up and trying to bring the inner strength out, and help them find the resiliency within to make the changes for themselves.

I truly do not believe that a young person is born "bad." It's a matter of the environments they were brought up in, along with other factors that have contributed to their makeup. The saying the "apple does not fall far from the tree" is a very true statement. Oftentimes, when I interview a youth and family—as long as the family and youth are very upfront and truthful—I will be able to find the issues that have led a youth to where they are today. It saddens me when I interview youth and family that the only family environment they know is one of abuse (either physical or mental), poor parenting, and they think this is the norm. There are often family generations that only know abuse and poor parenting as the norm. I would challenge our society to give every youth a fighting chance by introducing a mandatory course in school at some point in their academic career to introduce what a positive family atmosphere should, or could, look like.

> The saddest cases I've dealt with often involve substance use. I've had several clients' parents pimp their own children at very young ages to get high, or youth sell their own bodies to pay for drugs. When a youth is on drugs there is no effective way to work with them until they can come to terms with their addictions. I know people say that marijuana is not a gateway drug, but the majority of the youth I interview and have worked with over my 13-year career have smoked this at one point or another, and state that it was the core issue for them that initiated their downward spiral.
>
> At the end of the day, I believe probation officers have a very difficult role to play. We wear different hats depending on the situation, and all the while balance considerations for public safety with goals of rehabilitation with our clients. We are always involved with our clients and their families when they have reached their wit's end, and our challenge is to try and offer hope and positive change to them. Youth are always at varying stages of change, and in each stage we continually have to stay positive, motivate, advocate, encourage, and challenge them to make the positive changes themselves.

Overall, probation has proven to be a more effective approach (i.e., it reduces recidivism to a greater degree) than incarceration, and it is significantly cheaper. However, reintegrating youth who might not have been integrated into society in the first place is tremendously challenging work. This speaks to a social justice component that is often missing within justice systems. Scottish researcher Fergus McNeill has examined the practice of probation in depth. He argues that the effectiveness of probation will be limited if root causes are not addressed: "Probation services are not merely crime reduction agencies; they are justice agencies. In view of this ... our haste to control crime can sometimes lead to the neglect of questions of justice ... ultimately the pursuit of justice—social as well as criminal—is the only sure path to safer communities."[54]

TRACKING CHANGES TO THE YCJA

Although the YCJA was introduced as a counterbalance to the overincarceration of young people in Canada, in recent years, there's been a shift back toward making it more punitive to separate out serious from non-violent crimes,. Tracking these types of changes is relevant to understanding how society views young offenders. It's also important to continue to ask who benefits from legislative change(s). Is it victims, young people, or others? Youth justice needs to cast more of a critical eye on these types of changes, especially considering that law is like a tap. When it opens up further, more young people are collected into the bucket that is criminal justice. An important part of critiquing the dominant narrative of youth justice legislation is asking the question, "Why?"

In 2012, the principles of the YCJA were changed. This was precipitated in 2011 by the introduction of an Omnibus Crime bill. Without a doubt, the law was changed to (again) make it easier to put young people in prison. Sebastien's Law, as the YCJA portion of the bill was called, had a number of key elements. I will highlight three: First, the bill wanted to make the protection of society a primary principle of the YCJA. Canada's Justice Minister at the time, Rob Nicholson, argued in a speech to Parliament, "As it currently stands, the objective of protecting society is not stated strongly enough in either the preamble to the YCJA or its declaration of principles."[55] However, returning to the YCJA principles as they were originally written, the long-term protection of the public was already included in Section 3(1): "The following principles apply in this Act: (a) the youth criminal justice system is intended to ... (iii) ensure that a young person is subject to meaningful consequences for his or her offence in order to promote the long-term protection of the public."[56] Of course, this demands that we ask the question, "What is meant by making the protection of society a primary principle, when it was one already?"

Second, Sebastien's Law was intended to simplify pre-trial detention so that those at risk of hurting others would be remanded until their trials. Much of the impetus, with regard to evidence, for the government's proposal of strengthening public safety was the Nunn Inquiry of 2006, named for the judge who presided. Judge Nunn created a report titled *Spiralling Out of Control: Lessons Learned from a Boy in Trouble*. On October 14, 2004, a stolen car driven by a 16 year old sped through a red light and killed the occupant of another vehicle (53-year-old Theresa McEvoy). The youth had been released from custody two days earlier (on bail) despite having 38 outstanding criminal charges against him. The mandate of the inquiry was to explore specific questions regarding how this could have happened. Essentially, it asked (a) why the boy was not in custody at the time of the tragic October 14th crime, and (b) what policy implications would prevent this from happening in the future. As to the latter, Nunn hoped that his report would "contribute to the ongoing development of public policies that protect public safety, prevent crime and support youth at risk."[57]

However, it's noteworthy that the report entered a grey area in making federal-level recommendations (e.g., changes to YCJA), as it was a provincially ordered process. Nunn makes a strong argument that he's right in making these types of recommendations, as there's significant overlap between what's federal (Criminal Code, YCJA, etc.) and what's provincial (e.g., the implementation of these laws). However, he offers the following caution about the scope of his report:

> It appears from a review of some decisions of the Supreme Court of Canada that generally a provincial inquiry may inquire into some aspects of federal legislation, *but it may not explicitly undertake to assess the effectiveness of federal legislation....* A provincial inquiry may submit a report in which it appears that changes in a federal law would be appropriate. (emphasis added)[58]

With this in mind, out of the 34 recommendations in the report:

- Eight recommendations were for improving administrative procedures of the court (e.g., less delay in trials, better telecommunication tools, etc.)

Chapter 3: Youth Justice Today

- Two recommendations were for dedicated youth court police liaison officers and Crown attorneys
- Four recommendations were for improved bail supervision of young people in non-custodial settings
- Five recommendations were for common approaches to criminal justice proceedings for young people (i.e., issues related to pre-trial detention and findings of guilt)
- Six recommendations were for the province to advocate for changes to the YCJA
- Nine recommendations were for crime prevention initiatives targeting specific risk factors for youth.

Although crime prevention dominates Nunn's report, it's worth examining in more detail the six recommendations that follow related to the YCJA, as they are what the government picked up on.

- Recommendation 20 advocated for adding a clause to the YCJA that states protection of the public as a primary goal.
- Recommendation 21 was about making a change to the definition of a violent offence to include conduct that "endangers or is likely to endanger the life or safety of another person."
- Recommendation 22 suggested that pre-trial detention should be an option for people with a pattern of pending charges, not just for those with a pattern of findings of guilt.
- Recommendation 23 advocated to "amend and simplify the statutory provisions relating to the pre-trial detention of young persons," so there is less confusion for judges between Criminal Code and YCJA. The concern is that, as such, if YCJA takes precedence over the Criminal Code then it is difficult for judges to use custodial options for pre-trial detention.
- Recommendation 24 wanted to make sure that if a responsible person (for monitoring bail conditions of a young person) had to be relieved of their duties, the young person would still be required to fulfill the bail conditions.
- Recommendation 25 advocated that a new bail hearing should not be required for the young person before incarcerating them if the responsible person is relieved of their duties pre-trial.[59]

Fundamentally, these recommendations were about pre-trial detention and addressed the challenges judges had with keeping the young offenders in question incapacitated before their trials. Remember though, as Nunn said, a provincial report like this one is to be used to determine "efficacy" of legislation.

It's worth noting that, as a researcher, I'm unable to generalize from appearance, let alone from a single anecdote, such as the car crash that killed 53-year-old Theresa McEvoy. Of course, appearance can be used to build a set of rigorous and valid questions and a methodology from which to collect further research data, but if I overgeneralize as a researcher, my work is likely to be ignored. Still, that doesn't mean that appearance is false. In this case, there appeared to be some type of systemic legal problem that was creating opportunity for pre-trial, high-risk young offenders to slip through the cracks. However, for the government to have used this information to make the third recommendation (below) in the bill is a dramatic overgeneralization.

Here's another analogy to explain the risk of overgeneralization: On rare occasions, an offender escapes from a minimum-security prison in Canada by simply strolling off the property. (The doors are not locked in these institutions.) However, we don't build fences around minimum-security facilities to make them more "prison-like" because we know the value of having decreasing (cascading) levels of security. It eases an offender's transition back into society. Research tells us this is important both for reintegration and for reducing recidivism. Thus, reintegration policy isn't written based on these extreme and unique situations. If it were, our communities would be less safe, because the reintegration process would be more difficult on the individual offender—and it's known that the more difficult the reintegration process, the more likely it is that an offender will end up back behind bars.

What I'm suggesting by making this comparison is that we need to carefully consider the federal government's use of the Nunn Inquiry by examining more thoroughly the bail process for young offenders, and at the same time making sure that the policies we implement will make our society more, not less, safe. Is the bail process flawed? Or are there simply some extremely rare (and, sadly, tragic) situations where it doesn't work as intended? More research is needed in this area.

Third, Sebastien's Law proposed adding to the definition of what constitutes violent crime, and further strengthening sentencing provisions to include denunciation, or condemnation of crime, and deterrence as core elements. Shifting away from the Nunn report, the government at the time identified the following as the impetus for these changes: Ed Fast, Conservative member of Parliament, said, "All too often, a young offender who commits a serious crime such as murder or aggravated sexual assault receives a sentence that is much shorter than Canadians expect."[60] This was followed by more words from the Justice Minister of the time, Rob Nicholson, "Canadians lose confidence in the justice system when a sentence is insufficient to hold offenders accountable for their actions or to protect society."[61] What kinds of sentences do Canadians *expect*? What source is the government drawing on to say that Canadians are "losing confidence" in the justice system? If Canadians *are* losing confidence, does the general public want tougher laws to deal with young offenders? And, if so, should we allow public perceptions to shape policy if tougher laws actually make us less safe? Often, the only information the general public has is from media, which is racially biased and often ill-informed, and has its own particular agenda.

This whole process—seen in the government's (mis)use of the Nunn report and the way they played on public perceptions and fear of crime—is called the **politicization of crime**. Rather than being informed by evidence, politicians use tough-on-crime talk for their own gains. If the general public is ill-informed, and afraid of crime, it would likely be political suicide to promote approaches different than punishment. Of course, Canadians *expect* meaningful consequences and accountability in order to feel *confident* that our communities will be safer. Prisons do incapacitate. But, for young people in particular, they don't reduce recidivism. The proposed changes—at the time—to the YCJA suggested an expansive definition of violent crime, so that incarceration could be more of an option for young offenders. This helps politicians present a facade that youth crime is being dealt with effectively.

Ultimately, in March 2012, the government of the day used their majority to make the changes law. This move ran counter to the very report—the only one—used as evidence. Commissioner Nunn wanted a focus on prevention: "We should be able to halt the spiral into crime for our youth at risk: through prevention, through quick action, through creative thinking, through collaboration, through clear strategies and through programs that address clearly identified needs.... Our children and youth at risk deserve it. Their families deserve it. Our society deserves it."[62] It's hard to interpret the government's (mis)use of the Nunn report in any other way than it being about political gain. In their critical examination of the use of incarceration and tough-on-crime politics in the United States, *Prison Masculinities*, Don Sabo, Terry A. Kupers, and Willie London suggest that these approaches are only about political and economic gains:

> We need to ask about who benefits from the failures of imprisonment. Once we see through the media hype about "superpredators" and rising violence in our midst, it becomes evident who benefits from the "war on crime"— politicians who base their prospects for election on "tough-on-criminals" rhetoric, contractors who build the new prisons, vendors who supply the prisons, and corporations that run prisons for profit or utilize prisoner labour to undercut competition.[63]

Other than corporations being out to make a profit (youth detention facilities in Canada are not run for profit) all of these beneficiaries can be considered similar for the Canadian context. The politicization of crime means that political agendas, not victims, not communities, not evidence, shape law. In support of challenges in Parliament and the media to the new law, critics claimed that crime rates were down and asked why laws were being toughened. The then Justice Minister responded, "We don't govern on the basis of statistics."[64]

CONCLUSION

In a similar way to the era prior to 1984, the variables of power and race surface in the modern history of youth justice, from the YOA through to the YCJA. The quote that concluded the last section highlights the politicization of crime—the use of crime as a way to govern and to maintain power. In spite of progressive advances (for example, the increased reliance on alternative, restorative justice measures) youth justice remains vulnerable to misuses of power. Furthermore, these advances have done little to stem the flow of marginalized youth into the system. Indigenous peoples continue to be overrepresented. A deeper understanding of crime must be undertaken. In order to make communities safer and more livable, we must ask why young people commit crime. In the next chapter, I will start to advance more of a theoretical framework for this book: the idea that a trauma-informed approach makes the most sense for understanding root causes of crime and injustice.

GLOSSARY OF TERMS

Criminogenic means something is likely to cause crime or to be correlated with influencing criminal behaviour.
Extrajudicial means apart from, or outside of, the traditional justice system.
Iatrogenic is a Greek term referring to when harm (that is preventable) is brought on by the healer.
Politicization of crime is the assimilation of issues related to crime for partisan political purposes or to advance a particular political agenda.

QUESTIONS FOR REFLECTION

1. The history of youth justice in Canada shows a pendulum swing between social welfare and more punitive approaches. Although there are elements of restorative justice in current YCJA legislation and it straddles the line between both, there seems to be an impetus to change it in the direction of punishment. What do you think about this? Why does this happen?
2. Analyzing the topic of meaningful public apologies, Regan, whose work is cited in this chapter, builds on the work of political scientist Matt James and sociologist Nicholas Tavuchis to identify eight criteria for an authentic political apology:
   1. It is recorded in writing.
   2. It names the wrongdoing.
   3. It accepts responsibility.
   4. It states regret.
   5. It promises not to repeat the behaviour(s).
   6. It does not demand forgiveness.
   7. It is not hypocritical or arbitrary.
   8. It undertakes reparations to demonstrate sincerity.[65]

How would you score Canada's apology to Indigenous peoples for residential schools? Does it meet these criteria? What does it mean for the apologist to "accept responsibility" and to "be sincere"?

RECOMMENDED READING

McNeill, Fergus. "What Works and What's Just?" *European Journal of Probation* 1 (2009): 21–40.

This research article is by one of the leading academics on the topic of desistance, or how and why people stop offending. Rather than thinking about youth justice only through the technical lens of rehabilitation, McNeill pushes the reader to consider the bigger-picture questions of the moral character of criminal justice systems.

Regan, Paulette. *Unsettling the Settler Within: Indian Residential Schools, Truth Telling, and Reconciliation in Canada.* Vancouver: UBC Press, 2010.

Paulette Regan challenges the myth that Canadians are peacemakers by describing how settler practices toward Indigenous peoples have been incredibly harmful. She promotes the notion that settler people must decolonize, or stop colonizing, Indigenous peoples if society is to heal from the harms of residential schools.

Tanner, Julian. *Teenage Troubles: Youth and Deviance in Canada.* Don Mills: Oxford University Press, 2010.

Written from the perspective of social constructionism, Tanner clearly explains how the social problem of youth deviance in Canada is defined.

4 | Theory of Trauma-Informed Youth Justice—Why Do Young People Commit Crimes?

"Pain that is not transformed is transferred."

—Richard Rohr

One of the central tasks of youth justice should be to answer the question, "Why do youth commit crimes?" In this chapter, after exploring a variety of theories, I'll ultimately conclude that the best answer is "Because they've experienced trauma." Young people often hurt others because they are hurting. Of course, not everyone who experiences trauma goes on to cause trauma to others, or to commit other crimes, but the majority who commit crimes have their own experiences of trauma.

Acknowledging the fact that many young people who come into conflict with the law have experienced trauma in no way excuses harmful behaviours, nor does it diminish accountability. What it does instead is allow us to address individual behaviours in a more meaningful way, while also getting at root causes. A trauma-informed lens does this better than other current theoretical models for approaching crime. By understanding the trauma and pain experienced by young people, we can start to evolve youth justice responses in ways that heal victims, hold offenders more meaningfully accountable, and also provide opportunities for healing collective harms.

The astute reader should have a baseline understanding of the history of theoretical explanations for youth crime. Trying to explain why isn't a new phenomenon. However, in my experience of reading the academic literature, as well as working with people in conflict with the law, I have found most theories to be wanting. Still, it's important to understand them because they've given shape to various criminal justice policies, as well as to social attitudes about crime and deviant behaviour. At the outset of this chapter, I'll explore some traditional theories—biological, psychological, sociological, and criminological—that attempt to explain youth crime. Regardless of their merits, understanding these theories will help you to grasp how society has explained young offenders over time. This will help to position current practices, and give shape to new ones.

In the second half of the chapter, I'll put forward my own trauma-informed explanation for youth crime. Following a discussion about a theory of **cycles of violence**, I'll begin to explain why, as stated in the Richard Rohr quotation that opened this chapter, trauma that isn't transformed is transferred. If the best way to understand youth offending is, indeed, through a trauma-informed lens, we must ask whether other theoretical frameworks are simply—at worst—adding harm to harm or—at best—insufficiently explaining youth crime. To paraphrase President Roosevelt, justice is about finding what is right. For most of its existence, the discipline of criminology has sat in the shadows of power, claiming scientific objectivity toward issues of social and criminal justice. According to criminologists Larry Tifft and Dennis Sullivan, "The incessant apologia of social scientists that their methodologies are value-free comes from their unwillingness to consider their own mode of thinking about the world, to consider themselves as part of the one world of human struggle."[1] A trauma-informed lens calls the idea of scientific neutrality into question and argues instead that neutrality really sides with whoever is in power, to the detriment of marginalized populations.[2]

A HISTORY OF THEORETICAL EXPLANATIONS FOR YOUTH CRIME
By Judah Oudshoorn, with research assistance from Josiah Thorogood

A **theory** is an explanation for why something is as it is. The way I use this term is different than a hypothesis. A hypothesis is a guess: something yet to be tested. For me, a theory is a tested hypothesis. There must be some evidence for it. Below, a number of key theories that seek to explain youth crime will be described—some more insightful than others. Some of these theories have withstood empirical testing, while others have not. Each wrestles with questions related to responsibility. What is it about a young person that might predispose them to come into conflict with the law? Some of these theories put responsibility on the individual while others place it on the environment. Some focus on psychological factors, while others focus on sociology. Many of the theories related to biology have been rejected over time. However, from a trauma-informed perspective, it might prove useful to return to these—but in a different way. Traditionally, biological theories have tried to explain crime based on the appearance of the criminal. One more popular theory from over a hundred years ago presumed that criminals had large foreheads. Other theories were more racist, suggesting that particular races were more criminal than others. Neither of these theories is relevant to our discussion, as both have been discounted. Where biology might be of use, however, is in looking at the impact of trauma on the biological, the physiological, and the genetic structure of the victim's brain. More and more, research is demonstrating that the experience of trauma can create lasting physiological (or structural) changes in a person's brain and genes. I'll discuss this in more detail in chapter 5.

Classical Criminology

Criminology is the study of crime and its causes. In its early days, it was linked with the behavioural sciences, but today, more so with sociology. Criminological explanations for crime also come from other disciplines, including biology and psychology.

Cesare Beccaria (incorporating rational thinking into criminal justice) and Jeremy Bentham (utilitarianism) are regarded as the fathers of classical and neo-classical criminology respectively.[3] They both believed that individuals possessed free will—the capacity to act voluntarily. Neither Bentham or Beccaria celebrated the idea of free will.[4] Instead, they saw it as the state's responsibility to overcome this evil aspect of human cognition. They formed their approaches to criminal justice on the belief that human behaviour can be controlled through the imposition of sensible legislation. If penalties were chosen wisely by lawmakers, individuals would choose not to break laws in order to avoid punishment.[5] Beccaria's *On Crimes and Punishments* is considered a classical piece in the history of criminology. At the time of its writing (1764), it helped push forward a reformist agenda for criminal law throughout Europe and Britain. Beccaria was against torture and the death penalty.

At about the same time, Bentham developed utilitarianism: the idea that policy and law should focus on increasing pleasure over pain. According to Bentham, we all like pleasure and dislike pain.[6] Applying this idea to law, punishment should be just enough to deter someone from committing a future offence, no more, no less. He wrote on the principle of what he called a hedonistic calculus, or how a person goes about making what they believe to be the best moral—or right—choice.[7] Bentham believed that if punishments were sensible, yet harsh enough to deter criminal acts, individuals conducting a hedonistic calculus would see that the violation of law wasn't worthwhile and would decide not to commit an offence.[8]

Essentially, classical criminology assumed that human beings were self-interested and would act rationally with regard to crime. If punishments were justifiable, they would be sufficient to deter criminal activity. Regardless of its merit (punishment hasn't been shown to deter crime) or whether it was progressive enough (others at the time called for even more radical changes), utilitarian theory has played a central role in criminology, moving the explanations for crime beyond religious reasons (e.g., sin) to more naturalistic reasons.[9] On one hand, these reforms brought about some important safeguards: an attempt to implement due process into criminal law, as well as equality of punishment.[10] On the other hand, this theory continued to place responsibility for crime with the individual, or to overemphasize choice without recognizing the context in which choice is made. Overall, these premises have had a profound impact on the evolution of Western criminal justice systems. The idea of deterrence, especially—despite having been disproven—still holds strong in criminal justice spheres and beyond.

The Beginnings of Positivist Criminology

The classical school of criminology was closely followed by that of positivism.[11] Positivism employed the scientific method of controlled experiments in an attempt to differentiate between criminal and non-criminal people and behaviours.[12] Positivist thinkers believed that criminal acts were compulsive, meaning criminals were inherently different from others in society.[13] Criminal acts were believed to be preprogrammed into a person instead of being the result of free will or rooted in social causes.[14] One of the main supporters of positivism was Cesare Lombroso. He believed that criminals were merely less evolved than other human beings.[15] In a multi-volume study entitled *The Criminal Man*, Lombroso wrote that criminality was inherited and could be determined based solely on specific characteristics of the human body.[16] He came to this conclusion after undertaking a systematic study that involved measuring the bodies of many offenders.[17] He put forward the ideas that the "born criminal" was genetically defective[18] and that certain types of delinquents were impossible to reform.[19] In Lombroso's mind, society had a right to protect itself against these individuals, providing a justification for the use of the death penalty.[20] Although his findings have been proven incorrect, Lombroso's use of the scientific method remains important in criminology research today.

Early criminological theories were closely linked with biology, the scientific study of life. Biological theories tried to find explanations for criminal behaviour in the biological makeup of the criminal. Research in this area has provided many explanations using a variety of research methodologies. For example, some studies have examined twins and adopted children looking for hereditary explanations.[21] Other studies have examined the body types of criminals versus non-criminals, while still more have looked at the physiological characteristics of the criminal brain. Over time, biological theories have drifted more into the area of mental health, including studies on attention deficit hyperactive disorder (ADHD) and learning disabilities. While some studies have found high rates of antisocial disorders in adults who were hyperactive as children,[22] it's important to note that the results on adult criminality being linked to hyperactivity in children have been inconsistent. Stronger links have been found between ADHD and early childhood traumas, which might account for some connections between ADHD and crime.

Psychological Theories

Psychology is the study of mental life and its corresponding influence on how people choose to behave. As such, psychological explanations of crime tend to focus on the individual, studying personality and mental functioning alongside behaviour. Some examples include psychoanalytic theory, behaviourism, social learning theory, and moral development theory.

Psychoanalytic Theory
According to a Freudian psychoanalytic perspective, criminality is a result of instinct.[23] These criminologists believed that society—as represented by the superego (the moral part of the mind) and the ego (the rational mind)—redirects or represses the id (the instinct to commit crimes). Therefore, they view all types of criminal behaviour as a failure on the part of the superego and the ego to control the urges of the id to commit crimes.[24] In essence, Freudians believe criminal actions result when impulses aren't regulated.[25] Later, Erik Erikson modified—and diverged from—Freud's psychoanalytic theory in a number of ways, including redefining criminal behaviour. He stated that, in relation to the world around them, individuals develop positive and negative self-concepts that influence their choices over time.[26] Erikson argued that some studies published in his time were ignoring the influence of the process of identity formation that might lead to criminal behaviour.[27]

Behaviourism

Karl Lashley is credited with bringing behaviourism into the realm of credible scientific study of the mind.[28] Behaviourism focuses on analyzing observable events, or choices that individuals make, rather than characteristics in the mind. In order to illustrate the basic ideas of this perspective, it's helpful to look at the work of one of the field's best-known practitioners, B. F. Skinner. The highlight of his work was the "Skinner box," developed in the 1930s.[29] This was a box containing a rat, a lever for it to press, and a mechanism for delivering small amounts of food.[30] Skinner's focus was on "reinforcement schedules": controlling the rat's behaviour by changing the relationship between the pressing of the lever and the food being delivered.[31] In addition, Skinner's 1938 book, *The Behaviour of Organisms*, contained extensive discussions of the ideas of response and stimulus, as well as notes on his observations of behaviour.[32] Skinner's work culminated in his assertion that all behaviour is the result of reinforcement, and that everyone's environment should be engineered from birth in order to produce behaviour deemed desirable.[33] Extending this to criminology, some have suggested that criminal behaviour is simply reinforced for those who choose it, and in order to modify it, some version of punishment must follow closely. Skinner called this operant conditioning: "the basic process by which an individual's behaviour is shaped by reinforcement or punishment."[34] Behaviourism has been heavily critiqued by modern-day criminology for missing the mark on causality. There's much more going on internally and in the social environment for the individual who commits crime than behaviourism is able to explain.

Social Learning Theory

Alternatively, social learning theory sought broader explanations. Albert Bandura, the father of social learning theory, argued that a complete theory of aggression must explain what causes people to act in an aggressive manner, how patterns of aggression are developed, and what factors are linked to continued aggressive actions.[35] Bandura believed that individuals aren't simply born to act aggressively. While some very simple forms of aggression don't require great amounts of learning, most forms of aggression, he suggested (such as military combat or the hateful ridicule of another person) are learned behaviours.[36] Bandura claimed that observational learning is crucial for survival and development because it allows individuals to gain complex, integrated behaviour patterns by simply observing them, rather than by using a slow, gradual trial-and-error process. He specifically noted that family members, the impacts of an individual's subculture, and the large number of easily available models provided through the mass media are of particular importance in their impacts on the development of learned aggression.[37] Indeed, the idea of role-modelling is an important one to this text—especially in relation to patterns of male violence.

Moral Development Theory

French psychologist Jean Piaget's work was foundational in the area of moral development theory. As part of his research, he identified the first stage of moral development as one in which a person chooses how to act on the basis of maintaining societal norms, and for fear of being disciplined for actions that deviate from accepted norms.[38] Moral development theory is interested in explaining why some individuals act morally (according to society) while others don't. An American psychologist, Lawrence Kohlberg, advanced Piaget's theory by formulating six stages of moral reasoning, organized into three overall stages which he identified as:

1. *Preconventional*: moral decisions are made on the basis of punishment, what authority figures say is right and wrong, and what rules and laws say;
2. *Conventional*: wherein individuals make decisions based on the maintenance of good relationships with people around them; and
3. *Postconventional*: describing a state of moral decision-making where general moral principles are equal to or transcend concerns for the stability of society or relationships.[39]

Kohlberg created this paradigm for understanding moral reasoning on the basis of extensive interviews he conducted with adolescents and young adults over a period of almost 20 years, from the mid-1950s up till 1974. Of course, much of this demands the question: What counts as "moral"? Who decides? How does this factor into the research? Some researchers have criticized Kohlberg in particular for ignoring female perspectives (his research was male-centric).[40] There is some evidence to support the link between moral development and criminality, but further work needs to be done to integrate the social environment, as well as to include the variables of power and privilege in the discussion.

Sociological Theories

Sociology is primarily interested in studying the interactions between individuals and societies. Sociological explanations of youth crime look at individual young people, as well as at how they interact with and react to their environments. Examples include social disorganization theory, strain theory, subculture of violence theory, and techniques of neutralization.

Social Disorganization Theory
Social disorganization theorists believe that poverty, ethnic disparity, and population turnover all work together to contribute to the weakening of organization in communities and their ability to institute forms of social control.[41] This, in turn, leads to increases in the rates of delinquency and criminal activity. One of the focuses of researchers in this area is the breakdown of the family unit, which is thought to have negative impacts on social organization in communities. Specifically, the research of social disorganization theorists demonstrates that individuals from single-parent families or unstable families are generally involved in crime at greater rates than individuals from stable or two-parent homes.[42]

> **Emile Durkheim and Anomie**
>
> One early sociological explanation for criminal behaviour was Emile Durkheim's concept of anomie: "the absence of clear societal norms and values."[43] This concept is based on the assumption that individuals may act or think based on their own subjective values and individual meaning.[44] Subsequently, ethical and moral disorder occurs as society and its institutions fail to place normative limits on individuals' desires and pursuits. Durkheim described anomie as a state of affairs that occurs when societies are in transition, creating instability and a lack of moral regulation.[45] Ultimately, as people pursue individual interests rather than collective ones, social disorder and crime result.

Strain Theory

Sociologists Robert K. Merton (post-1935) and Stanley Cohen (post-1970) studied the topic of deviance. Their explanation for deviant behaviour, called strain theory, suggested that class, or socio-economic status, was the best predictor. Merton's work theorized that criminal behaviour is partly a consequence of individuals in lower socio-economic classes having less access to opportunities for legitimate advancement in society than those in the middle and upper classes.[46] Later, Cohen argued that lower classes of young boys are unable to achieve the social respect that's available to the middle class.[47] The strain of what is available to some (middle and upper classes) but not available to others (lower classes) tends to produce deviant behaviour in the marginalized category.

Sociologists Richard Cloward and Lloyd Ohlin expanded on and clarified the theories of Merton and Cohen. They suggested that a lack of access to legitimate opportunities can lead to a criminal lifestyle, because deviant opportunities give individuals a way to cope with their unfulfilled, legitimate aspirations.[48] Criminologist Robert Agnew built on earlier theories by articulating a general strain theory (GST). This widened the concept of strain theory to consider processes other than economic ones. In Agnew's explanation, crime is still an adaptive response to stress. An example includes conflict between an individual's desired life versus their actual reality.[49] GST claims that crime is a coping strategy, in the sense that strain creates negative emotions and pushes an individual toward crime in order to resolve these feelings.[50]

Subculture of Violence Theory

The thesis of subculture of violence theory is that certain groups are more violent than others as a result of adherence to values that support violence.[51] For example, according to this theory, where a group feels under threat, violence is permissible in order to protect their honour or status. Research in this area is focused on the impacts of socialization, or how individuals internalize the values of the group.[52] If a person living in a violent subculture is attacked or wronged in some way, others will expect a response involving some form of aggression. By retaliating in an aggressive way, the individual maintains their honour, or saves face, and fulfills the expectations of their social group.[53]

Techniques of Neutralization

Sociologist David Matza's contribution to this area of the literature represents a significant rejection of the approaches of his contemporaries.[54] He believed that rather than being continuous in nature, delinquency was episodic and represented occasional escapes from the rules and norms of society. From Matza's perspective, delinquency is never a foregone conclusion. Instead, under certain conditions, an individual may drift into delinquency for a period of time. The techniques of neutralization framework examines criminal behaviour committed by youth from the perspective of rationalizations, or the justifications they make in order to make violating the law possible.[55] David Matza, together with sociologist Gresham Sykes, describes five techniques of neutralization:

1. *Denial of responsibility:* A young person sees her or himself as lacking responsibility for their actions. It doesn't matter to the deviant person whether others approve or not.
2. *Denial of injury*: The young person justifies further criminal acts by causing a disconnection between such acts and their consequences. If a young person can convince him or herself that no one has been truly hurt, he or she won't see anything wrong with committing additional crimes.
3. *Denial of the victim*: This allows a young person to see her or his actions as ethically permissible in the specific circumstances because the victim may "deserve" the injury they have received.
4. *Condemnation of the condemners:* The young person transfers the focus from his or her criminal act and instead places the emphasis on the people who have shown they disapprove of his or her actions. In this situation, a youth may claim that the disapprovers, acting out of personal spite, are really criminals in disguise or are simply hypocrites.
5. *Appeal to higher loyalties rationalization*: The young person may neutralize her or his social controls by putting aside the demands of wider society and instead focusing on the demands of a sibling pair, friendship group, gang, or other social group within society to which they belong.[56]

In summary, the preceding discussion of theories was intended to be like a wine tasting, giving you a flavour of some of the more influential explanations for why young people commit crime. Although there is value in looking across the disciplines mentioned—biology, psychology, sociology, and criminology—none is sufficient for explaining crime from a trauma-informed perspective. However, trauma-informed theory can be richer for having tasted from a multidisciplinary cup.

TRAUMA-INFORMED THEORY: TRAUMA AS AN EXPLANATION FOR YOUTH CRIME

This book introduces the idea of trauma to the theoretical discussion. Returning to the metaphor of the tree from chapter 1, when we start at the roots with a values-based approach focused on critical thinking, human dignity, participation, peace, a holistic approach to addressing youth crime, and social change, we give shape to a restorative justice worldview (the trunk of the tree). This way of seeing broadens the theoretical landscape, represented by the branches. When testing explanations of why young people commit crime against the lived experiences of these young people, one consistent theme emerges. Trauma is often found to be a common denominator for young people who end up in conflict with the law.

Multiple studies in North America and Europe have confirmed that over 90 percent of justice-involved youth have experienced some form of trauma in their childhood.[57] Most youth detained in correctional facilities have a history of major psychological trauma.[58] Almost 50 percent of incarcerated youth have either moderate or severe depression, with child maltreatment being a major explanation for this.[59] A study of incarcerated youth in Illinois, USA, found that 92.5 percent had experienced one trauma, 84 percent more than one, and almost 57 percent had experienced six or more.[60] In comparison to non-delinquent youth, those deemed delinquent were more likely to have been exposed to trauma or to have experienced post-traumatic stress disorder or a major depressive episode.[61] A study of youth in the United Kingdom found that mental health challenges were three times more likely to be found in youth in the criminal justice system than in those who were not in the system.[62] A study of youth entering the criminal justice system in New York found that almost 70 percent had experienced some form of traumatic brain injury, with the majority of those being accounted for by an assault. The authors of the study suggest that the damage this does to regulating emotions and processing thoughts would likely have put these youth at risk of coming into conflict with the law.[63]

The effects of trauma are even more pronounced when talking about Indigenous youth.[64] As identified in the previous chapter, close to 50 percent of female and 25 percent of male young offenders in Canada are Indigenous. This is directly correlated with the intergenerational traumas of colonialism. As the Special Rapporteur on the Rights of Indigenous Peoples at the United Nations says about Indigenous peoples in Canada, *all* Indigenous young people have been impacted by settler colonialism and the trauma of cultural genocide.[65] Of course, one part of this is the reverberations of the "Indian" residential school system,[66] which have contributed to poverty[67] and serious housing and health crises (especially in the Northern parts of Canada) including drinking water that isn't potable,[68] as well as to the devastation of culture, identity, and family.[69] In the words of researchers Raymond R. Corrado, Sarah Kuehn, and Irina Margaritescu: "The consequences from Aboriginal children being routinely victimized in these schools have been causally associated with the loss of identity and self esteem and, in turn, inter-generational poverty, cycles of abuse, family adversity, high suicide rates, and high rates of substance abuse."[70] Furthermore, Indigenous women and girls are disproportionately victims of crime. The Native Women's Association of Canada has "documented over 660 cases of women and girls across Canada who have gone missing or been murdered in the last 20 years, many of which remain unresolved, although the exact number of unresolved cases remains to be determined."[71] Thus, one reason for adopting a trauma-informed lens is to understand and address the root cause of colonialism.

But what is the explanation for the high levels of trauma seen among non-Indigenous young offenders? Here, the main cause is patriarchal male violence as expressed in family and sexual violence. Research indicates that both male and female young offenders are likely to have experienced and witnessed domestic violence.[72] Furthermore, 65–75 percent of young offenders report being physically abused.[73]

Other traumas found in young offender populations include childhood neglect and traumas associated with poverty. Studies are one part of understanding this. Another part involves listening to the stories of young people. Most people who work in the field of youth justice would not be surprised by the statistics just given. Many will have heard stories about the horrific abuses suffered by young offenders during their childhoods. The Centre for Crime and Justice Studies put together a report called *My Story: Young People Talk about the Trauma and Violence in Their Lives*, to allow for young people who had committed serious crimes to speak about their childhoods. Here's a female young offender speaking about one childhood experience:

> [What happened that changed things] was just my mum and dad and the sort of fighting. Well, it was more my dad because he started drinking, and then when he'd be drunk he'd hit my mom. It used to happen a lot and then in the end she tried to get away from him.... When I was twelve she left him. Then she had to go in a hostel with me, my brother and my sister, to try and get away from him."[74]

A male young offender tells about some of his childhood: "I remember once my mum and dad were arguing over something and my dad smacked my mum over the head with a broom. He hit her over the head with a broom and she's still got a permanent lump on her head now, the lump's never ever gone down.... [At that time I was] probably about six."[75]

The lives of young offenders have often been characterized by **violence**, neglectful parenting, and—too often—poverty. Each of these factors contributes to their heightened levels of stress and, in turn, influences their choices. Of course, not all people who experience trauma in childhood go on to perpetrate violence. In fact, the majority don't. However, the common denominator in the lives of these children is that they have experienced one or more significant traumas. These traumas have shaped who they are and how they see the world, and have set them on paths that they did not necessarily choose. We don't get to choose the homes we're born into. We also don't choose our traumas. They're imposed on us, usually by the selfish, violent actions of others, whether individually or structurally.

As our understanding of trauma is deepening, we now know that the way traumatized people react to certain stimuli—and relate to other people—can largely be explained as a function of their (damaged) brain physiology. In the next chapter, I'll talk at great lengths about how trauma affects people. For now, however, the basic theory I am putting forward is that a history of trauma puts a child at risk of perpetrating trauma or committing crime. The quote at the outset of the chapter by Richard Rohr, "Pain that is not transformed is transferred," is accurate. Essentially, it sets up the theoretical explanation of this book: the best answer to the question of why young offenders do what they do is that they're caught up in a cycle of trauma/violence. If we wish to break this cycle, we need to do things differently in the youth justice system.

Before explaining how a cycle of violence works, it's worth repeating that this theory is not meant to excuse young offenders' actions or to minimize the impact of their choices. Some of the crimes young offenders commit are incredibly harmful. Accountability is vital. What I'm trying to suggest, however, is an alternative explanation beyond young offenders being "bad" or "sick," and to present an alternative to other ways of addressing crime that tend to individualize responsibility without looking at the context of offending. In later chapters, I'll discuss how accountability works best within a context of support. Even as we shift our focus toward trauma, I will not lose sight of meaningful consequences for harmful behaviours. Building peace is as much about accountability as it is about providing safe, supportive futures for all.

Theoretical Explanation for a Cycle of Violence Theory

In order to explain cycle of violence theory, I will tell a fictitious story. Let's imagine the following: Tim is a 16-year-old boy, recently charged with physically assaulting his elderly neighbour. For years, the senior had asked Tim not to cut across his lawn when walking into his townhouse complex. One day, as Tim walked across the neighbour's lawn, the older gentleman yelled, "You're useless, you damn kid. You never listen," and turned his garden hose away from his flower garden toward Tim. In an instant, Tim was on top of the old man, beating him with the nozzle end of the hose. Some people passing by managed to get Tim off the victim, and subdued him until police arrived—though not before the old man was bloodied and left with torn clothes and in need of medical attention. While arresting Tim, police found drugs in his backpack and charged him with possession.

The police officer, with the help of some colleagues, handcuffed Tim and put him in the back of a cruiser. Evidence was carefully collected and witness statements were taken. The case would be fairly open-and-shut. The teenager would be found guilty of assault and possession. The justice system would move from guilt (for breaking the law) to determining an appropriate punishment. Case closed.

But wait, does the context matter? Probably not to the elderly gentleman—although he might have interest in ensuring that what happened to him doesn't happen to anyone else. Maybe not to the other neighbours who might be glad to have Tim off the street. Where it does matter, however, is if we want to ask why. Why did Tim assault his neighbour? Why was Tim in possession of drugs? Did he assault his neighbour because he was tired of being called names? Was he using drugs because he was a troublemaker, or selling them because he was simply lazy, looking for quick money? From a trauma-informed perspective, these questions are relevant, not only for Tim but also for his victims and his community. A cycle of violence theory seeks to find an explanation, or at least influential factors, for why people do what they do. In this situation, Tim's violence communicates something about him, about the circumstances of his life.

Imagine that at the time of the assault, Tim had been couch surfing. He'd been staying at friends' houses, strangers' houses, and sometimes at a youth shelter — basically anywhere he could rest comfortably, not on the street or under the bridge where many other street-involved youth slept. On that day, Tim was stopping by his home, hoping his mom wasn't there, in order to get some money from his older sister. Going back further, imagine that Tim's family was relatively stable, relatively middle class, but his parents had kicked him out of the house when they had — for the third time — found drugs in his backpack. His parents couldn't understand his drug use, lack of interest in school, and his aggressive behaviour. (He was always getting into fights.)

Now imagine that, although neither his parents nor anyone else was aware, Tim had been sexually abused by the caretaker of the townhouse complex where he lived. When Tim was nine, he had started helping with chores on the properties, weeding gardens and cutting the grass. The caretaker was well liked by all, and Tim's parents were happy that he had taken Tim under his wing. The abuse lasted until Tim was kicked out of his house at age 15.

Tim's story isn't far removed from the stories of many young offenders. It describes harm the young offender has done, and harm done to them. Unfortunately, where the criminal justice system often stops listening would have been with Tim's behaviour. Once a punishment has been decided, little else is done to look at the circumstances. A probation officer would likely help Tim figure out what kinds of supports he might need in order to fulfill his obligations to the justice system. And while many probation offers do look more holistically at the circumstances surrounding youth crime, Tim isn't likely to disclose the sexual abuse, nor will the system do much about his familial circumstances.

Tim's story gives us a window into the cycle of violence that's often part of young offenders' lives. Tim's assaultive behaviour should be a red flag that there are deeper issues. Psychiatrist James Gilligan has spent his working life with people who have committed violent crimes. He theorizes that violence communicates something about the individual who uses it: "The basic psychological motive, or cause, of violent behaviour is the wish to ward off or eliminate the feeling of shame and humiliation — a feeling that is painful, and can even be intolerable and overwhelming — and replace it with the opposite, the feeling of pride."[76] It's not a stretch to imagine that Tim is having a difficult time coping with the experience of sexual abuse, as well as with being kicked out of his family home. According to Gilligan, trauma produces shame and humiliation. The violence, in turn, is about attempting to ward off these overwhelming feelings, to instead find a feeling of pride or self-worth. In fact, the words of Tim's neighbour — "You're useless" — may well have struck a chord with how he was feeling about himself. The intention here isn't to blame the victim. The elderly neighbour is not at fault. Tim is still at fault. Gilligan explains it like this, "People become *indignant* (and may become violent) when they suffer an *indignity*; language itself reveals the link between shame and rage."[77] In chapter 5, when I examine the issue of male violence, I'll explain how this issue is particularly problematic for men and boys because of toxic versions of masculinity that are often engrained in society. Canadian writer Margaret Atwood summed it up nicely when she said, "Men are afraid that women will laugh at them. Women are afraid that men will kill them." Ultimately, I would characterize a cycle of violence as having four basic components:

1. An experience of trauma or violence
2. The lack of opportunities to heal
3. The traumatized person reenacting trauma or violence as a way to ward off feelings of shame
4. Rather than warding it off, the perpetration of violence simply adding to the shame, which now includes regret, making it more difficult to escape the cycle

In her book titled *The Little Book of Trauma Healing: When Violence Strikes and Community Security Is Threatened*, Carolyn Yoder identifies 10 steps to explain a cycle of violence:

1. Traumatic event(s), act(s) of aggression
2. Physiological changes
3. Shock, injury, denial, anxiety, fear
4. Realization of loss—panic
5. Suppression of grief and fears—numbness and isolation
6. Anger, rage, spiritual questions, loss of meaning
7. Survivor guilt, shame, humiliation
8. (Learned) Helplessness
9. Re-experiencing events, intrusive thoughts, avoiding reminders, hypervigilance
10. Fantasies of revenge, need for justice[78]

Essentially, this list expands on the four components I have identified. It begins to articulate how a person moves from victim to aggressor, from pain to violence. Without an opportunity to heal, or the social support necessary to do so, Yoder suggests that it's possible for the victim to step into a cycle of violence. She characterizes this as a process. (Although numbered, she says the steps are not necessarily sequential.)

1. Seeing self as victim
2. Unmet needs for safety and justice—shame, humiliation, fear
3. Development of a good-versus-evil narrative
4. Dehumanization of the enemy
5. Seeing violence as redemptive
6. Decision to pursue own needs at the expense of others
7. Social and cultural pressures—pride
8. Attack in the name of self-defense, justice, or restoring of honour[79]

Furthermore, Yoder suggests that violence is directed inward, outward, or both. A person who "acts in" might abuse substances, self-mutilate, experience depression, or some combination of these, while a person who "acts out" could perpetrate domestic violence, child abuse, or other criminal activity.[80] Yoder, similarly to Gilligan, proposes that violence communicates a pained inner state of the individual. She suggests that other symptoms of trouble—or signs of trauma—include apathy, lack of empathy, impaired communication, and an inability to trust.[81] The literature on this topic is fairly consistent. Traumatized people often act in, or act out. In reality, then, it's a short—and often logical—step from victim to perpetrator.

Research on Cycle of Violence Theory

In 1989, researcher Cathy Spatz Widom set out to discover whether empirical evidence would support the claim that children who suffered abuse were more likely to come into conflict with the law later in life. She argued that prior to 1989 research studies on this topic were very limited, if not suspect, because of methodological problems (like the lack of a control group in some studies, or overreliance on participants self-reporting in others). Her work affirms a cycle of violence theory. Using confirmed reports of child abuse (from child protection records), she tracked a randomized group of individuals 20 years after the fact to see what paths their lives had followed. Children who had suffered abuse and neglect were more likely than a control group of non-abused children to come into conflict with the law.[82] Furthermore, she found that, although not inevitable, violence does beget violence in some situations: "Victims of physical abuse had the highest levels of arrest for violent criminal behaviour, followed by victims of neglect."[83]

A few decades later (in 2011), Widom, along with a few other researchers, completed a similar study. This time, however, the focus was on the traumas of neglect and poverty and whether these could be correlated with post-traumatic stress disorder (PTSD), major depressive episodes (MDD), and adult criminal activity. This particular study used an ecology theoretical framework, which views child development "as embedded within a family, a school, a community, and a neighbourhood, and recognizing the need to consider contextual factors in understanding outcomes for maltreated children."[84] The results were similar to those of the 1989 study. Neglected children were found to be at greater risk for future violent delinquency, as were children who had experienced poverty.[85]

A 2012 article in the *Journal of Interpersonal Violence*, "From Child Maltreatment to Violent Offending: An Examination of Mixed-Gender and Gender-Specific Models" by Topitzes et al., sought to answer similar questions, but by focusing on the variable of gender. The researchers wanted to know whether outcomes would be different for males and females. They aimed to answer the question: Does gender mediate risk of future violence for those who experienced victimization between the ages of 0 to 11? Ultimately, they concluded that gender did not mediate risk of violence. That is, both boys and girls who experienced victimization were at risk of perpetrating future violence.[86] An even larger study (N > 12.5 million) conducted by researchers in Sweden sought to find out if interpersonal violence clustered within families. The researchers found strong evidence of a correlation between violent behaviour and family of origin; that is, violent crime runs in families.[87] Their conclusion was that a public health approach was needed to address the genetic and environmental origins of violence.[88] Still other studies have demonstrated a correlation between early victimization and increased psychological distress and subsequent offending behaviours.[89] Each of these studies offers empirical support for a cycle of violence theory.

Indeed, there's a strong connection between traumatic experiences and future criminal behaviour. As cited in the previous paragraphs, one of the most common experiences of young offenders is witnessing or experiencing the violence of a (usually male) parent. A high percentage of boys with this trauma go on to repeat the cycle by being violent toward their own partners and children.[90] In fact, most research seems to indicate that boys who witness domestic violence in their home while growing up are three times more likely to perpetrate domestic violence as adults.[91] This is consistent with my own experience as a counsellor for men who have used violence toward partners and children. When I listen to their stories from childhood, I hear about abuse and violence, similar to what they have chosen to carry on. Again, this is not an excuse, but an explanation. The assumption has often been that domestic violence is a learned behaviour and it might, in part, be that boys mimic the behaviour of their fathers, yet when I articulate the impacts of trauma in the next chapter and its effect on attachment and relationships, it will become clearer that there's more at work. As we move along in this book, our question will become: How can we best interrupt cycles of violence? Understanding trauma will help.

Although some of the studies I've just mentioned indicated that both boys and girls are at risking of perpetrating violence when victimized, there is a gendered component to relational violence. Boys and men are much more likely to be violent toward partners, and others, than girls and women are. The Centers for Disease Control and Prevention tracks large amounts of data on this topic:

- Close to 75 percent of family violence perpetrators are men.[92]
- Eight out of 10 people who killed a family member were male.[93]
- A large majority (83 percent) of spousal murderers were male.[94]
- Two-thirds of people who killed a boyfriend or girlfriend were male.[95]

What this highlights is the need for a gendered analysis of violence, which feminist theoretical perspectives in criminology are well equipped to articulate. Therefore, the cycle of violence theory that I'm proposing requires a feminist overlay.

Trauma-Informed Theory Is Feminist, Anti-racist, and about Peacemaking

Feminism encompasses many theoretical perspectives, from more radical Marxist perspectives to cultural and social constructivist approaches. Instead of *feminism*, it's more appropriate to say *feminisms*. For the purposes of this text, I've found inspiration in the work of feminist leader bell hooks. She describes, in various writings, some of the distinct characteristics of feminism. Here, I name three: first, the culture in North America (and beyond) is patriarchal. This is characterized by unequal power relations, domination, and exploitation:[96] men over women and other genders (i.e., those who do not identify as either "male" or "female"), white over other races, rich over poor, and so on. Second, feminism is about struggle, about raising critical consciousness about these issues. About this, hooks says, "We had to educate for a critical consciousness in ways that enable women and men to see that patriarchy promotes pathological behavior in both genders and that our wounded psyches had to be attended to not as a secondary aspect of revolutionary struggle but as a central starting point."[97] Third, feminism as theory grows out of the lived experiences of women and other marginalized groups. Theory is only functional in conjunction with practical living. Personal testimony and personal experience is fertile ground for transformation that liberates the oppressed.[98] hooks tells a story of her childhood that explains this:

> I came to theory because I was hurting. Whenever I tried in childhood to compel folks around me to look at the world differently, I was punished. I remember trying to explain at a very young age to Mama why I thought it was inappropriate for Daddy, this man who hardly spoke to me, to have the right to punish me with whippings: her response was to suggest I was losing my mind and in need of more punishment. Imagine this young Black couple struggling to realize the patriarchal norm (the woman taking care of household and children while the man worked) even though such an arrangement meant that economically they would always be living with less. Try to imagine what it must have been like—each of them working hard all day, struggling to maintain seven children, then having to cope with one bright-eyed child relentlessly questioning, rebelling against the patriarchal norm they were trying so hard to institutionalize. No wonder Mama would say to me, exasperated: "I don't know where I got you from, but I wish I could give you back." Living in childhood without a sense of home, I found a sanctuary in "theorizing," where I could imagine possible futures. This "lived" experience of critical thinking, of reflection and analysis, became a place where I worked at explaining that theory could be a healing place. When our lived experience is fundamentally linked to processes of self-recovery, of collective liberation, no gap exists between theory and practice.[99]

Criminology has been slow on the feminist uptake, in spite of the richness feminism offers to the discipline. (Mainstream criminology has been referred to at times as "malestream."[100]) As sociologist Elizabeth Comack explains, feminist criminology, particularly in the 1980s, "sought to expose how the gendered nature of women's lives in a patriarchal society affected both their risk of victimization at the hands of violent men and their involvement in crime."[101] What feminist criminology also accomplished, though, was to turn the spotlight on the maleness of many people in conflict with the law, as well as the racialized and economically disadvantaged components of their identity.[102] The critical perspective feminism offered by bringing lived experience to the forefront has added much to criminological discourse. Furthermore, radical and Marxist feminisms have allowed for a more nuanced discussion of marginalization. Gender is only one component of identity.

The work of Kimberle Williams Crenshaw has been vital for understanding how social constructs related to identity interact with each other, sometimes in counterproductive ways. For example, in analyzing gender oppression, Crenshaw says racism must also be considered. That is, a gendered analysis alone will not fully explain oppression.[103] Thus, she coined the term "intersectionality" to explain a layered exploration:

> Consider an analogy to traffic in an intersection, coming and going in all four directions. Discrimination, like traffic through an intersection, may flow in one direction, and it may flow in another. If an accident happens in an intersection, it can be caused by cars traveling from any number of directions and, sometimes, from all of them. Similarly, if a Black woman is harmed because she is in an intersection, her injury could result from sex discrimination or race discrimination....But it is not always easy to reconstruct an accident: Sometimes the skid marks and the injuries simply indicate that they occurred simultaneously, frustrating efforts to determine which driver caused the harm.[104]

Crenshaw claims that her concern has not been to create an overarching theory, but to highlight how identity politics often ignores difference.[105]

A cycle of violence theory must account for an anti-racist perspective alongside a gendered analysis of trauma. Further to this, there are also class considerations. In chapter 1, I proposed the value of peace, and the perspectives of peacebuilders and peacemaking criminologists as a way to address racism, sexism, and classism. One final theory deserves discussion along with feminism, anti-racism, and peacemaking criminology: anarchist criminology. This tradition, which emerged in the late 1970s and early 1980s, has been largely sidelined within mainstream criminology. Its value, for the purposes of this book, is in problematizing mainstream theories for maintaining the status quo, not calling into question the marginalization of certain groups of people or offering alternative ways of being in community.

Two of the primary supporters of anarchist criminology have been Larry Tifft and Dennis Sullivan. Their early work *The Struggle to Be Human: Crime, Criminology and Anarchism* presents an alternative vision for criminology, and life, for that matter. In the introduction to this chapter, I began to describe their work. Fundamentally, anarchist criminologists are asking two questions: one, is the individual delinquent, or is their delinquent behaviour a normal reaction to a delinquent state? Or put another way, is the state criminal in its treatment of certain groups of people, which in turn causes them to lash out? Two, given the state marginalization of certain people, how might we live as communities in ways that eliminate harmful hierarchies and offer a dignified life for all? Other core components of anarchist criminology include:

- The awakening of the collective consciousness of all people to injustice, and its antidote, freedom
- Autonomy and inclusion for all people

- Mutual aid and care for all people
- A commitment to equal relationships or, more fundamentally, to equity
- A pursuit of freedom[106]

CONCLUSION: LIMITS OF A TRAUMA-INFORMED LENS

Of course, a trauma-informed lens—one that uses a cycle of violence theory—doesn't explain *all* young offending. Some can be explained by the developmental immaturity of young people, where a person might not have grown up in trauma, but still acts out for lack of foresight or clarity of thought. The teenage brain is less developed in cause-effect than the adult brain. I'm not trying to suggest to you that I have found *the* theoretical explanation for all crime and delinquency. It's important for you to assess this theoretical perspective against (and with) the other theories described in this chapter, as well as with your lived experience and worldviews. A multidisciplinary theoretical explanation for youth crime will be more robust than one explanation that seeks to explain it independently. In essence, I'm arguing that a trauma-informed approach should be the starting place for understanding the issue. Once we know that most youth who commit crime have in some way been hurt in their lives, we will do better in our justice responses. A trauma-informed perspective flows from a cycle of violence theory that is one part feminist, another part anti-racist, and primarily about peacemaking. In the next chapter, I'll provide a detailed account of trauma to help you better grasp how it affects the way that people relate to others.

GLOSSARY OF TERMS

Cycle of violence is an explanation for how violence tends to repeat from one generation to the next, as well as how once individuals use violence, they risk repeating it again in the future.

Theory is an explanation for why something is as it is. Beyond a hypothesis—or a guess—it is an explanation that has been tested, whether through empirical analysis, or by the lived experience of the theorist or those being observed.

Violence is an action that violates, or harms, something or someone psychologically, physically, emotionally, spiritually, financially, or sexually. For our purposes, we are mostly talking about human violence, though the definition could extend to the environment and to other living creatures.

QUESTIONS FOR REFLECTION

1. Which of the theories in the first half of the chapter do you find the least compelling? Which one do you find the most compelling?
2. What makes for a good criminological theory about young offenders? Researchers measure what they hypothesize. How might a hypothesis be limited by a researcher's privileged position within academia?
3. The cycle of violence theory proposed in this book operates on the principle of "intersectionality" suggested by Crenshaw; that is, it is a layered analysis,

including constructs of gender, race, and socio-economic status. What other constructs do you think should be included? Are there some that this text misses?

RECOMMENDED READING

Gilligan, James. *Preventing Violence*. New York: Thames & Hudson Inc., 2001.
   In this book, psychiatrist James Gilligan, after many decades of working with violent offenders, proposes making violence a public health issue, as a way to eradicate it.

hooks, bell. "Out of the Academy and into the Streets." *Ms* 3 (1992): 80–82.
   Any of the works of bell hooks, a feminist writer and activist, is helpful for thinking about how to do the work of trauma-informed youth justice well. I selected this article, though, because of its exquisite writing, and how it connects theory with practice — and lived experiences.

Tifft, Larry and Sullivan, Dennis. *The Struggle to Be Human: Crime, Criminology & Anarchism*. Orkney: Cienfuegos Press, 1980.
   I would recommend this book to readers interested in exploring anarchist criminology further. Larry Tifft and Dennis Sullivan ground the work of criminology in a values-base.

5 | Understanding Individual Trauma

A boy is regularly beaten and ridiculed by his dad. By the time he's a teenager, his friends mostly describe him as shy, if not reserved and withdrawn. However, he's known to explode when repeatedly provoked; and when he consumes alcohol at parties, he doesn't slow down until he's heavily inebriated. Furthermore, alcohol appears to precipitate the eruption of a Mr. Hyde persona from his normally quiet, stone-like, Dr. Jekyll demeanour. Nobody is very surprised when, at 17, he's charged with assault after knocking out another student's front teeth in a locker room dispute after a physical education class. It was only a matter of time.

I start this chapter on individual trauma by inviting you into a story. Although the vignette that opens the chapter is fictitious, the best way to understand trauma is to hear stories of survivors. As I engage in the work of youth justice, I'm not interested in a purely academic exercise—one that only challenges the mind to think critically about issues. I'm also interested in inviting the whole person—including feelings and experiences—to consider how these stories matter to me, to you, and to consider what we can do to improve the lives of those who live in our communities. The person in the story above might be known as a "criminal." He might be defined as "bad." These labels might help us in some ways to understand harmful behaviour, but labels also constrain. For example, they could limit future opportunities for growth and for a young person to contribute to society. Obviously, there's always much more to the story of the young person beyond the label. The "drug dealer" comes from hardship. The "angry boy" has a past that is none too kind. The label "lawbreaker" might be the reason the youth justice system is involved in their lives, but it should only be a starting point, not an ending. We have to dig deeper to understand. Otherwise, labels get in the way of stories, and better endings.

In the previous chapter, I laid the foundation for why youth justice should be trauma-informed: because trauma is *the* most common denominator across the lived experiences of young people who end up in conflict with the law. It's not the only reason; it would be simplistic to say so. However, trauma is widespread and deserves our full attention. I also talked about a cycle of violence theory, and how one generation is prone to repeating the previous generation's mistakes. Now, in chapter 5, we come to the point where we're ready to understand trauma more fully. What is it? What causes it? How does it affect people and communities? More specifically, how does it affect the way that people relate to each other? Our objective is to better understand harmful or criminal behaviour and how it can be better addressed.

This chapter will go as follows: Trauma will be defined. Individual trauma will be distinguished from collective trauma, as will episodic versus intergenerational trauma. Some causes of trauma will be identified, but the arena of causes will largely be reserved for chapter 6. The impacts of trauma will be described—from physiological, to emotional, to cognitive, to behavioural—as will trauma's after-effects. Some of this discussion will include highlighting the impacts on the brains of traumatized people. I'm not a neuroscientist, and can only skim the surface of this topic, but I feel that it's important for those involved in youth justice to acknowledge the physical wounds in the brain that trauma creates. Society tends to allow for special accommodation and extra support when a person has a broken leg. So why not when the brain has been damaged by trauma? Mental health and addictions will be examined. Some forms of these conditions have their roots in trauma. In fact, when it comes to substance abuse, one of the researchers I will discuss, Dr. Gabor Maté, claims that most, if not all, addictions can be correlated to early childhood traumas.

The chapter will conclude with a section on attachment theory. Ultimately, we can better understand why people hurt each other and commit crime if the issue is put in the context of relationships. People who have been traumatized often have disrupted attachments, and some—or much—difficulty relating to others in healthy ways. This can correlate with violence or other behaviours that society deems deviant.

A word of warning: In my years of teaching on this topic, I've found that most people have some indirect or direct experience with trauma. This topic is deeply personal for most. So, as I invite you into this topic, take care of yourself, and be sure to take it at an appropriate pace. Consider it personally, or more theoretically, whatever is more comfortable.

TRAUMA

For the purposes of this book, we'll be focusing primarily on psychological trauma rather than on the traumas typically talked about in the medical community. These other medical traumas tend to focus more on the emergency treatment of physical injuries. For example, a person physically injured in a car accident would be triaged at a hospital, and would likely see a trauma surgeon based on the extent of the injury. The surgeon might perform an invasive surgery to repair a broken bone or a damaged organ. This chapter isn't about that type of trauma. However, there can be some overlap. For example, the same car accident I just mentioned might also psychologically injure (or traumatize) the person who experiences it. There's also an element of physical injury in the brain caused by psychological trauma; however, my focus will be on how psychological trauma affects individual functioning. In this example, the victim might develop a fear of driving or avoid smells that remind them of cars (oil, gas, etc.) or anything that takes them back in time to the overwhelming fear of the car accident. Although I'm talking about psychological trauma, for the sake of simplicity from here on, I will simply refer to it as trauma.

What is trauma? Trauma is an incident or event experienced as so overwhelming that the person fears their life is over. It's an injury or a wound that results when a person's system of coping is breached. There are two parts to this definition: first, an incident (or ongoing incidents), and second, an individual's or community's experience of it. The latter, the experience, will determine whether the person, or people, are traumatized. Experts in this area offer the following definitions of trauma. Judith Herman says, "traumatic events overwhelm the ordinary systems of care that give people a sense of control, connection and meaning."[1] Bessel van der Kolk defines it as "an inescapably stressful event that overwhelms people's existing coping mechanisms."[2] Sandra Bloom claims that traumatic events produce "a physiological overload that the brain and body are unable to manage adequately, preventing us from continuing to function normally."[3] In their research, Lori Haskell and Melanie Randall say, "Trauma refers to the range of possible, typical and normal responses people have to an extreme and overwhelming event, or series of events."[4]

Trauma is different than what we typically call stress. Although there are similarities with how a person experiences regular stress, trauma is much more extreme. It hinders, rather than helps, human growth. For example, many students find studying for exams stressful. They might feel anxious, or even overwhelmed at times, but most find ways to cope and see the value in the overall experience or outcome (if they pass!). Writing an exam can create growth. It can provide a sense of accomplishment or create future opportunities for the student. Trauma is different. It impedes growth. It is more than simply difficult or stressful, and only happens when a person's capacity to cope is overwhelmed, usually by a matter of life or death. The person feels profoundly helpless or powerless, unable to stop the event.

It's important to note that the same event might traumatize some people, but not others, because it is how a person experiences an event and its after-effects that determine traumatization and not the event itself. Some more specific labels for trauma include: *episodic* (single incidents), *persistent* (consistent episodes), *intergenerational* (episodes that can carry over from one generation to the next), *collective* (a group that shares trauma), and *historical* (present-day trauma, explained by unresolved historical harms). The chart below gives some examples of events in each category that would likely cause any individual or group to be traumatized.

Trauma affects not only individuals, but also groups. (Focusing only on the individual would ignore issues like race and power, examples of structural causes of trauma.) Returning to the metaphor of a car accident, what if we discovered that crashes were more common in particular types of cars? We'd want to do more than help individual victims. We'd also want to address the systemic issues to prevent future harm. Similarly, an overly individualistic definition of trauma can lose sight of certain harms. Trauma isn't only incidental and episodic, but can happen across generations or among groups of people. This will be explored more in chapter 6.

Table 5.1: Types of Trauma

Type of Trauma	Example
Episodic	• Serious car accident • Natural disaster • Physical, emotional, sexual abuse
Persistent (can also be intergenerational)	• Family violence • Child abuse • Neglect • Bullying • Intimate partner violence • Imprisonment • Poverty
Collective (can also be intergenerational)	• Genocide • Violence against women • Refugee experiences • Colonialism • Poverty • Environmental degradation • War
Historical (intergenerational in nature)	• Holocaust • "Indian" residential schools • Slavery

THE IMPACTS OF TRAUMA

In this section, I'll start to explain in greater depth the impacts of trauma. We'll begin by looking at individual trauma and its emotional, mental, physical, cognitive, behavioural, relational, and identity effects.

As we've seen, trauma has a profoundly negative impact on the person who experiences it; however, it's important to understand that although trauma can lead to mental health issues, I will not consider a traumatized person as someone with a disorder. From a trauma-informed perspective, the traumatized person is responding normally to an abnormal situation. For a number of years, I've worked to support male survivors of sexual abuse. Like many sexual abuse survivors, their recovery can be long and it can be a struggle to find stability. Oftentimes they've told me, "I feel like I'm crazy. I don't know what 'normal' is." Although the survivor might feel as if she or he is "losing her or his mind," the brain is often responding normally to the abnormality of violence, of sexual abuse. Their brain has gone into survival mode. The following is a chronological account of the life of a male survivor of sexual abuse. It's a fictional account that represents a compilation of themes that exist in some survivor stories. I will use this as a starting place to explain some of the impacts of trauma.

Chapter 5: Understanding Individual Trauma

A young man, aged 25 (I'll call him Sean), decides to ask for help. For 10 years, he's been drinking until he blacks out, engaging in high-risk sexual activity and harming himself. Many of his family members have grown tired of his behaviour—including his volatile temper—and have distanced themselves from him. Talking to a social worker, Sean discloses that he was sexually abused by a relative when he was a child. Sean has conflicted feelings toward the abuser. On one hand, Sean hates the abuser and feels he has ruined his life. On the other hand, he doesn't want this person to go to prison. He's worried, though, that this man might be sexually abusing others.

Now let's backtrack a little ...

Age four: Sean's parents are in the process of going through a divorce. During this time of intense conflict in his family's life, Sean often sleeps over at his aunt and uncle's home. During these visits, under the guise of comfort, Sean's uncle John touches his genitals and coerces him into doing the same to him. Uncle John also does healthy, nurturing activities with Sean: teaching him how to ride a bike, playing catch, and watching TV with him. He's always complimentary of Sean's abilities and notices his accomplishments.

Age eight: The sexual abuse has been ongoing and has evolved into rape. Uncle John tells Sean that it's their secret, and that if he tells anyone, Sean will never be able to see his family again. Further, Sean is led to believe that women are dirty and what is happening between them is normal and proper—that Uncle John is teaching him how to be a man.

Age 12: Sean hates the abuse and hates that when he ejaculates it feels good. He is confused and angry—always angry. He continues to have problems in school. He's often aggressive toward teachers and has been caught taking things from classmates. Sean's mom is exasperated. What is she supposed to do with a child that everyone has labelled a "problem"?

Uncle John introduces Sean to alcohol.

Age 16: In an alcohol-fuelled rage, Sean tells his mom about the sexual abuse, but she refuses to believe him. In fact, she berates him, saying she's sickened that he would try to blame his problems on such a kind, hardworking man. Sean's mom threatens to stop talking to her son should he "make up such lies" again. Sean spirals: drops out of school and starts binge drinking.

Age 18 to 25: Sean is able to stop the abuse, but he can't stop the restless feelings or the constant reminders of it. Everywhere he turns it follows him, whether he's awake or asleep. He often wanders the streets at night, looking to buy sex. He has difficulty holding down a job and can't look at himself in the mirror. He hates himself and his life. He's tried to kill himself several times. The last time landed him in the hospital for a week, where he met the social worker.

A number of basic impacts can be articulated based on the story of Sean, including physical, emotional, and behavioural impacts as well as a change in how he might see the world.

Physical impacts: Sexual abuse is usually experienced as traumatic. Trauma typically creates an altered state in the brain whereby the stress response is damaged. Individuals might have difficulty coping with everyday life stresses or develop mental health challenges. Post-traumatic stress disorder, depression, anxiety, and so on are common in victims of sexual abuse. Victims also experience pain in their body and are reminded of victimization through their senses. Certain sights, sounds, smells, tastes, and touches bring them back to the times when they were terrorized. Nightmares ensue and sleep can be difficult. Sean walks the streets at night, trying, at all costs, to avoid reminders of the abuse he experienced.

Emotional impacts: Some primary emotional impacts of sexual abuse are shame, fear, and distrust. Victims often blame themselves. In the story above, the offender manipulated his victim into thinking he had initiated or wanted the abuse, and that it was somehow his fault. Shame makes us feel as if we are "bad," or, as researcher Brene Brown says, we are unworthy of human connection.[5] The victim might be afraid that the abuse will happen again. Sensory reminders mean that he's constantly on edge. Distrust is common; most offenders are known to victims. They are often family members and have established a close relationship by proximity or through grooming behaviours, contributing something positive to the victim's life as a way to build trust and to lure them in. This trust is then betrayed—leaving victims feeling confused and distrustful.

Behavioural impacts: When a person is traumatized, she or he often orient her or his life around trying to ensure that trauma is never repeated. This can take the form of withdrawal from relationships or other maladaptive ways of trying to calm their anxiety such as substance abuse, self-harm, and suicide. Sean uses alcohol and sex as a way to cope. Most sexual abuse survivors find relationships difficult. Some avoid them all together while others cling to them in an attempt to heal.

Worldview impacts: An experience of sexual abuse often alters how a victim sees the world and their place in it. Victims often wonder, "Why me?", and struggle to understand what life would have been like if the abuse hadn't happened. They begin to see the world as unsafe. This can lead to—if they believed in a higher power to begin with—questioning God. Ultimately, this is about identity, how they see themselves and others.

The next step in understanding the impacts of trauma is to consider physiological changes, or changes in the brain of the survivor.

Impacts of Trauma on the Brain and Body

When a person is traumatized, he or she is harmed in a way that dramatically affects future functioning. Trauma has after-effects that are physiological, especially in the still-developing brain of an infant, a child, or a teenager. Once you begin to understand how trauma affects the brain, Sean's responses will all start to make sense. As much as the development of our brains is dependent on genetics, it's also shaped by our experiences. Research has consistently demonstrated that a single event can alter a child's development, and this is even truer of ongoing, chronic, or traumatic events.[6] In their work on how psychological trauma affects the developing brain, psychiatric nurse Phyllis Stien and journalist Joshua C. Kendall say, "Not surprisingly, the clinical picture for children with histories of severe abuse and neglect is disturbing. As mental health professionals, educators, foster parents, and those in the juvenile court system have long observed, these children often develop self-defeating, provocative, and destructive patterns of behaviour."[7] Traumatic stress damages neurological pathways in the brain necessary for healthy functioning. Stien and Kendall claim the brain is impaired in the four following ways:[8]

1. A Damaged, or Dysregulated, Stress Response

Trauma triggers the stress response of the brain. This usually results in one of two survival options for a person: fight, or flight. The person's brain believes that in order to survive in the moment they must either fight whatever or whoever is triggering the stress or run away. Sometimes neither response is an option (as is often the case in sexual abuse), so instead of being able to run or fight, the person simply freezes and remains unable to act. The experience of traumatic stress creates long-lasting, if not permanent, changes in the brain.

The amygdala, the part of the brain that's responsible for processing memory and responding emotionally, can become hyper-reactive (or aroused) in the future from even very minor stimuli.[9] This produces a state of **hyperarousal** for the trauma survivor: a constant fear, or (hyper)vigilance, that the traumatic event will happen again. In her research and work with trauma survivors, psychiatrist Judith Herman talks about this as a baseline of arousal rather than one of relaxation: "Their bodies are always on alert for danger."[10] It becomes very difficult for a person to function and to carry out day-to-day tasks when the brain is on high alert.

In the past few years, researchers have begun to compare the brain functioning of combat veterans with that of children maltreated by caregivers. The results are astonishing—though perhaps not to those who work in shelters supporting women and children escaping family violence. The brain scans are almost identical. Researchers McCrory et al. found a heightened activation of the anterior insula and the amygdala in both populations.[11] These two components of the brain are associated with helping a person predict how painful a particular stimulus will be.[12] The researchers state that, although this is helpful in a moment of fear or actual threat, it seems to remain "turned on" in survivors of combat and child victims of maltreatment. The long-term impact is an increase in overall anxiety in response to many stimuli, even non-threatening ones. According to McCrory et al., it "may predispose [a person] to reactive aggression."[13] Normal human relationships become difficult for people who have experienced trauma. Conflict is inevitable in relationships, but each episode feels disproportionately exaggerated in the mind of the trauma survivor.

Furthermore, the brain begins to overreact to any type of sensory reminder of the traumatic event: sights, sounds, smells, tastes, and certain feelings. For example, in the scenario above, perhaps every time Sean smells cologne that reminds him of his uncle's, he'll be reminded of the abuse. This is called a **trigger**. The sensory reminder puts Sean back into the moment of abuse. He feels triggered and wants to run away from the present situation (the smell of the similar cologne), even if he's not actually unsafe at that moment.

As psychiatrists Bessel van der Kolk and Alexander McFarlane say, traumatized people tend to move from stimulus to response immediately, without necessarily understanding why.[14] They describe this as a "generalization of threat"—an inability to modulate arousal: "Their bodies continue to react to certain physical stimuli as if there were a continuing threat of annihilation."[15] The tension of constantly feeling threatened, yet wanting to avoid experiencing the traumatic event again, leaves the person simultaneously aroused and wanting to numb their feelings. For this reason, trauma survivors often withdraw from everyday life, as their physical, emotional, and psychological capacities become depleted.[16] The sum total of this is damage to the overall structure and function of the brain's stress response.

2. Decrease in Hippocampal Volume

Another area of the brain that's damaged by trauma is the hippocampus. This part is normally used for memory, processing emotions, and learning. It's believed that the hippocampus, along with the prefrontal cortex of the brain, helps by signalling the amygdala to stop the stress response.[17] In survivors of childhood trauma, the hippocampus has been shown to be smaller, less developed.[18] This diminishes the brain's capacity in two ways: first, in managing stress, and second, in integrating memory properly.

First, researchers believe that heightened levels of the steroid cortisol, released when the body is under stress, are part of what impacts the hippocampus. Actual damage, or interruption of blood flow, can result.[19] When trauma happens in childhood, this can have lifelong repercussions—the person can become brain damaged. This physiological impact is important for people working in the field of youth justice to understand. Sometimes youth are acting based on how their brains are functioning, not necessarily out of a spiteful, vindictive, or criminal nature. Traumatic stress, experienced as overwhelming to its victim unless allowed to heal, triggers a more permanent stressed state. This in turn affects the mental health of the trauma survivor.

Second, when a person is traumatized, they're unable to store memories of the event in the same way they store other experiences. Researchers believe that ordinary memory is linguistic in nature, or can easily be put into words, while traumatic memory is more sensory. Although a person might not always remember "normal" events, when they are able to remember them, it's easier to articulate what happened. If I've been on a camping trip, for example, I can talk about my tent, the campsite, and my overall experience without much difficulty. Conversely, trauma survivors often remember traumatic events more as feelings/emotions or sensations. This is why sensory triggers, as discussed above, are common. Instead of being able to recall traumatic events in a way that's easy to describe, memories often come and go as flashes, called **flashbacks**. Sensory memory is often experienced as intrusive, arriving unexpectedly. Flashbacks—intense emotions like panic and rage, and nightmares—are commonly associated with sensory memory.[20] It can be incredibly difficult for the survivor to articulate their experiences, and they often rely on metaphors or comparisons instead of on more matter-of-fact descriptions. This is as much a part of the pain of being traumatized (how can one put into words what it's like to be abused, or to experience violence at the hands of a loved one?) as it is about the impact on the brain of the survivor.

Memory science also describes this change in memory in declarative versus procedural terms. Ordinary memory is also known as declarative—the ability to be consciously aware of facts or events—while traumatic memory falls under the procedural category.[21] Procedural memory is more reflexive in nature. As trauma specialist Sandra Bloom explains it, procedural memory helps us drive a car or ride a bike—it allows people to develop habits, so we don't have to devote all our attention to recalling what to do every time.[22] Procedural memory is processed in a much more automatic way than declarative memory. On one hand, riding a bike is an example of this type of brain memory functioning well. On the other hand, when the hippocampus is damaged it doesn't function as it's supposed to, seeming to store memories as procedural when they should be declarative. Judith Herman says, "Traumatic memories lack verbal narrative and context; rather they're encoded in the form of vivid sensations and images."[23] As a result, a traumatized person is forced to continually relive the event through various sensory intrusions.

Table 5.2: Ordinary vs. Traumatic Memory

Ordinary Memory	Traumatic Memory
• Declarative	• Procedural
• Linguistic	• Sensory
• Integrated	• Disintegrated
• Controlled	• Out of Control

3. Underdevelopment of the Left Hemisphere and Communication Problems between Brain Hemispheres

Another cause for concern with individuals who have experienced trauma as children is damage to the cortex of the left hemisphere of the brain. Studies have consistently found there to be an increased likelihood of this among survivors of early childhood trauma.[24] This type of damage is associated with a number of psychiatric disorders as well as with an inability to process thought in more complex ways. Furthermore, something called lateralization can happen in the corpus callosum, the section that connects the two sides of the brain. This results in an overreliance on one particular side of the brain given certain tasks.[25] Most brain functioning requires that the brain work as a system. Ultimately, when the two sides of the brain aren't working in concert, or when a brain is underdeveloped, higher-order thinking and emotional processing can become impaired.[26] Van der Kolk and McFarlane suggest that this limits the person's ability to articulate their feelings.[27] When conditions are relatively normal, the brain appears to function well as a whole system. Under trauma, this is dramatically impaired.

4. Neuroendocrine and Immune System Dysfunction

Trauma's impact on physiology goes beyond the brain. Research has explored connections between certain illnesses and early childhood trauma, as well as trauma being passed genetically from one generation to the next. In the past decade or so, scientists have started to examine links between adverse childhood experiences (ACE) and future health outcomes. Typically, researchers look at seven ACE factors: physical, emotional, or sexual abuse; alcohol and drug abuse in the home; an incarcerated household member; chronic depression or suicidality in a family member; domestic violence; one or no parents; and neglect.[28] Studies then track a number of outcomes. Some outcomes are social in nature: education or employment. Others look at health outcomes: smoking, obesity, or chronic disease. One study of adults in Texas that looked at over 5,000 adults with at least one ACE factor found that there were significant increases in the likelihood of poor health outcomes.[29] These findings are not unique, having been replicated on numerous occasions. Chronic stress, created by trauma, heightens risk of future health problems.[30] Epigenetics, the study of changes in gene activity from one generation to the next, has also identified changes in the genetic structure of survivors. In their study titled "Child Maltreatment Is Associated with Distinct Genomic and Epigenetic Profiles in Posttraumatic Stress Disorder," a number of researchers working together concluded that trauma "engrave[s] long-lasting epigenetic marks, leading to adverse health outcomes in adulthood" for survivors.[31]

TRAUMA AND MENTAL HEALTH

There is a strong connection between trauma and certain mental health challenges. The four impacts on the brains of traumatized people that we saw in the last section are one explanation for why trauma survivors often develop mental health challenges. Clearly, brain functioning is altered. As a person struggles to cope with psychological pain, life becomes oriented toward avoiding revictimization. Often, people shut down internally to any form of difficult feeling or any reminder of the trauma. Externally, they commonly avoid "outside" life, for fear of experiencing any trigger. In combination, inner turmoil and external withdrawal have a profound impact on mental well-being. In this section, I'll describe five mental health challenges correlated with trauma: post-traumatic stress disorder, depression, borderline personality disorder, dissociative identity disorder, and fetal alcohol spectrum disorder along with a few disruptive behaviour disorders.

Post-traumatic Stress Disorder

In the previous section, I incorporated research associated with post-traumatic stress disorder (PTSD), together with research that looks at how children's brains are affected by trauma. In reality, in comparison with adults, psychiatrists don't diagnose children with PTSD nearly as often. Many psychiatrists argue that traumatized children have their own uniqueness, or nuances of impact, that still need to be better understood. In a 2012 article in the *American Journal of Orthopsychiatry*, Wendy D'Andrea, Julian Ford, Bradley Stolbach, Joseph Spinazzola, and Bessel van der Kolk identify some themes present in children who have experienced trauma:

- Disregulation of affect and behaviour: extremes between numb and explosive
- Disturbances of attention and consciousness: impulsivity, dissociation, and inability to concentrate
- Distortions in attributions: lower self-worth, shame, and self-blame
- Interpersonal difficulties: diminished social skills, and distrustful[32]

These themes do indeed relate to the two core themes of post-traumatic stress disorder: compulsive re-exposure to trauma and avoidance or numbing. Life for the trauma survivor is conflicted between reliving trauma and avoiding it. Of course, as stated earlier, the person doesn't want to live through the trauma again; however, survivors will often re-enact the trauma. In doing so, they're likely trying to master an experience that was previously out of their control and, at the same time, gain control over the associated feelings. Survivors are plagued by "what if" questions: What if I had done something differently? Would it have ended better? This is part of the self-blame of trauma. Re-enactment is a futile, and usually harmful, way to try to change the past. There are three ways that re-enactment of trauma occurs: self-harm, harm to others, or future victimization.

Self-harming is one way people numb feelings. When one hurts oneself, the person's body releases natural painkillers, or endorphins. Studies have found that self-destructive behaviour is common in children who have been abused. Examples include cutting, burning, or head banging.[33]

Hurting others is another way that trauma gets repeated. As indicated in the previous chapter, many youth in conflict with the law have experienced trauma. Studies consistently find that—although not all trauma survivors repeat their pasts—survivors of childhood trauma are at risk of future drug use, crime, and other forms of violence.[34] Some of this can be explained by a need to numb (drug use), while other aspects of it can be explained by feelings of worthlessness, isolation, or a lack of belonging (crime). Meanwhile, violence can be explained as a person feeling the need to thwart a sense of constant threat. A traumatized person is in survival mode. For some this means the "fight" of "fight or flight" has been switched on, and not successfully turned off. One rationale for violence is that people who use it do so to gain power or to control victims. What this explanation often misses is that by controlling the victim, the perpetrator is actually attempting to master his (or her) own feelings of powerlessness.

Future victimization can occur for a variety of reasons. Children who have been abused are more likely to enter into abusive relationships as adults.[35] Sometimes this is all a person knows as "normal." Or, future victimization can result from an inability to create safe boundaries from psychological exhaustion. Regardless, there is a compulsive re-exposure to trauma.

Avoidance or numbing is the other side of the re-exposure coin. When traumatized, a person's life can become oriented around not experiencing trauma again. However, the struggle can be ongoing; when memories aren't processed properly, there are constant reminders of the pain. Common coping strategies include drug and alcohol abuse, sexual promiscuity, and binge eating. Avoidance is a progression from trauma, to—sometimes harmful—coping strategies.

As we saw in the opening vignette of the chapter, being traumatized affects a person's behaviour. Recall the young boy being beaten by his father. Although the beatings are happening secretly, at home, some changes in the boy's behaviour will be observable to the outside world.

The boy, if traumatized, is likely to experience a constellation of intrusions, avoidances, and hyperarousal. He'll have moments where there will be forced reminders of the beatings. These might be triggered by a sight; for example, an angry look from a teacher that causes him to shut down. They might also be triggered by a sound; a bell at school could cause him to jump, or a door closing loudly could make his heart race. Or perhaps the smell of deodorant (someone using the same kind as his dad in the gym changeroom) will make him rush through changing as quickly as possible to escape. These traumatic memories intrude, because the young boy cannot control their recall. If it were his choice, he'd do anything possible to avoid remembering.

The young boy's behaviour becomes orientated around the trauma, because he's doing everything possible to avoid it. Rather than put himself in a position where a teacher might get angry with him, he might withdraw and become ultra-compliant. Or, perhaps he might fight back too early—becoming overly aggressive as a way of warding off a nonexistent attack from a teacher. Rather than be scared by a "silly bell," he might watch the clock closely as recess approaches, counting down the minutes. Rather than change with other students for physical education, he might avoid the deodorant smell by changing in advance in a different washroom. It's important to note that the boy isn't likely to be processing all of these experiences in the ways that I'm articulating them. That is, it isn't likely that he could put into words why he is avoidant. He's simply trying to escape a feeling of overwhelming angst that sits in the pit of his stomach. Furthermore, his own avoidant responses might produce a feeling of embarrassment and shame: "Why does the damn bell scare me every time it rings?" This paradoxical alertness as a way to avoid flashbacks happens because, physiologically, his body as a system is in a mode of hyperarousal. The initial trauma was so overwhelming that his body was put into survival mode—fight or flight. However, he wasn't able to run away or fight back when he was being beaten, so instead he froze, and now it's as if he's frozen in time, in that moment.

The boy is constantly anxious. At home, he might "walk on eggshells"; that is, he tiptoes around his father to ensure there are no further violent eruptions. He startles easily, he has a hard time focusing, and he might even have difficulty sleeping. He's constantly on alert. When danger presents itself, he avoids it. His range of options for dealing with stimuli is limited. He feels the only other tactic available when "danger" presents itself is to fight. This is why, as the vignette goes, he ends up getting into a fight in the locker room and comes into conflict with the law. Clinical psychologist Mary E. Vandergoot, talking about young offenders, says, "Often youth who attract the attention of police do so during a time in their lives fraught with other stressful events."[36]

All of this takes a toll on the survivor. Shame and fear are two predominant emotional responses I have mentioned. In her work and research with trauma survivors, Sandra Bloom describes others. She explains that emotions are important for survival, as well as for ordering, or structuring, our worlds.[37] When the process of ordering emotions is interrupted, there is a disconnect between thought and feeling. Learned helplessness sets in as the person feels like they can no longer control or trust their emotions and thoughts. Thus, people will do whatever they can to avoid negative feelings associated with the trauma.[38] Physiologists believe that, over time, this affects the body as a whole (inducing illness).[39] One form of avoiding negative feelings is dissociation, which Bloom describes as "... the brain mechanism that allows us to define individual reality to accommodate unsettling events, while remaining aware of another reality."[40] In other words, by dissociating, a person is able to go to another place in their mind while the body is present with a different event. This can be very useful. It allows a person to survive something horrific by moving out of their own body so as not to feel emotional or physical pain. Bloom describes it as an internal cast that the brain puts around broken emotions.[41] However, over time, dissociation can become a problematic pattern for trauma survivors. They might be trying to avoid reliving pain by using it as a strategy, but it can also get in the way of everyday life and, at times, can prevent them from facing pain and experiencing healing.

> **Eve Ensler on Dissociation**
>
> I think—from my own life experience, and certainly what I've discovered in many women and men across the planet—is [that] when we're traumatized, when we're beaten, when we're raped, we leave our bodies. We disconnect from ourselves. And if it's true that one out of every three women on the planet have been raped or beaten, which is a U.N. statistic, that's a billion women. Many, many of us have left our bodies—we're not embodied creatures, we're not living inside our own muscles and cells and sinews. And so we're not in our power, we're not in our energy. It's been a long journey to get fully back into my body. And, certainly, what I've seen everywhere in the world is that the more traumatized people are, the less connected they are to their own source of strength, their own source of inspiration, intuition, heart—everything.[42]

While advances continue to be made in psychiatry about PTSD, there is some backlash about limiting understandings of trauma by using medical diagnoses. Some medical professionals and community-based trauma healing practitioners are dissatisfied with labelling trauma as a "disorder." Instead, they prefer to use the term post-traumatic stress reaction. A reaction normalizes the experience of the survivor. Disorder indicates that something is wrong with the survivor, which possibly adds to self-blame. How we describe, or what labels we give, people when they are post-trauma will make a difference in how they see themselves, and in how they move toward healing.

> **Diagnostic and Statistical Manual-5 Critera for Medical Diagnosis of PTSD**
>
> Criterion A: stressor—exposure to a traumatic event
> Criterion B: intrusive symptoms—the event is re-experienced in some way
> Criterion C: avoidance—persistent efforts made to avoid trauma-related stimuli

> Criterion D: negative alterations in thought and mood—negative distortions and beliefs about reality and oneself, negative emotions, and feeling alienated from others
> Criterion E: alterations in arousal and reactivity—irritable, aggressive, hypervigilance, exaggerated startle response, problems in concentration and sleep
> Criterion F: duration—a persistence of symptoms
> Criterion G: functional significance—symptom-related impairment of social, occupational, and other abilities
> Criterion H: exclusion—symptoms not related to an illness or substance use[43]

Depression

One of the impacts of trauma is loss—the loss associated with how a person previously felt about the world (safe) or others in it, being replaced by new distrustful feelings (fear). Loss is associated with depression. As such, depression is one common impact of trauma.[44] Researchers J. Christopher Fowler, Jon Allen, John Oldham, and B. Christopher Frueh suggest that "evidence relating childhood trauma exposure to lifetime risk for major mental health and physical health disorders is substantial."[45] Diagnosis of depression, by a doctor, occurs when an individual has five of the following eight symptoms:

1. Depressed mood for long periods of time;
2. Diminished interest in normally pleasurable activities;
3. Significant weight loss;
4. Disturbed sleep, either too little, or too much;
5. Restlessness or sluggishness;
6. Fatigue;
7. Feelings of worthlessness;
8. Diminished ability to think, concentrate, and make decisions.[46]

Borderline Personality Disorder

Those afflicted with borderline personality disorder (BPD) exhibit an unstable identity, as well as unstable interpersonal relationships characterized by frantic efforts to avoid abandonment and by intense interpersonal relationships. Their mood too is often unstable, anxious, and irritable, as they have difficulty regulating it. Behaviours can be impulsive, often overindulgent—usually in the areas of spending, sex, or binge eating. What's more, self-injury and suicidal thoughts, with intense periods of anger or feelings of emptiness as well as some dissociative symptoms, are common.[47]

Psychiatrists Judith Herman, Christopher Perry, and Bessel van der Kolk have collaborated since the 1980s to better understand the connections between trauma and BPD.[48] They discovered that those with BPD often had histories of severe trauma, often physical or sexual abuse at the hands of a caregiver.[49] The researchers suggested that due to this early childhood trauma at the hands of caregiver, the child's development became arrested.[50] Van der Kolk describes these cases as a form of complex trauma, where the individual might display "permanent hostility and distrust, social withdrawal, feelings of emptiness and hopelessness, increased dependency and problems with modulation and aggression, hypervigilance and irritability, and feelings of alienation."[51] Furthermore, BPD is related to other mental health challenges, particularly depression.[52] Much of the research on BPD is still ongoing, and questions remain. Some researchers wonder whether BPD can intermingle, latently, with more stable personality traits, and only surface under stress or as a way to cope with difficult circumstances.[53]

Dissociative Identity Disorder

Previously known as multiple personality disorder, dissociative identity disorder (DID), like BPD, is usually found in people who have suffered significant or complex traumas. According to Dorahy et al., DID is "consistently linked to child relational trauma.... Many DID patients are conditioned 'not to tell' of their trauma.... Every study that has systematically examined etiology has found that antecedent severe, chronic childhood trauma is present in the histories of almost all individuals with DID."[54] DID, in some ways, is a natural result of survivors' attempts to dissociate—or to take their minds elsewhere—while experiencing violence. While dissociating in the moment is a way to survive, it becomes maladaptive later in life when survivors are unable to be present in normal day-to-day routines. Symptoms of DID include a fragmentation of identity, so that the person exhibits more than one personality. When feeling overwhelmed or afraid, the person escapes to a more comfortable identity. Research on DID has been somewhat limited, as there was debate about its validity until recently. This is changing, especially as people come to understand how it can be caused by trauma.

Fetal Alcohol Spectrum Disorder and Disruptive Behaviour Disorders

In *Justice for Young Offenders: Their Needs, Our Responses*, Mary E. Vandergoot writes of trauma and mental health: "Mental disabilities can be triggered by a traumatic event—witnessing a violent act or experiencing the death of a parent—or by chronic social stressors such as poverty, marginalization, and victimization."[55] She suggests that fetal alcohol spectrum disorder (FASD) and disruptive behaviour disorders are two mental disabilities that all youth justice professionals should be familiar with. FASD is a result of prenatal alcohol exposure. The yet-to-be-born child's brain development is impaired by maternal consumption of alcohol. It is a spectrum disorder, meaning that it manifests itself in a variety of ways. Most commonly across a variety of diagnoses under this umbrella term, individuals with FASD have deficits related to memory, judgment, abstract reasoning, and adaptive functioning.[56] Disruptive behaviour disorders are characterized by lying, aggressive behaviour, difficulty in sustaining attention, early substance use, and an inability to work toward a goal.[57] Examples include attention deficit hyperactivity disorder

(ADHD), oppositional defiant disorder (ODD), and conduct disorder (CD). Estimates suggest that 25 percent of children with disruptive behaviour disorders will come into contact with the law before the age of 12.[58]

TRAUMA AND ADDICTIONS

Dr. Gabor Maté is a medical doctor who has worked for many years in one of the poorest neighbourhoods in Canada: East Hastings, Vancouver, British Columbia. His writings on addiction are informed by his own experience of it, his relationships with others, and his work in the medical profession. I've found his work *In the Realm of Hungry Ghosts: Close Encounters with Addiction* to be particularly helpful in understanding addiction's roots in trauma. Maté defines an **addiction** as follows:

> Addiction is any repeated behaviour, substance-related or not, in which a person feels compelled to persist, regardless of its negative impact on his or her life and the lives of others. Addiction involves: one, compulsive engagement with the behaviour, a preoccupation with it; two, impaired control over the behaviour; three, persistence or relapse, despite evidence of harm; and, four, dissatisfaction, irritability or intense craving when the object—be it a drug, activity or other goal—is not immediately available.[59]

Maté suggests that addictions are a neurobiological disease—the addict is seeking an altered state, away from their current reality.[60] One of his clients described it like a hug: "'The first time I did heroin' she said to me, 'it felt like a soft warm hug.'"[61] Citing studies about Vietnam veterans who had become addicted to heroin, Maté suggests that addiction isn't about the substance. "Drugs, in short, do not make anyone into an addict, any more than food makes a person a compulsive eater. There has to be a pre-existing vulnerability."[62] The pre-existing vulnerability is usually some form of trauma.

Children are most vulnerable to trauma in utero and in early childhood, when their brains are going through significant development.[63] Children need nutrition, physical security, and emotional nurturing.[64] In the words of Maté, brain development is "sabotaged" when trauma happens.[65] Studies consistently show that drug addictions are highly correlated with trauma, especially physical and sexual abuse. Psychoneurobiologist Joyce Fowler says, "Pre-existing trauma exposure is a risk factor for addiction. Early trauma exposure, especially during early infant development has been cited as a primary risk factor for PTSD due to the developmental influences on brain development, particularly limbic system structures. Also ... sexual abuse has been cited as a risk factor for addiction."[66] She says that a medical explanation for addiction is its value for self-medicating the traumatized person: "sedatives, hypnotics, or alcohol are often used in an attempt to interrupt the stress response."[67] Research consistently indicates that most people, in the range of 55 to 99 percent, entering treatment for addictions have a history of interpersonal trauma.[68]

The role of the addiction, given trauma, is to provide short-term relief to provide an altered state in the brain. As researchers Nora LaFond Padykula and Philip Conklin state:

> Vulnerabilities to addiction exist for those with histories of interpersonal trauma. Specific risk factors include compromised abilities to form healthy attachments and a decreased capacity for self-regulation.... For the addicted individual with an attachment system that has also incurred trauma the chemical initially serves as a complex compensatory mechanism. This is done by maintaining an equilibrium, albeit addicted, through self-regulation and self-medication behaviors directed at adaptation.[69]

The internal world of the trauma survivor is in turmoil. An addiction creates calm, a sense that the world is "okay" and that they are "okay." Of course, this feeling is only temporary. And the tragedy of it all is that people don't usually feel good about their addiction the day after using. In this way, the addiction typically fuels feelings of worthlessness, and the cycle continues. In the words of therapist David Marjot:

> A patient of mine said that, for him, alcohol was his lover and heroin his mother. I now offer as an explanation to patients and those I teach that alcohol and heroin get into the brain through the back door, the blood stream, and subvert or take over the cerebral mechanisms of attachment. To alcohol as if to one's lover and to heroin as if to one's mother. These chemical attachments are endowed with all the power, passion and drive of such attachments to a real person. As an adult you can, and in some cases will, cheat, beg, borrow, steal, wound or even kill to maintain these attachments.[70]

TRAUMA AND RELATIONSHIPS—ATTACHMENT

In his photojournalistic work *Transcending: Reflections of Crime Victims*, Howard Zehr interviewed victims of serious crime about how their lives have been affected in the aftermath. Many talk about the impact of trauma on relationships. Lynn Shiner, whose ex-husband murdered her children, Jennifer and David, said that people would avoid her, unsure how to talk to her about her children. Relationships faded.[71] Diane Magnuson, who was sexually assaulted by a stranger, describes the difficulty of relating to men afterward: "I couldn't relate well to men because of the assault. I had been married three months when this happened, and my marriage fell apart. I would put myself down. I became very much of an introvert."[72] Pam and Robert Ayers, whose daughter Amy was murdered, share a similar perspective:

> People who have been around you for a long time all of a sudden aren't comfortable with you. They don't know what to say. They don't know how to act around you. They don't realize that even though they might mention Amy and we might cry, it's still good. Because if they don't mention her, it's like she never existed. People were supporting us, but one day it ended, and I was lost. You're getting all this support, and one day it's over. That's when you start to dig a hole.[73]

A predominant impact of trauma is that survivors feel disconnected from others. They feel alone, like no one understands, or could understand, the pain they're going through.

Relationships are essential to life, especially in the vulnerable years of early childhood development. Human development happens in the context of relationships. Yet trauma impedes this by circumventing a person's ability to trust. This is especially true where a loved one has perpetrated the trauma. Domestic violence and sexual abuse are the most common forms of traumas experienced by young people. More often than not, the perpetrator is a family member: a father, a mother, a brother, a sister, a grandparent, an uncle, or an aunt. This obviously affects the young person's ability to trust and to form healthy relationships. However, distrust of others, and of the world, can also occur where trauma does not originate from someone known to the victim.

Judith Herman writes about these impacts, suggesting that trauma disrupts attachments that connect individuals with others.[74] She claims that "traumatized people feel utterly abandoned, utterly alone, cast out of the human and divine systems of care and protection that sustain life. Thereafter, a sense of alienation, of disconnection, pervades every relationship, from the most intimate familial bonds to the abstract affiliations of community and religion."[75] This disconnection is often exacerbated when trauma survivors are doubted—like in our story of Sean. Often the response to a trauma, or lack thereof, can be equally traumatizing. When a child discloses sexual abuse and is not believed, she further doubts herself. When a child goes to school with bruises on his face, and no one asks why, he believes what happened to him doesn't matter.

In the pre-trauma world, if the person was lucky, they might have felt safe. Now, she no longer feels safe in her own body, nor in the world. This affects her ability to trust others, and to be in meaningful, reciprocal relationships. Of course, this affects behaviour. Violent actions are often explained by disrupted attachments. This discussion of the relational impacts of trauma requires a further understanding of the biological process of attachment as part of a child's relationship with a caregiver, especially in the early years of development. In attachment theory, **attachment** describes the biological process of human relationships, particularly those of a caregiver with a child. Psychologist Colby Pearce defines it as "a term used to describe the dependency relationship a child develops toward his or her primary caregiver."[76] An attachment figure is "someone who provides physical and emotional care, has continuity and consistency in the child's life, and who has an emotional investment in the child's life."[77] Attachment behaviour relates to the emotional bond between the child and the caregiver. Of particular importance for the formation of healthy attachment is for caregivers to respond to the needs of the child when the child is in distress. Attachment theory is premised on the notion that human beings are social by nature. In order to develop well (from a relational perspective), children must be protected from harm, and must learn appropriately how to survive.

Psychoanalyst John Bowlby developed attachment theory. In the 1940s, Bowlby was doing therapy and research in a mental health facility where children had been separated from caregivers. He became interested in understanding how children were affected by the temporary loss of a mother.[78] In the 1950s, the World Health Organization tasked Bowlby with examining the mental health of children who were homeless. His findings were similar. In both cases, what was needed for the well-being of the child was a "warm, intimate, and continuous relationship" with their mother.[79] Out of this work came attachment theory.

Attachment processes are especially important for children two and younger. Bowlby states:

> [Attachment theory] postulates that the child's tie to his mother is a product of the activity of a number of behavioural systems that have proximity to mother as a predictable outcome.... Once a child has entered his second year, however, and is mobile, fairly typical attachment behaviour is almost always seen. By that age in most children the integrate of behavioural systems concerned is readily activated, especially by a mother's departure or by anything frightening, and the stimuli that most effectively terminate the systems of are sound, sight, or touch of mother.[80]

Attachment, although rooted in social interaction between the caregiver and the child, is a biological function, as important as other basic functions.[81] Mikulincer and Shaver suggest that Bowlby was not only interested in how a disruption in this biological system affected the individual, but also societies at large, and future generations.[82] Quoting Bowlby, they say, "Thus it is seen how children who suffer deprivation grow up to become parents deficient in the capacity to care for their children and how adults deficient in this capacity are commonly those who suffered deprivation in childhood."[83] This has been further termed the "intergenerational transmission" of insecurity.[84]

Taking Bowlby's work further, Mary Ainsworth, a developmental psychologist, identified what happens when the biological process of attachment works well, and when it does not. She identified three attachment patterns in children:

1. Secure: relatively comfortable with relationships, with little worry or fear of abandonment.
2. Anxious: a strong desire for people or partners to be close or available, and strong worries or fears of abandonment.
3. Avoidant: uncomfortable with being too close to others. People who are avoidant prefer to remain distant and self-reliant.[85]

In her earlier PhD research, and together with the above patterns, Ainsworth coined the phrase "a secure base" to describe what all children need from caregivers. That is, in the developmental years, every human being needs someone who is sensitive and responsive, especially when she or he is distressed. As Bowlby says of her research: "What emerges from these studies is that the ordinary sensitive mother [and father, or caregiver] is quickly attuned to her infant's natural rhythms and, by attending to the details of his behaviour, discovers what suits and behaves accordingly."[86] With proper attunement, infants can develop well:

the provision by both parents of a secure base from which a child or adolescent can make sorties into the outside world and to which he can return knowing for sure that he will be welcomed when he gets there, nourished physically and emotionally, comforted if distressed, reassured if frightened. In essence this role is one of being available, ready to respond when called upon to encourage and perhaps assist, but to intervene actively only when clearly necessary.[87]

Attachment theory is a theory of human relationships, or the biological impacts of human relationships. As we understand better how attachment processes become disrupted by trauma, we can understand better why young people act out. Those of the avoidant stream are more likely to act out inwardly; however, the anxious category can become violent when they cannot control relationships in a way that alleviates their fears. This theory explains, to a certain degree, what might be going on in the inner world of youth who have come into conflict with the law. In later chapters, when I discuss principles of trauma-informed youth justice, creating a new or renewed secure base for these young people becomes exceedingly important. In the words of Bowlby, "Human infants, we can safely conclude, like infants of other species, are preprogrammed to develop in a socially cooperative way; whether they do so or not turns in high degree on how they are treated."[88] With trauma being a core characteristic of the experience of young offenders, it's imperative to understand that how they're choosing to relate to others is dramatically shaped by how others have related to them.

TRAUMA AND IDENTITY

In the previous sections, I have described the impacts of trauma on the brain and behaviour of the individual. The section on attachment then highlighted how those who have experienced trauma often have a difficult time in relationships (friendships, intimate relationships, etc.). Now we will go on to explore how, at its core, trauma not only affects functioning, but also impacts the very identity of the survivor.

People who have been traumatized will typically characterize life in two parts: pre-trauma and post-trauma. Survivors often wonder what their life would have been like had the trauma never happened. They ask: "Why did this happen? Why me? Why did that person do this? Why would a higher power allow this to happen?" Fundamentally, these kinds of questions come from feelings of hopelessness and helplessness. The meaning system—the worldview—of the trauma survivor is called into question. And, often, they can no longer make sense of the world or of their own life.

This puts a person at risk of shame and self-doubt.[89] Shame is a feeling, if not a belief, about oneself: the idea that one is unworthy of love or belonging. Shame makes a person feel that they are fundamentally flawed. When someone experiences violence at the hands of another, especially a loved one or a caregiver, they will often blame themselves. This creates confusion. "It must have been my fault," the survivor says, "because someone who loves and cares for me would never have done this." Furthermore, as Herman suggests: "To imagine that one could have done better may be more tolerable than to face the utter reality of helplessness."[90] The traumatized person becomes plagued by doubt. Human beings need to feel like they have some measure of control or autonomy over their lives. Yet, trauma is a profoundly out-of-control experience. Trauma survivors doubt themselves and other people.[91]

Impacts on identity are particularly profound in situations of ongoing child abuse. In this case, the child might only know the world as unsafe. Bloom explains: "Children who are traumatized do not have developed coping skills, a developed sense of self, or a developed sense of their self in relation to others.... As a consequence, all of the responses to trauma are amplified because they interfere with the normal process of development."[92] Survivors of trauma wonder who they are and how they fit into the world. One particularly profound change in identity post-trauma is a sense of disillusionment. In a study of war veterans with PTSD, researchers C. R. Brewin, R. Garnett, and B. Andrews found that most viewed the world as an evil place: "I have never seen so much hate in a bunch of people in all my life.... [Veterans] expressed an incredulity at [the] human capacity for nastiness."[93] This view of the world created cynicism and suspicion in the veterans.[94] It's hard not to see the world as an evil place when someone experiences the worst side of humanity.

Identity, then, is often formed in isolation. A feeling of loneliness can settle in because traumatized people feel like others cannot understand their pain, how badly people can treat each other, and so on. Compounded with the loss that trauma creates, recovery (forging a new identity) is an enormous, but not impossible, task. Joanne Vogt, another survivor of serious crime, interviewed by Howard Zehr, puts it like this: "You've just completed this beautiful puzzle. All of a sudden, someone comes along and just swishes it off the table and you have to start putting it back together. Then there's a piece missing that you just can't find anywhere. Your picture is completed, but there's a piece missing and you have to deal with that."[95]

CONCLUSION

As we have seen, trauma is nothing short of a devastating experience. It affects all areas of a person's life—how they feel physically, how they feel emotionally, how they behave, and how they see themselves and the world. A traumatized person's brain can be damaged. The physiological impacts of trauma affect how the brain functions. A person can become hypervigilant, simultaneously being re-exposed to trauma through triggers while doing their utmost to avoid being reminded of—or reliving—it. Long-term impacts include mental health challenges; the most common being PTSD, depression and other forms of anxiety disorders. Ultimately, trauma affects behaviour (how people relate to each other) and identity (how people see themselves and the world). It can be overwhelming reading about the sum total of the effects of trauma. I know that, at times, I become discouraged, if not cynical and disillusioned, about the pain that people inflict on each other. There is hope, though.

One of the promising findings of brain and attachment research is that the physiology—the brain wiring—of the traumatized individual is not fixed. This is true whether a person has PTSD or is diagnosed with some form of psychopathy. People can heal. Psychopaths can change and can learn to feel empathy. These findings should be especially motivating for those who work in the realm of youth justice. Our interventions hold power. The question is, will they contribute to further trauma, or will they help with healing? Will they reinforce why a person with psychopathy lacks empathy, or will it give them new reason to feel for others? Before turning to these questions, however, it's important to better understand some of the main sources of trauma for young people in Canada: male violence and colonialism. The next chapters will explore the connections between trauma, identity, and male violence, as well as collective trauma and colonialism.

GLOSSARY OF TERMS

An **addiction** is a repeated behaviour that a person feels compelled to persist in even when it brings harm to self, others, or both.[96]
Attachment is the biological process of how human beings, particularly young children, bond with caregivers.
A **flashback** is when the memory of a traumatic experience comes back as a "flash," putting the person (back) into a state of fear.
Hyperarousal is a physiological state of increased fear—fight or flight—or anxiety that a traumatic event will happen again.
A **trigger** is a sensory reminder of an experience of trauma, typically outside of the survivor's ability to control.

QUESTIONS FOR REFLECTION

1. Why do you think people would rather blame people struggling with addictions as morally deficient rather than acknowledge the correlation between trauma and addictions?
2. Given what you know so far about attachment theory, why are young people who have experienced trauma at greater risk of coming into conflict with the law than those who have not?

RECOMMENDED READING

Herman, Judith. *Trauma and Recovery: The Aftermath of Violence—From Domestic Abuse to Political Terror*. New York: Basic Books, 1997.

Considered to be a classic, one of the most important works in the field of trauma. In it, Judith Lewis Herman, a psychiatrist, articulates the impacts of trauma, as well as how to best support survivors.

Maté, Gabor. *In the Realm of Hungry Ghosts: Close Encounters with Addiction*. Toronto: Alfred A. Knopf Canada, 2008.

In this book, medical doctor Gabor Maté describes his experience working with vulnerable populations and the effects of addictions and traces the cause of addiction to early childhood trauma.

Zehr, Howard. *Transcending: Reflections of Crime Victims*. Intercourse: Good Books, 2001.

In this photojournalistic book, the grandfather of restorative justice, Howard Zehr, shares the stories of victims of serious crime alongside their portraits.

6 | Collective Trauma, Colonialism, and Patriarchy

When we come to it
We, this people on this wayward, floating body
Created on this earth, of this earth
Have the power to fashion for this earth
A climate where every man and every woman
Can live freely without sanctimonious piety
Without crippling fear

—Maya Angelou[1]

Imagine: A boy grows up in the suburbs of London, Ontario, largely unaware of his Indigenous heritage. Only later in life does he discover that his mom is Munsee, a residential school survivor of the Mount Elgin Industrial Institute, and that she has suffered cultural and physical abuse. His dad, too, is an Onondaga and a survivor of cultural, sexual, and physical abuse at the Mohawk Institute residential school. The Indigenous boy, now a man, wonders if his troubles during his teenage years (conflict with the law because of selling drugs) might have something to do with his parents' distance and his dad's violence while he was growing up. There was a lack of love, affection and, at times, physical care in the boy's childhood home.

This chapter explores the topic of **collective trauma**. Trauma isn't limited to individuals. At times, it can be a group experience. Without opportunities for grieving and healing, the trauma of one generation can impact the next. When unresolved trauma becomes intergenerational, it can not only haunt the children of survivors, but their children too, sometimes carrying forward over many generations. If we fail to look beyond the individual, there's risk that harms will be perpetuated and that the reasons youth come into conflict with the law will never be truly addressed. For this reason, a trauma-informed perspective focuses both on individuals, as well as on group and structural causes of harm.

In earlier chapters, I began to tell the story of youth justice in Canada in tandem with the history of "Indian" residential schools. This system was premised on racism and was founded on settler colonialism—a desire to displace Indigenous peoples from their lands. The cloak of "helping" that residential schools hid beneath has long since been lifted. We know that residential schools, along with other aspects of settler colonialism, have contributed to a collective trauma for Indigenous peoples, which has persisted across generations. Today it manifests itself in many ways—one being the overrepresentation of Indigenous youth in the Canadian youth justice system. Residential schools may be a thing of the past, but Canada continues to treat Indigenous peoples in oppressive ways. Ongoing practices, legislation, the reserve system, reduced educational funding, resource extraction, and land theft continue to allow traumas to fester. Many Indigenous communities in Canada live in conditions that are worse than those of third world countries. The poor treatment, the colonization of Indigenous peoples is *the* primary issue facing youth justice.

Another primary issue affecting youth justice is male violence, which is epidemic in Canada. Rates of sexual abuse, domestic, and interpersonal violence perpetrated by men continue to be high. Patriarchy is alive and well. Having grown up a boy in a man's world, and living now as a man in a man's world, I'll speak about some of my own experiences of victimization, as well as privilege and responsibility.

Before diving deeper into these root causes of youth injustice—colonialism and patriarchy—I'll begin the chapter by defining and explaining historical, collective, and intergenerational traumas. Following this, I'll advance the notion that collective trauma typically has a political aim; that is, one group having power over another. A trauma-informed approach must find ways to resist this type of oppression. Collective impacts of trauma will be described, as well as the limits of a medical model, or the diagnostic framework of PTSD, for encapsulating these impacts. The chapter will conclude with a push for decolonization and the dismantling of patriarchy as a precursor to later chapters on trauma-informed practices and prevention.

COLLECTIVE TRAUMA

The terms *historical*, *collective*, and *intergenerational trauma* can be used interchangeably. Fundamentally, the shift we're discussing here is from individual trauma to trauma that affects an entire group of people. The principle is that unresolved trauma moves from one generation to the next, similar to a cycle of violence theory. I recall at some point hearing in my work, "The future is the past that lies before us." This has stayed with me because it speaks to the reverberations—or generational impacts—of both harm and good. I've often thought that violence ripples, while kindness makes waves. In this section, we'll focus on the ripples.

The work of Maria Yellow Horse Brave Heart, a Lakota person (Indigenous to what is now the United States of America) describes how historical trauma is often an experience of marginalized peoples. Specifically, in her research, she explores the historical traumas like genocide and land dispossessions of her people, and how group trauma is often ignored by a Western individualistic focus. According to her, historical trauma is:

cumulative trauma—collective and compounding emotional and psychic wounding—both over the life span and across generations.... For American Indians, historical unresolved grief involves the profound, unsettled bereavement that results from generations of devastating losses which have been disqualified by prohibiting indigenous ceremonies by larger society's denial of the magnitude of its genocidal policies.[2]

This devastating loss features a constellation of reactions, something Brave Heart calls historical trauma response.[3] Others have also studied this phenomenon. Literary scholar Gabriele Schwab researched children growing up in Germany after World War II. She observed what she calls transgenerational trauma: "the legacies of violence not only haunt the actual victims but also are passed on through the generations ... the damages of violent histories can hibernate in the unconscious, only to be transmitted to the next generation like an undetected disease."[4] The powerful metaphor of haunting is used by many researchers. To describe how collective trauma carries from one generation to the next, researcher S. Amy Desjarlais personifies collective trauma like this, "a Nightmarish figure, come to devour them, claim their mind, sear the flesh, devour their spirit."[5] The following box highlights some examples of the causes of structural, or large-scale, trauma.

Causes of Structural Trauma

- Poverty
- Family Violence
- Colonialism
- Genocide
- War
- Slavery
- Racism
- Patriarchy

A shift in focus from the individual to the group allows for proper diagnosis of the source(s) of harm, and thus for appropriate solutions. A deeper look at the source—or **etiology**—of trauma is needed. If a Band-Aid is put on a cancer, it doesn't get at the root cause. If a leaking pipe is fixed without turning off the water source, the problem will continue to overrun the solution. This type of shortsighted approach is often taken; groups are examined as collections of individuals. The problem is individualized. And, sadly, sometimes individuals are blamed. Without proper attention and care, traumas are often passed from one generation to the next.

Scholars have used the work of Brave Heart to describe how this happens: Eduardo Duran, Judith Firehammer, and John Gonzalez claim that historical trauma "continues to cause confusion and suffering in the present. If the historical soul wounding is not effectively dealt with, each person, as well as her or his descendants, is doomed to experience and perpetuate various forms of psychic and spiritual suffering in the future."[6] Lori Haskell and Melanie Randall, referring to Indigenous peoples in Canada, suggest that colonialism has disrupted and dislocated entire communities, which has in turn affected a transmission across generations of families.[7] Scholars argue that without proper remembering and integration of traumatic experiences, maladaptive social and behavioural patterns will develop.[8] As Schwab explains, the current generation will then display symptoms of traumas that they themselves have not directly experienced, as if that generation is haunted by ghosts.[9] The Aboriginal Healing Foundation in Canada suggests this is why sexual and physical abuse has remained in some Indigenous families for generations. Harms, if they are experienced as "normal," can be passed from one generation to the next.[10]

To summarize, two themes emerge when talking about intergenerational trauma. First, present troubles are rooted in historical harms, transmitted from one generation to the next. Gabriele Schwab's *Haunting Legacies: Violent Histories and Transgenerational Trauma* explains that trauma tends to shift across generations, like a ghost or a haunting.[11] This often has to do with the behaviour of the older, traumatized generation. If unable to cope with their experiences, they might behave in harmful ways toward their children. This can occur in such seemingly benign ways as keeping secrets (denying the past) or in more overt ways that include being abusive toward their children, perhaps in ways that are similar to the ways they were abused themselves. Either way, the trauma of one generation is transmitted to the next. Of course, this isn't always the case. There are many who break from the trauma of their pasts, but they must do the hard work of finding ways to heal.

The second theme that emerges when talking about intergenerational trauma is that it's often caused by structural inequality. For example, Indigenous children and youth in Canada experienced the harm of settler colonialism (structural inequality) through harmful residential schools, while many were also physically and sexually harmed (subjected to individual trauma) during this time. Making connections between systemic issues and individual issues is helpful for getting at root causes.

SETTLER COLONIALISM AS A ROOT CAUSE OF WHY INDIGENOUS YOUTH ARE OVERREPRESENTED IN YOUTH JUSTICE

> "The great aim of our legislation is to do away with the tribal system and assimilate the Indian people in all respects with other inhabitants of the Dominion as speedily as they are fit to change."
> —Canada's first Prime Minister, Sir John A. MacDonald, in 1887[12]

In 2011, Statistics Canada reported that close to 50 percent of female and 25 percent of male young offenders in Canada were Indigenous. This is a significant overrepresentation, as Indigenous youth make up only 7 percent of the general youth population in Canada. Furthermore, Indigenous people, especially women and girls, are more likely to be the victims of crime than others.[13] At the heart of this is collective trauma—the impact of settler colonialism. Criminologists Raymond Corrado, Sarah Kuehn, and Irina Margaritescu claim that the intergenerational impacts of colonialism have filtered down to impact family dynamics:

> The more recent 20th-century policies in Canada included cultural assimilation, the destruction of traditional Aboriginal families resulting from children forcefully being removed from their families and sent to largely Christian residential schools. The consequences from Aboriginal children being routinely victimized in these schools have been causally associated with the loss of identity and self esteem and, in turn, inter-generational poverty, cycles of abuse, family adversity, high suicide rates, and high rates of substance abuse.[14]

Excerpt from *Clearing the Plains: Disease, Politics of Starvation, and the Loss of Aboriginal Life*, by James Daschuk

The annexation of the northwest by the Dominion of Canada in 1870 changed the political, economic, and medical history of the region forever. Although acute contagious disease continued to strike the indigenous population, an epidemic transition took place within a decade of transfer. Widespread vaccination measures diminished the threat of smallpox, but almost immediately a new pathogen emerged to take its place as the primary cause of sickness and death—tuberculosis. Appearing in tandem with a region-wide famine, tuberculosis exploded and cut down the indigenous population. An epidemic unlike anything the region had ever seen, it swept through the entire newly imposed reserve system. In contrast to smallpox and other infections that had swept through the region like wildfire, to a significant degree the TB outbreak was defined by human rather than simply biological parameters. The most significant factor under human control was the failure of the Canadian government to meet its treaty obligations and its decision to use food as a means to control the Indian population to meet its development agenda rather than as a response to a humanitarian crisis.[15]

A central premise of this book is that youth justice interventions cannot be divorced from a historical, contextual analysis. The purpose isn't to immobilize the (white, settler) reader with guilt, but to help settler Canadians take responsibility for wrongdoing. Many Canadians don't have an accurate understanding of the history of Indigenous peoples or of the negative consequences of colonialism. I, for one, didn't learn this history in elementary or high school. It wasn't until I was invited to participate in the healing circles described in chapter 1 that my eyes—and mind— began to be opened to a different version of history. The Canadian justice system also needs to remove its blindfold. From police, to courts, to corrections, cultural sensitivity isn't enough. A trauma-informed approach means treaties and Indigenous self-governance must be honoured. To do so requires a broader framework, including an expansive definition of trauma.

Starting from individual trauma, and from our reliance on a medical PTSD-type model to diagnose trauma, is also insufficient. Researchers studying collective trauma have been quick to point out the limits of a medical model—or a diagnostic framework like PTSD—to explain community or group trauma. As researcher Derek Summerfield says in *Beyond Trauma: Cultural and Societal Dynamics*: "Medical models are limited because they do not embody a socialized view of mental health. Exposure to a massive trauma, and its aftermath, is not generally a private experience."[16] Using the example of Vietnam veterans returning from war, Summerfield describes how their trauma of war was compounded by the way the United States disowned its guilt over the war, and displaced it instead on individual service men and women. Summerfield uses this example to show how there are aspects of trauma that are culturally and socially constructed: "Victims react to extreme trauma in accordance with what it means to them. Generating these meanings is an activity that is socially, culturally, and often politically framed. Enduring, evolving over time, meanings are what count rather than diagnoses."[17] This is true across many groups of people: Syrian refugees, Somalis impacted by war, and Indigenous people in Canada.

When we examine the traumas caused by residential schools, and then begin to examine the climate of blame directed toward Indigenous peoples in Canada via settler colonial laws, policies, and practices, it's no wonder that trauma is carrying from one generation to the next. Chronic trauma is the result. Researcher David Becker, writing in the same volume as Summerfield, argues that trauma is sequential. First comes the traumatic event, but second, Becker suggests, "Chronic trauma can develop whenever the content of the traumatic situation is persecution and political repression."[18] Making an argument against the diagnosis of PTSD, or at least describing its limitations, Becker makes four points. First, when clinical language disempowers victims it can be problematic. Becker says that collective trauma victims are often called disordered—or dehumanized—by perpetrators, and clinicians often reinforce this by also applying the "disordered" label. Second, it's inappropriate to say someone is disordered when she or he has been traumatized. Likely speaking tongue in cheek, Becker suggests it might be better to say that the person who doesn't become traumatized by a certain event is actually disordered. Third, calling someone disordered, as PTSD does, can get in the way of people accessing help: "It makes an enormous difference that we regard them less as individually disturbed and more as persons suffering the consequences of a disturbed society."[19] Finally, the diagnostic criteria of PTSD fails to adequately describe the impact of collective trauma on survivors.[20]

PTSD, then, tends toward individualizing the problem, rather than diagnosing the structural inequalities at the root of collective trauma. Imagine the young Indigenous boy from the vignette at the outset of the chapter being diagnosed with PTSD, without any consideration for the larger context: his parents' residential school experience or other Canadian colonial impositions. While possibly helpful for treating some symptoms, the diagnosis would fail to get at the most significant root causes of his pain. How is his mental health to improve without changing the harmful conditions that traumatize?

In *The Trauma-Informed Toolkit* researchers identify the multiple layers of impact of collective trauma, starting from individual effects, spreading outward to families, and even into communities. Individually, people might experience feelings of isolation, shame, anger, self-hatred, internalized racism, and distrust of authority. Externally, they might act out through destructive behaviours, like substance abuse, gambling, and alcoholism. Within families, there has been a loss of traditions, identities, and stories. Many Indigenous families have experienced violence, where parents lacked proper role-modelling for how to raise children. At the community level, there's a loss of connection with languages, traditions, land, and resources. There are also increased rates of poverty and suicide.[21] Looking at the impacts of collective trauma in this manner helps us identify the ripple effect that moves in both directions from individual to community, and from community to individual.

Studying the topic of social support and Indigenous communities, geographer and First Nations researcher Chantelle Richmond identifies how settler colonialism has disrupted normal pathways of health. She argues that the dispossession of land has created significant inequalities:

> The after-effects of [colonialism] contribute to the health and social inequalities we witness across Indigenous populations today, including lowered life expectancies, elevated infant mortality, persistence of infectious disease, and increased rates of noncommunicable diseases, accidents, violence and suicide ... the kinds of health problems most closely associated with poverty.[22]

Life expectancy is six years less for Indigenous peoples than for non-Indigenous people in Canada, while infant mortality is two times higher.[23] In a more recent work, Richmond suggests that limited access to traditional lands has caused an imbalance in Indigenous ways of life.[24]

Ultimately, collective trauma affects both individual and group identity. In *From Violence to Blessing: How an Understanding of Deep-Rooted Conflict Can Open Paths to Reconciliation*, Canadian scholar Vern Neufeld Redekop creates a framework for understanding human identity. Although he focuses on the self, or the individual, his work can be mapped onto social identity. Redekop suggests there are five fundamentals of human identity:

1. Meaning
2. Connectedness
3. Security
4. Recognition
5. Action[25]

With a sense of meaning, or purpose, a person knows their place in the world. Meaning is a form of recognition, or recognizance, as Redekop calls it.[26] Relationships are essential to identity; when people belong they feel connectedness and self-respect.[27] Security leads to self-confidence, through physical, emotional, intellectual, and spiritual safety.[28] Healthy identity includes recognition, what Redekop describes as self-worth and actualization, which in turn promotes action, agency, and self-esteem.[29] Redekop suggests that violence interrupts, or undermines, these basic identity needs. Without meaning, there is anger; without connectedness, sadness; without security, fear; without recognition, shame; and without action, depression.[30] He makes a strong argument that when trauma occurs, people need each other and community: "satisfiers to human needs tend to be derived from community and connectedness."[31] This puts an exclamation point on the need to create a functional social identity.

One important aspect of identity that this framework misses for Indigenous peoples is that of place. In *Red Skin White Masks: Rejecting the Colonial Politics of Recognition*, scholar Glen Sean Coulthard explains from his perspective as an Indigenous person (Yellowknives Dene) that place, or land, is central to the identity of his community. He explains that while land is a resource it is also, "constitutive of who we are as a people,"[32] meaning his people have a mutually beneficial relationship with the land—not one of superiority or ownership. Coulthard explains how colonialism has been profoundly disorienting to Indigenous identities. Of course, displacement from traditional lands is a part of this disorientation. Capitalism as an economic system has also had devastating effects, changing the very nature of Indigenous relationships with the land.[33] These systems of domination (white/settler over Indigenous, rich above poor, people taking resources from land for a profit) are radically different from the traditional ways of the Yellowknives Dene.

The best term to describe the impact of settler colonialism on Indigenous peoples is **cultural genocide**. The United Nations Convention on the Prevention and Punishment of the Crime of Genocide defines genocide as any act "committed with intent to destroy in whole or in part, a national, ethnic, racial or religious group." This includes such acts as: "Deliberately inflicting on the group conditions of life calculated to bring about its physical destruction in whole or in part;... Forcibly transferring children of the group to another group."[34] The cultural genocide of Indigenous peoples ripped apart the social fabric of their communities. Normal systems of care have been devastated. The ongoing government policies of assimilation and paternalism continue to negatively impact the well-being of Indigenous peoples.[35]

Part of the work of trauma-informed youth justice is decolonizing, taking apart the system of colonialism in Canada. In this book generally, and in this chapter more specifically, I have simply begun to acknowledge some of the devastation of colonialism. In later chapters, I will discuss some practical ways of decolonizing.

PATRIARCHY AS A ROOT CAUSE OF YOUNG OFFENDING

> All the world's a stage,
> And all the men and women merely players:
> They have their exits and their entrances;
> And one man in his time plays many parts
> —from Shakespeare's *As You Like It*, 1600

"All the world's a stage," wrote William Shakespeare. Men and women are merely players on it. What character(s) am I playing? Who am I? What character(s) do you portray? Who are you? What scripts are we following? These are questions of identity. Certainly trauma interferes with how we see ourselves and the world. A significant component of identity related to trauma and violence is gender. Gender is a performance, wrote gender theorist Judith Butler. All of us perform certain parts of our identity, including gender, to varying degrees. Sometimes we put on a face—quiet with one group, outgoing with another. Or we may put on a mask at work to hide our true feelings when a supervisor does something we dislike or a colleague gripes incessantly. The metaphor of being a performer on a stage is particularly apt when it comes to discussing gender, however, especially in Western society, where masculinity is being performed with traumatic consequences. A 2010 survey in the United States found that one in five women and nearly one in seven men experienced some form of intimate partner violence between the ages 11 and 17, including rape, physical abuse, stalking, and other forms of violence.[36]

Even though, in the words of Shakespeare, a man plays many parts, all appearances indicate that there's a dominant script that many men are following and that this script is strongly linked to patriarchy and violence. The script of masculinity has negative impacts on all women. It has negative impacts on many children, and on many men, too. In fact, relating this topic to youth justice, the most common form of trauma experienced by young offenders is violence in their family home, usually (although not always) perpetrated by a man. Male violence is an essential topic when we consider the etiology of trauma. In fact, along with settler colonialism, a trauma-informed approach to youth justice must also get at the root causes of male violence in order to cause positive change.

WHAT IS A MAN?
By Judah Oudshoorn

He awakes to the sound of breaking glass.
His mother cries his father only laughs.
"Go back to bed, young boy"

He is hurt on the pitch intercepting a pass.
He can't stifle his tears, teammates laugh.
"Don't be a bitch, fat boy"

He has used his fists at last.
Victim bleeds, he trembles a bit, the crowd jeers like loud laughs.
"Way to man-up, tough guy"

He looks to a chaplain for mass.
Only person in the prison who will not laugh.
"Take time to just be, boy"

He awakes to a concrete overpass.
His cries empty to the sound of rich laughs.
"Pull up your socks, lazy boy"

He buries his head deep in the past.
He is frozen and cold, alone with the laughs.
"What the fuck is a man?"

Patriarchy, as defined by criminologist Rick Linden in *Criminology: A Canadian Perspective* is "a system of male domination that includes both a structure and an ideology that privileges men over women."[37] Oftentimes, the assumption is that patriarchy is a thing of the past, or that it simply describes the way a family can be structured—a 1950s family, for example, where the man works and the woman stays at home with the children. Unfortunately, patriarchy is neither limited to the past nor about family structures. It is very much present in the political, economical, legal, educational, social, familial, and other structures of society.

Of course, some changes have occurred over time. For example, in 1918, (white) women were finally able to vote in Canada, and in 1983, the law of consortium was finally struck down in Canada.[38] Consortium was the husband's legally enshrined right "with respect to the 'consummation of marriage, cohabitation, maintenance of conjugal rights, sexual fidelity, and general obedience and respect for his wishes.'"[39] However, despite these reforms, there's still significant lag in overall change. Two examples include violence against women and income inequality. Rates of violence against women (perpetrated by men) continue to be high in Canada, especially incidents involving young men being violent toward their partners. A 2013 Statistics Canada report titled *Measuring Violence Against Women* found:

> As with most crimes, males were most often identified as the perpetrator of violence against girls (79%). However, not all male perpetrators of violence against girls were adult men, as one-third (30%) of male accused were under the age of 18 years. Overall, male accused represented 85% of stranger-perpetrated violence, 80% of family violence, and 77% of offences committed by acquaintances or friends.[40]

As well, income inequality still exists between women and men. The Conference Board of Canada says that women continue to make 19 percent less than men in similar jobs.[41]

Patriarchy affects everyone's lives to varying degrees; however, it affects young offenders especially. As cited in chapter 4, research by Erin M. Espinosa, Jon R. Sorensen, and Molly A. Lopez (among many others), titled "Youth Pathways to Placement: The Influence of Gender, Mental Health Need and Trauma on Confinement in the Juvenile Justice System," published in the *Journal of Youth Adolescence*, found that most male and female young offenders are likely to have experienced or witnessed domestic violence.[42]

A Brief Autobiographical Sketch by Judah Oudshoorn

In the following section, I include some of my own life story. Why would I provide an autobiographical section in a textbook? Doesn't sharing my story get in the way of looking objectively at this subject matter? I come from an academic perspective that says there's no such thing as pure objectivity. In reality, in my research, no matter how distanced I am from my subject matter, my actions are influenced by my life experiences, ideas, and values. The questions I ask during a research project are influenced by my understandings of the subject matter. My understandings are influenced in a variety of ways—as much by what I've read as by what I've lived. My analysis, too, will be interpreted through a similar lens of my worldview and experiences. As such, I believe that including some of my own story is an attempt to be more authentic with you. It bridges some of the (false) divide between what I'm theoretically proposing—a trauma-informed lens for approaching youth justice—and my own practical experiences of why this approach might be helpful. In research language, this is called **positionality**. Who am I in relation to my subject matter? My gender, sexual orientation, race, and other social constructs influence how I do research. As a researcher and writer, I come at these topics having had many advantages over others. I cannot divorce the privileges of being male, white, and heterosexual, for example, from my analysis, but I can think critically about what they mean, including how to draw more attention to those who are typically marginalized.

I also choose to share some of my story because I want to offer it to others. Maybe there's something in it that will resonate. Maybe it will give hope or create new questions to help people think critically about their world. I've experienced some trauma, but I won't go into the gory details. Instead, I'll focus on the theme of male violence as it has played out in my life.

I grew up in male violence, under the thumb of familial patriarchy. It stunted my emotional growth and well-being. Nonetheless, as is common in many homes where violence surfaces, there was also love and affection. It wasn't "bad" all of the time. There were parts of my childhood that were nurturing, but the overwhelming nature of other aspects left me largely destabilized. I was timid, compliant, and at times withdrawn. I knew that it was best to obey and not stand out. I'd been scared and hurt—physically and emotionally—enough times that I became rigidly obedient. I also became stoic, dissociating from most feelings. Every once in a while I'd have an outburst, but these were few and far between. In short, I was a good kid.

Sporadic violence made me scared and anxious. From time to time I was beaten. One time my head was smashed off my bunk bed so hard I had a headache for a week. My Opa made that bed by hand. I remember when he hammered it together in my basement. I love the smell of sawdust, but its scent also reminds me of violence. Often, I worried about my brothers and my mom. A stifling air—the dark storm cloud of the dominant parent—didn't make for a hospitable environment for my happy-go-lucky personality. I distracted myself with sports, and later with alcohol. I had a hard time standing up for myself. Rigidity stunted my creativity, as well as my ability to relate to others and to trust.

When people talk about family violence, I know it. I've lived it. When people talk about patriarchy, I can intimately recognize its tentacles in the life of a family. When people talk about depression as a result of traumatic childhood experiences, I can identify. My depression drove me to try to want to be alone, on my bike, in the woods, reading a book. As I got older I worked a lot, first cutting lawns, and then in the fast food industry. I took as many late-night shifts as I could. When I finally got home, I would lie in my bed and stare out the dark window, listening to music to fall asleep.

In 1994 (when I was 17) Pink Floyd released their Division Bell album. I played and replayed "Coming Back to Life" in my room on my Walkman. The words, "Where were you when I was burned and broken.... Where were you when I was hurt and I was helpless," echoed what I felt toward my parents at the time. The music took me outside of my home: "I took a heavenly ride through our silence. I knew the moment had arrived. For killing the past and coming back to life." I knew there was something I wanted to be liberated from. However, it wasn't until my early thirties that I really confronted some of the pains of the past.

Becoming a parent forced me into a position where I needed to ask for help if I didn't want to risk repeating the past. I remember clearly one night, one of my beautiful, toddler children had a temper tantrum. This is quite normal for that age; however, I didn't experience it as normal. It triggered anger in me ... actually, more like terror. I had to escape. I ran out of my house into the street, hurling punches at my own face. I felt a strong urge to hurl myself into traffic. I knew I needed to get help, and so I asked for it.

I went to a therapist and talked. This helped a bit, but it wasn't enough. I went to my doctor and talked. He diagnosed me with depression. Ever since, I've taken medication to help with it.

Since navigating my own pains I've been incredibly motivated to help others. I see this book project as part of that motivation to help. I'm interested in working toward ending male violence and in helping others to see how a toxic version of masculinity is harmful to all.

I know others aren't so lucky. In spite of the violence I experienced, I had other things going for me in my childhood. I'm male, I'm white, the family I was born into was never hungry, and I was taught how to do well in school. As much as I give myself credit for surviving, I recognize that other aspects of my privilege helped. For example, I was never doubted by those who helped me. I had money to pay for therapy and a job with benefits for medications. I had social support: brothers who cared for me when I was young, and a partner, now, who is unwavering in her support and love. So I focus on gratitude, on acceptance, and on acting maturely—with kindness and respect—toward other people. And I also focus on giving back.

Sometimes I want to minimize the darker aspects of my childhood, and to say it wasn't that bad, or at least not as bad as what some people experience. In some ways the latter is true, although it isn't overly helpful to compare traumas. If I'm honest, though, I really didn't feel safe as a child. Confronting it in this way, for me, has been helpful. It has allowed me to better understand who I am, as well as to engage in the struggle of shaking off the darker parts of my past by getting help.

I no longer feel held down.

The Purpose of Identifying Men (Masculinity) as a Problem

All men receive privilege from patriarchy—and all women are affected by patriarchy and sexual assault. Oftentimes, in response to comments about the problem of male violence, men will say, "Not all men are like this." But this distracts from the responsibility that *all* men need to take to disrupt patriarchy, and from the work they need to do to help construct new, healthier versions of masculinity. This isn't about bashing men or saying that "men are bad." In fact, the philosophy of this book is that even those who perpetrate horrific violence aren't "bad." Rather, they are people who have done something horrific—often because the circumstances in their lives and the trauma they have experienced have led them down a certain path. The distinction is important. The same applies to this section on male violence. It isn't intended to convey that men are inherently bad, but rather to indicate that the way some men have been taught to perform their gender is negatively impacting others. And, if other men remain silent, and refuse to help address a culture of violent masculinity, they are complicit. Some might argue that highlighting the issue of violence in gendered terms limits the discussion, pitting men against women, and women against men. My discussion here is not meant to create a divide between genders, between women and men. Ultimately, people are people, whether they identify as "man" or "woman" or some other construction of gender. My hope would be that someday we simply talk about the problem—violence—and focus less on the gendered component. But, we aren't there yet. Talking about violence as a gendered phenomenon is one of the first steps toward ending it. This is not to say that men and boys cannot (and have not) been victims of female violence. However, when it comes to intimate partner violence and sexual abuse, perpetrators are predominantly male. Some questions must be asked, including "why?"

My purpose in shifting our focus onto male violence and talking about violence as gendered is twofold; first, to draw attention to the inequalities that still persist between women and men, and second, to identify male violence as a root cause of youth trauma, and thus young offending. Once young offenders—and their histories of trauma—are better understood, more helpful justice practices that also get at root causes can be implemented. This *is* about helping all men to take responsibility for changing the definition of masculinity. In the words of anti-violence educator Jackson Katz:

> I believe that men who are silent in the face of other men's violence—whether the silence is intentional or not—are complicit in the perpetuation of that violence. We're not guilty because we're men. We're responsible—because we're men—either for speaking out or for not speaking out about other men's violence.[43]

The perpetrators of violence in North America are overwhelmingly male:

- 83 percent of violence committed against women in Canada is perpetrated by men.[44]
- 98 percent of intimate partner violence is perpetrated by men (Canada).[45]

- 75 percent of people who killed a boyfriend or girlfriend were male.[46]
- 96 percent of family violence convictions in Federal Court were male (USA).[47]
- 93 percent of family violence offenders in State Prison, in 1997, were male.[48]
- The primary risk factor for perpetrating intimate partner violence is being male.[49]
- The National Intimate Partner and Sexual Survivor Survey conducted by the Centers for Disease Control and Prevention found that across all types of violence—sexual assault, stalking, intimate partner violence, and so on—victims identified the perpetrator as male.[50]
- Female rape victims report that the majority—98.1 percent—of perpetrators are male.[51]
- Female stalking victims reported over 80 percent of perpetrators as male.[52]
- Male rape victims reported predominantly male perpetrators.[53]

Statistics paint a troubling picture about violence and about its perpetrators—men. An article in *MacLean's* magazine in 2000 written by Chris Wood tackled this issue. At the outset, he stated, "If there is a gene for murder, it is a safe bet it will be found first in someone who carries XY chromosomes. That is, a man. There may be no such gene. Many experts insist violence is learned, not inherited. But as a spate of domestic tragedies and a powerful new study by Statistics Canada both establish beyond doubt, when murder happens in the home, it is men who do most of the killing. And women and children who do most of the dying."[54] Although overall official (reported) rates of family violence have declined over the past few decades, its gendered component must be illuminated. Why are men much more likely than women to perpetrate violence? To answer this question, I'll follow two lines of thought; one that looks at the question from a sociological perspective, the other from a trauma-informed approach. Both of these lines of thought reject biological explanations of male violence—the idea that men are inherently predisposed to act violently toward others.

Male Violence: Hegemonic Masculinity Gives Men Permission

From the perspective of social learning theory (sociology), people learn to act based on what they're taught by their social environment. Those who "teach" can include family of origin, peer groups, the education system, the workplace, religion and other social institutions. The leading theorist in this area, Albert Bandura, argues that there are three primary sources of learning: family, subculture, and symbolic sources. Families that model aggression often produce children who are aggressive. Communities where peers or other social models demonstrate that aggression is valued tend to create members who live by this code. And, finally, media can play a role in providing examples of aggressive behaviour for children to copy. Social learning theory is premised on the notion of modelling, that individuals will learn from the experience of observing others.[55] What do boys growing up learn about what it means to be a man? There's a dominant, or hegemonic, form of masculinity that persists, providing a script that boys can violently act out in order to be a "real man." In essence, this script gives boys and men permission to be violent.

Even though it is contested by some, I tend to support a hegemonic understanding of masculinity, as it relates to male violence. Sociologist Raewyn Connell first put forward this idea.[56] Drawing on the Marxist work of theorist Antonio Gramsci, hegemony represents the notion that there are dominant, overarching social constructs that infiltrate all areas of society. Or, as critical legal scholar Douglas Litowitz describes it, there are singular, large-scale phenomena that permeate individual life.[57] Bringing the concepts of hegemony and masculinity together, Connell explains:

> Hegemonic masculinity was understood as the pattern of practice (i.e., things done, not just a set of role expectations or an identity) that allowed men's dominance over women to continue. Hegemonic masculinity was distinguished from other masculinities, especially subordinated masculinities. Hegemonic masculinity was not assumed to be normal in the statistical sense; only a minority of men might enact it. But it was certainly normative. It embodied the currently most honored way of being a man, it required all other men to position themselves in relation to it, and it ideologically legitimated the global subordination of women to men.[58]

Put more clearly, **hegemonic masculinity** represents a dominant version, or way, of being a "man."

Male violence isn't understood as arising from hegemony, but in pursuit of it. What does this mean? I used to facilitate a pscyho-educational anger management group for male probation clients. Many of the men were able to identify versions of masculinity that supported violence—tough-guy image, powerful, in control, dominant, commanding subordination—and how they pursued these versions of masculinity, often to their detriment and to the detriment of those around them. Thus, when asked what a "real man" is, most men (as well as most women) associate the idea with toughness, control, dominance, stoicism, and physical strength. In educator Jackson Katz's exploration of this image in the documentary *Tough Guise*, he asks young men what they're NOT supposed to be. The responses, or what a "real man" does not include: a pussy, a bitch, a girl.[59] Notice how one of the worst things a male can be is a female. This is indicative of a powerful, negative, hegemonic script.

Of course, some object to the idea of hegemony (singular) preferring instead to speak about hegemonies (plural).[60] According to this perspective, pluralities of masculinities better account for complexity, and ideas of masculinity play out differently among individual men.[61] Not all men follow the hegemonic script of masculinity. Researcher Tony Coles cites examples of men dominating other men or men who resist stereotypical notions of masculinity to explain his objection to a hegemonic version as relevant to the social construct of masculinity.[62] However, having grown up a man in a man's world, I find it hard to ignore, or to minimize, hegemonic masculinity. I've heard the violent locker-room talk about women. And I've experienced the benefits of being a man—whether it relates to my own recovery from trauma, as shared above, or to how easy it has been for me to gain employment. Yes, men also dominate other men, but my gender definitely colludes with my race and class to my advantage. In some ways, this is similar to what Connell describes as the "patriarchal dividend"—or how all men benefit from the subordination of women.[63] Furthermore, having worked with hundreds of men who have used violence toward partners and children, there seems to be a common language they understand about what it means to be a man and how this impedes meaningful—safe and healthy—relationships.

Masculinity as a performance is violent. It's about being the tough guy. This violence is further amplified when one considers hegemonic masculine attitudes about sex. In this case, sex is blurred—or confused—with violence. Over the past few decades there have been a few studies that examined men's attitudes toward sexually assaulting women, and in fact, whether they would perpetrate sexual assault if they knew they wouldn't get caught or be held accountable. A study conducted in 1980 asked a sample of college males this question; 51 percent reported a likelihood to rape.[64] A study in 1987 replicated the methodology and found similar results: 22 percent of men would be likely to rape if they knew they wouldn't be caught; 49 percent would be willing to commit some form of sexual assault.[65] Others, too, have repeated the study but in different contexts. In 1996, researchers Osland et al. completed similar research, but with a sample from a Protestant-church-affiliated liberal arts school: "34% of the 159 participants questioned at this small, Protestant-church-affiliated, Midwestern liberal arts college admitted some proclivity to rape and/or to force sex."[66] Researchers—and others—have wondered how this could be possible. Clearly, there's something wrong with this picture. In 1982, Timothy Beneke wrote a book called *Men on Rape: What They Have to Say about Sexual Violence*. One of his discoveries was that the pursuit of hegemonic masculinity blurs sexuality with violence. He uses a series of metaphors that surfaced in his interviews in order to explain this:

- Sex is a hunt, a conquest: I'm going *to go out and get a piece of ass* tonight.
- Sex is a game: I hope I *score* tonight. I *struck out* with her.
- Sex is war: I tried to get her into bed but *got shot down*. If I can *wear down her resistance*, I'll score. He's always *hitting on* women.
- Sex is being serviced by a woman: She wouldn't *put out for me*.
- Sex is triumph: I really *put it to her!* I really *stuck it to her!*
- Sex is possession: I'd like to *have her* for a night. I bet I could *get her* if I tried….
- Sex is hitting a woman: I'd like to *bang* her.
- A penis is a gun; sperm is ammunition: He *shot his load* into her." (italics in original text)[67]

In some ways these metaphors are just the tip of the iceberg. They don't only describe the way that some men talk, but also how they act. Sexual assault is a common trauma. It's estimated that one in three women, and one in six men, will experience some sort of sexual trauma in their lifetime.[68] College women are particularly vulnerable to sexual assault, with some statistics indicating that one in five is sexually assaulted during her college years.[69]

All of this is indicative of attitudes, beliefs, and behaviours that permeate hegemonic male culture. The attitudes and beliefs give men social permission to choose violence as a viable option. Lundy Bancroft, a counsellor who has worked with men who use violence, writes in *Why Does He Do That?: Inside the Minds of Angry and Controlling*

Men that abuse is a mentality. Bancroft identifies what he calls "realities" of men who use abuse. He says the abusive man feels entitled to physical, sexual, and emotional caretaking and comments on "the abuser's belief that he has a special status and that it provides him with exclusive rights and privileges that do not apply to his partner."[70] He goes further to say that men who use violence often feel justified, externalizing their responsibility on to their partners. "'She knows how to push my buttons.... She pushed me too far.... You expect me to just let her walk all over me'" are some common refrains cited by Bancroft.[71] Entitlement and justification are both available to men through patriarchial social values. If men are superior to women, then caretaking is assumed. If women are responsible for this caretaking, then justifications for male violence will include blaming women. The sum total of these patriarchal values is permission for male violence.

Male Violence: Cycles of Trauma Influence Violent Choices

Permission is only one part of the story of male violence. It is sufficient to account for a percentage of domestic, family, and intimate partner violence—but there's more at play. Certain men are much more prone than others to perpetrate violence toward partners and children. Research indicates that most male perpetrators of domestic violence witnessed similar violent acts committed by their own fathers growing up. Most children who experience family violence do not go on to perpetrate it, but those who do often experienced it growing up. There's evidence of a trauma etiology in domestic violence. Aggression and conduct problems in children and youth are common where a child has been affected by domestic violence.[72] In their work on the topic, researchers Angela J. Narayan, Michelle M. Englund, and Byron Egeland conclude, "Witnessing violence against one's mother in early childhood is ... the greatest risk factor for violence in the next generation."[73]

What happens when a young person experiences violence in the home? The Centre for Children and Families in the Justice System has put together a research report titled *Little Eyes, Little Ears: How Violence Against a Mother Shapes Children as They Grow*. The authors, Alison Cunningham and Linda Baker, cite a number of ways a child can be changed by violence in the home, including abuse destroying a child's view of the world as a safe place, while also possibly causing them to believe that victimization is normal.[74] These findings connect with Bancroft's explanation above, as children might adopt certain attitudes and beliefs that support violence. However, the point I want to make in this section has more to do with the trauma of growing up in a home where parents choose violence—in this particular case the father or father-figure. It's important to add to this discussion how children are shaped by experiences of violence in their homes.[75] The psychological theory of attachment, discussed in the previous chapter, provides a useful reference point for this.

Those operating out of a psychological framework argue that sociology (e.g., social learning theory) is limited in its explanation of intimate partner violence (IPV).[76] Researchers Donald G. Dutton and Katherine White suggest that the best predictor for chronic, repetitive IPV is attachment insecurity in the perpetrator, which, as described earlier, is often present in those who have experienced child abuse.[77] They define attachment insecurity as "any set of psychological factors that have anxiety or fear as a component affect of intimacy. Hence, [it] encompasses all fearful attachment patterns as an 'attachment insecurity spectrum' (e.g., fearful, avoidant, disorganized) and borderline personality disorder (BPD)."[78] Given one thing that's known about IPV (that a woman is most at risk of harm when leaving a relationship), it makes sense that perpetrators, acting out of insecure attachment or BPD, are frantically trying to avoid abandonment. When considering youth or adolescent violence, a similar theory holds true. Violent behaviours, and other criminality, are strongly associated with insecure attachments.[79] For this reason, attachment insecurity is the central condition to watch for in perpetrators of IPV. This highlights the impact of abusive or neglectful parenting on the process of attachment and the corresponding impact on the development of personality. There's good reason to believe that the violent behaviour of young offenders has roots in harms they experienced growing up.

In conclusion, social learning theory provides an account of the permission available to men; that violence is a viable option in relationships. Attachment insecurity describes the mediating factor, why certain men are more likely than others to perpetrate violence. This second explanation of the roots of male violence fits within our trauma-informed story of youth justice. Attachment insecurity typically follows from childhood trauma perpetrated by a caregiver who is failing to perform their role of providing a secure base. Neither explanation is an excuse for men who use violence. These factors should, however, inform justice interventions. In later chapters, when I explore the topic of accountability, I'll use this as evidence that a context of support is the best way to hold offenders accountable for their actions.

COLLECTIVE TRAUMA IS POLITICAL

What starts to emerge in the stories of colonialism and partriarchy is that collective trauma can have, as psychiatrist Judith Lewis Herman indicates, a political aim.[80] This isn't meant in the mainstream sense of the word *political*—as in a type of government or a particular political party—but is about one group controlling, or having power over, another. Both colonialism and patriarchy are examples of this type of domination. To say that structural trauma is political means that there's an agenda behind it, or some advantage to be gained by those who inflict it on others. For settler Canadians, that advantage is land and resources. The quotation from Sir John A. MacDonald found earlier in this chapter identifies this. For some individual men who use violence toward partners and children, the advantage or agenda is to dominate and control. For all men, the advantage is to gain privileges that other genders don't have. In both cases, there is an unwillingness to relate in an equal manner, which ultimately disadvantages the victim group.

As the history of trauma studies is explored, an insidious political agenda emerges. Herman argues that, historically, in trauma studies and interventions, victim voices have been silenced. More specifically, she suggests, given that it's mostly men who perpetrate domestic violence and sexual abuse, and mostly women and girls who have been victims of this male violence, patriarchy has infiltrated our ability to respond effectively to trauma. She uses the history of psychoanalysis, particularly

Sigmund Freud, to explain this. In the late 1890s, Freud had identified early sexual experiences, or what we would call sexual abuse, as the primary reason why his clients suffered hysteria (the name given to psychological trauma at that time).[81] Herman suggests that Freud stumbled upon what he could only describe as an epidemic of "perverted acts against children."[82] However, before long, he backpedalled from this finding, suspecting that no one would believe him.[83] Instead, the focus of Freudian psychoanalysis became conflicting inner desires. Rather than naming what he was seeing—sexual abuse and male violence—as the cause of hysteria in his female patients, he chose to focus on the inner, psychological world of the victim; in essence, shifting blame onto the victims.[84] As such, Herman concluded, "the study of trauma in sexual and domestic life becomes legitimate only in a context that challenges the subordination of women and children."[85]

In their research article titled "The Political is Personal," psychologists Nicole M. Else-Quest and Shelley Grabe discuss how a feminist lens broadens the view of violence against women, from personal harms to political realities.[86] They highlight the relationship between political realities and women's personal lives. More to the point, they discuss how inequities at a structural level, and disadvantages in social systems, affect the well-being of individual women. It is their argument, and that of other social psychologists, that efforts to ensure the well-being of women must also challenge structural inequities.[87] Feminist scholar Judith Butler, talking about disparity between the genders, says, "To counter oppression requires that one understand that lives are supported and maintained differentially, that there are radically different ways in which human physical vulnerability is distributed across the globe. Certain lives will be highly protected."[88] Part of the work of trauma-informed youth justice is dismantling patriarchy. Social activist bell hooks says of race in North America, "Living in a White-Supremacist culture, Black people receive the message daily, through both mass media and our interactions with an unenlightened White world, that to be Black is to be inferior and subordinate."[89] Indigenous communities in Canada have a similar experience. The work of trauma-informed youth justice is also to dismantle colonialism, or decolonize.

CONCLUSION: COLLECTIVE TRAUMA AFFECTS COMMUNITY HEALTH, WELL-BEING, AND CARE

In the previous chapter, I wrote that a person becomes traumatized when their system of coping is overwhelmed. A psychological injury results. In this chapter, we've seen that trauma isn't limited to the individual; it can also be a collective experience. When we start to understand the structural causes of trauma we find that certain incidents or events are more likely to traumatize than others, and many of these incidents or events originate from a certain political agenda—the domination of one group over another. Trauma is an oppressive event, whether experienced by an individual victim or by a group.

Aside from the collective trauma Indigenous people have experienced at the hands of settler Canadians, and the trauma male violence has caused women and children, there are many other examples of communities impacted by collective trauma. The most well-known example is the Holocaust. Collective trauma became a better-known concept when researchers started to study long-term impacts on the children of Holocaust survivors, as well as the children of Nazi perpetrators. Collective trauma is part of the story of war, of refugee life, of poverty, of racism, of environmental degradation, and of so many other social ills of humanity that are relevant yet beyond the scope of this book. Collective trauma has an impact on communities that is nothing short of all-encompassing. According to sociologist Kai Erikson, it "is a blow to the basic tissues of social life that damages the bonds attaching people together and impairs the prevailing sense of community."[90] In the 1970s, Erikson was studying the after-effects of a few communities obliterated by a negligent coal company in West Virginia: a "massive refuse pile dam unleashed 132 million gallons of water and coal waste materials on the unsuspecting residents of Buffalo Creek ... 125 people were killed, and over four thousand survivors were left homeless.[91] Erikson concluded that survivors faced the world in a demoralized state, weighed down by guilt, numbness, feelings of fear, and a loss of moral anchors.[92] The important point was the communal nature of the trauma, which impacted the group's ability to relate well to each other afterward:

> Lonesomeness increases and is reinforced. People have heavy loads of grief to deal with, strong feelings of inadequacy to overcome, blighted lives to restore.... The inability to come to terms with their own isolated selves is counterpointed by an inability to relate to others on an interpersonal, one-to-one basis ... the community seems to have lost its most significant quality—the power it generated in people to care for each other in times of need, to console each other in times of distress, to protect each other in times of danger.[93]

In summary, collective trauma affects community health, well-being, and care. Impacts often described as affecting the individual, like distrust, disorientation, and demoralizing, come to pervade an entire community. But it doesn't have to be this way.

In the opening epigraph, the quotation from poet Maya Angelou states we have the power to fashion a better world, for all peoples, where everyone can live freely. What version of youth justice would choose this type of better world? Unfortunately, as I explain in the next chapter, it isn't the current system. However, there are helpful elements in the current system that can be built on, and new elements that can be made to create a trauma-informed youth justice system that will lead to safer, more livable communities.

GLOSSARY OF TERMS

Collective trauma is harm that traumatizes a group of people, whether a family, a community, or a nation.
Cultural genocide is the attempted elimination of the uniqueness of a people group. In Canada, the process of assimilation of Indigenous peoples is an example.
Etiology is the study of the cause of something.
Hegemonic masculinity refers to one dominant system that controls others. When connecting this with masculinity, it means that there is a particular type of

masculinity that is reinforced through various social institutions, like education, religion, work, family, and so on.

Positionality is the relationship of the researcher to their subject matter.

QUESTIONS FOR REFLECTION

1. How do you understand your own identity? What experiences do you think have most profoundly shaped how you understand yourself? What influence has colonialism and patriarchy had on this?
2. Most Canadians are not taught in school about colonialism, or patriarchy, for that matter. Why do you think we do not learn about these things?
3. Apart from colonialism and patriarchy, what other causes of collective trauma should be of concern to Canadians?

RECOMMENDED READING

Katz, Jackson. *The Macho Paradox: Why Some Men Hurt Women and How All Men Can Help*. Naperville: Sourcebooks, 2006.

Jackson Katz is a leading educator in North America on the topics of male violence and masculinity.

Vancouver Status of Women. *History in Our Faces on Occupied Land: A Race Relations Timeline*. Vancouver: Vancouver Status of Women, Feminist Working Group, 2008.

This book—available online as a PDF—is an excellent resource for understanding the timeline of colonialism in Canada.

7 | Prison, Risk, and Punishment— A Trauma-Inducing Justice System

"The basic problem, I have come to conclude, is neither a lack of awareness nor a lack of alternatives but rather that our culture is captive to a spirit of punishment."

—T. Richard Snyder[1]

The purpose of a criminal justice system is to catch wrongdoers (this is the role of police), determine guilt (this is the role of courts), and apply a punishment (this is the role of corrections). However, making this discussion too simplistic disguises the **normative** nature of law and criminal justice. Normative questions ask, "What's the ideal?" or "How *should* things be?" We would hope that certain acts are defined as crimes because they're collectively agreed to be harmful. Really, though, when applying a critical lens—thinking about race, gender, and class—there's an element of oppression to definitions of crime. Lawmakers are typically white, male, upper-class individuals, while lawbreakers are typically from marginalized communities. The answer to how things should be is not straightforward. Considering the overrepresentation of Indigenous peoples in the youth justice system, and the epidemic rates of male violence in our society, Canada has failed to adequately engage normative questions of law and justice. This chapter shines a spotlight on the problems of current youth justice practices. Incarceration and an overemphasis on risk, two primary mechanisms of punishment, tend to create more traumas, which lead to more crimes. The justice system needs a different litmus test—a new way of measuring—than whether or not someone is caught, found guilty, and punished, for determining if it is accomplishing its purposes.

My argument is that we should define certain actions as criminal in order to make our communities safer, and ultimately more livable. A justice system, then, should serve these purposes:

1. **Safer communities:** Everyone should have the right to live a life as free as possible from harm. For example, at a personal level, this means children

should not have to grow up at risk of sexual abuse or domestic violence, while at a community level, people should not live impoverished or in other ways disadvantaged. Defining actions as criminal means looking at what is harmful—individually and structurally—and finding ways to minimize these conditions.

2. **Livable communities:** Everyone should have full opportunity to live a meaningful life as they see fit. Crime and harm can get in the way of this. Livable communities mean that people should have some measure of choice, or control, over their lives and that everyone belongs in some way. A justice system should be about creating livable communities. One way to achieve this is by starting from a values base. For example, some of the values at the heart of this text (like human dignity and peace) could be used to start a conversation on this front.

With this normative stance about crime and justice, we have the ability to measure—to ask whether the youth justice system in Canada is actually creating safer, livable communities for young people.

Someone might counter, "How can we measure the justice system against something it isn't intended to accomplish? Justice might be about safe communities, but it certainly isn't about livable communities." This is a fair argument. Sections 38 and 83 of the Youth Criminal Justice Act (YCJA) describe the purposes of applying sanctions to young offenders:

> 38. (1) The purpose of sentencing under section 42 (youth sentences) is to hold a young person accountable for an offence through the imposition of just sanctions that have meaningful consequences for the young person and that promote his or her rehabilitation and reintegration into society, thereby contributing to the long-term protection of the public.
>
> (2) (f) (i) to denounce unlawful conduct, and
> (ii) to deter the young person from committing offences.
>
> 83. (1) The purpose of the youth custody and supervision system is to contribute to the protection of society by
> (a) carrying out sentences imposed by courts through the safe, fair and humane custody and supervision of young persons; and
> (b) assisting young persons to be rehabilitated and reintegrated into the community as law-abiding citizens, by providing effective programs to young persons in custody and while under supervision in the community.[2]

According to the YCJA legislation, the primary purpose of law, police, courts, and corrections is the protection of society. This is even easier to measure than my proposed yardstick. Is society being protected from young offenders? The answer is fairly straightforward: the youth criminal justice system typically has a negative effect on young offenders. Society isn't being well protected. This isn't because we aren't being harsh enough. In fact, the opposite is true. Our protection agenda—rehabilitation cloaked in punishment—is counterproductive. Punishment is simply contributing to the cycle of violence that many young people are already caught up in. In the previous chapters, I've identified the two leading causes of trauma among young offenders, one, colonialism, and two, male violence. To this I now add a provocative third cause, the youth justice system.

This chapter will unfold as follows: Current youth justice practices will be described as iatrogenic, when harm (that is preventable) is brought on by the healer. A (perhaps) surprising discovery about the youth justice system is that it's better to do nothing than it is to intervene; that is, once the youth justice system gets involved in a young person's life, they're more likely to come into conflict with the law again than they would have been if nothing had been done. I will explain the iatrogenic nature of youth justice in four ways: first, I'll describe the impacts of incarceration on young people (its hypermasculine and traumatizing nature); second, I'll identify the inherent risks of a risk focus (how risk assessments focus on everything that's wrong with a young person, rather than on what's right, and how this gets in the way of resilience and growth); third, I'll consider the often-ignored victim (where is the place of the victim in youth criminal justice?); and, fourth, I'll consider the problems with punishment. Rehabilitation with punishment means the focus is on punishment. Reintegration with punishment means punishment wins again. A system premised on retribution is incompatible with other purposes of justice.

ARE CURRENT YOUTH JUSTICE PRACTICES TRAUMA-INFORMED?

> Well, I'm goin' to a place where the tough guys go
> And come out even tougher
> A place where a man don't show his feelings
> A place where a man don't cry
>
> Well, they say I'm bein' punished
> And they say I can be reformed
> But some day I'll return
> Did they really think that
> This time it would work.
> —from the song "Prison Bound" by Social Distortion[3]

Sometimes a punk rock song, in this case "Prison Bound" by Social Distortion lyricist Mike Ness, communicates more clearly than a whole set of empirical research—or the author of a textbook on youth justice. This song gets at the heart of the problems with prison justice; the punished person may never know another way of living—or relating to others—if the punishment fosters, or mirrors, the very environment that produced the criminality in the first place. This begs the question, are current youth justice practices helping to interrupt cycles of violence, or are they further aggravating them? The answer is that our current system is doing more harm than good. There are some specific programs, as well as individuals, who work from a more trauma-informed perspective; however as a whole the criminal justice system does a poor job of accounting for trauma. In fact, the criminal justice system is responsible for adding to it.[4] A meta-analysis (a study of a collection of studies) by Gatti et al. found a positive correlation between intervention by the juvenile justice system and the perpetration of adult crime:

> For boys who had been through the juvenile justice system, the odds of adult judicial intervention increased by a factor of 6.98 ... it was found that the more restrictive and more intense the justice system intervention was, the greater its negative impact ... placement in an institution exerts by far the strongest criminogenic effect.[5]

Take a moment to digest the previous sentences. The information is so important that it bears repeating in a different way, as a question. Is it better not to intervene at all than to do what we're currently doing in the area of youth justice? Yes, it is. How can this be? This is, in fact, the iatrogenic effect of the current youth justice system. An iatrogenic effect in the area of youth justice means that the system that's meant to deal with youth crime is causing further—preventable—harm.

The same is true in adult corrections. A number of studies have looked at the iatrogenic nature of prison for adult offenders by focusing on recidivism. Two particularly large studies, one in Italy, the other in the United States, have examined this issue and have found that prisons have a criminogenic effect.[6] When comparing incarcerated offenders with a similar group of offenders on probation, those imprisoned had a much greater chance of reoffending than those based in community corrections.[7] What's more, the harsher the conditions of the prison environment (e.g., overcrowding, violence, lockdowns, overuse of solitary confinement, etc.), the greater the likelihood of reoffending.[8] Tougher prison conditions create increasingly violent conditions between inmates and staff. When asking if tougher is better, researcher David M. Bierie concludes that communities bear the brunt of "tough-on-crime" practices: "Communities may experience increased costs in as much as prison victimization and violence imply offenders become more risky upon release than they otherwise would have been."[9]

In order to explore this issue further, let's consider the area where iatrogenesis is most often discussed: health care. When a system is geared toward improving the health of individuals, it's important to ask whether interventions are, in fact, hurting or having unintended consequences. One focus of health research has been on the risk of infection for those staying in hospitals. Annually in Canada, close to 10 percent of patients who stay in hospital contract a harmful infection.[10] This amounts to about 200,000 people.[11] Of these, about 10,000 die.[12] Obviously, this is a serious issue. These are infections not present in the individuals when they arrive at hospital, but contracted on site. In fact, research by the Canadian Medical Association has determined that Canada has one of the worst track records in the developing world when it comes to this issue.[13] As such, much effort has been put toward preventing the spread of infections in hospitals. For example, a huge priority is put on hand washing practices—making sure that health care professionals are not transmitting antibiotic-resistant bacteria. If health care sites want to improve the health of the sick individuals they serve, focusing on iatrogenic issues is vital.

The efforts put toward preventing iatrogenesis in youth justice should be similar. The problem is that justice isn't focused on healing, but on punishment. **Punishment** is the deliberate infliction of pain. Some people wrongly assume that punishment is a useful vehicle for changing behaviour. Esteemed social psychologist Hans Toch explains that punishment invites undesirable repercussions:

> Among prevailing views about how one goes about producing behaviour change (especially change in other people) a cherished notion has always been that it helps to engender discomfort in the person to be changed.... We assume that pain and discomfort can produce an impetus to self-reviews.... The problem is that this confidence in the long-term effectiveness of punishment as a behaviour modifying strategy happens to run counter to the evidence.... B.F. Skinner, the founding father of behaviour management, deplored the presumption as a dangerous and self-serving delusion. Skinner maintained that using punishment to try to modify behaviour not only does not work but also reliably invites undesirable repercussions.[14]

If justice is about public safety, the fact that punishment doesn't bring about behaviour change should be troubling to us. And it should trouble us even more if we start to consider justice as being about healing and about creating livable communities. From a trauma-informed youth justice perspective, at minimum, we must consider justice to be about improving community safety. Taking it a step further, we must learn to recognize that community safety outcomes improve when victims, offenders, and communities are provided opportunities for healing. A shift from punishment toward healing heeds iatrogenesis.

PRISON: THE WORST OFFENDER

"The degree of civilization in a society can be judged by entering its prisons."
—Fyodor Dostoyevsky

Having worked with offenders for the past decade, teaching in the area of criminal justice and researching for this book, I've come close to positioning myself as a prison abolitionist—at least for children and youth. I do think there's a need to incapacitate some young people, when they're bent on hurting themselves or others, but I'm increasingly convinced that prison does much more harm than good—not only for offenders, but also for victims and for safe, livable communities. The poem below by Judge Dennis A. Challeen sets up my explanation for this.

We want prisoners to be responsible.
So we take away all their responsibilities.

We want them to be a part of our communities.
So we isolate them from our communities.

We want them to be positive and constructive.
So we degrade them and make them useless.

We want them to be trustworthy.
So we put them where there is no trust.

We want them to be non-violent.
So we put them where there is violence all around them.

We want them to be kind and loving people.
So we subject them to hatred and cruelty.

We want them to quit being tough guys.
So we put them where the tough guy is respected...

We want them to take control of their lives, own their own problems and quit being a parasite.
So we make them totally dependent on us.

—Judge Dennis A. Challeen[15]

If trauma is highly correlated with criminal behaviour, then we want to do our best to help people heal from trauma so they won't hurt others. Prison, however, is a traumatic place. Maybe society is okay with this. Some might think that criminals deserve to be punished and to suffer for the wrongs they have done. In this text, I'm not contesting whether it's appropriate to hold young people accountable for their criminal actions. I am, however, arguing against punishment over meaningful consequences. There's a difference, and it's a significant one. We need to understand the impacts of imprisonment on young people—because, ultimately, prisons are making our communities less safe. In 2011, the Annie E. Casey Foundation in the United States of America released a research report titled, *No Place for Kids: The Case for Reducing Juvenile Incarceration*. The foundation is dedicated to improving the lives of young people in the USA. Their report claims that juvenile incarceration is dangerous, ineffective, unnecessary, obsolete, wasteful, and inadequate:

1. Dangerous: The study concludes that correctional institutions are difficult to operate in a humane, safe fashion. This conclusion comes about from decades of research data that suggests that many youth in institutions have been mistreated both by other inmates and by staff, including "epidemics" of physical and sexual abuse, and "rampant overreliance" on solitary confinement and use of restraints.[16] Incarcerating youth makes their mental health worse and increases their likelihood of self-harm.[17] Non-white young people are more likely than white youth to be incarcerated. In Canada, Indigenous youth are dramatically overrepresented. In the United States, it's African-American, Latino, and Native American youth.[18] This overrepresentation of certain groups tends to disenfranchise entire populations of young people.

2. Ineffective: Pulling together numerous studies, the report suggests that the incarceration of young people increases the likelihood of recidivism and leads to poor future employment and educational outcomes.[19] In fact, longitudinal studies show the re-arrest rate for a new crime three years after release to be in the range of 73 to 89 percent.[20] Furthermore, the author of the study, Richard Mendel, says that "a number of well-designed studies indicate that correctional placements exacerbate criminality."[21] The author also cites a Canadian study of young people in Montreal: "involvement in the juvenile justice systems proved by far the strongest predictor of adult criminality of all the many variables examined."[22] Indeed, exposure to the violent environments of correctional facilities puts youth at further risk of aggressive behaviours.[23] The Justice Policy Institute in the United States put together a policy brief called *The Dangers of Detention: The Impact of Incarcerating Youth in Detention and Other Secure Facilities*. They found similar results: that incarceration increases recidivism and slows the natural "aging out of delinquency" that happens with most youth.[24] In one example of a state's track record, 86 percent of children who spend time in Illinois (USA) prisons end up going back.[25]

Excerpt from *The Prisoner*, edited by Ben Crewe and Jamie Bennett

A young offender speaking about becoming institutionalized: "I grew up with my parents until I was ten years old. And then I went through the local authority care systems and through various children's foster homes, foster placements all up and down the country. I started getting into trouble from when I was about 12. One day I decided that it would be funny to set fire to my room while I was in it. From then on I was remanded into a secure children's home. I think it's prepared me to come into YOIs [Young Offender Institutions] as well. I mean, I know it's the wrong word to use, but I probably would call me 'institutionalised.' I've been here that many times. You get so used to one thing and it just becomes the norm, becomes easier to be in here than it does out there … I didn't have the love and support of family and stuff. I suppose I've become numb to feelings and emotions and stuff like that, and I do think I missed out on a lot of years, but obviously, I had to be locked up, for my good and for other people's good. I don't think it's good to be locked up so young … I was very scared. It's intimidating, very intimidating."[26]

3. Unnecessary: In the United States, many of the young people incarcerated actually pose a low risk of harming their communities. In Canada, the Youth Criminal Justice Act was effective in correcting inflated rates of young people in Canadian prisons during the 1980s and 1990s; however, the incarceration of low-risk young offenders is still an issue in Canada. Youth in custody tend to have committed non-violent crimes. Approximately 60 percent of admissions are related to property crimes.[27]

4. Obsolete: Mendel claims that there are a number of alternatives to incarceration that are more effective, and in fact, as he says, "inconsistent" with imprisonment.[28] When it comes to young offenders, prison isn't necessary for community safety. Treatment and counselling tend to reduce recidivism, while coercion and control do not.[29] A number of alternatives are highlighted—some that focus on substance abuse and mental health, others that support the families of young offenders.

5. Wasteful: Prison is expensive. In fact, it's the most expensive youth justice option. In the United States it costs $66,000 to $88,000 to incarcerate a young person for 9 to 12 months.[30] In Canada it's even more expensive: approximately $100,000 per youth per year (in 2007).[31] Alternatives are much cheaper.

6. Inadequate: *No Place for Kids* highlights that, in spite of the high cost of incarceration, prisons provide inadequate support for the needs of youth incarcerated. Mental health services and substance abuse recovery supports are lacking, and educational services catering to specific cultural needs are insufficient.

The *No Place for Kids: The Case for Reducing Juvenile Incarceration* report also offers some discussion about what can be done. It suggests funding alternatives as a start, but also proposes changing laws to prevent the incarceration of youth who commit non-violent crimes.

Why does incarceration lead to worse outcomes for youth? To answer this question, I'll explore two themes: first, prison tends to draw in traumatized young people then add to their trauma; and second, it tends to reinforce a negative version of masculinity—both root causes of crime.

Incarceration Is Traumatic

In his study of prisons, medical doctor Terry Kupers has examined the impacts of incarceration. From his perspective, prisons are traumatic—a recipe for creating madness:

> The recipe for creating madness in our prisons is easy enough to explicate, one merely needs to identify the steps that were taken to reach the current state of affairs. Here is the recipe:
>
> - Begin by over-crowding the prisons with unprecedented numbers of drug-users and petty offenders, and make sentences longer across the board.

- Dismantle many of the rehabilitation and education programs so prisoners are relatively idle.
- Add to the mix a large number of prisoners suffering from serious mental illness.
- Obstruct and restrict visiting, thus cutting prisoners off even more from the outside world.
- Respond to the enlarging violence and psychosis by segregating a growing proportion of prisoners in isolative settings such as supermaximum security units.
- Ignore the many traumas in the pre-incarceration histories of prisoners as well as traumas such as prison rape that take place inside the prisons.
- Discount many cases of mental disorder as "malingering."
- Label out-of-control prisoners "psychopaths."
- Deny the "malingerers" and "psychopaths" mental health treatment and leave them warehoused in cells within supermaximum security units.
- Watch the recidivism rate rise and proclaim the rise a reflection of a new breed of incorrigible criminals and "superpredators."[32]

Kupers is looking at the overall picture of corrections in the United States, while also identifying specific traumatizing components of incarceration. A similar recipe could be written about the Canadian context. Prisons are hostile environments and, as Kupers says, this breeds fear, which in turn births violence.[33] Prisons are characterized by violence and social isolation, two traumatizing factors for young people.[34]

One of the tragedies of incarceration is the use of solitary confinement. In 2011, the United Nations took a stand on this issue, claiming that solitary confinement, because of its impacts, was a form of torture. In a report to the General Assembly, *Torture and Other Cruel, Inhuman or Degrading Treatment or Punishment*, the following was stated: "Solitary confinement ... when used as a punishment during pre-trial detention, indefinitely, prolonged, on juveniles or persons with mental disabilities ... can amount to cruel, inhuman or degrading treatment or punishment."[35] The report goes further to suggest that negative health effects can be seen within a few days of solitary confinement and can get increasingly worse with each additional day.[36] Most individuals confined like this will experience psychotic disturbances and other symptoms like "anxiety, depression, anger, cognitive disturbances, perceptual distortions, paranoia and psychosis and self-harm."[37] Even after release from solitary confinement, research has found that seven days in solitary confinement can have a lasting negative impact on brain functioning.[38] As such, the United Nations recommends that juveniles not be held in solitary confinement.[39]

UN Standard Minimum Rules for the Administration of Juvenile Justice

17.1 (c) Deprivation of personal liberty shall not be imposed unless the juvenile is adjudicated of a serious act involving violence against another person or of persistence in committing other serious offences and unless there is no other appropriate response;

17.1 (d) The well-being of the juvenile shall be the guiding factor in the consideration of her or his case.

17.2 Capital punishment shall not be imposed for any crime committed by juveniles.

Commentary
The main difficulty in formulating guidelines for the adjudication of young persons stems from the fact that there are unresolved conflicts of a philosophical nature, such as the following:

(a) Rehabilitation versus just desert;
(b) Assistance versus repression and punishment;
(c) Reaction according to the singular merits of an individual case versus reaction according to the protection of society in general;
(d) General deterrence versus individual incapacitation.[40]

Of course, there's more to look at than solitary confinement when trying to understand the traumatic impacts of current forms of incarceration. Hans Toch, a social psychologist writing in the area of criminal justice has studied the impact of incarceration for many decades. In one study from the 1980s, as incarceration rates were growing astronomically, he wrote about poor outcomes for inmates, simply because prisons were too crowded and weren't focused on rehabilitation. He suggested that, in youth, this typically leads to disruptive behaviour, while in older generations it usually affects physical and mental health.[41] Although his labelling might be problematic, ultimately, Toch says the sick are getting sicker and the bad "badder," as a result of incarceration.[42]

Much of the literature on trauma and incarceration focuses on the pre-incarceration trauma histories of inmates. As I have written in this book, rates of trauma are disproportionately high among young offenders in comparison to the general population. However, in comparison, very little is written about the fact that prison is itself trauma-inducing. The studies that do exist in this area tend to focus on female inmates. Similar to youth populations, research shows that over 90 percent of incarcerated women have experienced some form of trauma in their lives.[43] Ethnographic research designed to study the phenomenon of women's experiences in prison explains that they have worsened mental health, are under tremendous stress, experience extreme isolation, and receive very little support to help them with these feelings and experiences.[44] A woman who participated in one of these studies said:

> This place is set up for the worst-case scenario, but not for the everyday needs of women. By the grace of God, we are surviving. I didn't get the help

I needed because I wasn't homicidal or suicidal. It is the squeaky wheel that gets the groups in here. I wrote to mental health and waited for six weeks to talk to someone ... I tried to speak with the counselor on my unit and [the counselor] said, "... I have too many files and not enough hours in the day. You have fifteen minutes. What would you like to talk about?" Now how therapeutic is that?[45]

As indicated in the research above, outcomes are similar for young people. Increases in mental health challenges are common, as is self-harm.

As the United Nations indicates, there are some significant tensions—if not contradictions—in how prison justice is carried out. Do people go to prison as punishment, or to be punished? Or asked another way, should people in prisons be punished beyond the loss of their freedom? I remember interviewing an inmate in the bowels of Kingston Penitentiary, Canada's first (although now recently closed) penitentiary. I was on one side of a small, concrete interview room and the inmate was on the other. We were separated by glass. I seem to recall green, or maybe some kind of aquamarine blue on the walls, although it was probably grey. We talked for about 45 minutes. The purpose of my visit was for me to understand how much responsibility this man took for his crimes. He tried to speak, but we were constantly interrupted by blood-curdling screams. The screams reminded me of something else. Once I saw a teenage boy crash his bike while taking a corner too fast. He was wearing no helmet and landed on his face. When I ran over to him, I saw that his upper lip was ripped bare. His gums were all lacerated. He was screaming—those same blood-curdling screams. Blood-curdling screams in a prison meant that someone's psyche was being lacerated.

And that wasn't all. There were thuds: the thud of a human body launching itself against a concrete wall. Each time there was a thud, the man I was meeting with would close his eyes, bow his head, and hold up a hand with one pointer finger in the air. "Just a moment," he would say, "it'll pass." But it didn't. More screams. More thuds. We were down the hall and around the corner from solitary lock up. Some person—someone's son, perhaps someone's brother, or someone's dad—was writhing in animalistic pain—an incarcerated human being.

I didn't get much information from that meeting. I had to come back later because the man I was meeting with couldn't concentrate. Each scream was like a stone through glass, shattering the opportunity for accountability. The man was prepared to tell me how he thought his own crimes had affected the lives of others, but it wasn't to be.

In his work *Corrections and Post-traumatic Stress Symptoms*, Daniel S. Murphy suggests that prison is a traumatizing environment. For inmates, "incarceration is socially and psychologically debilitating. Negative aspects of the prison experience may result in psychological damage."[46] Something similar holds true for those who work in correctional environments, especially correctional officers (guards). Prison conditions like violence and overcrowding have also been found to affect the psychological well-being of staff. Bierie, cited above, claims that as conditions worsen, staff are more likely to smoke, drink, have headaches, stomachaches, back pain, and psychological problems.[47] Examining the experiences of correctional officers in British Columbia, criminologist Neil Boyd found that over a six-month period most reported exposure to biohazards—blood, feces, saliva, urine, and vomit—and to violence, like verbal threats and threatening gestures.[48] Over one-third reported being physically assaulted.[49]

Incarceration Is Hypermasculine, in a Toxic Way

Returning to the lyrics of "Prison Bound," the other problem with prison is that it's the place "where the tough guy goes, and comes out tougher." Prisons are a hypermasculine environment—a place where to be a man means to be violent. The worst of hegemonic masculinity is pursued there. In her foundational work on this topic *Out There, In Here: Masculinity, Violence and Prisoning*, sociologist Elizabeth Comack describes how assaultive violence is a (masculine) gendered practice on the streets for many youth, and also inside young offender facilities.[50] She shares an interview with one young offender:

> It's like an initiation. That's what it's like.... When I was little, I was a bigger kid, right? I was big for my age, that's how my family is, they're all stocky, right? And, I don't know, guys that go look at a big kid coming in [to prison] and everything, you know, they tried to fight me, they tried to see if they could beat me up and stuff like that.... But I took it, when I first came in. I thought, I don't wanna fight, you know I don't wanna do nothing. And this guy, I remember this guy, like, every time we'd go for supper we had to line up, right. And I knew he was gonna bug me, he bugged me everyday, always at supper time, he always bugged me, always there calling me names and giving me pushes and everything. And just one day, I just couldn't take it. As soon as he pushed me I grabbed him, threw him against the door. But I never hit him. I just threw him against the door and I said, "Leave me alone." And he did, just left me alone.[51]

The prison code is an example of hegemonic masculinity in prison. Another inmate describing life on the outside, as well as on the inside, had this to say: "'Violence solves everything. It's acceptable for the crowds I'm with. If you're not listening, I give you a shot in the head. Then you'll listen to me. It's just the way it is.'"[52] Don Sabo, Terry A. Kupers, and Willie London in *Prison Masculinities* highlight the following as rules of the prison code:

- Act tough, even if you do not feel it.
- Suffer in silence.
- Never admit fear.
- Do not trust anyone.
- Do not snitch on anyone.
- Fight when manhood is disrespected: unrestrained retaliation.
- Be willing to inflict pain on others.[53]

About the last point, Sabo, Kupers, and London say, "Not surprisingly prison violence reflects the kind of everyday violence that men have become accustomed to in larger society. In fact, for men on the outside prison—with its exaggerated forms of violence and insensitivity—provides a spectacle that serves to normalize the seemingly less-perverse forms of violence that are part of daily life on the outside."[54] The seamless transition between hegemonic masculinity on the outside, and hegemonic masculinity on the inside, provides inmates with little opportunity for rehabilitation or for reflection about the nature of their choices. Male violence as a root cause of youth criminality persists—and is, in fact, reinforced—in the justice system in the same way it is in everyday life.

> **Excerpt from "Night Crier," by Rudy Chato Paul Sr.**
>
> The silence is broken by a scream, followed by lengthy cries and jumbled words that I can't quite make out. I recognize "god" and "c.o." The cries swell and fade in a crazy rhythm, a mantra of pain. "Ahhhhhhhhhhh...," he moans...
>
> ... I go to the window and see lights flicking on in the cells adjoining the hospital building. The cries are reaching ears in these cells as well. "Ahhhhhhhhhhh..." This time the cries sound more agonized...
>
> ... I don't know if I should feel sorry for the individual or not. The night crier continues his refrain. He's shrieking now, and the sentences are getting longer. My feeling of indifference bothers me. Am I no longer able to care? Have I lost touch with human compassion entirely?
>
> ... How do I feel? "Ahhhhhhhhhhh..." No long sentences this time. No mention of c.o.'s or god. He seems to have decided to moan just for the satisfaction it provides him. I realize that it takes a great deal of courage to cry out the way he's doing. Crying in prison is taboo. In a maximum-security prison like Attica, it's an even greater breach of the manly codes. I wonder how much pain I could endure before I cried out like he does. Or would I merely cry into my pillow instead, as I have done in the past?[55]

RISK ASSESSMENT: THE WRONG FOCUS FOR YOUTH JUSTICE

> Sometimes I wonder what it's gonna take
> To find dignity
>
> —Bob Dylan, "Dignity"[56]

Another troubling aspect of the youth justice system is its incessant focus on risk—the use, if not overuse, of **risk assessment** measures. Risk assessment measures are actuarial tools that criminal justice system professionals use to predict whether a young person will reoffend in the future. Understandably, justice system professionals want to know, or to be able to predict with some accuracy, which youth are likely to reoffend. After all, they have an obligation to work in the interest of public safety. Properly matching young offenders with appropriate interventions and treatment is part of this. However, problems arise when we become over-reliant on these tools. Human behaviour is difficult to predict. Psychologists remind us of this, as do other professionals who work in this arena, as do young people themselves. Nonetheless, the justice system in Canada relies heavily upon risk assessment tools, both with adults and with young people. In the section below, I'll describe a few risk assessment tools that are used with youth. I will problematize their use by discussing how narrowly they understand human behaviour, as well as the human condition (e.g., the traumas of young people).

Risk Assessment Tools

In this section I'll describe three risk assessment tools: first, the Psychopathy Checklist–Youth Version (PCL-YV); second, the Structured Assessment of Violence Risk in Youth (SAVRY); and, third, Level of Service Inventory models (LSI).

The PCL-YV measures a young person's psychopathic or antisocial tendencies. It was not initially designed to predict recidivism, but is now used in this manner, as it is believed to have some statistical significance in this area.[57] When using the tool, a professional asks a young person a series of questions in a semi-structured interview related to 20 items:

1. *Impression management:* Presents in a good light, is superficially charming
2. *Grandiose sense of self-worth:* Is dominating, opinionated, has an inflated view of own ability
3. *Stimulation-seeking:* Needs novelty, excitement, is prone to boredom and risk-taking behaviours
4. *Pathological lying:* Exhibits pervasive lying
5. *Manipulation for personal gain:* Is deceitful, manipulates
6. *Lack of remorse:* Has no guilt, lacks concern about the impact of his or her actions on others; justifies and rationalizes their abuse of others
7. *Shallow affect:* Has only superficial bonds with others, feigns emotion
8. *Callous or lacking empathy:* Has no appreciation of the needs or feelings of others
9. *Parasitic orientation:* Exploits others, lives at the expense of friends and family
10. *Poor anger control:* Easily offended and reacts aggressively; is easily provoked to violence
11. *Impersonal sexual behaviour:* Has multiple casual sexual encounters, indiscriminate sexual relationships, uses coercion and threats
12. *Early behavioural problems:* Lying, thieving, fire-setting before 10 years of age
13. *Lacks goals:* Has no interest for education, lives day-to-day, has unrealistic aspirations for the future
14. *Impulsivity:* Acts out frequently

15. *Irresponsibility:* Habitually fails to honour obligations
16. *Failure to accept responsibility:* Blames other for his or her problems
17. *Unstable interpersonal relationships:* Has turbulent extrafamilial relationships, lacks commitment and loyalty
18. *Serious criminal behaviour:* Has multiple charges or convictions
19. *Serious violations of conditional release:* Has two or more escapes from security or breaches of probation
20. *Criminal versatility:* Engages in at least six different categories of offending behaviour.[58]

Significantly, there's considerable debate about whether it's possible to measure psychopathy in young people, as the baseline for it is higher among young people than adults.[59] Researchers suspect that some of the characteristics of psychopathy are related to natural child and youth development. In other words, many teenagers would fit in some ways into the categories above. That being said, the tool is still used in the youth justice system.

The second tool I will describe, the SAVRY, measures both static (unchanging) and dynamic (changing) risk factors for future violent behaviour. It uses a 30-item checklist and requires the use of some professional judgment rather than simply an actuarial (or counted) total.[60] The items on the checklist are divided into four categories: one, historical risk factors, like a history of violence, criminal activity, experiences of abuse, and caregiver criminality; two, contextual risk factors, examining quality of peers and other social supports, like parental and community connections; three, clinical risk factors, measuring attitudes, impulsiveness, and other mental health challenges; and four, protective factors, looking at social support, attachments, and the commitment of the individual to positive social activities.

Finally, the third risk assessment tool I'll describe is the Level of Service Inventory models (LSI). The most common of the LSI models is the Risk Needs Assessment—Case Management Review (RNA). It is one of the main tools used by probation officers, and is an adaptation of the Young Offender Level of Service Inventory/Case Management Inventory (YO-LSI/CMI). It is an actuarial too designed to measure the risk of a young person to reoffend. A risk assessment is completed to match youth with appropriate punishments and treatments. Data is collected by interviewing individual youth, as well as by gathering corroborating evidence from a young person's social and professional networks (e.g., family, school, social services, etc.). The YO-LSI/CMI collects information based on eight criminogenic (crime-causing) factors: education, employment, attitudes, peer relations, leisure activities, substance abuse, personality/behaviour, and family circumstances/parenting. After totalling up items in each category, the youth justice professional (e.g., a probation officer) will assign a young offender to either low, medium, or high risk category.

Together, these three tools are used to measure risk, needs, and responsivity—the foundational principles of a risk assessment model. Developed in reaction to an era where it was believed that nothing was working in criminal justice to rehabilitate offenders, these new psychologically based models were an attempt to create a "what works" approach. The *risk principle* means that higher levels of service should be associated with those most at risk of reoffending.[61] Furthermore, the system should be careful not to pull those at low risk too far into its grasp. The *needs principle* indicates what a young person needs in order to be successful. That is, what protective factors can be implemented to mitigate each risk factor. The *responsivity principle* means that service should be matched to the capacity of the young person.[62] Risk assessment tools have followed four phases since the 1970s. Initially, first-generation tools were mainly about professional or clinical judgment. However, disparate outcomes resulted. To address this, second-generation tools started using shared measurement criteria. Today, risk assessment involves a combination of actuarial and clinical judgments.

The (In)effectiveness of Risk Assessment Tools

One of the most important questions, given the widespread use of risk assessment tools and principles, is how effective they are in assessing what they claim to measure. If a young person is deemed a high risk to reoffend, are they actually likely to go out and commit another crime? These tools claim to be evidence-based; meta-analyses have been collected over time to build the case for their use. The results are promising from a psychological perspective, but perhaps not from a human perspective.

Most risk assessments are only able to accurately predict future recidivism in a range of about 5 to 20 percent. This should be cause for concern. Many meta-analyses have been done on the three risk assessment tools just described. A particularly useful study by researchers Olver et al. found that: (1) the PCL-YV could account for 7.8 percent of the variance in recidivism for offenders who were assessed using this tool; (2) the LSI could account for 10.24 percent of the variance in recidivism for offenders who were assessed using this tool; and (3) the SAVRY could account for 10.24 percent of the variance in recidivism for offenders who were assessed using this tool.[63] Ultimately, what this means is that the statistical models do not account for most of the variance in recidivism; that is, the PCL-YV, LSI, and SAVRY have limited value in predicting future offending. Therefore, we should be critical of their widespread use. In discussing their findings, Olver et al. remind readers that, indeed, risk assessment tools are better used for preventing future offending behaviour (because offenders can at least be matched with appropriate programming) than as a predictor for it.[64] In text box below, I explain in greater detail how these particular statistical models attempt to predict recidivism.

Understanding Statistical Models That Try to Predict Recidivism

- **Correlation Coefficient (r):** This indicates the strength and direction of a linear relationship between two or more variables.
- **Coefficient of Determination; R-squared (r^2):** This is the amount of the variance in the y (dependent/predicted) variable explained for by x (independent/predictor) variable, or by the model, given multiple dependent

variables. In the case of recidivism (y), how much of it can be explained by a given risk assessment model?
- **Effect size:** This is the estimated strength of relationship between independent and dependent variables.

The findings cited by Olver et al.:

- PCL-YV: general recidivism $r = .28$, violent recidivism $r = .25$
- LSI: general recidivism $r = .32$ (.35 in Canadian studies), violent recidivism $r = .28$
- SAVRY: general recidivism $r = .32$, violent recidivism $r = .30$[65]

In order to find r^2, simply square the Correlation Coefficient (r) data above, and multiply by 100 to get a percentage:

- 7.8 percent of the variance in general recidivism can be accounted for by the PCL-YV model
- 6.25 percent of the variance in violent recidivism can be accounted for by the PCL-YV model
- 10.24 percent of the variance in general recidivism can be accounted for by the LSI model
- 7.8 percent of the variance in violent recidivism can be accounted for by the LSI model
- 10.24 percent of the variance in general recidivism can be accounted for by the SAVRY model
- 9 percent of the variance in violent recidivism can be accounted for by the SAVRY model

When doing statistical research, software is used to test whether there's a correlation, or a relationship, between variables; that is, between predictor (x) variables and a variable (y) that they are trying to predict. One type of statistical research is multiple regression analysis. In this type of analysis, data collected about the variables is randomly sampled a number of times in order to create a statistical model. This allows a researcher to use sample data to make inferences about the properties of a population. In the case of the PCL-YV, LSI, and SAVRY, statistical models of these tools would be created by repeated random sampling of data collected about them. Then, inferences could be made about how effective they are in predicting whether or not a young offender is likely to reoffend.

How does multiple regression analysis work? After each random sampling of data a statistic is produced. This statistic indicates a relationship between the x variables and y. A statistic specifies for every change in the value of x, y will increase by a certain value. Repeated random sampling will create a number of statistics. Pictorially, this can be plotted on an x-y axis graph (see Figure 7.1). The x-axis represents the explanatory or predictor (independent) variables, while the *y*-axis indicates the response or predicted (dependent) variables. Subsequently, using a formula, a regression line (or a line of best fit, positioned in such a way that all of the data points are as close as possible to the line) is drawn. The regression line indicates the direction (positive or negative) and strength (strong or weak) of a relationship between *x* and *y* variables. Essentially, the regression line models the relationship between *x* and *y*, which is why it is called a statistical model. Based on the statistical model, a researcher can then infer the probability of *y* occurring based on *x*.

Figure 7.1

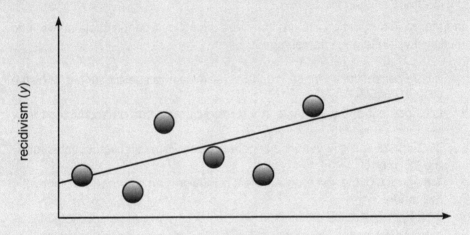

Risk assessment tools are the predictor (*x*) variables. Recidivism goes on the *y*-axis. Based on multiple regression analyses, researchers have determined that offender recidivism can be inferred from risk assessment tools—but only to a certain degree.

Returning to the percentages from the Olver et al. meta-analysis; the higher the percentage, or r^2, the better the predictor (*x*) variables are able to predict the response variable (*y*)—or, stated more accurately, the more the variance in recidivism is accounted for by a risk assessment model. The r^2 values from studies of the PCL-YV, LSI, and SAVRY were at best 10.24 percent, and at worst 6.25 percent. The conclusion is that only a small amount of the variance in recidivism can be accounted for by statistical models of these risk assessment tools.

However, before being overly critical, a low r^2 isn't necessarily a bad thing. The r^2 values of the PCL-YV, LSI, and SAVRY are fairly indicative of how well psychological assessment can predict human behaviour; it really only captures a small percentage of what human beings will do in the future. In statistical research, there's no set bar for how high r^2 should be in order for a model to be meaningful. I've seen some research where the authors claim that around 25 percent makes

> for a helpful model. In fact, some people are suspicious if the value is too high. Furthermore, there's some theoretical debate about whether r or r^2 is better at explaining effect size (estimated strength of the relationship between variables).[66] If the former (r) is used, this would put the statistical models of risk assessment tools closer to a 28 percent to 32 percent predictive range. Our conclusion should be that there is some validity in risk assessment models, but they cannot account for most reoffending. Therefore, we should be wary of the overuse of risk assessment in youth justice.

Where we do need to further problematize—or ask critical questions—is in the use of risk assessment tools for sentencing purposes under the Youth Criminal Justice Act (YCJA). Most provinces and territories now require probation officers to complete risk assessments as part of their pre-sentence reports (PSR), which judges use for sentencing purposes. Two sociologists at the University of Toronto, Paula Maurutto and Kelly Hannah-Moffat, have raised the following questions about this practice: Are we simply relying on a form of statistical justice?[67] And, perhaps more importantly, is it defensible or fair? One of the problems with risk assessments is that marginalized people are often framed by them as higher risk.[68] If we examine the themes of the tools above, the issue of growing up in violence or having unstable caregivers, for example, factors into whether a person is labelled a higher risk. Is it fair to deem people who have been negatively affected by a family or a community of origin as higher risk? This question is essential for the work of trauma-informed youth justice.

Essentially, I see three main problems with an over-emphasis on risk. First, and fundamentally, risk assessment tools are poor predictors of future behaviour. Yes, there's statistical correlation between the tools and recidivism, yet these tools leave out more than they tell us. Second, risk assessment tools haven't been developed in partnership between clients and professionals. Rather, they are tools imposed on clients by professionals. This is especially problematic when clients are marginalized peoples and professionals are mostly from privileged classes. This is not an accusation against psychology, particularly, but a general statement of the risk—to use the word appropriately—of professionalization and privilege potentially causing further harm. Indicative of this problem is the fact that risk tools are especially unhelpful with Indigenous and female offenders.[69] This should be a clue. Given the use of risk assessments under the YCJA, if I were a psychologist, I would be wary of my newfound power. According to the New World Encyclopedia, the purpose of a psychologist is to understand human nature, to help people overcome difficulties, and to help people live up to their potential.[70] However, in some ways, yesterday's psychologist has become today's judge, because under the YCJA part of their role is also to punish.

Third, a focus on risk is a narrow way to understand a human being. It tends to look more at what's "wrong" with a person than at what's "right." What if we looked instead at the strengths of a young person? What if we understood their risk factors regarding their previous traumas as indicators of their resilience; their ability to survive hardship? Or, what if we understood other risk factors—like substance abuse, even violent behaviour—as ways of coping with or surviving trauma? One of the principles we will discuss in chapter 9 is the need for a strengths-based approach to working with young offenders. Human beings function best when others believe in their ability to live meaningful lives.

Moving beyond tools and thinking about society's aversion to risk is also important to youth justice. One example of this is the requirement of background checks on individuals hoping to work in the field of criminal justice, policing, probation, corrections, and so on. A criminal record usually makes it impossible for a person to find employment in these areas. Yet, I can't help but wonder what value a person with lived experience of "the system" could bring to this type of work. Are we missing an opportunity for bettering youth justice by being too risk-averse?

VICTIM (DIS)SATISFACTION WITH CRIMINAL JUSTICE

One way that I'm critical of my own work here is that, so far, we have been (over)focused on offenders. Here we are in chapter 7, and I've had very little to say about victims. Yes, I've identified how many (most) young offenders have experienced victimization; however, most victims don't go on to become offenders. What about people who are "purely" victims? If, as we've identified above, the justice system is doing little to accomplish its purposes toward offenders, perhaps it's doing so for the sake of victims. After all, justice is designed to punish offenders, making them suffer the same amount that they've caused others to suffer (an eye for an eye). Some believe this is meant to satisfy victims' desires for revenge. Yet, studies show that only about 20 percent of victims of violent crime really want revenge.[71] And, furthermore, the overall experience of justice does little to satisfy this feeling.[72]

Not surprisingly then, overall, Western justice systems are doing little to satisfy victims. In the same way that criminal justice doesn't take a trauma-informed approach toward offenders, it also fails to address the traumas of victims. Research on victim satisfaction in the justice system is generally mixed; however, where the results are not mixed—where victims are largely dissatisfied—is in cases of violent crime, particularly sexual assault and domestic violence. In fact, victims of these crimes often experience the justice system as revictimizing and retraumatizing.

- The criminal justice system often causes secondary victimization in crime victims.[73]
- In particular, survivors of sexual assault often feel blamed, doubted, and revictimized by criminal justice.[74]

A more in-depth discussion and analysis of the fact that victims feel revictimized by the criminal justice system will occur in chapter 11, where I present the idea that trauma-informed youth justice should take a victim-centred approach.

THE PROBLEMS OF PUNISHMENT

> The answer my friend is blowin' in the wind,
> The answer is blowin' in the wind.
> —Bob Dylan, "Blowin' in the Wind"[75]

I'm convinced that the agenda of punishment—the overarching concern of giving offenders what they deserve—gets in the way of justice, for victims, for offenders, and for communities. This orientation skews justice toward focusing on offenders, rather than on those who've been harmed by crime. Why do we continue to carry out justice in this way?

Our current criminal justice system has stood on the premise of punishment since well before Canada became a nation—for almost a thousand years, in fact. Since about the 13th century, the criminal justice system has been punishing criminals—by death, through torture, and more recently through incarceration. In earlier times (at the risk of being overly simplistic) it was about atonement, an eye for an eye, making an offender suffer for the suffering they had caused. In the 18th century, criminal justice reforms started putting limits to punishment. Today the principle of retribution still holds true, yet the question remains: Is this fair? Perhaps. But, here's an even more important question: Is it working? Does this approach meet the needs of victims? Does it meet the needs for communities to be safe? Much as the lyrics of the Bob Dylan song "Blowin' in the Wind" describe, our approaches have been shown to be futile, yet we keep repeating them: "How many times will this mountain exist before it is washed to the sea"?

Table 7.1: Major Euro-Canadian Philosophies of Criminal Justice

Philosophy	Description	Principles
Retribution	• Judeo-Christian • 13th Century • Blood Atonement	(1) Wrong is right by inflicting similar harm. (2) Offender (morally) deserves this (just deserts).
Utilitarian	• Rational Choice Theory • 18th Century • Criminal Law Reform	(1) Punishment must maximize social good. (2) Least amount that will deter (specific & general).
Rehabilitation	• Behavioural Sciences • 19th Century	(1) Crime is an "illness" that needs to be treated. (2) Therefore, offenders need to be reformed.
Restitution	• Neoclassical Economics • Political Libertarianism • Mid to Late 20th Century	(1) Some shifts toward victims based on financial restitution. (2) Offender should pay debt to society and victim.

Justice is traditionally equated with three values: fairness, equality, and impartiality. Let's look at each of those values in turn. One: fairness. When we think of fairness, we often think of balance—like the image of lady justice holding the scales, tipping the scale away from offenders and back toward victims and the community. Anyone who has young children knows they exude a desire for fairness. "That's not fair," is a common statement from children, imploring an authority figure to treat them the same as another child. Two: equality. This is the idea that everyone deserves the same amount or the same treatment. Over time, as we have become more aware of the need to listen to voices on the margins, we've come to understand that this is better termed equity. After all, what happens when we treat unequals equally? We perpetuate inequality. Equity means we have to consider peoples' prior circumstances. Three: impartiality. Lady justice is blindfolded, so that regardless of who the person is, they will be treated the same as any other. The notion was originally conceptualized so that the rich wouldn't receive special treatment. Of course, this begs the question of whether we should remove the blindfold, having discovered that our current justice system entangles many individuals with mental health issues, as well as other marginalized peoples. None of these values necessarily implies punishment. Yet, somehow, punishment still seems to be the central concern of criminal justice.

Punishment, as I've defined it, is the deliberate infliction of pain. In spite of significant criminal justice reforms over the past thousand years, nothing has changed about the fact that our consequences are primarily about inflicting pain. One thing that has perhaps changed, however, is the location in which we're inflicting the pain. As philosopher Michel Foucault argues in *Discipline and Punish: The Birth of the Prison*, punishment has shifted from a very public attack on the body of the criminal, to a very private assault on the soul.[76] He described the public torture—for example, quartering—of criminals that happened prior to the birth of the prison. This torture was a gruesome public spectacle. Four horses tied to the four limbs of the convict, pulled him or her apart by moving in opposite directions. He argues that punishment is still grotesque, but now it is private. Today it is inmates, out of the public eye, being tortured psychologically by incarceration. Danish criminologist Nils Christie describes the current state of affairs like this: "Crime control has become a clean, hygienic operation. Pain and suffering have vanished from the text-books [sic] and from the applied labels. But of course not from the experience of those punished. The targets of penal action are just as they used to be: scared, ashamed, unhappy."[77] Punishment, whether public or private, whether corporal or psychological, is painful.

The torture of previous centuries is looked down upon from the vantage point of today. We ask ourselves how humanity could stand by, watching—celebrating, in fact—as a human being was ripped apart by horses. Such barbarism! Yet, now we stand by silently while inmates suffer. Prisons are known to damage the psyches of their inhabitants, especially so where solitary confinement and restraints are used. Will people of the future look with similar disapproval on our practices? How will the history of the prison read a few hundred years from now?

Of course, all of this begs the question, what do criminals deserve? In its time, maybe people believed that quartering was exactly what a criminal deserved. After all, people today seem to believe that prison is just and that inmates deserve it. There is little political or public will to discuss the suffering and pain of inmates. This text cannot resolve the dilemma of just deserts. Some—maybe most—will always believe that criminals deserve punishment. In fact, many criminals may believe they deserve it, too. What this book can do, however, is question the usefulness of orienting so much of criminal justice machinery on punishment.

Questioning the usefulness of punishment is particularly important from a trauma-informed perspective. Is punishment accomplishing what we want it to? The answer would be yes if our purpose were to inflict pain on an inmate. The answer would be no if our purpose was community safety. I have heard it said that you cannot punish someone into changing. In *Security With Care: Restorative Justice and Healthy Societies*, criminologist Elizabeth Elliott says, "The dark side of punishment is that it not only does not work to achieve its goal, it actually exacerbates anti-social behaviour."[78] Punishment might deal with the guilt of an offender, but it only increases their shame. It acknowledges their culpability—that they have done something harmful—but the way we do it, through incarceration and through stigmatizing reintegration practices, exacerbates feelings of shame, worthlessness, and disconnection.

Some might argue that I'm missing the point that other perspectives are also fundamental to criminal justice—for example, that deterrence and rehabilitation are as important to sentencing as retribution. However, when we examine each of these perspectives, the baseline (the launching pad) is always retribution. Punishment is meant to be *the* deterrent. Rehabilitation is supposed to happen within the context of a prison, the tool of punishment. We know that punishment does not deter. And, we know—from the perspective of young offenders—that prison contact increases the likelihood that a young person will commit a crime again in the future. Rehabilitation in this context is far from a sure thing. As such, we might argue that punishment gets in the way of deterrence, and similarly impedes rehabilitation.

The question then becomes, who is punishment satisfying? We might answer: victims. (In later chapters, we'll explore the complex needs of victims further.) A victim once told me that prisons are not victim services. Sure, some victims might want to see an offender suffer like they have, but more often than not victims have other needs, for care, for attention to their traumas, and so on. Is it really possible to meet the complex needs of victims by punishing offenders? If punishment doesn't work, does little to meet the needs of victims and is only a small part of what people would describe as justice, why does it play an exaggerated role in criminal justice? The darker side to this answer might be that it meets the needs of politicians. Punishing offenders and get-tough-on-crime agendas seem to be a way to garner political points. Another answer might be capitalists. There's significant profit to be made in the building and sustaining of prisons. As Sabo, Kupers, and London argue, in order for profits to continue to rise, the prison system must not work to rehabilitate, it must consistently bring people back behind bars: "It is becoming apparent that the prison system is designed to fail ... this is precisely the point."[79]

Still another answer could be that it benefits settler society. With increasing numbers of Indigenous peoples behind bars, it deflects from the moral obligation Canada has to take responsibility for harm done to Original peoples, and to return the land and resources that rightfully belong to them. Who else is overrepresented in Canadian prisons? Black Canadians, people with mental health challenges, and people living in poverty—essentially, those who are often on the margins of society. What does this tell us about why we punish? Maybe that we do it because we're afraid.

Punishment conveys a moral message.[80] Crime is wrong. From a sociological perspective, some argue that by punishing criminals we're actually trying to separate out "good" from "bad" in order to make society more cohesive and ordered.[81] Sociologist Emile Durkheim claimed that by excluding delinquents, "the rest of the community ... feels better for it."[82] This explains, then, that some of this morality is rooted in anxiety—a fear of the "criminal other." In exploring why Anglophone societies imprison people in excess—or in a way that's disproportionate to the amount of crime committed—sociologists John Pratt and Anna Eriksson argue that excessive use of prisons gives "messages of reassurance to anxious and insecure communities: inflammatory speeches are thus made by politicians about the need for more use of imprisonment and longer sentences and curtailment of early release mechanisms."[83] When we examine which people are in our prisons, it becomes clearer who is afraid, and who we are afraid of. Those in power—those who own homes, those who have jobs, the middle- and upper-class white community—are scared. And they are afraid of marginalized communities.

In an article for *Psychology Today*, Robert Wilson explains a correlation between fear and power. He writes that the amount of power a person pursues is related to the amount of fear they have. Use of power, then, is an attempt to control their environment. He states:

> An individual's motivation for power is to acquire control over his environment. A certain amount of controlling behavior is a healthy natural survival instinct, but after a point it becomes harmful. When that happens normal survival is no longer the motivator. Underlying the quest for power is fear, and the desire for power is to eliminate fear. The more fearful a person is the more control over their environment they believe they need to feel safe.[84]

From this perspective, punishment becomes the tool for attempting to control their environment.

Putting this all together, punishment benefits the powerful through harmful control of the less powerful. Men continue to dominate women and other genders. White supremacy harms Indigenous peoples and others. The rich control the poor. Punishment is used because it meets the agenda of politicians, capitalists, and a fearful public. Yet, punishment gets in the way of justice. It makes offenders worse, it revictimizes victims, and does little for public safety. Safer, more livable communities desperately need new—trauma-informed—conceptions of justice.

CONCLUSION

Many of the practices of the current youth justice system are trauma-inducing. The use of incarceration, an over-emphasis on risk, victim retraumatization by justice systems, and an overall punishment agenda means that a system intended to bring about justice is actually causing more harm. The tragedy is that the information I've presented here isn't new. What do we call it when we keep doing the same thing and expecting different results? Some might call it insanity. What do we call it when we compulsively seek relief in a system that adds further harm? To me, it sounds a lot like an addiction. As T. Richard Snyder claims in the opening epigraph, Western society has become captive to a spirit of punishment. In the remaining chapters of the book, I'll describe what can be done, and how a trauma-informed framework for approaching youth justice is a better way to go.

GLOSSARY OF TERMS

Normative, as used in the law, means establishing or relating to a standard of how things should or ought to be.

Punishment is the deliberate infliction of pain.

Risk assessment is the use of actuarial tools by criminal justice system professionals to predict whether a young person will reoffend in the future. One of the primary purposes of risk assessment is to create a correctional plan for a young person, based on criminogenic needs.

QUESTIONS FOR REFLECTION

1. From Bob Dylan to Social Distortion, I've quoted various songs in this chapter that resonate with my work. In your studies and life, do you find certain music or artists are able to express something that relates to your experiences? How so?
2. Why do you think we're so risk-averse in North America? In your opinion, what balance between taking risks and avoiding risks should the youth justice system be aiming for?
3. Do you think people who break the law deserve to be punished? Is punishment primarily about revenge or is it a natural consequence of wrongdoing? Can you imagine a time in the future where punishment is no longer a part of the justice system? Would this be a good or a bad thing?

RECOMMENDED READING

Foucault, Michel. *Discipline & Punish: The Birth of the Prison*. New York: Vintage Books, 1975.

Using historical and discourse analyses, French philosopher Michel Foucault traces the reasons for the emergence of the modern penitentiary as a way to replace the more public practices of torture.

Mendel, Richard A. *No Place for Kids: The Case for Reducing Juvenile Incarceration*. Baltimore: The Annie E. Casey Foundation, 2011.

Researcher Richard A. Mendel provides an essential analysis of the harm of incarceration on young people and the need for alternatives.

Sabo, Don, Kupers, Terry A., and London, Willie. *Prison Masculinities*. Philadelphia: Temple University Press, 2001.
   In this edited collection, authors describe connections between violence, masculinity, and incarceration.

8 | Restorative Justice—The Worldview of Trauma-Informed Youth Justice

"Restorative justice is a process to involve to the extent possible, those who have a stake in a specific offense and to collectively identify and address harms, needs, and obligations, in order to heal and put things as right as possible."

—Howard Zehr

This chapter is a transition toward solutions. In the first three chapters of the book, I discussed trauma-informed youth justice as a framework and gave a history of youth justice in Canada. I then outlined the impacts of individual and collective trauma, and identified colonialism, patriarchy, and the iatrogenic nature of youth justice as traumatizing structures. Now, I'll turn from an analysis of problems toward outlining possible solutions. The starting point is **restorative justice**. As Howard Zehr defines it, "restorative justice is a process to involve, to the extent possible, those who have a stake in a specific offense and to collectively identify and address harms, needs, and obligations, in order to heal and put things as right as possible."[1]

Restorative justice provides a framework, or a worldview, for guiding trauma-informed youth justice. The Youth Criminal Justice Act makes restorative justice legally possible. Police and the courts are to consider it as an alternative to traditional criminal justice system options. However, I'll be describing restorative justice as more than simply an alternative—a way to divert youth from the criminal justice system. Restorative justice is about healing harms. A restorative justice worldview is necessary to create a safe, secure base—both for young offenders (so that they don't offend again in the future) and for victims and communities (to allow them to heal).

In this chapter, I'll describe how restorative justice holds offenders accountable in a meaningful way, while also working to better support victims. In traditional criminal justice, accountability means "doing time" or serving out a sentence. In restorative justice, it means being directly accountable toward those harmed, including taking steps to repair damage. In criminal justice, victims become witnesses to their harm. In restorative justice, they're given more choice and more power to identify their needs and the processes that will help them. I'll explain how restorative justice is rooted in some Indigenous philosophies, and in the modern era, by the influence of some Mennonite people in North America. Following this, I'll discuss how a restorative justice worldview is put into practice and will present evidence for its effectiveness. Finally, we'll conclude the chapter by looking at some critiques of these approaches.

RESTORATIVE JUSTICE

In the opening chapter I identified Howard Zehr's guiding questions for restorative justice as contrasted with traditional criminal justice. To review, traditional justice asks:

1. What law has been broken?
2. Who did it?
3. Are they guilty?
4. What punishment fits the crime?

Alternatively, restorative justice asks:

1. Who has been hurt?
2. What are their needs?
3. Whose obligation is it to meet those needs?
4. What are the root causes?
5. Who needs to be involved in a justice process?
6. What is the best process for making things as right as possible?[2]

One of the central tasks of restorative justice is to determine the needs of people affected by crime and harm: victims, offenders, and communities. This shift from focusing on punishment (criminal justice) to needs (restorative justice) cannot be understated. The first is rather one-dimensional, while the second allows for more nuances. The hope is that by using a restorative justice process some of the following victim, offender, and community needs can be met.

Victim Needs

- Safety and choice
- Information and answers to questions
- Acknowledgement that what happened to them was wrong
- Support—personal, professional, and financial
- Space for healing
- Opportunities for mourning and meaningful (re)connection with others

After a crime has been committed, the first priority is ensuring safety. This is the most important task of restorative justice and of trauma recovery. Included in this task of ensuring safety is the need for victims to be empowered to make choices in their recovery. As well, victims need information. Some of this information will be specifically related to understanding how the justice system works, while other parts will be related to seeking answers to various questions. Victims often want to know why the crime happened, and how people—especially the offender—will take steps to make sure it never happens again. Victims need acknowledgement, a formal denunciation that what happened to them was wrong. Victims also need supports: personal, professional, and financial. They need spaces to heal, to grieve the harm, and to be able to connect with others and know that they won't be ostracized or isolated.

Sometimes people confuse restorative justice with a particular form of practice—a face-to-face meeting between victims and offenders. Although this isn't all that restorative justice is, face-to-face meetings are one aspect. As a result of this confusion, people often assume that restorative justice means that victims are pushed to forgive or to reconcile with offenders. Restorative justice is not forgiveness or reconciliation. Although this might be a goal for some victims, it isn't for all. It's especially important that victims are able to define for themselves what they need. I do some work as a facilitator with the Restorative Opportunities program of Correctional Service of Canada (CSC). The program offers opportunities, where appropriate, for victims and offenders to have contact to address harms. A client I worked with named Heather White, who courageously shared some of her story in *Let's Talk*—a newsletter of CSC—highlights how restorative justice allows a victim's needs to shape the process. Heather's sister Wendy and Wendy's young children (Victoria and Jessy) were murdered by Wendy's estranged husband. In Heather's words:

> I didn't know what to expect. I felt so comfortable and was able to share how I felt. Talking to a complete stranger about intimate details of my life was scary at first. But we bonded right away and I was able to be very open with him. Once I started telling my story, I realized I had forgotten how angry I was, how devastated I was.... I had forgotten a lot of emotions because I had just been trying to move on and live a normal life. My husband attended one of our meetings and he said things that he hadn't planned to say. He was also shocked at how his buried feelings just came out. This process helped me realize that I do not need to forgive and it is okay. It allowed my feelings and anger to be validated.... We will never forgive the offender for what he has done to us. I realized that meeting with the offender was no longer necessary. Being able to express my feelings to Judah had helped me deal with my pain. I felt that putting myself through a face-to-face meeting would probably throw me back into a very bad space. But I know if I change my mind in the future that this restorative justice opportunity is still available.... I would highly recommend restorative justice to anyone who has been through a terrible crime.[3]

As a framework, restorative justice puts victims' needs first. It recognizes that it is their lives that have been most affected by a crime. Even though the state swoops in and takes on the role of victim, it isn't the state whose house was broken into, or whose family member was murdered. It isn't the state that has to deal with the ongoing aftermath. Criminal justice is so busy giving offenders what they deserve that it mostly forgets to give victims what they deserve: care and attention paid to the needs created by harm. Criminologists Sullivan and Tifft argue that punitive approaches ignore, if not destroy, human presence.[4] From their perspective, retribution simply satisfies the person who wields the power—the governments who write laws and the criminal justice system professionals who implement them. This type of justice ignores needs. A needs-based approach, like restorative justice, shifts power into the hands of everyone, but particularly those most affected by harm. Sullivan and Tifft argue that "such an approach toward justice puts a great premium on the participation of everyone, and on the expression of the voice of each ... everyone involved is listened to, interacted with, or responded to on the basis of her or his present needs."[5] This isn't limited to meeting needs after the fact, but also focuses on structuring relationships based on equity—fairly meeting the needs of all, which works to prevent crime in the first place.[6]

Of course, not all victims will want to be involved with a particular restorative justice practice. Some might need for the criminal justice system to handle their case fully. In other instances, like in the story of Heather White, the criminal justice system can work in tandem with a restorative justice process. The important part of a restorative justice orientation is that it creates options for victims. Choice is fundamental to healing and to establishing safety.

Offender Needs

- Accountability
  "I did it."
  "It was wrong."
  "I will make amends."
  "I will get the support necessary to change."
- Recognition of their humanity
- Transformation—opportunities to heal from their own hurts
- Incapacitation

The starting place for meeting offender needs is making them accountable for their actions by having them acknowledge harm, understand impacts, and take steps toward responsibility. In practice this can involve four steps: "I did it," "It was wrong," "I will make amends," and "I will get the support necessary to change." The objective is accountability within a context of support. This works best when the humanity of the offender is acknowledged, by recognizing that a person is never fully defined by the worst thing they've done. This means that offenders will need opportunities to heal from their own hurts and to be supported through a transformative process. At times where offenders are a risk to themselves and to others, incapacitation is necessary—although this, too, should take a restorative justice approach.

Certain restorative justice practices—like face-to-face meetings between victims and offenders—aren't well suited where an offender denies guilt. These practices need, as a baseline, an offender to admit to having perpetrated harm. In my experience doing restorative justice work, offender accountability is often a slowly opening door. The door opens at the point of acknowledgement. The next step is recognition that their actions were wrong, that people have been hurt by their choices. This can be complicated. For example, I've helped to facilitate contact between victims and offenders in a number of manslaughter cases. Manslaughter means that an offender didn't plan, or necessarily intend, to kill the other person. I've heard it said by a number of offenders convicted of this crime that the tables could easily have been turned. Given a different set of circumstances, or the opposite outcome, they could be deceased and the victim behind bars. Of course, this isn't always true in manslaughter cases. What it does represent, however, is the complexity of accountability. In relation to accountability, one offender I worked with said, "I don't regret what I did, but I feel remorse." Even if the crime wasn't intentional or carried out with malice, it's still important for offenders to own wrongdoing. Most family members of victims in these cases still want accountability—their loved one lost their life, and the offender bears this responsibility.

Accountability should include some measure of remorse, a feeling of sorrow for choices made. This, too, can be convoluted. On one side, some offenders feel this selfishly. They feel sorry for themselves and for their circumstances. They regret that they've lost their freedom. This isn't remorse. Remorse is feeling sorry for harm done to others. On the flip side, I've worked with many offenders who feel a tremendous amount of remorse and who would give anything for an opportunity to apologize. However, without changed behaviour, an apology or expression of remorse is insufficient. Once a person acknowledges wrongdoing, feels remorse, and works toward making change, then the door to accountability is more fully open. Harmful choices don't happen in a vacuum. They're indicative of a person's inner state, as well as a pattern of behaviours. Until offenders understand their pattern of thinking, feeling, and acting, they're likely to commit further harm. Especially with violent crimes, like sexual assault and domestic violence, a restorative justice process of accountability is important. Oftentimes, when the door to accountability first opens, offenders will say things like, "I lost it," or "I saw black," or "I have no idea why I did it, I just did," indicating that violence came out of nowhere. Accountability requires a deeper understanding and the creation of a new, healthy pattern of behaviour.

Restorative justice processes can play a central role in this. Sometimes the questions of a mediator might cause a young person to reflect in a new way on their choices. Other times an offender might not move toward changed behaviour until they hear directly from a victim about the impacts of the crime. Sometimes it takes a combination of the two. Development of empathy for victims, for communities, and for others generally is consistent with restorative justice. Within the current criminal justice system, it's possible for an offender to be sentenced and to serve their time without ever having to discuss what happened and their role in it. In this regard, restorative justice is very different.

Community Needs

- Attention to their needs as victims
- Taking ownership for root causes regarding offending behaviours

A restorative justice worldview looks beyond direct victims and offenders to think about who else has been harmed. A common analogy used to explain the effects of crime is that of a pebble dropping into water. The ripples created represent how crime's effects spread. If my home is broken into, I might experience a sense of violation, as well as a loss of material goods. My neighbours, too, are victims. They might feel nervous and vulnerable, wondering if their homes will be next. The offender's family is also victimized. For example, if the offender serves time, their children suffer. Restorative justice takes an expansive view to consider these and other layers to harm. It recognizes that, when a crime is committed, the community is also a victim with needs.

Conversely, something not often talked about is that the community is also an offender, and bears a responsibility to address harm and root causes. A quotation that continues to resonate with me is the one by Emma Goldman that "every society has the criminals it deserves." It is my suggestion in *Trauma-Informed Youth Justice in Canada* that individual accountability will rarely happen unless society takes responsibility for why some young people end up in conflict with the law in the first place. After all, why should a young person take responsibility when no one is accountable for the harm done to her? Why should a young person change when nothing about the circumstances that influenced his choices is changing? As we've noted, most young offenders have been (and are) victims of crimes themselves. This cannot be understated. It's why, from my perspective, our efforts toward youth justice are falling short. When we focus solely on individual offender responsibility, we fail to get at root causes.

In *So You Think You Know Me?*, his wonderful and troubling autobiographical account of growing up as a young offender in Scotland, Allan Weaver eloquently highlights how the justice system, in its effort to punish, largely ignored the trouble that was going on in his home.[7] I often use this text as a teaching resource to help students better understand the lived experience of a young person who struggled through the justice system and came out the other side better, not because of, but in spite of it.

Feeling unsafe at home due to domestic/family violence, Weaver found a sense of belonging among a peer group that was increasingly involved with crime. At one point, he tells the story of breaking into his school, where he finds a number of reports written about him:

> "Not long out of assessment centre and mainstream education is perhaps not suited to his needs." These people barely knew me, I thought, though being the experts, both they and everyone else *thought* they did; they did not actually need to, I supposed, they knew my type. They rarely even acknowledged me and they did not know what went on in other parts of my life, nor were there any attempts to find out. "So you think you know me!" I shouted bitterly.[8]

In a culture of punishment that ignores the responsibility of community in shaping young people, including their offending behaviour, questions about root causes are ignored. More significantly, young people, like Weaver, don't feel like they belong:

> Going back to school was expectedly difficult; I was unsure, at first, how I would be received but it was rapidly made clear to me that my return was slightly

more difficult and far less welcomed by some teachers than it ever was going to be for me. A couple of them felt the need to make reference to the fact that I had just been "released" ... "Weaver, you don't belong here." He could have had a point I thought quietly to myself at the time, as I certainly didn't feel as if I belonged, but that said, I didn't really know where I *did* belong. Not only had nothing changed through my admission to the centre but things appeared to have got worse: I felt increasingly isolated and excluded at school, my [dad] was still causing mayhem at home and the guys and the Street seemed to be the only stability and source of acceptance in my life at the time.[9]

The need for connection and stability is particularly important as efforts toward criminal justice often isolate and separate offenders from communities with little regard for the concept of belonging. Of course, some of this is done with good intent, trying to separate those who are at risk of harming themselves or others. However, this one-size-fits-all approach is often to the detriment of safe communities. What does it mean when we further isolate and exclude young people who are often already feeling alone? Do we put our communities at risk for further harm? What does it mean for them, for their sense of purpose and meaning in life?

While getting to know young people and ensuring belonging are central, so too are getting at other root causes of crime:

- Poverty
- Domestic and sexual violence
- Neglect
- Addictions and mental health
- Colonialism
- Male violence

The community needs to be accountable for all of these things. A restorative justice approach means adopting a dual focus: not only considering interventions, but also focusing on programs that prevent harm.

HISTORY OF RESTORATIVE JUSTICE

In a broad sense, restorative justice is not new. In fact, it's quite old, having roots in Indigenous worldviews and practices. Its notions of justice as healing are also common across many spiritual traditions. Within Western criminal justice systems, however, it is relatively new. One of the first examples can be traced back to a case in Elmira, Ontario, in 1974, facilitated by a Mennonite man named Mark Yantzi. In this section, I'll describe these two parallel foundations of the growth of restorative justice.

1. Roots of Restorative Justice in Indigenous Traditions

Settlers in Canada wrongly assumed that Indigenous peoples didn't have their own legal systems, when, in fact, the oral traditions of these diverse peoples indicate robust legal practices. Canada is lesser as a nation today because we failed to learn from Indigenous peoples about restorative ways to address harm.

Myeengun Henry and I have been teaching a course together for the past few years. It's called "Social Issues III: Aboriginal Peoples" and is part of a Bachelor of Community and Criminal Justice degree program at Conestoga College in Kitchener, Ontario. One of the purposes of the course is to help students understand why there's an overrepresentation of Indigenous peoples in Canadian prisons while also helping them to learn more about Indigenous perspectives and cultures. The professor who was assigned the course before me, Jennifer Robinson, had the foresight to invite Myeengun to lead it. Myeengun is the Aboriginal Services Manager at the college. He's also an Ojibway Elder and a traditional healer. The last thing the college needed was for someone other than an Indigenous person to take the lead on a course such as this. Presently, Myeengun and I co-teach. On the days he leads, we sit in a circle, and he teaches through stories and ceremony. He's incredibly generous with the students. On the days I lead, we focus on settler responsibility: how Canada has failed First Nations, and what can be done to take responsibility to end ongoing colonialism.

As serendipity would have it, both Myeengun and I have daughters the same age playing soccer. One muggy June evening in 2014, our children were playing against each other and we sat together, talking about parenting and also about a variety of issues related to the course. I told him how I was trying to incorporate a story that isn't often told about Canadians as settlers. Myeengun, in his quiet, calm way, said it needed to be told, but that we didn't need to dwell on it. I answered that I thought Canadians have an obligation to stop imposing themselves on Indigenous peoples, to allow for self-determination. I also added that Canadians need to adequately give restitution to Indigenous communities. Myeengun smiled. Again, quietly, calmly, he said that he wasn't looking for compensation, but for Canada to honour treaties with Indigenous peoples. If they did, there would be enough for everyone. There wouldn't be situations like in Attiwapiskat (where there are housing, poverty, and suicide crises). The conversation was good, as was the soccer game. My daughter was the goalkeeper; his was a forward. She scored three goals on mine.

Later in the summer, I went to Myeengun's office to learn more about justice from the Ojibway perspective. His space was inviting. Many hundreds of Indigenous students travel through it. He told me that the Ojibway view community holistically. This also extends to their conception of justice. When harm occurs, everyone has a responsibility to repair it. Within this there are some specific roles. The warriors help with peacekeeping; the Elders remind people of their responsibilities to each other. Offenders are encouraged to take responsibility and to heal. Victims are given safe space to heal. The traditional healers share medicines.

When there's been a violent act, the Ojibway warriors are expected to help. According to Myeengun, these are not camouflaged, masked, or aggressive people. The Ojibway warrior is a peacekeeper; someone who looks after the best interests of the community. Their efforts toward justice aren't about punishment. In fact, the Ojibway language doesn't have a word or a term for punishment. Instead, justice is about reminding everyone of their responsibility to each other, to the Creator, and to Mother Earth. Everyone in the community has a responsibility to live up to. By committing harm, they're failing to do this.

Together with the Elders, warriors ensure that the person who caused harm acknowledges it and resolves it together with the families of those harmed. If the parties themselves are unable to do this on their own, the Elders intervene using spiritual ceremonies and traditional practices to encourage peace. If still unsuccessful, the Elders make a decision about how to resolve the situation in the best interests of the whole community. Elders don't take sides; there's no "us" and "them"—only one community. Elders want to know what led to a person causing harm—where and why they stopped living up to their obligations. It is understood that crime comes from somewhere deeper. Elders want to create space where those hurt can talk about it. In very rare cases, where nothing else has worked, an offender might be banished from the community. However, Ojibway from other regions often take them in. As a medicine person, Myeengun helps investigate, probe, and get people talking in a safe way, in circles, about what is happening. These can be tough conversations.

Significantly, Ojibway justice is much more about a way of living than it is a particular intervention. Justice is never separate from a relationship with the land. About this, Myeengun says:

> We are the Indigenous peoples of this land. The land is everything. It's our mother. That's our link between Indigenous peoples—it's the land. The land is where we find our link. Being a part of creation, not above or below it. We need to be here like plants, medicines, and water. What we see in life today are scientists, people being separate or superior to the earth. We are equal to the earth. We're part of it. We're not separate. We feel separate, though, because of our relationship with Canadian government. We have to show people that we are the defenders of the land. We have to look after generations to come for the safety and well-being of the land. Defending the land in their actions—that's what Native people are doing. When we see a Native person disrupting a government process, it's because of environmental disruption of land, medicines, and waters. That's what we teach our kids right now. The land carries us from life to death. Mother earth gives health. She is a twin to the moon. Out of her everything is born.

I'm grateful to learn from Myeengun's wisdom. Ojibway justice isn't representative of how all Indigenous peoples view, or live, justice. However, from the little I've come to know, most forms of Indigenous justice are premised on similar themes of interconnection, wholeness, and healing, and many Indigenous justice practices are based on the idea that humans exist in a web of relationships, with each other and with creation. Rupert Ross, a Crown attorney, writes this after observing a circle justice meeting in his work with Indigenous communities in Northern Canada: "I stood at that door, looking into that room, seeing not empty chairs but a circle of people experiencing together the strength of interconnecting Creation through the drum, the circle and songs.... Until that moment I would have said, 'I, Rupert Ross, *have* relationships,' whereas the new perspective would require me to say, 'I, Rupert

Ross, *am* relationships."'[10] The shift from having, or owning relationships, to existing because of connection with other people was, for Ross, of the utmost importance. The Indigenous peoples he worked with didn't identify as individuals separate from community, but as individuals because of community.

To many Indigenous communities, the central premise of justice is healing. This is about wholeness, or the pursuit of it.[11] Métis scholar Craig Proulx says that following the teachings of the medicine wheel is the way to find wholeness: "The commission of a crime indicates a lack of spiritual balance within a person, and the healing process is intended to restore balance by uniting the four elements of the person: the spiritual, emotional, physical, and mental."[12] Balance must also be restored in the community, as justice is about healthy relationships.[13] The Anishinaabe people talk about "all my relations" as a way of describing living together, of which Proulx says: "A good life, respectfully lived is holistically based upon the seven grandfathers of caring, sharing, kindness, honesty, respect, bravery, and courage."[14]

Although distinct in some ways, Indigenous justice is often likened to restorative justice.[15] There are similarities in a focus on relationships and healing, particularly the healing of victims. In his book *Aboriginal Justice and the Charter: Realizing a Culturally Sensitive Interpretation of Legal Rights*, Cree law professor David Milward suggests that many Indigenous peoples—the Cree, the Anishinaabe, the Navajo, the Dene, the Twanas, the Clallams, the Puyallups, the Nisquallys, the Mi'kmaq, and the Coast Salish—had formal gift-giving procedures as a form of offender recompense and acknowledgement to victims.[16] The overall goal of Aboriginal justice is peacemaking— restoring harmony in relationships—and a constant acknowledgement of relationships in social practices.[17]

2. Roots of Restorative Justice in a Mennonite Peace Tradition

In 1974, in Kitchener, Ontario, a young probation officer named Mark Yantzi came up with another idea for "punishing" two young vandals who had damaged a number of properties in Elmira, Ontario. After meeting with a local peace club at the Mennonite Central Committee—a peace, justice, and development organization—Yantzi decided to suggest in a pre-sentence report that two young offenders should meet with their victims to better understand the harm they had done. In a 2004 article titled "How a Drunken Rampage Changed Legal History," the *Ottawa Citizen* describes it like this:

> Mr. Yantzi mentioned a pre-sentence report on two teens who had gone on a vandalism rampage in nearby Elmira. Wouldn't it be neat, he asked, if the two teens could meet their victims and find a way to compensate them for their losses?
>
> "I just threw it out as a kind of a brainstorm," he recalls. "And people said, 'yeah, that's a great idea.'" [...]
>
> The judge in the case, Gordon McConnell, considered himself a law-and-order magistrate. But he was tired of revolving-door justice, of seeing the same offenders back before him again and again. He was ready to try something different.

> Though Mr. Yantzi's idea was without precedent, Judge McConnell ordered Mr. Kelly and his co-accused to meet their victims, find out the cost of their damage, and pay for anything not covered by insurance.
>
> With that order, Mark Yantzi, the probation officer, and Russ Kelly, the youthful vandal, were forever linked as pioneers in the world's first restorative justice project.[18]

Without him realizing it, Yantzi's decision opened up a floodgate of possibility. This was the first instance of (modern) restorative justice in action. Yantzi was simply acting on some of his own cherished Mennonite values; however, since then, programs based on the Elmira Case have emerged all over the world.

As the restorative justice movement evolved in the 1980s, other Mennonites became involved. One of those was Howard Zehr, who started the first Victim Offender Reconciliation Program in the United States of America, modelled after Yantzi's work in Canada. In an effort to articulate their experiences, Zehr wrote a number of publications, including *Changing Lenses: A New Focus for Crime and Justice*, published in 1990. In it, Zehr describes a framework for understanding restorative justice, including the Mennonite (Christian) value of shalom as a unifying force for justice: "Shalom has to do with social relationships. God intends for people to live in right relationships with one another and with God. To live in shalom means that people live in peace, without enmity (but not necessarily without conflict!)"[19] With this central value, Mennonites like Yantzi and Zehr worked toward justice practices that value human relationships and that attempt to make things as right as possible when there is wrongdoing.

The worldview of restorative justice I'm proposing and describing in this book isn't necessarily Indigenous or Mennonite (Christian). Personally, I don't look at restorative justice as a spiritual practice or as a practice of which one group of people has ownership. As significant as the two histories I've just described are, restorative justice ultimately means a community coming together to determine what is most just in their context.

RESTORATIVE JUSTICE IN PRACTICE

Since its advent in youth justice in the 1970s, restorative justice has become a social movement. Its practices go well beyond criminal justice and it has been written about in many academic disciplines, like criminology, social work, and education. Restorative justice is used in schools, child welfare systems, workplaces, and so on. Its practices fall into two main streams: contact-based, involving some type of encounter between victims, offenders, and communities; and support-based, or focusing solely on one group of stakeholders, like offenders.

Contact-based restorative justice practices are mainly about bringing together victims and offenders, where appropriate, for some type of dialogue or encounter. I have called these practices "contact," because face-to-face dialogue isn't always an appropriate option. Sometimes programs use letters, video exchanges, or even shuttle mediation (where the mediator carries messages back and forth between the parties). Typically, these encounters are mediated by someone trained in the practices of restorative justice and, ideally, someone who has an understanding about the dynamics of harm, crime, and trauma. Processes are always voluntary, with participants deciding whether or not they would like to be involved.

Prior to bringing people together, mediators explain the process separately to participants and assess victims and offenders for suitability. Offenders should be willing to take some responsibility for their behaviour, acknowledging that they've perpetrated harm and recognizing that it was wrong. Victims should be prepared for the difficult nature of meeting face to face with someone who has caused them harm. This can be emotionally taxing, and requires preparation and support on both sides.

The process of preparation is called case development. During this time, mediators will get a sense of participants' willingness and readiness to engage with the process. This usually involves discussion in the following areas:

- What happened
- How participants have been affected
- Building in supports: personal and professional
- Any underlying mental health challenges
- Any underlying addictions or coping strategies
- Goals for participating in restorative justice
- What they would like to say or ask during a restorative justice encounter
- Understanding what will make them feel as safe as possible during the process
- Other people they might want to be present during the encounter
- What they will need for follow up

Case development can take many meetings. Sometimes mediators will stop the process, realizing that a person isn't ready for it. Or sometimes participants themselves will realize that a restorative justice meeting isn't what they need. In her research on victim-offender meetings in the aftermath of violent crime, Susan L. Miller has found that victims at times experience case development as more meaningful than the encounter itself.[20]

Depending on the participants' readiness, and the seriousness of the crime, case development can take months or even years. Encounters have different purposes. Some encounters are agreement focused. Their purpose is to craft an agreement that will be returned to courts as an outcome. Some of these agreements include what has been discussed, as well as proposed steps for restitution and taking responsibility. Other practices focus primarily on dialogue. These types of encounters are more concerned with people being able to express thoughts and feelings to each other. As well, some mediators, like those who follow the restorative practice approach of the International Institute of Restorative Practices (a graduate school that teaches on the topic of restorative justice), use a more scripted approach to dialogue, where mediators/practitioners follow a specific set of questions. Other approaches are more fluid.

Furthermore, contact programs typically fall under three streams: victim-offender mediation, family group conferencing, or Circle processes. Each has particular nuances in how the process functions. The primary difference, though, is in who is included. In the first category (victim-offender mediation), the group is small—victim, offender, mediator(s), and maybe a support person or two. In the second (family group conferencing), the families of victims and, particularly, offenders are included. This model, in fact, is used in New Zealand as the primary way of dealing with youth crime. The third category (Circle processes), involve family members and the extended community. As can be seen from type one to type three, the number of stakeholders is not only increasing, so is the idea of whose voice matters in the process. As family and community members become involved, they too have an equal say about the impacts and outcomes of restorative justice.

Within the contact-based stream of restorative justice practices, there are also programs that exist outside of the criminal justice system. For example, many school boards are using restorative justice to handle conflict and violent situations. As well, some movement is occurring within child protection systems to give family more power in decision-making. These programs are often called Family Group Decision Making. Here, practitioners function more like facilitators, making sure that all the necessary parties are invited to a meeting. Once child protection experts establish the parameters of child safety, families are left alone to decide a plan of care for a child. Although outside the scope of this book, this type of restorative justice is worth further exploration in relation to youth justice, as there's significant crossover between youth justice and child protection systems.

Support-based restorative justice programs have been developed where contact between direct victims and offenders is either not needed, or undesirable. Some support programs work solely with victims, others only with offenders. Similar to encounter-based restorative justice, the focus of support-based initiatives is to work toward meeting the needs of the population being served.

In the sections that follow, I'll describe four different restorative justice practices. Three of these fall into the category of contact-based and one is representative of support-based interventions.

Peacemaking Circles

The purpose of a peacemaking Circle is to respond to a crime in ways that respect the needs and concerns of everyone involved, with the ultimate goal being community or human development.[21] That is, the aim of a Circle process is the holistic healing of all and the restoration of unity.[22]

Why a Circle? In North America, Circle processes emerged from Indigenous traditions and teachings. Indigenous teacher and Circle keeper Antone Grafton says that, "the circle is an expression of life itself."[23] Furthermore, a Circle is symbolic of the medicine wheel, an Indigenous representation of the universe. The medicine wheel is depicted by a circle divided up into four quadrants. Each quadrant can represent, among other things, one of four gifts of life: the emotional, the spiritual, the physical, and the mental.[24] The medicine wheel balances diversity and there is no hierarchical order to these quadrants.[25] It's a reminder that there's wholeness, unity, and connectedness in the universe.

Crime disrupts this unity. When a disruption occurs the connection is broken and people must relearn to be connected to each other.[26] According to this worldview of interconnectedness, circle experts Kay Pranis, Barry Stuart, and Mark Wedge in *Peacemaking Circles: From Crime to Community* suggest that, "our connectedness gives us the responsibility to care for each other and to help mend the webs that hold us."[27] A Circle process provides an avenue for doing this.

How do Circles work? According to Circle practitioners Pranis et al., the first step toward accomplishing a successful Circle is to create a safe space where everyone can talk and be heard.[28] To accomplish this there are essential values, understood and created by all during a Circle, that act as a guide. Pranis et al., who have conducted Circles all over the world, have discovered that people from all regions identify similar values as important for human interaction.[29] The 10 most cited values are respect, honesty, humility, sharing, courage, inclusivity, empathy, trust, forgiveness, and love.[30]

Figure 8.1: Ten Most Commonly Cited Circle Values

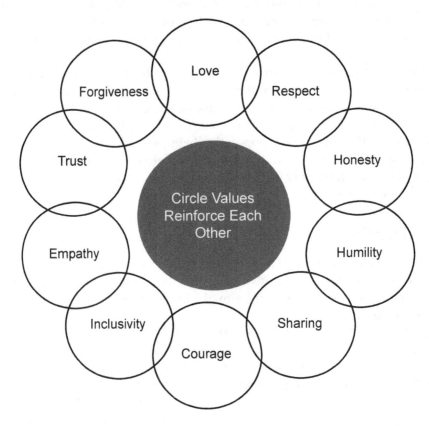

Source: Pranis et al., *Peacemaking Circles*, 47.

It should be noted that people understand individual values differently. Thus, as Pranis et al. say, it's important for participants to identify and define values at the beginning of a Circle process.[31] This is an ongoing process and can often take days to accomplish, but is essential for the success of a Circle.[32]

There are five elements that support the operation of a Circle: Circle keeping, a talking piece, guidelines, ceremonies, and consensus decision-making.[33] The Circle keeper plays an important role in a Circle process. According to Pranis et al.: "[k]eepers are the caretakers and servants of the Circle."[34] It's their responsibility to support the process, but the keeper isn't solely responsible for the outcome.[35] The keeper's power is limited to that which is given by the participants in a Circle, and all are responsible for the outcome of the process.[36] At a logistical level, the Circle keeper does the preparation leading up to a Circle, such as inviting all attendees. During the Circle process it's their job to ensure that the process is equally empowering to all participants. The Circle keeper sets the tone, facilitates the dialogue, balances all interests and perspectives, helps to protect the integrity of the process, regulates the pace of the Circle, welcomes new people, and maintains focus by proposing appropriate questions or themes for sharing. Moreover, the Circle keeper is to participate as themselves, not as an arm's-length professional, and never using their position to impose their own views on others.[37]

A Circle can operate as follows: Each person takes a turn sharing. While one person is talking, no one else talks. Sharing proceeds in one direction, often clockwise, depending on the tradition. Often a talking piece is used to promote healthy sharing. A talking piece is an object held by whoever is sharing. When the speaker has finished, they pass it on to an adjacent person. Usually, a talking piece is an object of significance to the participating members. For example, some Indigenous communities use an eagle feather. (The eagle is considered to be close to the Creator, and reserved for those who have done something remarkable for their community.)[38] What's more, choosing a meaningful talking piece promotes the idea that a Circle is a sacred space.[39]

Circles have guidelines. These are based on the aforementioned principles and values. It's the responsibility of the keeper to explain to participants this connection between guidelines and principles, thus, assisting in putting values into practice.[40] Here are some guidelines suggested by Pranis et al.: respect the talking piece, speak from the heart, speak with respect, listen with respect, remain in the Circle, and honour confidentiality.[41]

Finally, Circle processes are logistically about consensus decision-making. All of the components I've described—values, the Circle keeper, the talking piece, guidelines and ceremonies—indicate this very fact. As much as possible, these components create avenues for using human potential to respond to crime in ways that cultivate positive development and create consensus decision-making.

This is the transformative nature of Circle processes, the ability that Circle processes have to put things as right as possible. Together, a group decides which values are most important to them and to their process. These values shape the guidelines of the process and the process itself. The Circle keeper provides a safe space where these values are put into action. The talking piece fosters a safe space and allows opportunities for all to share, listen and reflect to transform crime. Ceremonies remind participants of their interconnectedness and encourage respect for all.

Figure 8.2: Circle Guidelines

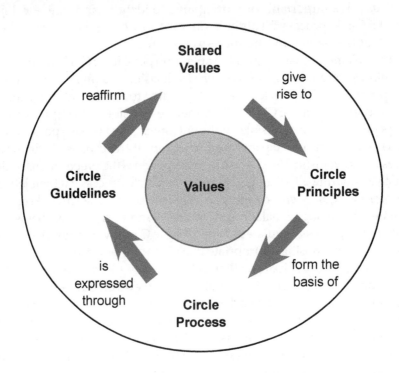

Source: Pranis et al., Peacemaking Circles, 104.

Family Group Conferencing

In their work *The Little Book of Family Group Conferences New Zealand Style*, Allan MacRae and Howard Zehr describe the beginnings of family group conferencing (FGC). Similar to the troubles seen in the Canadian youth justice system today, in the 1980s New Zealand faced an overrepresentation of Maori—their Indigenous population—in the youth justice system. The Maori people argued that the New Zealand model of justice was a colonial imposition, foreign to how they would traditionally carry out justice. As such, in 1989, the entire youth justice system was revamped to make restorative justice, or FGC, the primary response of youth justice. According to MacRae and Zehr:

> Although it did not use this terminology until later, the New Zealand legal system became the first in the world to institutionalize a form of restorative justice. Family Group Conferences became the hub of New Zealand's entire juvenile justice system. In New Zealand today, an FGC, not a courtroom, is intended to be the normal site for making such decisions.[42]

MacRae and Zehr identify seven goals and seven principles of FGCs:

Goals:

1. Diversion: keeping young people out of courts.
2. Accountability: young people are encouraged to accept responsibility.
3. Involving the victim: victims' needs are an important part of the process.
4. Involving and strengthening offenders' families: Family members should be involved.
5. Consensus decision-making: outcomes are to be agreed upon by all participants.
6. Cultural appropriateness: adaptations should be made depending on the culture of participants.
7. Due process: the young person's rights must be protected.[43]

Principles:

1. Criminal proceedings should be avoided unless the public interest requires otherwise.
2. Criminal justice processes should not be used to provide assistance (i.e., for child welfare decisions).
3. Families should be strengthened.
4. Children should be kept in the community if at all possible.
5. The child or young person's age must be taken into account.
6. Personal development should be promoted using the least restrictive option.
7. The interests of victims should be considered.[44]

One judge, Fred McElrea, who has been involved with FGC since its inception in New Zealand, describes it as a shift from state control of justice toward restorative justice: "[There is a] transfer of power from the state, principally the courts' power, to the community; the FGC as a mechanism for producing a negotiated, community response; the involvement of victims as key participants, making possible a healing process for both offender and victim."[45]

What have the results been? Within a year of implementation, FGC was able to reduce the number of youth justice cases coming before the courts by half.[46] To date, victims and offenders have been largely satisfied both with the process and outcomes. Some FGC has also been implemented in Australia, and one study in New South Wales found that 90 percent of offenders and 79 percent of victims were satisfied with their conference.[47] Particularly in the area of violent crime, young people who went to a conference were much less likely to reoffend than those who had not.[48] Conferencing, overall, in one study was found to reduce reoffending by 15 to 20 percent.[49] Reporting on another study, researchers Hennessey Hayes and Kathleen Daly describe the successes of FGC:

> Maxwell and Morris (2001) followed 108 young offenders who attended family group conferences in 1990 and 1991 for 6.5 years to learn how features of the conference relate to future offending. Using data from post-conference

convictions, they found that more than a quarter (28 percent) of young offenders were "persistent reconvicted" (i.e., appeared in court on criminal matters five or more times during the follow-up period). A similar proportion (29 percent) were not reconvicted at all during the follow-up period. They developed a model of reoffending, which showed that early negative life events (e.g., poverty and parental neglect) and what happened after the conference (e.g., unemployment, criminal associates) were predictive of future offending behaviour. However, several features of the conference also were predictive. When young offenders' conferences were memorable, when they were not made to feel a bad person, when they participated in, agreed to and complied with the outcome decision, when they met the victim and offered an apology and when they felt sorry for what they had done, reoffending was less likely.[50]

Hayes and Daly summarize the research on FGC, saying that reoffending is less likely when offenders are remorseful and conference outcomes are consensual.[51] Research has consistently demonstrated that the younger the offender, the more likely they are to reoffend in the future. However, Hayes and Daly discovered that conferencing actually works best for younger offenders.[52]

Victim–Offender Conferencing

People often wonder why a victim would want to meet with an offender. Why would someone who has been sexually assaulted want to meet with the person who offended against them? Why would a mother want to meet with the person who murdered her child? In *After the Crime: The Power of Restorative Justice Dialogues Between Victims and Violent Offenders*, Susan L. Miller describes an encounter between a victim and an offender:

> In May 2001, a drunk driver killed eighteen-year-old Cameron. Jenny, the driver, was nineteen years old when she crashed into Cameron's car, having run a red light at eighty-two miles per hour. Her blood-alcohol concentration was 0.14. She pled guilty and was convicted of first-degree vehicular homicide.... She received three years in prison and two years of house arrest ... Since Jenny was on work release and no longer incarcerated, the dialogue occurred in a conference room at a private business. Leigh [Cameron's mother] and Jenny faced each other across a table.... Leigh began by reading a statement to Jenny that detailed the impact that Jenny's choices had on her family. Leigh was very articulate in describing the grief they had experienced, how impotent she felt in helping her other children grieve and move forward ... Leigh concluded with the questions she wanted to raise: "What about [you]? How has this affected you? Are you the same person now as when you killed my son? What were you then? What will you become?"[53]

There are many reasons for offenders and victims to meet, some explained in the section above on victim needs. In Leigh's case, she seemed to want to know how Jenny would make the most of the tragedy.

Two themes often emerge when I'm facilitating dialogue between victims and offenders in cases of serious crime. One, victims have questions. Why did you do this? Why me? What were my loved one's last words? What actually happened? Second, victims want to ensure that what happened to them never happens to anyone else. As such, they want to know that the offender is taking responsibility by making changes. For example, if the offender is a person who has offended sexually, the victim will want to know that the offender is in therapy, working to understand why they did what they did. If the offender was drinking and driving, victims want to know how an offender is managing their substance abuse problem. If the offender is someone who has killed another person, a victim might want to know what they're doing to "get on the right track" to make healthy choices in the future.

In a similar vein, people often wonder why an offender would want to meet with a victim. In some ways—and according to some offenders—it's easier to do their time in prison than it is to face the people they've hurt. All the same, offenders often feel an obligation to meet with their victims, a desire to apologize, and to demonstrate to victims that they're more than their offence. Many offenders have told me they wanted to apologize during a court process, but that their lawyers recommended that they not. Offenders often carry heavy feelings of shame and are looking for opportunities to restore a sense of dignity for themselves and for others. In fact, many scholars and practitioners within the restorative justice movement have explored the topic of shame at great length to demonstrate that it's often a root cause of violence, as well as something that increases after a person behaves violently toward another.

A Case Study of Victim-Offender Conferencing
By Arley Irvine, Youth Service Coordinator, Community Justice Initiatives, Kitchener

One winter night Steve was out partying with his friends, using drugs and alcohol. They decided to walk to someone else's house. While on the way Steve got separated from his friends and became disorientated and cold.

Steve has little recollection of the night. At 3:30 a.m., an elderly couple, Martin and June, were awoken by the sound of a window in their sunroom being smashed. Martin got out of bed and walked with his cane to their sunroom to find glass everywhere, and a young man lying on the floor, not moving, with obvious signs of injury. June called the police, and when the officers arrived they woke up Steve, arrested him, and took him to the station.

The officers politely told the couple that they would take care of it from here—as if this statement was to answer all their questions and put their fears at ease. The criminal justice system had now taken over, and the first thing done was the removal of the victim from the process. The elderly couple spent the night at their son's house.

Steve was later released to his father and went through the typical proceedings. However, the elderly couple was still reeling from the experience. They no longer felt comfortable sleeping in their home and spent most of their time at their son's place. They were left with many questions. Who was this boy? Was he alright? What did he want from us, to rob us, hurt us? Will he or his friends be back; are we a target in this neighbourhood?

Steve's case was diverted from the court to Community Justice Initiatives (CJI). He met with volunteer mediators to tell his story about how this was just a bad night for him, there was no ill intent, and he stated that he had hoped his blood didn't stain their carpet.

The elderly couple was invited but reluctant to participate in mediation. However, they chose to do so with the accompaniment of their son—who was also very angry.

Mediation began and everyone was very nervous. The first statement spoken was by Martin, and he asked, "Were you alright?" Steve looked up and said, "Yes... I'm sorry." Later Steve told CJI staff that he couldn't believe the first thing Martin asked was how he was doing. Steve thought he was going to yell and call him names. The mediation was transformative for everyone involved. Steve wanted to pay back the cost for the window. The couple told him not to worry about it, but Steve insisted he wanted to do something. They agreed Steve would shovel their driveway for the next month.

As restitution, Steve would go over after school and shovel the driveway. June often baked cookies for Steve to take home. This relationship lasted longer than the initial agreed-upon month, and in the spring Steve cleaned up their yard and continued to visit. Six months later, Steve, Martin and June were still in contact, and Steve would help out with the odd job. All participants agreed this restorative justice process tremendously exceeded their expectations.

Support-Based Restorative Justice

Obviously, in many situations of crime, contact between victims and offenders isn't appropriate. Furthermore, not all victims, or offenders for that matter, want or need contact. However, each person affected by crime needs some kind of support to address harms. For this reason, restorative justice programs that are simply about supporting victims have been developed, as have other programs that attempt to meet the needs of offenders alone. Support programs typically have therapeutic goals.

One example of a relationship-based support program working with offenders is Circles of Support and Accountability (CoSA). Although CoSA primarily works with adults, it provides a model of what might be possible for youth. CoSA is a reintegration and community-building program that works with high-risk sex offenders upon their release from prison. In Canada, rather than release a person partway through their sentence at Statutory Release (two-thirds of sentence in prison, one-third in community), those offenders who are considered to be most dangerous to public safety can be held in prison until warrant expiry, or until the very last day of their sentence. CoSA is mandated to work with these individuals.

CoSA's mission is twofold: first, no more victims, and second, do no harm. Recognizing that offenders, especially this population, need healthy relationships in order to reduce isolation, CoSA, as its name highlights, is one part support, another part accountability. The Circles of Support and Accountability training manual created by Correctional Service of Canada mentions, among others, the following values as foundational:

- We **affirm** that the community bears a responsibility for the safe restoration and healing of victims as well as the safe re-entry of released sex offenders to the community.
- We **acknowledge** the ongoing pain and need for healing among victims and survivors of sexual abuse and sexual assault.
- We **seek** to "recreate community" with former offenders in responsible, safe, healthy, and life-giving ways.
- We **accept** the challenge of radical hospitality, sharing our lives with one another in community and taking risks in the service of love.[54]

One of the incredible things about this program is that it is primarily community volunteers who walk with the men (and a few women) upon release. The offender, or core member (as he or she is called), meets regularly with a circle of volunteers. These volunteers help with day-to-day needs, such as housing and medical or other appointments. Volunteers also keep the core member accountable. What have they been doing? Who have they been connecting with? How are they doing? And it works! Longitudinal studies of CoSA have found that in comparison to a control group it dramatically reduces recidivism. Psychologist Robin Wilson and his colleagues have tracked the program for a number of years and have found a 70 percent reduction in sexual recidivism.[55] CoSA is a prime example of a trauma-informed approach to justice. Core members are made to feel safe, connected, and supported, while also being held to account for their harmful behaviour.

CRITIQUES OF RESTORATIVE JUSTICE

Many critiques of restorative justice have been made since its implementation. A number of early critiques have been from the victim services movement. However, critiques have diminished over time, as restorative justice programs have done well to listen and to respond. In this section, I'll outline eight common critiques of restorative justice.

1. Restorative justice risks framing domestic and sexual violence as non-serious crimes: This line of critique states that, as crimes of domestic and sexual violence get diverted to restorative justice programs, people might perceive that these crimes are not "serious."[56] That is, the public associates diversionary programs such as restorative justice programs with less serious crimes. This would be a step backward for the victim movement, which has struggled throughout the last four decades to make domestic and sexual violence "legitimate" crimes with serious consequences. For example, male violence directly impacts victims, but also all women through a culture that promotes rape and sexual violence. Critics are concerned that restorative justice practices, by only focusing on a single incident of violence, are detrimental to eliminating a culture that promotes rape and sexual violence.

2. Restorative justice practitioners aren't sensitive to victim needs and trauma: Victim advocates are, understandably, concerned for the safety of victims. Some feel that restorative justice practitioners have, at times, failed to adequately consider safety issues in bringing together victims and offenders.[57] There has also been some concern that, at times, victims aren't being included in the planning of restorative justice programs, and that practitioners aren't receiving sufficient training about trauma.[58] As the restorative justice movement has evolved, this issue has become less of a concern. Most practitioners are now trained in trauma. However, more needs to be done to help practitioners understand feminist and post-colonial perspectives.

3. Restorative justice practitioners aren't sensitive to manipulative offenders: Researchers Lois Presser and Emily Gaarder argue that practitioners need to be more aware of when engagement of victim with offender is an appropriate restorative justice response. Many offenders who commit domestic or sexual violence are manipulative and, as such, the worry is that a restorative justice response may do more damage to victims.[59]

4. Restorative justice offers no role for the government in these situations: Critics wonder if restorative justice adequately denounces criminal offences or, in other words, if it clearly shows society-at-large that an offence is wrong.[60] Trauma expert Judith Herman suggests that governments must play a role in condemning criminal acts, as this is what truly vindicates and allows victims to reintegrate into communities.[61]

5. Restorative justice definitions, terms, and goals are problematic: There are many restorative justice terms that those in the victim movement are uncomfortable with, especially when it comes to using these terms in response to crimes of domestic and sexual violence. For example, terms such as restorative, restitution, reconciliation, and mediation can be problematic. Many restorative justice programs are called Victim Offender Mediation (VOM). Victims groups are uncomfortable with the term mediation because it suggests that the parties enter the process on an equal footing and minimizes a crime to the level of a dispute, thereby erasing the experience of victimization.[62] Furthermore, many restorative justice programs encourage reconciliation. In fact, early VOM programs were often called Victim Offender Reconciliation Programs. Reconciliation implies, for many victim advocates, that a woman is to be reconciled with her abuser, and as such is supposed to stay in a violent relationship.[63] Moreover, with regard to restorative justice goals, critics of restorative justice consider some goals to be unrealistic, promising much more than they can deliver.[64]

6. Restorative justice is offender-oriented: While claiming to be victim-centred, some restorative justice programs have actually been quite the opposite and have been much more focused on offenders. Judith Herman wonders how a movement like restorative justice, which grew out of wanting to help offenders, can speak to victim needs.[65] Indeed, many restorative justice programs provide little victim relief while offering much for offenders.[66] Furthermore, restorative justice programs are reactive and limited to processes where the offender is caught, admits guilt, and wants to participate—as such, few victims will benefit.[67]

7. Restorative justice programming is limited: Encounter- or contact-based restorative justice between victim and offender isn't appropriate in some situations, yet restorative justice programs usually only offer encounter-based programs.[68] Moreover, restorative justice programs have historically not been properly evaluated and held accountable for their actions and decisions.[69]

8. Restorative justice programming further individualizes crime: By using the same starting point as the criminal justice system, and with little attention to root causes, restorative justice risks over-individualizing crime.[70]

In light of these criticisms, restorative justice advocates have worked hard to do better. There are still some areas for growth; however, restorative justice programs—especially in the areas of youth justice, and more serious crimes—continue to score well in evaluations. Both victims and offenders are typically satisfied with restorative justice experiences.

CONCLUSION: RESTORATIVE JUSTICE IS AN EFFECTIVE INTERVENTION FOR YOUTH

Similar to the track records of family group conferences I described earlier in this chapter, most restorative justice programs for youth have very positive outcomes, including victim and offender satisfaction and reductions in recidivism. Young offenders who go through restorative justice programming had significantly less future police contact, and fewer serious behaviours than those processed through the traditional criminal justice system.[71] Even with serious crimes, like sexual assault, research into restorative justice methods is demonstrating promising results. In a 2013 study titled "Youth Sex Offending, Recidivism and Restorative Justice: Comparing Court and Conference Cases," researchers Daly, Bouhours, Broadhurst, and Loh found evidence that restorative justice reduced recidivism. Although there were some challenges with the methodology, overall, the researchers found a decrease in future offences in low-risk youth sex offenders and no increase in future offences for those deemed high risk.[72] A study of Teen Courts (a diversionary, restorative justice approach in the United States) also found reduced recidivism, even with second-time offenders. Those who went through the Teen Court were also more successful in completing sentencing requirements. The authors conclude that juvenile offenders experienced restorative justice as more fair, and valued the opportunity to provide input into how to make things right.[73] Using researcher Heather Strang's benchmarks for identifying victim satisfaction, "a less formal process where their views count, more information about both the processing and the outcome of their case, to participate in their case, to be treated respectfully and fairly, material restoration, [and] emotional restoration, including apology,"[74] criminologist John Braithwaite conducted a literature review of numerous restorative justice evaluations. He found victim satisfaction to be higher overall than in traditional criminal justice.[75] Ultimately, much of the success of restorative justice appears to be its orientation toward a more relational focus for justice. It is this that makes it suitable as a framework for supporting trauma-informed youth justice.

Dr. Daniel Reisel, a neuroscientist from the United Kingdom, articulates some of his perspective on restorative justice in an evocative TED talk: "The Neuroscience of Restorative Justice." According to Reisel, the brain is able to change and grow, even into adulthood. This is called **neurogenesis**: the growth of new neurons. In his study of offenders with a history of psychopathy, Reisel discovered deficits in the amygdala, which in turn impacted their ability to empathize. Psychopathic offenders know the words, but not the music of empathy.[76] Reisel makes a pitch for restorative justice—relationally based—programming. He argues that stressful environments like prisons stunt future growth of the amygdala, while restorative justice programming creates new opportunities for neurogenesis, and thus the development of empathy.[77] In his view, this understanding is important for social change and can help us to evolve from our medieval approaches to criminal justice.[78]

Recall the work of Jennifer Llewellyn (**relational theory**) and the research of Lori Haskell and Melanie Randall (restorative justice in healing trauma), cited in chapter 1. Restorative justice provides a relational framework for healing the damage of trauma. It's a justice response that's premised on rebuilding connections and acknowledging that individuals exist because of relationships. And it's in the context of healthy relationships that a justice response can create a sensitive and secure base from which trauma can be healed.

GLOSSARY OF TERMS

Neurogenesis is the development of new neural pathways: brain regeneration. Neuroscientist Daniel Reisel researches how restorative justice processes allow for neurogenesis to occur.

Relational theory is premised on the idea that self-identity can only be defined in relation to others; that is, human beings are fundamentally relational creatures. Relational theory as applied to justice considers the individual in the context of relationships.

Restorative justice is a process to involve, to the extent possible, those who have a stake in a specific offence and to collectively identify and address harms, needs, and obligations in order to heal and put things as right as possible (as defined by Howard Zehr[79]).

QUESTIONS FOR REFLECTION

1. Given your own traditions—whether spiritual, familial, or other—is there anything familiar about a restorative justice framework that resonates with you? If so, what?
2. Research suggests that restorative justice is even more effective with serious crimes than with non-serious crimes. Does this surprise you? What might account for this?
3. Do you think it would be possible for Canada to create a youth justice system similar to New Zealand's, where the restorative justice option is the starting point? How might this be accomplished? What barriers to change would you identify?

RECOMMENDED READING

Miller, Susan L. *After the Crime: The Power of Restorative Justice Dialogues Between Victims and Violent Offenders.* New York: New York University Press, 2011.

This book describes the research of Susan Miller with victims and offenders of serious crime who have completed encounter-based restorative justice programs.

Pranis, Kay, Stuart, Barry, and Wedge, Mark. *Peacemaking Circles: From Crime to Community.* St. Paul: Living Justice Press, 2003.

A practical, as well as theoretical, guide to the restorative justice process of peacemaking Circles.

Weaver, Allan. *So You Think You Know Me?* Sheffield: Waterside Press, 2008.

In this autobiographical account, Allan Weaver describes how he grew up in a violent home, came in conflict with the law at a young age, served time in prison, and ultimately desisted from crime.

9 | Youth Justice as Trauma-Informed Care

"Unless someone like you cares a whole awful lot,
Nothing is going to get better. It's not."

—Dr. Seuss, *The Lorax*

This chapter outlines how youth justice might begin to work more carefully and effectively with the issues of individual and collective trauma. Trauma-informed youth justice means caring for victims, offenders, and communities who have been impacted by crime. One aspect of this is fostering resilience in survivors and communities. Another involves resisting systems that traumatize. Yet another aspect involves creativity—tapping into individuals' and communities' capacities for change, for wonder, for creativity, and for working toward creating a meaningful, fulfilling life for all. Fundamentally, this is about creating attachments to build a sensitive, secure base for trauma survivors and, for the purposes of our discussions, young people in the youth justice system. This means adopting an approach of trauma-informed care.

The term **trauma-informed care** is relatively new. Recently, people working in the field of trauma healing have talked about the need for practitioners to understand the impacts of trauma and to become sensitive to how certain practices can retraumatize people.[1] The expression "do no harm" is central to this way of addressing trauma.[2] This approach seeks to understand any iatrogenic affects of helping and justice practices. Treatment centres, child welfare, and—slowly—some areas of criminal justice have begun to adopt trauma-informed care.

This chapter will take a decidedly practical stance. After all, the work of trauma-informed care is hands-on. It's about how people relate to young offenders and to victims. It's about communication, about listening, about adopting a caring posture, and about creating a secure, relational base. When a young person has committed a crime, trauma-informed care doesn't let them avoid accountability. Rather, it holds them accountable from a place of kindness and respect. This isn't theoretical pie-in-the-sky. Trauma-informed care is possible, but it requires a certain belief about people. As human beings, we have the capacity to hurt each other, but we have an even greater ability to take responsibility and to care for one another. With young offenders, this means seeing beyond the facade—the tough-guy posturing. It means recognizing that behind the tattoos, piercings, or facial hair, and beyond the stoicism or erratic behaviour, is a person in need of nurturing, of connection, and of a meaningful existence.

Personally, I've found the work of writer Shannon Moroney to be inspiring in this regard. In her memoir *Through the Glass*, she writes about the devastation of being married to someone who has committed a violent crime.[3] Her journey toward resilience and healing hasn't been without anger and significant pain. Yet, she also talks about the need to attempt to understand why offenders do what they do. This isn't about letting them off the hook. From her perspective, it's a compassionate stance. When meeting with someone who has committed violent crimes, she talks about imagining that person as a five year old. This resonates with me. Behind the stone exterior of many offenders is a child, often someone who has shut down emotionally because of trauma. This person needs proper care: trauma-informed care.

This chapter is divided into two sections. The first examines a model for trauma-informed care based on resilience and relationships. I'll provide some practical tools for working with trauma survivors. The second section looks more specifically at trauma-informed care in the field of criminal justice—with victims, offenders, and communities impacted by crime.

TRAUMA-INFORMED CARE WITH INDIVIDUALS: RESILIENCE THROUGH RELATIONSHIPS

The purpose of trauma-informed care is to help foster resilience in the survivor. **Resilience** represents a person's capacity to deal with stress or adversity. It cannot be overstated that this is a fundamental shift needed in youth justice. As we saw in chapter 7, many of the efforts of the justice system are focused on risk (or deficits) and punishment. Transforming youth justice toward resilience means two things:

1. Tapping into the pre-existing strengths of people who have experienced trauma, and
2. Helping them to develop new, stronger capacities.

Essentially, a focus on resilience means developing well-being in individuals and communities. In their 2013 editorial in the *Journal of Child Psychology and Psychiatry*, researchers Catherine Panter-Brick and James F. Leckman state the following about resilience:

> Resilience offers the promise of a paradigm shift in many fields of research, clinical practice, and policy. A lens on resilience shifts the focus of attention—from efforts to appraise risk and vulnerability, towards concerted efforts to enhance strength or capability. It also shifts the focus of analysis—from asking relatively limited questions regarding health outcomes, such as what are the linkages between risk exposures and functional deficits, to asking

more complex questions regarding wellbeing, such as when, how, why and for whom do resources truly matter.[4]

Panter-Brick and Leckman define resilience as "the process of harnessing biological, psychological, structural, and cultural resources to sustain wellbeing."[5] Resilience is related to a person's internal capacities, like their ability to form attachments and to self-regulate. It also has to do with a person's access to relationships and with the availability of community resources.[6] As such, there's both an individual and a relational component. However, one of the lessons of resilience research is that it's less a character trait (although personality and temperament matter) and more a product of a person's environment. People often wonder why one person survives a certain type of situation and another does not. In the realm of youth justice, we know that most young people who experience trauma don't come into conflict with the law; however, those who do come into conflict with the law have predominantly had traumatic experiences in their lives. What differentiates the two groups? The answer typically lies in the young person's environment.

Resilience as a process isn't always available to everyone. Michael Ungar, the principal researcher at the Resilience Research Centre, Dalhousie University, says that resistance to trauma (or resilience) is "less a reflection of the individual's capacity to overcome life challenges as it is the capacity of the child's informal and formal social networks to facilitate positive development under stress."[7] Not only is this a fundamental shift in understanding how people survive—turning the focus away from the individual and toward the environment—but it also puts significant responsibility on those around a survivor of trauma (friends, family, professionals, and society) to help ensure that a process of resilience is available.

Alongside other international researchers, Ungar has developed a 28-point scale for studying resilience in youth, the Child and Youth Resilience Measure-28 (CYRM-28):

1. I cooperate with people around me.
2. I aim to finish what I start.
3. People think I am fun to be with.
4. I solve problems without drugs or alcohol.
5. I am aware of my own strengths.
6. Spiritual beliefs are a source of strength for me.
7. I think it is important to serve my community.
8. I feel supported by my friends.
9. My friends stand by me during difficult times.
10. My caregivers watch me closely.
11. My caregivers know a lot about me.
12. I eat enough most days.
13. I talk to my caregivers about how I feel.
14. My caregivers stand by me during difficult times.
15. I feel safe when I am with my caregivers.
16. I enjoy my caregivers' cultural and family traditions.
17. Getting an education is important to me.

18. I feel I belong at my school.
19. I have people I look up to.
20. I know how to behave in different social situations.
21. I am given opportunities to become an adult.
22. I know where to go to get help.
23. I have opportunities to develop job skills.
24. I am proud of my ethnic background.
25. I am treated fairly in my community.
26. I participate in organized religious activities.
27. I enjoy my community's traditions.
28. I am proud of my citizenship.[8]

Research on the Child and Youth Resilience Measure-28 has found the factors it outlines to be significant, although Ungar and his co-authors suggest that there are particular nuances based on the culture of the young person that must be recognized. Resilience has some global components (i.e., that relate to everyone) but it also has some culturally specific aspects.[9] Notice how numbers 8 to 18 are about friends, family, caregivers, and whether a person feels like they belong at school. These are all components of a process of resilience, and explain why it isn't available to everyone. Ultimately, Ungar makes three conclusions about resilience: First, nurture trumps nature when coping with trauma; that is, biology is less important than the environment. Second, the environment can have different impacts on resilience; when faced with a difficult situation, some grow while others are traumatized. As much as there are general themes in resilience, each case must be considered uniquely. Third, cultural variations matter; people from different cultures tend to process traumas in different ways.[10]

A MODEL FOR TRAUMA-INFORMED CARE

Trauma-informed care is about promoting well-being. Its purpose is to increase the resilience of individuals and communities. The more we can help young people to face adversity, the less likely they'll be to cause harm in their communities. Furthermore, when we increase resilience in victims they're better able to cope with the damage caused by crime. The foundation of trauma-informed care is safety. Victims won't be able to heal until they feel safe, and the same is true for offenders. What's more, until they feel safe, offenders will not become fully accountable for their crimes.

The need for trauma survivors to feel safe cannot be overstated. After all, the predominant experience of trauma is one of feeling unsafe, both in the moment of trauma and afterwards. As psychiatrist Sandra Bloom says:

> Psychological trauma refers to the ability to be safe with oneself, to rely on one's ability to self-protect against any destructive impulses coming from within oneself or deriving from other people and to keep oneself out of harm's way. This ability to self-protect is one of the most shattering losses that occurs as a result of traumatic experience, particularly childhood trauma.[11]

As such, re-establishing a feeling of safety is the first step to trauma-informed care. Trauma expert Judith Lewis Herman argues that "the guiding principle of trauma recovery is to restore power and control to the survivor."[12] In the following section I will give some practical examples for how to work with trauma survivors to re-establish a sense of safety. The examples will fall under the following categories: helpful ways to communicate with a survivor, taking a position of respect, using strengths-based practice, and being a healthy practitioner.

1. Communicate in a Way That's Safe

Validate: It's vital that survivors' stories be believed. As a general rule, people don't make up stories of trauma. Secondly, one of the impacts of trauma is that survivors often blame themselves, which only adds to their trauma. (Even though survivors might know intellectually that it wasn't their fault, believing it at an emotional level can be difficult.) For this reason, communicating to the survivor that you believe their story and that what happened to them wasn't their fault can help with healing. Validating their experiences is the first step in establishing safety.

Acknowledge: Validation is a form of acknowledgement. What happened to the trauma survivor was wrong. It's okay for them to feel whatever they might feel about it. Some will be angry or devastated, others confused or numb. Acknowledge the person's feelings. Acknowledge their pain. Don't pretend to know what they're going through, but name what you hear.

Normalize: When people are traumatized, they often feel like they're going crazy. The flood of emotions and triggers can be destabilizing. It's helpful to normalize their response to trauma by saying something like, "It makes sense to me that you'd feel that way, given what you've experienced."

Listen: Listening is a skill. It can be developed over time. It's about paying close attention and adopting an open posture. Reflect back to the person what you're hearing, sometimes summarizing, other times asking questions. It takes patience, stamina, and self care to be present with a person as they talk about their pain. Avoid over-talking (i.e., saying things to fill space). Silence is okay. Be present. As Winston Churchill famously said about listening: "Courage is what it takes to stand up and speak; courage is also what it takes to sit down and listen."

Allow mourning: Provide space for grieving the loss caused by trauma. Give space for survivors to tell their stories.

Work toward empathy: Validation and acknowledgement are forms of empathizing. I'm convinced that the criminal justice system needs more professionals willing to put themselves in the shoes of victims and offenders. We know how to build walls to keep inmates in prison, but do we know how to build bridges to create understanding and empathy?

2. Take a Position of Respect

Seek informed consent: Be clear about the purpose or agenda of the task, or of your role. As much as possible, give people an opportunity to opt out. (Voluntary participation is better than coerced participation.) Of course, giving this choice isn't always possible. A young offender might be court ordered to participate in a program. As much as possible, however, find ways to give the person power and control over tasks.

Be nonjudgmental: Everyone brings their judgments, perspectives, and attitudes into work. Be aware of your own and of how they might impact your work. This is where empathy is vital. Try to remind yourself, "If I'd been through a similar life as this young offender, I'd likely be in the same spot as them now."

Honour diversity: People are diverse. They come from all walks of life, cultures, and perspectives, and have differing abilities. How will your work honour this? Does a person need help with language translation? Does a person have difficulty understanding a concept, or do they see the world in a very different way than you do? A position of respect honours diversity. Keep in mind that survivors might interpret experiences in very different ways than you would.

Be trustworthy: Survivors of trauma have diminished trust. It's vital that those involved in the work of trauma-informed care do what they say they're going to do. Follow through. Be authentic. Have integrity.

3. Use a Strengths-Based Approach

Foster resilience: Rather than focusing on what's "wrong" with the individual, trauma-informed care is strengths-based. It considers what's "right" with the person. What have they survived? How can this accomplishment of survival be built upon? This is about both internal and external resources. How can a support network be constructed for this person? Focusing on the deficits of individuals has proven to be limiting; however, research on strengths-based approaches has demonstrated that well-being improves through the development of positive self-regard, creativity, and affirmation.[13] Strengths-based approaches have been used with victims and offenders alike. Even where offenders have committed violence toward partners and children, this approach has been used as a way to promote accountability and change. In their research on this topic, Catherine A. Simmons and Peter Lehmann suggest the following as strengths-based core constructs for working with male batterers:

- facilitate client-directed change,
- focus on strengths and resources, not deficits and problems,
- [be] fair and respectful of clients regardless of the harm they have inflicted on others,
- put values of respect and social justice into action,

- enable clients to identify and embrace their unique personal, social, and cultural strengths and abilities, and
- assist clients in making changes that are meaningful, significant, and reflect how they want their lives to be lived.[14]

In her work written together with young people with mental health challenges, some of whom have experienced trauma, Angie Hart from Brighton University and her young co-authors suggest that a focus on resilience involves some "noble truths," or principles and beliefs that are of the utmost importance, for young peoples' parents.[15] They identify four principles that trauma-informed practitioners would do well to consider applying: one, accepting the situation as it is; two, focusing on good steps, even small ones; three, committing to be consistent and in for the long haul; and four, enlisting support when and where necessary.[16]

> **Resilience Tree Guidelines, the Resilience Research Centre**
>
> Ensure youth are involved in every step of their case plan and service delivery. Ask them:
>
> - What do you want to work on while you are here?
> - What is the biggest issue/challenge you are facing that you want help with?
> - Is there anything that you don't want to do while here?
> - What can I do to support you?
> - What are your goals and future plans?
> - What do you need in order to meet these goals?
>
> Provide youth with unconditional positive regard:
>
> - They will mess up, and that's okay. Continue to support them and help them to learn from the mistake.
> - Be consistent with them and leave your personal problems at home.
> - Youth appreciate when they know that you will react the same way each day. Don't let an occasional bad mood influence your work.
>
> Give youth power and choice:
>
> - Explain why rules are in place and consistently enforce the rules.
> - Rather than tell youth to do something, give them an option. For example, you can continue yelling at me and you will have to leave for the rest of the day, or you stop can yelling and continue with this activity.
> - When the rules can be bent, it is often helpful to bend them to show you care. For example, if there is a 5 minute phone call rule and the youth is in crisis and needs to use the phone for longer or is having the first good talk with his/her parents in years, let them talk a bit longer.[17]

Use the method of appreciative inquiry: As a methodology, Appreciative Inquiry (AI) was developed in the realm of organizational behaviour, as a participatory way of advancing the strengths of an organization.[18] According to AI, what we focus on becomes our reality.[19] Therefore, the more we focus on the positive, the more energy will be available for advancement. Social workers Avril Bellinger and Tish Elliott, citing the work of Hammond, describe other principles of AI:

- In every society, organization or group, something works.
- What we focus on becomes our reality.
- Reality is created in the moment, and there are a multitude of realities.
- The act of asking questions of an organization or group influences the group in some way.
- People have more confidence and comfort to journey to the future (the unknown) when they carry forward parts of the past (the known).
- If we carry parts of the past forward, they should be what is best about the past.
- It is important to value differences.
- The language we use creates our reality.[20]

Appreciative Inquiry Questions

The Kansas Coalition Against Sexual and Domestic Violence has created a resource for using Appreciative Inquiry to craft powerful questions. They offer some examples of Appreciative Inquiry questions in three areas: focusing attention, connecting ideas to gain deeper insight, and questions that foster forward movement.

Questions for focusing attention:

- What question, if answered, could make the most difference to the future of (your situation)?
- What's important to you about (your situation) and why do you care?
- What opportunities can you see in (your situation)?
- What are the dilemmas/opportunities in (your situation)?
- What assumptions do we need to test or challenge here in thinking about (your situation)?

Questions for connecting ideas and finding deeper insights:

- What had real meaning for you from what you've heard? What surprised you? What challenged you?
- What's missing from this picture so far? What is it we're not seeing? What do we need more clarity about?
- What's been your/our major learning, insight, or discovery so far?

- If there was one thing that hasn't yet been said in order to reach a deeper level of understanding/clarity, what would that be?

Questions that create forward movement:

- What would it take to create change on this issue?
- What's possible here and who cares?
- What needs our immediate attention going forward?
- If our success was completely guaranteed, what bold steps might we choose?
- How can we support each other in taking the next steps?
- What challenges might come our way and how might we meet them?
- What conversation, if begun today, could ripple out in a way that created new possibilities for the future of (your situation)?
- What seed might we plant together today that could make the most difference to the future of (your situation)?[21]

4. Be a Healthy Practitioner

Take a trauma-informed approach: It almost goes without saying that the starting point for the healthy practitioner is knowledge of trauma and its impacts. The next step is knowing how to support someone in a way that does no further harm. Being trauma-informed also means being comfortable hearing about—and talking about—traumatic issues. Grieving is a part of this. How comfortable are you being present with people as they mourn horrific experiences? Being self-aware is another component. In *The Trauma-Informed Toolkit*, the Klinic Community Health Centre has created some other important questions for trauma-informed practitioners to ask themselves:

- Is establishing trust and safety a priority in your work with people?
- Do you try to establish a genuine, caring connection with clients?
- Do you acknowledge to the client the difficulty and courage involved in talking about trauma?
- Do you respond to disclosure with belief and validation?
- Do you encourage the client to disclose only what they are comfortable sharing?
- Do you ask clients how they cope with the difficult feelings surrounding the trauma?
- Do you ask how they cope with difficult behaviours that may result from the trauma experience, such as substance abuse?
- Do you acknowledge the link between trauma, mental health, and addiction?
- Do you believe that trauma survivors are resilient and able to recover?
- Do you believe that you can affect positive change for clients?
- Do you dispel the many myths surrounding trauma in your work with people?
- Are you familiar with community resources for trauma survivors?

- Do you refer clients to trauma-recovery services?
- Do you advocate on behalf of clients who need assistance in accessing resources?
- Do you focus on clients' strengths and resources?
- Do you try to instill a sense of hope and change for clients?
- Do you work as a team with the client, letting them make decisions about their care?
- Do you consider clients' cultural backgrounds when making referrals and discussing community resources?
- Do you get an understanding of their issues from their cultural perspective?[22]

Practice selfcare: Judith Herman reminds us that "trauma is contagious."[23] Put another way, it can be traumatic to hear stories of trauma. Service providers sometimes experience feelings of despair and hopelessness. Self care must be a priority. Understanding why you do the work you do will give you some perspective. Also, having healthy boundaries and appropriate outlets for stress allows practitioners to take care of themselves while doing difficult work. Personally, my work gives me a sense of purpose. As much as it can be hard to hear stories of trauma, I find meaning in being able to offer support and care to people. At times, I do run out of steam. I get angry at systems that make things worse. I get angry when I observe people making things worse, and I want to give up. Over time, I've learned to accept what I can change and what I cannot. I'm also learning to accept what my role is. In the early stages of my career, a wise mentor once told me about the value of being a "half-hearted fanatic," someone who is passionate, but also realistic. Someone who works hard, but also rests. Someone who cares for others while also caring for themselves.

TRAUMA-INFORMED CARE WITH VICTIMS

> "A lot of activists hate the word 'victim,' but the truth is that we are. And the truth is that we've survived. I want to use both terms: I am a victim and I am a triumphant survivor. At first I was really a zombie, a walking dead woman. Now I'm alive."
>
> —Sandra Murphy[24]

It's important not to fully conflate the needs of victims with those of offenders, although there is some overlap. Part of the purpose of this book is to explain that most young offenders have been victims of crime. However, most victims don't go on to be offenders. And, if—as I'll be recommending in the upcoming chapters—we employ a restorative justice framework to a trauma-informed approach to youth justice, the needs of victims must come first. A number of scholars have tackled the issue of how best to support survivors. In the field of trauma, Sandra Bloom has developed the Sanctuary Model. In restorative justice, Howard Zehr has written at length about the needs of crime victims, and the work of Angie Hart focuses on resilience.

Sandra Bloom has created something called the Sanctuary Model of care with trauma survivors. As part of this work—implementing it in hospitals, as well as with youth in care facilities—she has found it helpful for service providers to start from the same basic set of assumptions about trauma. This allows for practitioners to avoid being distracted by difficult behaviours—anger, suicidality, self-harm—that can express themselves in survivors. Some of the shared assumptions guiding the Sanctuary Model are adapted in the box below. These represent a part of the knowledge component for the healthy practitioner (in the model articulated earlier in this chapter):

Shared Assumptions for the Sanctuary Model of Trauma Treatment
Taken and adapted from the work of Sandra Bloom

1. Post-traumatic stress reactions are the reactions of normal people to abnormal stress.
2. When people are traumatized in early life, the effects of trauma frequently interfere with normal development.
3. Trauma has impacts that spread across and down through the generations.
4. Many symptoms and syndromes are manifestations of adaptions, originally useful as coping skills that have now become maladaptive.
5. Victims of trauma can become trapped in time, caught in the repetitive re-experiencing of the trauma.
6. Dissociation and repression are core defences against overwhelming affect and are present, to a varying extent, in all survivors of trauma.
7. Memories of traumatic experiences must be assumed to have at least a basis in reality.
8. Traumatic experience and disrupted attachments combine to produce defects in the regulation and modulation of affect, of emotional experience.
9. People who are repeatedly traumatized may develop "learned helplessness," a condition that has serious biochemical implications.
10. Trauma survivors discover that various addictive behaviours restore at least a temporary sense of control over intrusive phenomena.
11. Many survivors develop secondary psychiatric symptomology. They become guilt-ridden, depressed, and exhibit low self-esteem and feelings of hopelessness and helplessness.
12. Trauma victims often have difficulty managing aggression.
13. Childhood abuse often leads to disrupted attachment behaviour, inability to modulate arousal and aggression toward self and others, impaired cognitive functioning, and impaired capacity to form stable relationships.
14. Although it may be a lifelong process, recovery from traumatic experiences is possible.[25]

In *Transcending: Reflections of Crime Victims*, Howard Zehr talks about crime victimization as comprehensive—affecting the whole person. He suggests that it creates a crisis of self-image, a crisis of meaning, and a crisis of relationship.[26] Since trauma affects identity a person asks, "Who am I really?" When meaning is undermined, they think, "What do I believe?" Relational damage, meanwhile, makes them wonder, "Whom can I trust?"[27] In response to these crises, Zehr uses the metaphor of a journey to describe the unique process of moving toward healing that victims must embark on. These four journeys represent pathways to resilience for victims:

1. **Journey toward meaning:** Zehr argues that human identity is created, and recreated, through storytelling. Victims, then, need to have safe space to share their stories and to make new ones, "To heal we have to recover our stories, but not just the old stories. We must create new or revised narratives that take into account the awful things that have happened. The suffering must become part of our stories. The re-creation of meaning requires the 're-storying' of our lives."[28]
2. **Journey toward honour:** Part of "re-storying" means transforming stories of humiliation and shame into stories of honour and dignity.[29] Zehr states, "When we are victimized, our status is lowered. We are humiliated by that event, but also often by the ways that we respond to that event—the things we did or didn't do at the time, the ways it affects us afterwards."[30] Victims need care in ways that help them to honour how they've survived.
3. **Journey toward vindication:** Zehr argues that victims seek reciprocity from the justice system.[31] In other words, victims need to experience some kind of payback for the wrong done to them. They also need a clear indication that what happened to them was inappropriate, or wrong. Revenge can be part of this, but as Zehr says, it is not the deepest need, or the only way to experience vindication.[32]
4. **Journey toward justice:** Advancing some of his previous ideas about restorative justice, Zehr suggests that justice for victims includes safe space, restitution, answers to questions, and "truth-telling"—or an opportunity to share their stories in a way that they define.[33] Zehr argues that the criminal justice system often gets in the way of this.[34] If it became more trauma-informed or gave victims more control (i.e., allowed them to better define their needs) some of this could be rectified.

Working with Young Youth and Children Who Have Been Victims
Taken and adapted from the work of Angie Hart et al.

Basics—the basic necessities needed for life:

Good enough housing

- Enough money to live
- Being safe
- Access and transport
- Healthy diet

- Exercise and fresh air
- Playtime and leisure
- Being free from prejudice and discrimination

Coping—help the child:

- Understand boundaries and keep within them
- Be brave
- Solve problems
- Put on rose-tinted glasses
- Foster their interests
- Calm her/himself down, self-soothe
- Remember that tomorrow is another day
- Lean on others when necessary

Learning—learning not only includes school education, but also helping with their life skills, talents, and interests:

- Make school life work as well as possible
- Engage mentors for children
- Help the child to organize her/himself
- Highlight achievements
- Develop life skills

Belonging—helping a child make good relationships with family and friends:

- Find somewhere for the child to belong
- Tap into good influences
- Keep relationships going
- Get together people the child can count on
- Belonging involves responsibilities and obligations too
- Focus on good times and places
- Make sense of where a child has come from
- Predict a good experience of someone/something new
- Help child make friends and mix with other children
- Help child understand her/his place in the world

Core self—working to shape a child's character:

- Instill a sense of hope
- Teach the child to understand other people's feelings
- Help the child know her/himself
- Help child take responsibility for her/himself
- Foster their talents
- There are tried and tested treatments for specific problems, use them[35]

TRAUMA-INFORMED CARE WITH OFFENDERS

The criminal justice system stops harmful behaviour in the immediate. Yet, in the long term, it tends to exacerbate criminal behaviour, like violence. A trauma-informed approach thinks both short- and long-term. It is first and foremost about accountability—seeking transformation. Trauma-informed accountability, like trauma-informed care, begins with establishing safety for offenders. Safety speaks to the need for healthy relationships. Yet, many young offenders will not have had positive relational experiences growing up, in the home, at school, or in other environments. They're likely to be distrustful—for good reason—and their trust will need to be earned. After all, as we've seen, opportunities for processes of resilience (for healing) happen best within the context of healthy relationships. Furthermore, there's a real tension between how justice is carried out and what people need for well-being. The justice system takes control of a young person, telling them where to be, when to be there, and how to act. It does the same for victims. This is a largely disempowering experience for the trauma survivor, who has already experienced feelings of the trauma being out of their control. For this reason, establishing safety is about giving control over to the trauma survivor. Judith Herman emphatically makes this point when she says, "No intervention that takes power away from the survivor can possibly foster her recovery, no matter how much it appears to be in her immediate best interest."[36] This tension between controlling young offenders and empowering them is the core challenge of trauma-informed youth justice. It doesn't mean that accountability or the need for clear (behavioural) boundaries are not part of the process. It does mean, however, that we must find ways to work together with youth. The principles of working with victims that I've described in this chapter so far also apply to young offenders who have experienced trauma.

TRAUMA-INFORMED ACCOUNTABILITY WITH OFFENDERS

In the previous chapter, I introduced a restorative justice understanding of accountability and contrasted it with the typical legal understanding of accountability. The typical legal version of offenders taking responsibility for their actions means paying for crimes by serving sentences or "doing time." This accountability is focused on "just deserts" or "redress"; that is, offenders are held accountable by being given what they deserve, proportional punishment.[37] However, there are some significant problems with this form of accountability. Beyond a guilty plea (if they plead guilty), nowhere in the punishment/accountability process of the legal system does a person have to say, "I did it." Furthermore, a person can serve their entire sentence without having to reflect on or work to understand the root causes of their offending behaviour. Trauma-informed accountability, although concerned with "redress" and "just deserts," approaches this quite differently. It is based in a framework of restorative justice. Here, to be accountable is to take responsibility for your harmful behaviour.[38] This might sound like the same thing, yet it has quite different implications. It's a four-part process. First, it means acknowledging, or owning, criminal behaviour. Second, offenders need to say that what they did was wrong. By doing so, they're acknowledging harm done to others. Third, they must make amends, attempting to—in the language of restorative justice, and as Howard Zehr said, "put things as right as possible."[39] And, fourth, they must get the support necessary to change. After all, victims are acutely interested in making sure that what happened to them never happens to anyone else, and acknowledgement and amends mean little if the offender simply goes on to do the same thing again. In summary, the process of trauma-informed accountability goes like this:

1. I did it.
2. It was wrong.
3. I will make amends.
4. I will get the support necessary to change.

Accountability is fundamentally about change. After all, what's the point of criminal justice processes unless they create change? When a victim dies, the family doesn't want the loss of their loved one's life to have been in vain. They want the offender to honour the tragedy by changing. Someday all young offenders who are incarcerated will be released back to the community, and although acknowledgement is an important first step, without amends and accountability, it is simply rhetoric.

For an offender to become accountable involves asking *why* they did it. Human behaviour is often cyclical, or habitual. Is a crime part of a pattern of behaviour? What are the reasons for the person acting the way they did? Is it a result of their own traumas, mental health issues, or addictions? What else explains it? This process involves taking ownership of behaviour in a way that avoids minimizing, manipulation, and justification.

Accountability for an offender also means developing empathy toward people they have harmed.[40] What does empathy mean? Clearly, it's different than apathy, *not* caring for someone, or sympathy, which is concern *for* someone. Empathy is feeling concern *with* another person. It's about trying to step into the shoes of another person and working toward feeling their hurts.

Have you ever tried to mentally put yourself in the place of a person you've hurt? Someone you've laughed at or insulted, perhaps? It's not easy! As much as we may feel sorry for what we've done, we tend to avoid (at all costs) considering what the other person might be feeling. At times, we may only feel sorry that we've been caught and that we have to deal with the consequences. In those cases, our sorrow might present itself as self-pity, instead of as concern for the other person. In the same way, trauma-informed accountability is a difficult task. It can be easier for an offender to simply "do their time," where they can avoid facing the consequences.

Think about a person who has violated another (perhaps by committing a violent crime), and consider the accompanying shame. Young offenders sometimes hurt people in the ways they, themselves, have been hurt. For example, sometimes a young offender who has been sexually abused will go on to sexually abuse other children. It's incredibly difficult to want to empathize, let alone to actually feel with another person, in these circumstances. Nevertheless, this is the obligation and the expectation of trauma-informed accountability. Encounter-based restorative justice programs are particularly good at moving offenders in this direction. It's hard to understand the impacts of our actions until we hear directly from those we have hurt.

Accountability is painful. However, the alternative—ignoring the impacts of harmful actions—is worse. The context in the process of becoming accountable is very important. Earlier, I mentioned the incredible amount of shame that many people who have offended feel. Trauma-informed practitioners must be comfortable working with shame. In fact, many people who have been working with violent offenders suggest that shame is a, if not *the*, root cause of crime. Clearly, something must be done about it.

It is to address shame that trauma-informed accountability takes place within a context of care. A context of care means a context that's nonjudgmental—one in which violent actions like sexual abuse are labelled as "monstrous," but the people who commit them are not. To this end, some restorative justice programs working with sex offenders call these offenders "persons who have offended sexually" rather than "sex offenders," removing the "badness" from the person and placing it onto the action. A context of care is safe, respectful, and empowering. Trauma-informed justice is about sharing control of healing (including accountability), even with those who have caused great harm. We give space for people to do the work in their own time. Working with people in this way takes a certain amount of trust—if not belief—in the human capacity and desire to change.

Providing a context of care is so important for allowing offenders to become accountable. As mentioned in chapter 7, the criminal justice system has some positive elements, but perhaps its greatest failure is the context it puts many offenders in. Among other things, it asks people to stop being violent, yet places them in some of the most violent places on earth. The criminal justice system asks people to take control of their behaviour, yet it puts them in an environment where they have no control. It asks them to be more human, but replaces their human identity with a number, a costume, and a cage. Of course, sometimes restraint is necessary. But, this should be a last resort, not status quo.

TRAUMA-INFORMED INCAPACITATION WITH OFFENDERS

To address the tension between "do no harm" and the limited need for the incapacitation of some offenders, there have been some initiatives within correctional environments that have sought to be trauma-informed. In an article in the *European Journal of Psychotraumatology*, titled "Creating Trauma-Informed Correctional Care: A Balance of Goals and Environments," researchers Niki A. Miller and Lisa M. Najavits acknowledge the difficulty of incorporating trauma-Informed practices into prisons, but suggest that it isn't impossible. On one hand, the researchers say prisons are full of trauma-inducing practices: "The correctional environment is full of unavoidable triggers, such as pat downs and strip searches, frequent discipline from authority figures, and restricted movement. This is likely to increase trauma-related behaviours and symptoms that can be difficult for prison staff to manage."[41] On the other hand, Miller and Najavits argue that incorporating trauma-informed approaches is still a worthwhile goal: "Yet, if trauma-informed practices are introduced, all staff can play a major role in minimizing triggers, stabilizing offenders, reducing critical incidents, deescalating situations, and avoiding restraint, seclusion or other measures that may repeat aspects of past abuse."[42] Miller and Najavits argue for trauma-informed practices that are present-focused. That is, instead of digging too much into the past, which they suggest might be too much in a prison environment, focus should instead be placed on increasing coping skills by using psychoeducational models.[43] Although this article is somewhat narrow in scope, highlighting a specific model of programming rather than thinking about the whole environment, it argues that reduced recidivism will be an outcome.

Other researchers have suggested approaches that look at the entire environmental context of prisons, including the physical space and the structured living environment. The work of Barb Toews and Deanna Van Buren explores creating physical spaces that reduce trauma—or architecture for peacebuilding. This includes prison environments. In a graduate course at Eastern Mennonite University's Center for Justice and Peacebuilding, taught by Toews and Van Buren, the syllabus offers the rationale for architecture that promotes peacebuilding:

> The work of peacebuilding occurs in a myriad of spaces—mediation, negotiation, and training rooms, NGO and government offices, detention and correctional facilities, shelters and refugee camps, homes, and even outside. In each of these settings, peacebuilders strive to create a physical and psychological atmosphere that is safe, respectful, and supportive of the work occurring in the space. This means paying attention to, for instance, the layout of break out rooms, shape of dialogue tables, access to nature, and the cultural significance of objects in the room. These efforts suggest that the design and architecture of peacebuilding spaces is integral to peacebuilding itself and that, just as we design training and dialogue processes, we are called to intentionally design peacebuilding space. Architecture and design subsequently become a visual representation of a commitment to peace and justice. These efforts also raise important questions about how to design spaces in which peacebuilding occurs. For instance:
>
> - How does design influence the emotional, physical, and psychological well-being of people and the way they behave and interact with each other?
> - What designs can be used to enhance and promote the aims of peacebuilding work—e.g., build community vs. marginalize, reduce anxiety vs. create stress?
> - How does one create designs that are culturally respectful?
> - How can spaces be (re)designed within financial and material restrictions?
> - What can people engaged in peace and justice work practically do to design spaces well? The questions also hold true for development, trauma healing, and restorative justice work.[44]

Some attempts have been made to make prison environments more focused on restorative justice. Research conducted by Tania Petrellis with Correctional Service of Canada explored a living unit (RJU), structured on the principles of restorative justice at Grande Cache Institution, an adult, male, federal prison, in Alberta, Canada. This unit, while it existed, demonstrated positive outcomes for inmates in terms of attitudes and behaviours.[45] Based on the objective of creating an environment that created accountability and healing, inmates were invited to apply to participate and to live in the unit.[46] As part of living in RJU, inmates were expected to take an active approach with their correctional plans.[47] Correctional plans outline a risk management strategy for each offender, including necessary interventions (i.e., programs) that offenders should complete before their release.[48] Inmates were also invited to attend weekly restorative justice meetings. Furthermore, two inmates were appointed as mediators to help resolve any conflicts in the unit.[49] A number of indicators suggest this to be a more trauma-informed approach: one, inmates claimed to feel safer in this environment than in the general prison population; two, more agency was given to offenders; and three, there was a focus on accountability and healing.

Parenting Behind Bars
By Marion Evans, Professor, Community and Criminal Justice, Conestoga College

In the late 1990s, the Correctional Service of Canada introduced progressive new programming for women offenders. One initiative provided an opportunity for a small number of eligible offenders to care for their children while serving a sentence. For eight years, it was my privilege to manage the Mother-Child program at the Grand Valley Institution for Women, a federal penitentiary in Kitchener, Ontario. Recent years have seen the deterioration of this program across the country due to rising offender populations, operational constraints, changing government policy, and high profile institutional incidents that distracted from positive correctional results. However, in its early years the Mother-Child program helped a number of women move beyond their past to become pro-social citizens and effective parents.

Unlike other programs in a penitentiary, where intake procedures focus on risk, determine program needs, and assess individual motivation to address criminogenic factors (factors that contribute to criminal behaviour), the Mother-Child program operated from the opposite premise. The "pre-eminent consideration" to determine participation in the program was the "best interests of the child." The process of applying and determining eligibility for the program is detailed in Commissioner's Directive 768, Institutional Mother-Child Program (http://www.csc-scc.gc.ca/text/plcy/cdshtm/768-cd-eng.shtml).

One element of the application process was an assessment by a child welfare organization or a child care specialist. While this assessment was vital to assessing whether a mother had the skill and capacity to parent, it was also a time when biases against people who had broken the law can appear. Individuals who spend their career protecting children from abusive or neglectful environments are understandably sensitive to the results of trauma. The idea of a child being cared for within the confines of a prison can be difficult to contemplate. Building a system relationship between the prison and the child welfare agency was necessary in order to educate and build trust toward a common goal of effective parenting and healthy families.

The biases and challenges did not end there. Some staff questioned the existence of a mother-child program within a prison. Were they responsible for the child as well as the inmate? Was this program beyond their duty to carry out the sentence of the court? Should inmates be allowed to parent? More education was needed about the legal duty to report suspected abuse or neglect. The constant reminder to skeptics and concerned individuals was that people should not be defined wholly by their crime. It was a challenge to convince people that some offenders can be good parents.

What about the other inmates? Were they a risk to the child? Other inmates who lived in the same house as the mother and child were scrutinized carefully. On the compound, however, I observed that the conduct of the offender population was improved, and women even chastised each other for swearing or raising voices within the vicinity of the baby. Many women were eager to assist the mother, offer words of advice or encouragement, and admire the baby. Indeed, it seemed that a child had many "aunts" when they were in the Mother-Child program. Under the watchful eyes of institutional staff, community stakeholders, and offenders, the safety and nurture of each child was ensured. There was something sacred about the presence of a child in an environment where many are deprived of the mother-child relationship due to incarceration.

Few of the women who participated in the Mother-Child program had ongoing relationships with the father of their child. Without this program, the child of an offender would ordinarily be placed with a child welfare agency, or with a family member or friend. The majority of the women who participated in the program had experienced trauma and abuse as a child, as an adult, or both. All exhibited low self-esteem. Yet what seemed to propel a woman toward personal change more than any institutional program was the child who needed her love. Maybe she could be a good parent to her child if she just had the opportunity and some help? With the tireless efforts of staff and a community social worker, parenting skills were learned, and mothers were encouraged and supported as new little family units grew. The spectre of attachment issues was being swept away.

The issue of power and control is multi-layered within a prison environment. Many women come to prison having already experienced loss of power and control as a result of trauma. Once in prison, the expectation is that she must follow orders, abide by prison rules, and live within a structured context (i.e., more loss of power and control). Yet within the Mother-Child program, the mother was advised that she was responsible for all decisions related to her child. I remember the look of complete confusion when I reminded a young mother that she could decide who could hold her baby, and that she had permission to say no to anyone who asked, including me! In an environment where power and control are pervasive, the program returned some power and control to the inmate.

How can we assist people who are incarcerated and who have been traumatized?

1. Recognize that many offenders are victims of trauma themselves. This may remind us to question our own negative biases.
2. Return power and control to the offender when possible by allowing her to make choices. In so doing, we help to restore respect and dignity.
3. Build resiliency and relationships by offering support and encouragement, and celebrating achievements, however small.

As she was released, one mother said that the Mother-Child program had changed her life. Now, she had a reason to live and move forward. That "reason" was held lovingly in her arms as she walked out the door. Another young mother in the program had four other children whom she had never been able to parent due to multiple incarcerations. Her mother was raising them. While in custody, she embraced the care and responsibility for her new daughter with passion and fervour. Her attention to her correctional programs showed a new level of commitment. Toward the end of her time in the program, she said, "This baby is different. She is mine and I am going to raise her. I can do it now."

Trauma is not the end of the story; there can be a new beginning.

TRAUMA-INFORMED CARE WITH COMMUNITIES

Trauma-informed care with communities is necessary, both to alleviate individual traumas as well as to provide opportunities for the healing of collective traumas. Similar to work with individuals, community work should foster the development of resilience. However, there are some differences in terms of process. In the next chapter, I'll discuss the need for more preventative efforts, for resisting structures—like law and policy—that cause harm. I'll also discuss some models being used for trauma-informed work at the community level. In this second part of chapter 9, I'll share one model for trauma-informed work at the community level, and will discuss the value of strong leadership and creativity to transform violent situations into healing.

In some ways, working with communities post-trauma is similar to working with individuals. There's a need to establish safety, to mourn, and to find healthy ways of moving forward. In the "snail model" of trauma healing, developed post–9/11 by the Strategies for Trauma Awareness and Recovery (STAR) program at Eastern Mennonite University, these three themes are divided into 12 components. Trauma expert Carolyn Yoder writes about these steps toward healing in *The Little Book of Trauma Healing*. First is finding safety. It's difficult for survivors to heal while violence remains, and a certain degree of safety is necessary before healing can begin. Second is mourning and grieving.

Survivors need to be able to tell their stories. As stories are memorialized, isolation is reduced. Yoder suggests that artistic expressions are often helpful here. Third, it's important to accept the reality of loss and to come to terms with the fact that the past cannot be changed. Fourth, Yoder argues that healing is more likely to happen when the humanity of the enemy is acknowledged. Yoder says at some point groups must ask "why them?" questions about perpetrators in order to move on from asking "why me/us?" questions. Fifth, there must be a commitment to taking risks and to trying new things. Sixth, tolerance is necessary in order for people to coexist. In many contexts, post–group trauma, victims and perpetrators will be living in the same communities. As well, people are often simultaneously victim and offender. Seventh, this requires that offenders be engaged and involved in healing processes. Eighth, for some, forgiveness will help with moving forward. That being said, Yoder calls forgiveness "an obscene word."[50] It's controversial, and it isn't for everyone. Yoder's point is that forgiveness helps some survivors heal. However, whether or not their steps toward healing involve forgiveness will depend on the person or group. Ninth, everyone in the community has a responsibility to work toward dealing with the past in order to make the future positive. Sometimes, when caught in a cycle of victimhood, a community can minimize their own responsibility. This model challenges everyone to be involved in creating justice. Tenth, it is necessary to negotiate solutions between survivors, perpetrators, and other community members. Eleventh, experiences of trauma must be integrated into a new self and group identity, not as the central component, but as a part of it. All of this works toward the twelfth step, the possibility of reconciliation and the healing of communities.[51]

Some of the elements in Yoder's theory should be familiar to you by now. We have seen that creating a foundation of safety for trauma healing is the starting point, whether working with individuals or groups. This involves the work of communicating in a safe way and of building a foundation of respect, as described earlier in this chapter. However, what's new to us in Yoder's work is more of a consideration for the humanity of the "enemy" or the "other." The premise is that, without some form of acknowledgement of people or groups who have caused harm, it's difficult for communities to move forward. Why? If perpetrators are only punished, or only separated from others in the community, the work of healing is simply postponed. At some point, particularly in the realm of criminal justice, but also where collective trauma has been perpetrated by groups, people must find ways to safely coexist. As such, the work of healing from collective trauma involves healthy leadership that promotes progressive community dialogue.

Having worked for many decades in the area of intergenerational trauma, Vamik Volkan, a Turkish psychiatrist, writes about the need for transformative leadership. Believing that group identity can regress following trauma, Volkan suggests groups need reparative leaders willing to rise above violence.[52] Without strong leadership, groups can become stuck in cycles of victimization and revenge, trading harm for harm. What's more, Volkan argues that groups need ways to tell their history because the experience of collective trauma is often one of erasure, an attempt by one group to eliminate another.[53] The assimilation of Indigenous peoples in Canada is one example of this. Groups that are able to talk about their history and its impacts are better able to survive:

> Psychoanalysts who have studied the trans-generational transmission of massive social trauma inform us that if the impact of such trauma is denied or repressed, it will still manifest itself in various ways in new generations. The "therapeutic" way of dealing with previous generations' massive social trauma is not to deny or repress what happened to the ancestors, but to be aware of the history and the nature of the devastating events faced by the previous generations. When historical continuity is available for new generations, they have a better chance of strengthening their large-group identity.[54]

One way of making it easier to talk about difficult subject matter with collective trauma survivors is through the use of arts-based approaches.

Arts-based community dialogue offers a number of opportunities for trauma healing. Art provides a mechanism for communicating about difficult subject matter. As a creative act, it is inherently a strengthening process. It provides a visual representation of trauma, outside of the person, allowing them to reflect on its impacts and to move toward recovery, a memorial of subject matter that's often hidden or repressed. Art allows for groups to create a collective memory and a positive group identity.

Trauma is difficult to express or to put into words. Art offers one form of expression. Through metaphors and symbols, survivors are able to put horrible experiences into images that can be better understood and integrated. Studying the use of art with survivors of war, art therapist Barbara Ann Baker says, "Through art expression, fractured parts of the self are brought to the surface to be observed and evaluated for change. In the process of creating visual dialogue through art, survivors of trauma are able to resolve conflict, develop personal strengths, and heal their invisible wounds.... Art becomes a pathway to empower clients to become survivors instead of victims."[55] Furthermore, through art, survivors are able to memorialize, and create a collective memory of trauma. In *Memory, War and Trauma*, Nigel Hunt defines collective memory as "joint memories held by a community about the past."[56] He explains that a person might not have been present at the actual event, but that it still affects their life through the transgenerational transmission of trauma.[57] Linking this to the work of Volkan above, we can see how art allows for the creation of a positive self and group identity. Representations of the past present opportunities for groups to identify harms and to forge a new way forward.[58] So much more has been written about the use of creative enterprises for trauma healing—from the use of literature, to drama, to yoga—and I invite you to explore the topic further on your own.

CONCLUSION: MOVING TOWARD A NEW UNDERSTANDING OF TRAUMA-INFORMED CARE

Being trauma-informed isn't overly complicated. It has a twofold agenda: (1) understand trauma and its effects, and in light of this (2) implement practices that help people get better. It almost goes without saying that practices that do further harm should be abolished. However, given the information in chapter 7 about the iatrogenic youth justice system, it's worth repeating. The field of youth justice should adopt a restorative justice approach. That is, justice should shift from being about punishment toward being about healing. This will serve victims, communities, and offenders better. Trauma-informed care for each of these populations means establishing safety, promoting accountability, and creatively finding ways to talk about harms and make things as right as possible. The case study about the Mother-Child program at Grand Valley Institution for Women by Marion Evans highlights that even where people need to be incapacitated there are ways of doing it that promote healing. This requires leadership. Traditional criminal justice is often regressive, making things worse. What's needed is a new generation of practitioners in youth justice who understand trauma and who establish practices based on trauma-informed care.

GLOSSARY OF TERMS

Resilience is a person's capacity to deal with stress and adversity. Resilience is a process, not a character trait.

Trauma-informed care is supporting people who have experienced trauma toward healing by understanding the impacts of trauma, and implementing practices that do no further harm.

QUESTIONS FOR REFLECTION

1. Look again at the Psychopathy Checklist–Youth Version (PCL-YV) in chapter 7. Based on what you have learned in this chapter about strengths-based practice, why might the PCL-YV checklist be a narrow way to understand a human being, even a person with a significant mental challenge?
2. What do you think about the Mother-Child program at Grand Valley Institution for Women described by Marion Evans—is it a good idea? Why or why not?

RECOMMENDED READING

Cameron, Julia. *The Artist's Way*. New York: Jeremy P. Tarcher/Putnam, 1992.
   Although not a book about art therapy, this book helps readers unlock their own creativity. I include it on my recommended list because doing the work of trauma-informed youth justice is as much a challenge to think critically, as it is to creatively explore new ways of helping victims, offenders, and communities heal in the aftermath of crime.

Klinic Community Health Centre. *The Trauma-Informed Toolkit*. Available online: http://trauma-informed.ca/wp-content/uploads/2013/10/Trauma-informed_Toolkit.pdf, 2013.
   A very helpful resource for understanding the basics of what it means to be trauma-informed.

Yoder, Carolyn. *The Little Book of Trauma Healing: When Violence Strikes and Community Security Is Threatened*. Intercourse: Good Books, 2005.
   This little book by Carolyn Yoder provides an excellent summary of the impacts of trauma, as well as how communities can move out of cycles of violence toward healing.

10 | Trauma-Informed Prevention— Ending Cycles of Violence

"My ancestors resisted and survived what must have seemed like an apocalyptic reality of occupation and subjugation in a context where they had few choices. They resisted by simply surviving and being alive. They resisted by holding onto their stories. They resisted by taking the seeds of our culture and political systems and packing them away, so that one day another generation of *Michi Saagiig Nishnaabeg* might be able to plant them. I am sure of their resistance because I am here today, living as a contemporary *Michi Saagiig Nishnaabeg* woman. I am the evidence. *Michi Saagiig Nishnaabeg* people are the evidence. Now, nearly two hundred years after surviving an attempted political and cultural genocide, it is the responsibility of my generation to plant and nurture those seeds and to make our Ancestors proud."
—Leanne Simpson, *Michi Saagiig Nishnaabeg* writer and educator[1]

Trauma-informed care is a powerful tool, but it can only take us so far. Supporting individual youth to heal and to be accountable is only a part of the story. The larger story is about finding ways to address root causes of injustice and crime. There are massive social structures and institutions that continue to marginalize certain young people. The work of trauma-informed prevention is to end this violence. Youth are coming into conflict with the law because of structural violence—especially, as we've seen, because of the colonization of Indigenous peoples and patriarchal male violence—and it's time to more meaningfully address these issues.

This chapter is divided into two parts. The first part is focused on decolonization. **Decolonization** is the process of dismantling systems of colonialism. This is a massive undertaking. The Canadian state is rather illegitimate given its foundations on stealing Indigenous lands. Hopefully, at this point in the text, you'll have a fairly clear sense of the historical harm done through colonization including the dispossession of lands, the dishonouring of treaties, legislation aimed at assimilation, residential schools, the sixties scoop, and so on. Colonization, however, isn't a thing of the past. Current structures, including laws like the "Indian Act," maintain a harmful relationship as settlers continue to be violent toward Indigenous peoples. As a settler person myself, I'm trying to learn what I need to do to take responsibility and to work toward decolonization. I can follow the path of accountability described in chapter 8: admission of responsibility, admission of wrongness, making amends, and getting the support necessary to change. The first two steps are rather straightforward. As a settler, even though I didn't personally take part in some practices, like residential schools, I continue to colonize by allowing Indigenous peoples to be mistreated through ongoing assimilative practices. I can acknowledge this—I do it; it is wrong. As to the fourth step, I'm working toward listening to and understanding members of Indigenous communities, like my friend Myeengun Henry, to understand what I need to do to change. This chapter, then, will focus on the third step, making amends, and working toward making things right. This is about me, as a settler, talking to other settlers and identifying settler privilege as a form of white supremacy that continues to hurt Indigenous peoples.

There are many elements to taking responsibility for this, and in this chapter I'll describe three: one, the responsibility to honour all treaties; two, the responsibility to engage in justice using a pluralistic lens; and three, the need to learn from Indigenous peoples. Were we to honour these three responsibilities, the impact on youth justice—for both young offenders and victims—would be profound.

The second section of this chapter is about dismantling patriarchy. As someone who identifies as male, I'm learning to take responsibility for a society imbued with male privilege. To work toward making things right, I've begun to talk to other men and boys about male violence, how hegemonic masculinity influences violent choices and affects all women, children, and even other men. The focus of the second section, then, will be on these types of preventative practices.

TRAUMA-INFORMED PREVENTION: DECOLONIZATION

> "The colonized can see right away if decolonization is taking place or not: The minimum demand is that the last become the first."
> —Frantz Fanon

Current youth justice practices are an injustice. Rather than acting as a dividing line, separating people who are deemed "bad" from those thought to be "good," justice systems could be more like bridges of peace. Frantz Fanon, a psychiatrist and later a revolutionary opposing the French government's colonization of Algeria, describes the importance of a justice system. In his work *The Wretched of the Earth*, he says that justice systems are the dividing line between colonizer and colonized: "The colonized world is a world divided into two. The dividing line, the border, is represented by the barracks and the police stations. In the colonies, the official legitimate agent, the spokesperson for the colonizer and the regime of oppression, is the police officer."[2] This raises important questions about the role of the Canadian justice system toward Indigenous peoples: What is its purpose? Is it about public safety, about maintaining colonialism—or perhaps both? Furthermore, whose interests does the justice system serve? For those who are marginalized, the justice system can become like a wall—a way of keeping them out. As Fanon claims, the opulence of rich society is built on the backs of those who are poor. The marginalized are relegated to being a criminal class: "The colonized's sector, or at least the 'native' quarters, the shanty town, the Medina, the reservation, is a disreputable place inhabited by disreputable people."[3] This process of dehumanization should be of concern to all Canadians, but especially those who work in the field of youth justice.

The more people are dehumanized, the more others are able to justify actions against them that wouldn't be acceptable were they considered "human." The "criminal" can languish, forgotten in solitary confinement. The "Indian" can suffer behind bars. But, if the criminal is our brother, the "Indian" our sister—if both are our fellow human beings—justice as punishment is less viable, and justice as healing is more possible. Colonial justice builds walls and focuses on separating "them" from "us." The process of decolonizing, on the other hand, is one of peacemaking, of taking down walls and instead building bridges. Who better to do this work than all of us?

In recent years, there's been much talk of reconciliation in Canada, especially with Truth and Reconciliation Commission events related to repairing the damage caused by Indian residential schools. Yet, reconciliation without proper decolonization on the part of settler society seems rather two-faced. A trauma-informed youth justice approach must confront the settler-colonial reality of Canada's history and work toward decolonization. Decolonization requires a practical approach—not simply an apology from a Prime Minister. In their article, "Decolonization Is Not a Metaphor" in the journal of *Decolonization: Indigeneity, Education & Society*, authors Eve Tuck and K. Wayne Yang highlight that decolonization is "about the repatriation of indigenous land and life."[4]

Jeff Corntassel, a Cherokee professor at the University of Victoria in Canada, talks about decolonization among his people as a process of resurgence, of living in traditional ways. He says, "Decolonization offers different pathways for reconnecting Indigenous nations with their traditional land-based and water-based cultural practices. The decolonization process operates at multiple levels and necessitates moving from an awareness of being in struggle, to actively engaging in everyday practices of resurgence."[5] For settlers, there are two components to decolonization. First, it begins with treating Indigenous peoples as sovereign peoples, recognizing their inherent right to self-determination, and supporting their (re)connection with traditional lands. This will mean that Canadian society needs to become better acquainted with our colonial history, as well as with our treaty obligations. Secondly, decolonization requires a systematic analysis and subsequent dismantling of policies and practices (whether economic, legal, political, etc.) that are about the assimilation and subjugation of Indigenous peoples.

In earlier chapters, I argued that the focus of trauma-informed youth justice is on creating resilient communities. However, the development of resilience isn't possible without some forms of resistance. In their important article, "From Resilience to Resistance: A Reconstruction of the Strengths Perspective in Social Work Practice," in the journal *International Social Work*, researchers Wei-he Guo and Ming-sum Tsui make an argument for this. They believe that strengths-based approaches generally, and in social work in particular, neglect the role that resistance plays in establishing resilience for traumatized and marginalized communities.[6] A fundamental shift in power relations is necessary for change and for the building of resilience. Guo and Tsui summarize this perspective:

> If social work's mission is to emancipate, empower and enable people in vulnerable situations; then it must acknowledge the weapons used by people to facilitate social justice. Social workers should support the attempts of people to enhance their strength by resisting and even subverting power relations instead of forcing them to be rehabilitated according to middle-class values and behaviours. If social workers do not actively address power relations, their emancipation projects will fail, despite efforts to enhance personal resilience and communicative competence.[7]

Drawing on the work of social theorist Pierre Bourdieu, Guo and Tsui propose a framework for a more liberating practice. Core questions include:

- What is the difference between service users' behaviour and the behaviour of the dominant class?
- What resources (i.e., social capital, personal capital, and symbolic capital) do disadvantaged people possess that will enable them to change their lifestyle?
- What kinds of strategies do disadvantaged people employ to further their interests and resist exploitation?[8]

Resistance can take many forms, from advocacy, to non-violent protest, to property destruction, to violence. For some Indigenous communities in Canada, it has meant (re)occupying traditional lands. Sometimes it has involved blockading a rail route. Other times, it has been walking around a lake to demonstrate the value of caring for the water. Another example: in 2013 six young people from the Cree community of Whapmagoostui walked over 1,500 kilometers from their homes to Parliament Hill in Ottawa, Ontario, to push for change in how Indigenous peoples are treated in Canada.[9] Regardless of the tactic used, it isn't the job of settlers, like me, to debate whether we agree with how the message is being communicated. Rather, it's our job to listen to the message. Why are Indigenous peoples occupying lands by force? Why are children walking thousands of miles to share their stories? Sometimes options for resistance are limited.

In a provocative work called *Endgame: Volume 1 The Problem of Civilization*, writer Derrick Jensen argues that civilization isn't progressive; that it tends to favour an elite few who conquer abroad and repress at home. He quotes Herbert V. Prochnow, a rich banking executive, "A visitor from Mars could easily pick out the civilized nations. They have the best implements of war."[10] Jensen claims that civilization is inherently hierarchical and that the violence of those at the top is usually invisible, while any attempts at violence by those on the bottom is treated with shock and horror.[11] I'm not making an argument in favour of violence as a tactic of resistance. What I am suggesting, however, is that it's often a tactic used by those in power to oppress others and that a trauma-informed approach must work toward ending this type of violence. Furthermore, when marginalized groups do use violence, it's better to find ways to use dialogue, and to move toward livable communities for all, than it is to punish. I have cited a few examples of Indigenous resistance, but the point of my work here is to highlight that settlers, too, must resist violent forms of domination by following the lead of Indigenous peoples.

Responsibility 1: Honour Treaties

One of the central problems of colonialism has been Canada's blatant disregard for treaties made with Indigenous peoples. Of course, some of these treaties predate Confederation, but Canada still has an obligation to honour them. In 1991, George Erasmus, a Dene and leader of the Assembly of First Nations, was tasked with co-chairing a Canadian Royal Commission on Aboriginal Peoples (RCAP). Royal Commissions are established to look at national problems or issues that affect all Canadians. Since 1868 there have been 48 Royal Commissions conducted in Canada on topics ranging from electoral reform, to energy issues, to revisions to the Criminal Code. Part of the impetus for the RCAP was the fallout from the Meech Lake Accord, as well as the Oka crisis at Kanesatake, both in 1990. In the first instance, a member of Parliament in the Manitoba Legislature, Elijah Harper, an Indigenous person from Red Sucker Lake, blocked a constitutional amendment called the Meech Lake Accord. Among other changes, the government of the day was attempting to change the constitution to make Quebec a distinct society. Many Indigenous communities were opposed because of a lack of government consultation. In the second instance, the Oka crisis was a standoff—and confrontation—with the Canadian military by the Mohawks of Kanesatake over encroachment onto their land by the town of Oka, because of the development of a golf course.

Over the course of five years, Erasmus and the other Commissioners of the RCAP held 196 public hearings, visited 96 Indigenous communities, and commissioned many research reports. They concluded that: "The main policy direction, pursued for more than 150 years, first by colonial then by Canadian governments, has been wrong."[12] Essentially, they characterized the governments' approach as one of assimilation, an attempt to do away with Aboriginal culture and sovereignty. The RCAP was a forward-looking document. While identifying the harmful nature of the relationship between governments and Aboriginal peoples, it attempted to rearrange this relationship through a 20-year plan. Some of the recommendations included doing away with the Indian Act and the Band, or reserve, system. Fundamentally, though, the document suggested transfer of powers and land, which would mean "honouring the treaties for sharing of land and resources. Land and resources must be returned where taken."[13] The RCAP called for the renewal of treaties:

- The parties implement the historical treaties from the perspective of both justice and reconciliation.
- The federal government establish a continuing bilateral process to implement and renew the Crown's relationship with and obligations to the treaty nations under the historical treaties, in accordance with the treaties' spirit and intent.

- The federal government establish a process for making new treaties to replace the existing comprehensive claims policy.[14]

The RCAP recommended accomplishing this, among many other recommendations, over the next 20 years. Unfortunately, at the time of this writing, that timeframe has almost elapsed and almost all of the recommendations are collecting dust as the report sits idle on a bookshelf in Ottawa. The Special Rapporteur on the rights of Indigenous peoples from the United Nations has also recommended that Canada take more seriously the task of honouring treaties:

> Concerted measures should be adopted to deal with the outstanding problems that have impeded progress with the treaty negotiation and claims processes. Moreover, within these processes the Government should take a less adversarial, position-based approach than the one in which it typically seeks the most restrictive interpretation of aboriginal and treaty rights possible. In this regard, the Government should instead acknowledge that the public interest is not opposed to, but rather includes, aboriginal concerns.... Canada should take active measures to develop a procedure for addressing outstanding Métis land claims, to avoid having to litigate cases individually, and enter into negotiations with Métis representatives to reach agreements towards this end.[15]

Responsibility 2: Pluralism in Youth Criminal Justice

In the process of assimilating Indigenous peoples in Canada, a plurality of people groups has been subsumed together into one nation, in spite of the fact that the sovereignty of Indigenous peoples was never surrendered (remember, the term *Indigenous peoples* represents hundreds of nations and communities). This means that criminal law, and youth justice from a Canadian perspective, is illegitimately imposing itself on Indigenous peoples, who look at law and justice in different terms. There is some (limited) accommodation for Indigenous peoples through the *Gladue* principle, which allows for judges to consider Indigenous heritage when sentencing. Yet, this has done nothing to change the overrepresentation of Indigenous youth in the justice system. Since the implementation of *Gladue*, rates of incarceration for Indigenous youth have actually climbed. The problem is that Indigenous sovereignty is still being ignored. What's required then, as an interim measure until treaties are honoured, is an implementation of **legal pluralism**. When a crime is committed by a young Indigenous person, or when a victim is Indigenous—alongside the Youth Criminal Justice Act, the Criminal Code, and the Charter of Rights and Freedoms—Indigenous law and ways of carrying out justice need to be given precedence.

In essence, I'm arguing—as I have done elsewhere (in a chapter in *Reconstructing Restorative Justice Philosophy*, edited by Theo Gavrielides and Vasso Artinopoulou)—that we need to return justice processes to Indigenous peoples. Indigenous legal scholar Taiaiake Alfred says that a fundamental shift is required, to pluralist relations between autonomous peoples, in order to end colonialism.[16] Another Indigenous legal scholar, John Borrows, has written extensively and persuasively on this topic. He argues that Canada has redefined Indigenous status to that of subjugation, without any legal justification or any sound juridical reasoning: "What could be more arbitrary than one nation substantially invalidating a politically distinct peoples' rights without providing elementarily persuasive legal explanation?"[17] He goes further to say that the Supreme Court has not articulated how Indigenous governance has been replaced, and that the idea that settlers discovered, or conquered, "Canada" has been discredited in law.[18] In a later work, *Canada's Indigenous Constitution*, Borrows gives examples of the richness of various Indigenous legal traditions, including Mi'kmaq, Haudenosaunee, Anishinabek, Cree, Métis, Carrier, Nisga'a, and Inuit legal histories.[19] His point is to give examples of what has been largely ignored in Canadian law, and to position these legal traditions as predating settler society. What is involved in the task of creating a pluralistic youth justice system? The case study below explores this question.

Restorative Justice: It's Complex[20]
By Judah Oudshoorn

When Del Louie assaulted bus driver Charles Dixon, he injured him so badly that he shattered his orbital bone and damaged his brain. Rather than sending Louie to prison, the judge, citing the *Gladue* Principle—acknowledging the offender's Aboriginal heritage—instead gave him an 18-month conditional, treatment-oriented sentence. However, the outcome of court was unsatisfying for Dixon. He was quoted as saying, "He knew exactly how to throw one hell of a good punch.... I don't care what ancestry he's from" (http://www.news1130.com/).

This case invites complex questions. What is the value of a sentence to a victim? More specifically, what are broken facial bones and brain damage worth, let alone psychological costs? Was the court outcome fair? The social context of the offence is also important: what about the offender and *R. v. Gladue*? How do we balance a legacy of social wrongs with an individual's crimes? And, what are the challenges for restorative justice practitioners inherent within these questions?

(A) Victims and Vindication
Social psychologist Michael McCullough suggests that when we are significantly harmed our desire for revenge universally kicks in. At its core, he describes a need for people to replace feelings of shame with those of honour.[21] Restorative justice professor Howard Zehr describes this as vindication. In order for victims to be satisfied, offenders must go through a process of balancing the score that is deemed difficult, reciprocal to the pain they have suffered (www.emu.edu/restorative-justice).

In my experience as a restorative justice mediator, I have come across two specific ways this happens. One, victims want offenders to understand how their lives have been affected. In essence, it is about an offender learning to feel, at least in part, what the victim has. Two, because of their suffering, victims want to make sure what happened to them never happens to anyone else. This requires an offender to understand what influenced them to make harmful choices and to make change.

When our only tool for addressing this need is a prison sentence, we run into the challenge of quantifying harm purely based on a punishment. How much is a crime worth? How much punishment is enough? What if it is a physical assault like the one described above? Or, what about long-term sexual abuse or murder? Counterintuitively, beyond acknowledging that something wrong was done, punishment rarely equates with what has been lost. Efforts toward justice need to pay more meaningful attention to the desire for revenge.

(B) Aboriginal Offenders and Social Transformation

Tuning in to root causes of crime is as important as meeting victim needs. Without work in this area, restorative justice practitioners might simply be perpetuating some of the inequality that contributes to crime in the first place.

Although Louie's Aboriginal heritage is rightly irrelevant to Dixon, it has to be to Canadian society. For 100 years of Canada's less than 200-year history, over 150,000 Aboriginal children were removed from homes and communities into residential schools. The purpose was explicitly racist: a forced assimilation, described as civilizing the "savage."[22] In these schools, children were not allowed to speak their languages, practice their cultures nor live with their families. As if this was not criminal enough, many children were also physically and sexually abused. These colonial behaviours have had a traumatic impact on Aboriginal people and communities.

Recognizing the effect of this, which today translates into rampant drug abuse, violence and disorder in many Aboriginal communities and, as such, an overrepresentation of Aboriginal people in Canadian prisons, the Supreme Court of Canada in *R. v. Gladue* ruled that the Criminal Code of Canada should be changed to include: "718.2(e), all available sanctions other than imprisonment that are reasonable in the circumstances should be considered for all offenders, with particular attention to the circumstances of Aboriginal offenders." What has been the result of this? In spite of the *Gladue* decision, the number of aboriginal offenders increased by 22 percent in the eight years following it. Today, while only being 3 percent of the Canadian population, Aboriginals represent 20 percent of those behind bars. Is this not colonialism in repeat?

What does this mean for restorative justice practitioners? Clearly, law has not been able to ameliorate negative social conditions underlying crime. And if restorative justice practitioners simply facilitate dialogue between victims and offenders without calling public attention to the injustices experienced by Aboriginal peoples, our processes will have the same result on these vicious cycles: nil. Like one offender recently said to me: "Prisons are like putting a Band-Aid on cancer." Will restorative justice approaches be the same? By attending as much to the complexity of victimization as to the harms of human history, efforts toward justice can resist oversimplification.

Clearly the Dixon case presents the challenge of applying a pluralistic legal framework. Fundamentally, Canada has no right to incarcerate Indigenous people—who have never surrendered their sovereignty—on land that was forcibly taken from them. If Canada does incarcerate Indigenous people (as it is currently doing) the nation is repeating historical harms, caught up in a cycle of violence. I have written about this in other places, as well. In the 2013 edited volume, *Reconstructing Restorative Justice Philosophy*, I write:

> Bryan Stevenson, an anti–death penalty advocate, argues that without a knowledge of their history a people group is bound to repeat the ills of the past (www.TED.com, 2012). He wonders why African-Americans are being given the death penalty at dramatically higher rates than white Americans, on the very land where people of colour were lynched in the decades of segregation (*ibid*). Comparing this to Nazi Germany, he states that German scholars have deemed it unconscionable to imagine the death penalty being legal in their country (*ibid*). How could a country that systematically imprisoned, tortured and executed millions of Jews reinstitute a similar scheme? It would be outrageous. To implement one would be a denial of history and responsibility for mass atrocities and genocide. Put another way, what would the national reaction be if today the largest proportion of inmates in German prisons were Jewish? There would be an outcry, not only locally but also globally. Really, it is inconceivable. Nonetheless, in Canada the harmful legacy of residential schools has now translated into a disproportionate imprisonment for Aboriginal people. Yesterday's residential student is today's inmate.[23]

Pluralism is still interested in accountability; it matters that someone has been harmed, and this harm should be dealt with appropriately. What a pluralistic approach means, however, is that when a youth crime is committed, and it is determined that either the victim or offender (or both) are of Indigenous heritage, the appropriate Indigenous community must be engaged. Power—process and decision-making—needs to be shared between this community and the youth justice system. Legal pluralism acknowledges that there are multiple systems of law at work in a given conflict or crime.

Responsibility 3: Learn from Indigenous Peoples

For over 100 years, the youth justice system has struggled to reduce youth crime. However, the same issues (poverty, racism, and male violence) continue to bring young people into conflict with the law. Often these issues persist for generations. As I started to explain in chapter 8 on restorative justice, there's much to be learned from Indigenous communities about how to better carry out justice. A holistic approach, centred on peacemaking, has proven to be an effective way of dealing with some intergenerational harms. The First Nation community of Hollow Water in Manitoba is one example. This community dramatically reduced the amount of sexual abuse (which had been a pervasive problem for them for many generations). Of 48 sexual offenders who went through an Indigenous healing program, only two went on to commit another sexual offence.[24] This recidivism rate of 4 percent is much lower than the 13.4 percent Canadian national average.[25] How did this come about?

In 1984, in the small (home to approximately 600 people) First Nation of Hollow Water, a concerned group of people began to collaborate and discuss the pervasive problem of sexual abuse within the community.[26] Together, they formed the Community Holistic Circle Healing (CHCH) program. The program began in response to concerns about substance abuse, vandalism, truancy, suicide, and violence amongst the youth of the community. However, as the team explored the sources of these behaviours, they quickly realized that most family homes were full of violence and sexual abuse.[27] As Crown attorney Rupert Ross says after researching this situation, "underneath [all the other problems] lay generations of sexual abuse, primarily within families and involving children."[28]

For this reason, as the 1997 Ministry of the Solicitor General report *The Four Circles of Hollow Water* suggests, the CHCH program decided to face the sexual abuse "head on"; for "by comparison, repressing and forgetting are easy. Healing must take place under the steady gaze of the traumatic reality of sexual abuse. That this task is formidable is softened only by the fact that it takes place in a community that refuses to give up on any of its members no matter how deeply they have been wounded, nor how despicable their acts."[29] Significantly, the CHCH program and the Hollow Water community are noted as having come further than any other community in Canada in preventing reoffending of domestic and sexual violence and in developing approaches that support and heal victims of domestic and sexual violence.[30]

The CHCH accomplished this in five ways. First, it began by acknowledging the pervasive sexual violence and the profound effects it had had on *everyone* in the community.[31] It was estimated that three out of every four people in Hollow Water had been victims of sexual abuse, and that one out of three people had been a victimizer. In fact, virtually no community member remained untouched by victimization.[32] Second, the CHCH committee began a five-year training process of discovering possible healing journeys for victims and offenders of domestic and sexual violence.[33] Third, the CHCH identified the criminal justice system as a barrier to healing. They noted that the adversarial legal system was further exacerbating the problem by not creating a safe space for victims, and that the threat of incarceration was preventing offenders from coming forward to acknowledge wrongdoing.[34] Furthermore, the CHCH felt that these offences were too serious to be dealt with by incarceration.[35] That is, the negative feelings associated with incarcerating a person—anger, revenge, guilt, and shame—were the very ones the community was trying to address and transform, not perpetuate.[36] The CHCH also recognized that years of marginalization within Canada had damaged the community and its traditions. A centrally important Ojibway value is that of *p'madaziwin*. This term refers to living life in the fullest sense in health, longevity, and well-being, both individually and as family.[37] In the same way the water level of a river rises and falls, so too can *p'madaziwin* in a person's life.[38] Researcher Christine Sivell-Ferri suggests that throughout Canada's history—as white traditions imposed themselves on the Ojibway tradition in Hollow Water;[39] as residential schools removed Ojibway children from their parents, communities, and traditions;[40] as Treaties appropriated land from First Nations communities[41]—levels of *p'madaziwin* fell in Hollow Water, and the community became defined by hurt and pain, substance abuse, and violence. To set things right again, the CHCH intervention involved traditional Ojibway practices.[42]

Fourth, the CHCH understood the importance of healing to restore balance.[43] Healing, in their view, is about addressing all the elements that make up a person—the physical, mental, emotional, and spiritual.[44] It's about letting go of hurt; and, instead of being defined by anger, guilt, shame, and vulnerability, becoming honest, loving, courageous, truthful, wise, humble, and respectful.[45] Certainly this was a radical shift, and no easy task. Fifth, and finally, the process the CHCH followed was very important. The process for an offender began with the Canadian federal police (RCMP) contacting CHCH to say they had enough evidence to prosecute an offender.[46] At this stage an offender was given the option to either go the criminal justice route, and face typical prosecution, or to admit guilt, disclose the offence, and enter the CHCH Circle healing process. The CHCH Circle process involves 13 phases directed toward healing, as outlined in Figure 10.1.

Figure 10.1: The CHCH Process

Source: Sivell-Ferri, *The Four Circles of Hollow Water*, 121.

All of these factors combined—acknowledging the issue of domestic and sexual violence, breaking down professional barriers and extensively studying victim and offender trauma, identifying barriers to healing, returning to traditional Circle practices, being clear about how healing journeys may happen, and having many Circle processes—have led the community of Hollow Water to a place where it is recognized as a leader in helping to heal victims and perpetrators of domestic and sexual violence. The CHCH used peacemaking Circles, as well as other traditional forms of Indigenous healing, to support victims and to hold offenders accountable within a context of support.

Other Indigenous communities have also applied their own healing frameworks to similar complex problems. Peter Menzies, Head of Aboriginal Services at the Centre for Addiction and Mental Health in Toronto, Canada, suggests that Indigenous approaches work holistically, at multiple levels: individually, in families, in the community, and for nations or groups. Often, these approaches try to counter collective trauma through traditional methods:

- Sweat ceremonies
- Medicine wheel teachings
- Fasting
- Healing circles
- Traditional medicines[47]

The importance of this focus on traditional ways cannot be overstated. For so long, assimilation processes have traumatized Indigenous societies by attempting to separate them from their languages, cultures, and practices. The purpose of colonization was to create shame in Indigenous societies about their ways of life. Returning to these ways is healing in and of itself for many Indigenous peoples.

In her doctoral work, *Reconciliation, Repatriation and Reconnection: A Framework for Building Resilience in Canadian Indigenous Families*, Métis researcher Patti Laboucane-Benson connects healing with decolonization.[48] She articulates a three-phase model of healing from a Cree (Alberta) perspective. In her view, the first step is being about decolonization, connecting the person needing healing with a healer who can articulate traditional teachings and ceremonies, thus reinforcing a connection with culture.[49] The second phase of a healing program is about education, helping participants understand the impacts of colonialism and intergenerational trauma and allowing them to grieve associated losses.[50] The third phase Laboucane-Benson describes as follows:

> Within the allocated program time, healing programs cannot actually "heal" the participants; rather, the program is structured to provide the information, orientation and support required for a life-long pursuit of **mino-pimatisiwin** [Cree term for seeking the good life, being on the healing path, or red road], which is achieved through the building and maintaining of healthy, respectful relationships with one's family, community, nation and the natural/spiritual world.[51]

Laboucane-Benson's first step draws on the work of Indigenous researcher Linda Archibald, as it is similar to establishing safety in the trauma-informed care model. However, its focus is instead to rediscover pride in culture of origin.[52] The second and third steps, too, share similarities with a general model of trauma-recovery for individuals, creating space for remembering, mourning, and building connections.

In summary, there's much for settler society to learn from Indigenous peoples about healing collective and intergenerational traumas. A holistic approach that focuses on healing identity and relationships through culturally appropriate practices is one that can inform a restorative justice framework for trauma-informed youth justice. To date, youth justice in Canada has largely focused on the individual young offender, divorcing them from community and context. This punishment agenda is about separation. Indigenous justice, instead, focuses on inclusion and on repairing harm. It's about helping a young person to understand who they are, where they've come from, and who they want to be. My argument in this section isn't about co-opting an Indigenous model of healing, but about learning from it in order to develop forms of justice that address the whole person while taking into account the community that influences their choices.

TRAUMA-INFORMED PREVENTION: DISMANTLING PATRIARCHY

When it comes to dismantling patriarchy, trauma-informed prevention could learn a few things from crime prevention theory. The work of crime prevention is primarily about identifying risk factors (things that might lead to harm) and developing protective factors (things that prevent harm). I've already identified colonialism and male violence as two risk factors for crime. Other common risk factors identified in crime prevention theory are shame, low income, addiction, experiencing abuse as a child, little or no social support, and inadequate parenting (at the individual level); poverty and lack of access to community support services (at the local level); and racism, income disparity, and a culture of violence (at the societal level).[53] Risk factors aren't a guarantee of future crime, but only a possible indicator, or correlate. The Waterloo Region Community Safety and Crime Prevention Council says, "We cannot talk about violence in absolute terms. Violence is not caused by poverty, poor childhood development, or being male. We know this because if circumstances like poverty or being male *caused* violence most people with those traits would be violent—and most are not."[54] They go further to say that people who share certain risk factors "are more likely to become violent or to become the victims of violence than those who don't."[55] This is the difference between causation and correlation.

On the preventative side, common protective factors are support, empowerment, positive values, social competencies, and positive identity (at the individual level); caring neighbourhood, safety, and support programs (at the local level); and education and awareness (at the societal level).[56] These are all factors that individuals, local communities, and societies can develop in order to prevent future violence.

Interventions must find ways to work individually, locally, and at societal levels. An example of a restorative justice program that works in all of these areas is the Revive program of Community Justice Initiatives (CJI) in Kitchener, Ontario. CJI is a restorative justice agency. The Revive program works with people who have offended sexually, as well as with survivors of sexual abuse. Using this program as an example, I'll explain how a multi-level approach can prevent future harm.

Revive addresses the following risk factors: shame, experiencing abuse as a child, lack of support (at the individual/local level), and a culture of violence and the trauma of disconnection (at the societal level). Programming prevents future violence by creating the following protective factors: education and peer support groups (at the individual and local levels) and community outreach (at the societal level). These protective factors provide support and empowerment, and foster the development of positive values, identity, and social competencies (at the individual and local level) and raise awareness and educate (at the societal level).

Figure 10.2: Restorative Justice as a Means of Crime Prevention

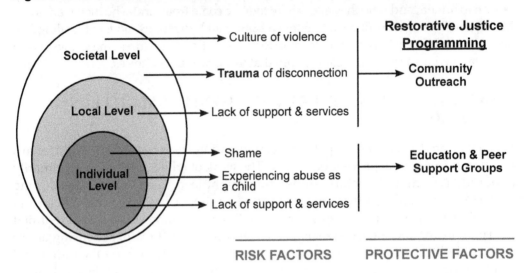

It should be noted that the use of restorative justice in the area of sexual violence is contentious. As we saw in chapter 8, critics of restorative justice have some concerns. Four of these commonly cited concerns relate to sexual violence and are worth revisiting here. One, critics are concerned that restorative justice, because of its community-based approach, often distant from government, risks framing sexual violence as a non-serious crime.[57] Second, critics have concerns that restorative justice practitioners are not sensitive enough to victim needs, and third, on the offender side are not sufficiently aware of offenders' manipulative natures.[58] Finally, restorative justice terms are considered problematic by some. For example, the term "restorative" creates an unattainable goal for survivors of sexual abuse, as they can never go back to (or restore) how things were before the harm occurred.

The Revive program has listened to these concerns and, in response, has incorporated important safeguards and mechanisms for accountability into their programming. With these important critiques in mind, I'll now describe the restorative justice programming that CJI has used for 25 years in the area of sexual abuse, focusing on their work with offenders. Following this description, I'll explain how the program addresses risk factors and creates protective factors while simultaneously answering critics' concerns.

The Revive program is best explained using the metaphor of a four-spoke wheel, driven by values.

At the hub (the central objective) is the prevention of future child sexual abuse through restorative justice practices. This is accomplished through a four-pronged approach, public education and public consultation (both forms of community outreach), and education groups and peer support groups (both forms of support).

Community outreach involves public education and consultation. The primary goal here is to make communities more aware of sexual abuse, its effects, its pervasiveness,

Figure 10.3: The Revive Program of Community Justice Initiatives as a Wheel

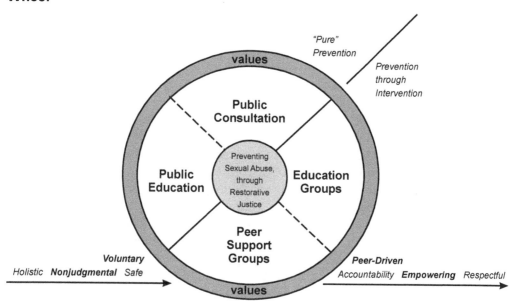

and the ways it can be prevented. *Public education* involves discussing these topics in various community settings such as schools and faith communities. *Public consultation* is about collaborating with agencies working with survivors of sexual abuse. For instance, CJI has maintained close connections over the years with the local sexual assault support centre.

Similar to community outreach, the support group half of the wheel involves education and peer support groups. The principle goal of support groups is to restoratively address the issue of sexual abuse by holding offenders accountable. Groups are facilitated by trained community volunteers who guide offenders through topics raised by the group, as well as through peer reviews—where offenders tell their story of offending, as well as what they're doing to ensure it doesn't happen again. Prior to entering peer support groups, offenders attend an educational program. General topics of the education group include understandings of sexual abuse and its impacts, victim empathy, self-awareness, relapse prevention, and non-violent conflict resolution. These groups can be used as an entry point into peer support groups, which are, as mentioned, about both support and accountability. They offer support in the sense that they are to be a safe, respectful, nonjudgmental place where people can talk about their abuse with others who have had similar experiences. They also hold people accountable, as one component of support is about encouraging people to maintain healthy boundaries in relationships.

As defined above, risk factors are commonly understood as those traits or experiences that make people more likely to become violent or to be the victim of violence.[59] By developing protective factors that respond directly to risk factors, research shows that violence and victimization can be reduced.[60] I would argue that the Revive program identifies some real risk factors existing in Canadian society and that the named protective factors directly challenge these. Therefore, logically speaking, by employing these protective factors, violence and victimization should be reduced, creating a safer society—one less traumatized by sexual abuse. How does this happen?

Looking at Figures 10.2 and 10.3, we can see that support groups primarily address individual and local level risk factors, while community outreach predominantly concentrates on local and societal risk factors. Even though these risk factors are interconnected, it's best to discuss each one independently to be as clear as possible about the preventative potential of Revive. There are three specific risk factors related to offenders who enter the Revive program that need to be addressed: lack of support, a culture of violence, and the trauma of disconnection.

Lack of support can be briefly explained as follows: when someone experiences trauma and lacks the support needed to heal, they often go on to harm others. For this reason, Revive supports offenders in finding a more positive self-identity. Two core values of restorative justice are respect and empowerment. If we want people to be able to replace shame with a positive self-identity, we need to allow them to talk about and find ways to work through shameful things. When I was a student, I volunteered as a facilitator for Revive groups for people who had offended sexually. I recall one participant who used to talk about hating himself. After a year in the group, this hate shifted from self-hatred, toward hate for his offence. This healing process was important both for accountability and for the offender finding a more meaningful existence.

Furthermore, Revive is about accountability. Offenders must acknowledge and face what they've done. The peer support environment, if well facilitated, promotes accountability. Offenders who are further along in the process of taking responsibility are good at spotting—and challenging—others who want to minimize the harm they've inflicted or who try to blame others.

The second risk factor to address is a culture of violence. There's a general lack of awareness, and apathy, in the form of violence acceptance in society (e.g., myths about sexual abuse abound and language is often used that blurs the lines between sexual activity and sexual assault). Community outreach and public education challenge this. Another example of a program working to counter male violence is the Male Allies Against Sexual Violence program of the Waterloo Region Sexual Assault Support Centre. Public Education Manager Joan Tuchlinsky describes it:

Men Engaged in the Work of Ending Male Violence
By Joan Tuchlinsky, Public Education Manager, Sexual Assault Support Centre of Waterloo Region

One in five men (21 percent) reported that they did not actively support community efforts to stop violence against women because no one had asked them to get involved, and another 13 percent reported that they did not know how to help.[61]

> The Sexual Assault Support Centre of Waterloo Region (SASC) responded by inviting men in their community to join them in addressing sexual violence and the Male Allies Against Sexual Violence (MAASV) program was born. In January 2008, 10 men gathered to learn, through activities and discussions, about the root causes of male violence and how men, individually and collectively, can work with women to address it. The program, which now has a male coordinator, has expanded to include workshops for male youth on healthy masculinity, healthy relationships/consent, self-esteem, and body image. Hundreds of males have participated in a MAASV workshop since the program began. Participants use the training in their paid or volunteer work, personal lives, or through volunteering for SASC. Monthly meetings for male allies are well-attended, and help break down the isolation and provide an opportunity for continual learning. MAASV's new 12-week Building on Youth Strengths (BOYS) Club for Grade 7 and 8 boys has been well received by schools and youth. One participant shared, "I enjoyed how we talked about our feelings at the beginning of each session."
>
> Violence prevention educator and activist Rus Ervin Funk reminds men that "men working to end sexism and violence also have a particular accountability ... to those who are harmed, the movements to end sexism and violence, the local agencies and programs that work with the people who are harmed, the local communities, themselves, and each other."[62] Funk goes on to encourage the creation of processes and structures of accountability, so that the survivors of male violence and agencies that provide support to survivors know *what* the men are doing and *how* they are doing it.[63]
>
> The challenge now is to take the increased awareness of individual men and boys and translate it into a collective awareness and belief that by working together, we can bring about the social change needed to end male violence.

The third risk factor to address is the trauma of disconnection. The more we marginalize and "other" people who have offended sexually, the more we compromise community safety. This does not mean that we should allow their full, unsupervised participation in society, but rather that we should carefully consider how to involve people who have offended sexually as members of our communities. As shame, disempowerment, and lack of supports perpetuate offending behaviour, so too does disconnection. In fact, disconnection can be a source of shame, as it pushes people out of communities and into hiding. The more people who have offended sexually have to hide, the greater the risk for reoffence becomes. Furthermore, offending behaviour is cyclical, starting from stress points (e.g., shame), moving to justifications of inappropriate behaviour (e.g., "It doesn't really hurt anyone"), then progressing into relapses through more stressful triggers and more justifications. This cycle has to be broken in individuals, families, and communities.

What happens when instead of "othering" people who have offended sexually and treating them like "garbage" we instead draw out positive values in them? Restorative justice agencies have seen firsthand that people can and do change, even in the area of sexual abuse. Mark Yantzi, former Executive Director of CJI and the founder of the Revive program in the early 1980s, confirms this:

> I have been affirmed in my belief that people can change. I have met men and women who have offended sexually and yet are facing their issues and previous irresponsibility in a responsible manner. Such actions give me hope that committed people can eventually disentangle the multilayered problem of sexual abuse. I am impressed by the number of individuals who can experience significant and sustainable change if we give them a supportive environment that respects them as people in spite of their past actions.[64]

Change happens when people are held accountable within a context of care. The values-based approach of restorative justice can break through the traumatic symptom of disconnection and therefore, prevent future harms.

There are two types of prevention I have written about in this chapter. One is "pure" prevention, or primary prevention. This is the community outreach half of the wheel model, and is about prevention through education and raising awareness. The second type is prevention through intervention, or secondary prevention. This is the other half of the wheel: the support groups. Traditionally, this is thought of as an intervention, and indeed it is. The Office of Child and Family Services Advocacy in Ontario has recently identified that as many as 50 percent of adults incarcerated for sexual offending began committing these offences as adolescents,[65] underscoring that interventions must take a trauma-informed and preventative orientation.

Figure 10.4: Prevention through Intervention

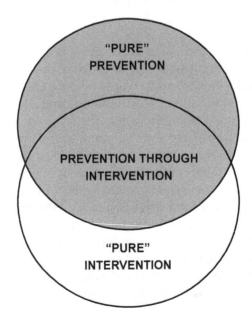

Draw the Line
By Julie S. Lalonde, Manager of Draw-the-line.ca

Draw-the-line.ca / Tracons-les-limites.ca is an interactive public education campaign that aims to provoke discussion on the role of bystanders in ending sexual violence. Developed and managed by the Ontario Coalition of Rape Crisis Centres (OCRCC) and Action ontarienne contre la violence faite aux femmes (AOcVF), the campaign was launched in 2012 as part of Ontario's Sexual Violence Action Plan. It includes a website, social media, YouTube videos, postcard-style pamphlets, and posters. All campaign materials are free and can be ordered at info@draw-the-line.ca.

Draw the Line / Traçons les limites believes that by engaging bystanders, sexual violence can be prevented.

Draw the Line is unique from many other public education campaigns in a few ways. Rather than focusing on the actions of victims or potential victims, the campaign's messages are targeted at bystanders. It uses accessible language to educate bystanders on concrete, tangible ways that they can make a difference. Using infographics to tell a story, the campaign is able to represent the diversity of Ontario without having 100 posters with 100 different faces.

The campaign does this by posing a series of "what would you do?" type questions to get users thinking about the reality of sexual violence in Ontario. Draw the Line / Traçons les limites believes that building an environment where people can honestly reflect on their actions is an effective means of creating social change.

The campaign also employs a casual and accessible tone, preferring to spark conversation than immediately dictating the right or wrong answer to each question. For example, instead of preaching about alcohol-facilitated sexual assault, Draw the Line/Traçons les limites gives a real-life example and asks folks how they would react: "Your wasted friend staggers out of the bar with some guy. Do you stay and keep dancing?" By creating a space for people to respond honestly, the campaign is able to expose the many myths and stereotypes surrounding alcohol-facilitated sexual assault. Through workshops and discussions with users, the overwhelming majority of respondents indicated that they *would* keep dancing and let their friend leave. As public educators and support workers to sexual assault survivors, this information was difficult to accept. But OCRCC and AOcVF knew that without creating a space for people to be honest, it's nearly impossible to challenge the behaviour.

Addressing issues as diverse as online sexual violence (e.g., non-consensual "sexting"), workplace sexual harassment, and assault by a person of authority, the campaign aims to reach outside the social justice "bubble" and make bystander intervention accessible for the general public.

Draw-the-line.ca/Tracons-les-limites.ca has proven effective at creating honest dialogue about sexual violence by focusing on bystanders (rather than victims or perpetrators), employing real-life scenarios, using accessible language, and focusing on tangible ways that people can make a difference. OCRCC and AOcVF believe that this campaign is a great model for developing effective prevention tools.

The process of dismantling patriarchy is similar to that of decolonization. Although I have identified one type of layered restorative justice intervention and have focused on highlighting some educational practices—especially for men and boys—that promotes change, other efforts toward improving policy and altering structures are also needed.

CONCLUSION: FROM DESPAIR TO HOPE

I find it hard at times not to fall into despair or to become cynical about society's unwillingness to end the colonization of Indigenous peoples and to put a stop to patriarchal male violence. Both seem to be relentless. White, male privilege continues to rule the day, and the impacts are devastating. There continue to be high rates of sexual and physical abuse in families, perpetrated by men, and Indigenous societies still struggle under the thumb of harmful policies. It feels at times that trauma is everywhere. Still, I find hope in reading the work of people like *Michi Saagiig Nishnaabeg* writer and educator Leanne Simpson, who talks about how she—and her people—continue to survive and thrive in spite of violence. I find hope in working with Joan Tuchlinsky as part of the Male Allies Against Sexual Violence program. During my time there, I have met many boys and men who long for a different version of masculinity, one that's kinder and based in equity. I find hope in the strong, fiery advocacy of Julie S. Lalonde, who has done incredible work raising awareness about the issue of sexual violence on university campuses, and generally about male violence. These people not only suggest that change is possible, they demonstrate it. In this chapter, I highlighted some ways to work toward ending colonization—by honouring treaties, bringing pluralism to youth justice, and learning from Indigenous peoples. I've also presented some thoughts on dismantling patriarchy—through interventions and education that promote change. But all of this is just a start. There's still much work to be done.

GLOSSARY OF TERMS

Decolonization is the process of dismantling systems of colonialism. Examples in the Canadian context include: honouring treaties, returning Indigenous lands, abolishing the Indian Act, recognizing Indigenous sovereignty, and so on.
Legal pluralism is multiple legal realities coexisting. In this chapter, this pertains to Canadian laws in conjunction with Indigenous ones. The argument in this book is that youth justice with Indigenous peoples must recognize a legal plurality.
mino-pimatisiwin is a Cree term for seeking the good life, being on a healing path, or the "red road."
p'madaziwin is an Ojibway word that refers to living life in the fullest sense in health, longevity, and well-being, personally and for your family.

QUESTIONS FOR REFLECTION

1. Why do you think colonization persists? Is Canadian society ignorant, apathetic, or intentionally harmful in the way we treat Indigenous peoples?

2. Consider the question posed by Julie S. Lalonde of the Draw the Line/Traçons les limites campaign: "Your wasted friend staggers out of the bar with some guy. Do you stay and keep dancing?" What would you do?

RECOMMENDED READING

Anaya, James. *Report of the Special Rapporteur on the Rights of Indigenous Peoples: The Situation of Indigenous Peoples in Canada.* Geneva: United Nations General Assembly, 2014.

In 2014 James Anaya, the Special Rapporteur on the rights of Indigenous peoples for the United Nations, released a report condemning Canada's treatment of Indigenous peoples. While being critical it also gave dozens of helpful recommendations.

Metatawabin, Edmund, with Alexandro Shimo. *Up Ghost River: A Chief's Journey Through the Turbulent Waters of Native History.* Toronto: Alfred A. Knopf Canada, 2014.

In this powerful account of his life, Edmund Metatawabin describes his experiences attending "Indian" residential school, the horrors and trauma of it, as well as how he relied on traditional, Indigenous ways for healing.

Sivell-Ferri, Christine. *The Four Circles of Hollow Water.* Public Works & Government Services Canada, Aboriginal Peoples Collection: APC 15 CA, 1997.

Hollow Water, a First Nations community in Manitoba, Canada, developed a uniquely Indigenous approach to dealing with the aftermath of sexual violence—with incredibly promising results. This report describes Indigenous justice in action, one that addresses individual and collective traumas, as well as root causes.

Yantzi, Mark. *Sexual Offending and Restoration.* Waterloo: Herald Press, 1998.

One of very few books written on the topic of restorative justice and sexual violence, written by the founder of the Revive program (described in this chapter).

11 | Victim-Centred Justice

"That night, back at home, I got out a new canvas. I painted it a very soft, washed-out blue, blending a pale yellow into the top-left corner. The sun was coming out. I glued a mosaic of clear glass to form a bumpy landscape along the bottom of the painting—sharp ground, but solid enough to walk on. Then from a photo I'd taken of the front garden of my former home, I clipped out the pink ballerina tulips and placed them on the canvas, growing out of the broken glass landscape. Hope personified in flowers."

—Shannon Moroney[1]

Young people are much more likely to be victims of crimes than to be offenders. For this reason, the question of what it means to be victim-centred is increasingly important for the work of trauma-informed youth justice. Within a restorative justice framework the central questions are: "Who has been hurt?" followed by "What do they need?" Using this as a starting place puts victims at the forefront of justice responses. As I've written in earlier chapters, sometimes justice responses end up creating more injustice and harm. Furthermore, a risk focus detracts from creating resilience in young people who commit crime, and prison makes youth more likely to reoffend. In a similar way, police, the courts, and other justice mechanisms can often affect victims negatively, making it more difficult for them to heal and, at times, leaving them dissatisfied with justice processes and outcomes. As we've seen, victims are often sidelined in the justice processes—made witnesses to the proceedings rather than active participants in the justice process. The case is no longer about them. It is about the state, *R. v.* [last name of offender].

Some of this is intended to help victims. Making the state the victim creates an element of safety for the real victim and ensures that victims don't have to decide for themselves how to deal with an offender. However, the overall effect is often one of disempowerment. Recall how we saw in chapter 9 that establishing safety for someone who has experienced trauma is of primary importance. Psychiatrist and trauma expert Judith Herman claims that this is fundamentally about empowering, or giving control over to victims. Justice processes often do the opposite. What's needed, then, is justice that gives an appropriate amount of control to victims of crime. This is trauma-informed. This will help victims to heal. In the epigraph above, author Shannon Moroney eloquently describes healing after crime. She creates a painting based on her victimization, incorporating parts of an old life (pre-trauma) together with a new one (post-trauma). We can offer victims hope for this type of healing and renewal when we move their needs to the centre of justice processes.

This chapter will go as follows: The place of the victim in criminal justice will be discussed. A history of the victim movement, as a social movement, will then describe why victims are often dissatisfied with criminal justice. In the final section, I'll advocate for trauma-informed youth justice to become victim-centred by putting the needs of crime victims at the forefront of justice processes. Finally, the chapter will conclude with a piece that was inspired by a focus group I did with a group of victims (survivors!), as I sought their input in order to ensure that, as should be the case in justice proceedings, their voices were given space and heard in this chapter.

THE HISTORICAL SIDELINING OF VICTIMS

A history of the Western criminal justice system reveals a gradual sidelining of victims. Prior to the emergence of the "modern" Western justice system, crime was understood as a "private" interpersonal conflict.[2] However, from the 13th century onward, the state began to slowly occupy the place of victims. Some have suggested that the state substituted itself as victim to counteract the vengeful outcomes of conflicts. In studying the formation of the Western criminal justice system, law professors Gerry Johnstone and Tony Ward describe the transition from more communitarian approaches to national, formalized criminal justice. They suggest that the state adopted the vengeance component of justice, without realizing some of the more reparative elements of communitarian justice.[3] Some theorize that public justice—or state-sanctioned criminal justice—was a way to contain, or control, the unwieldy nature of private justice, or vengeance:

> Criminal law has its roots in the ancient practice of private vengeance. The state tames private vengeance. It formalizes the customary norms which determine the actions for which vengeance is permitted and the severity of vengeful actions, makes rules about who is a legitimate target of vengeance, and gradually replaces violent killings and mutilations with gentler forms of punishments.[4]

However, what this interpretation seems to miss altogether is that communitarian justice often did not involve tit-for-tat violence. Johnstone and Ward discuss how cyclical violence or revenge, although possibly helpful for restoring honour to a community, might simply have been too risky or costly for certain people groups.[5] Furthermore, restorative justice professor Howard Zehr argues that it's a myth to say that the outcome of "private" justice in pre-modernity was uncontained vengeance.[6] Justice wasn't necessarily a blood sport. In fact, Zehr states that it was primarily about settlement:

The feud was one way of resolving situations, but so was negotiation, restitution, and reconciliation. Victim and offender as well as kin and community played vital roles in this process. Since crime created obligations, a typical outcome of the justice process was some sort of settlement.... Laws and customs frequently specified a range of appropriate compensations for both property and personal offenses.[7]

Outcomes were sometimes punitive, but not necessarily in the way we might imagine. Punishment may not, in fact, have been about retribution. Zehr says, "The Greek *pune* refers to an exchange of money for harm done and may be the origin of the word punishment."[8] Ironically, it appears that with the emergence of the nation state, the focus of criminal justice became more about vengeance and less about compensation. As the state began to occupy the space previously held by victims, justice became more retributive.

The question is: Why would communities relinquish control of private conflicts, or of crime, to the state? Johnstone and Ward put forward two theories:

1. **Social Contract Theory:** This theory assumes that people give up control to a state for the sake of security—as such, the belief is that rational people will obey the laws because they have agreed to do so.[9]
2. **Self-Help Theory:** This theory claims that without the help of a sovereign, or state, the resolution of conflicts will be caught up in a never-ending need for private vengeance. The state provides law, and thus controls the means to vengeance.[10]

As communities gave up control of conflict, criminal justice services became increasingly professionalized through magistrates (later judges) and advocates (or lawyers). Rather than remaining in the hands of victims, power and decision-making now resided with professionals. The diagram below maps out the place of victims in the current criminal justice system.

Figure 11.1: Hierarchical Power and Decision-Making in the Court System

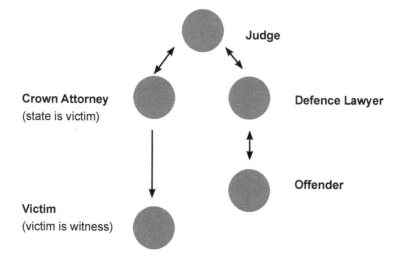

The diagram indicates the hierarchical nature of power in a criminal justice process. At the top is the judge, all powerful, responsible for process and outcomes. Below are the lawyers. On the right, is the defence lawyer representing the offender. On the left is the Crown attorney, representing the state (the substitute victim). Below is the offender. Even further below is the actual victim, or victims. The arrows indicate communication flow. Notice how the victim is the only one who doesn't necessarily influence process or outcomes. They are a witness to the case. Of course, if the offender is found guilty, they're supposed to have the right to make a victim impact statement, which in turn is supposed to influence a judge's decision at sentencing. However, communication still flows from Crown attorney to the victim/witness. Because impact statements are prescriptive, the state decides the parameters of what can be said, basically what's allowed. All of this represents a significant shift in decision-making and power, from the community to the state, from individuals harmed to professional decision-makers. This reliance on the state to resolve criminal conflicts has come at a cost, particularly to victims.

In a troubling account, *The Story of Jane Doe: A Book About Rape*, Jane Doe describes how she was raped and subsequently retraumatized by criminal justice processes that discounted her. This story puts an exclamation point on the disempowering experience of criminal justice, showing how far victims have been displaced. In a chapter titled "How to Survive a Rape Trial" she says about judges:

> Most of the officials of [the court] are still old white guys who wear long black priest-like robes. If they were priests, the judge would be pope. Everyone is required to stand when the judge leaves or enters the room. He can interrupt you at any time and tell you what to say. He can banish you from his sight. His word cannot be questioned. He does not have to explain. He answers to no one. Latecomers must bow their heads in supplication for disturbing his court. When you are a witness, he is the one you must impress (unless there is a jury), for he is the one who will decide if you are lying or telling the truth. He will decide how serious your rape was and what penance or sentence the rapist will receive. If any. His decisions will be based, among other things, on his impressions of you. How you are dressed. How angry you are and if that anger is justifiable or in proportion. If he sees that your friends and family are with you, he usually considers that a good thing. If you speak English and speak it well, that is even better.[11]

All of this raises the question: If criminal proceedings are no longer about victims, then what is justice for victims? To consider this question further, I will now tell a case story about a crime that my family and I experienced a few years ago.

A CASE STORY: THE VICTIM IN A BREAK-AND-ENTER

In 2011, my house was broken into and ransacked. Many items were stolen. Below, in four parts, I'm going to tell this story. The first part reads like a newspaper report, written after the fact. The second part focuses on my family and our victimization, from my perspective. The third part is primarily about the offender, and the fourth part centres on the outcome. As I tell the story, I invite you to pause after each of the four parts and ask yourself: What is justice?

Case Story: Part 1

In February, a man who was well known to the Waterloo Regional Police Service Break & Enter Unit was tailed and caught by some officers breaking into a house in the East Ward of Kitchener. On his person, they discovered items belonging to other people: an iPod, a wedding ring, and some children's jewelry.

- *What is justice?*

Case Story: Part 2

It's the end of January, a Sunday evening. My family and I are just returning from a nice weekend away at my partner's parents' house. After a two-and-a-half-hour drive, we pull into our driveway at about 9:30 p.m.

My partner enters the house first. I stumble in, close behind, tired from the drive. I'm immediately jolted by her gasping noises of panic. "Jude, Jude," she says, "I think our house has been broken into." My stomach drops. I look around. Our living room is a disaster—stuff strewn everywhere, a desk tossed to the side. Immediately, I notice that our computer is gone. I run upstairs; it's the same sight in the bedrooms. We've been completely ransacked.

With a shaky hand and a sick stomach I call the police. An officer arrives within minutes.

His first question: "Have you checked to see if there's anyone in the house? Looked in all the closets?"

"No," I say, thinking I've just tucked my eldest daughter (who is five), still asleep from the drive, into her bed. I run upstairs, the officer a few steps behind me. Nobody. I run downstairs. Nobody.

I look at the officer and he says, "You might want your wife to count her intimates."

"What?" I say.

"Her underwear. We're checking on that kind of stuff these days." Russell Williams (a convicted Canadian murderer and rapist), who is all over the news at the time, pops into my head. I stare blankly back at the officer.

The forensic team arrives. Our house is dusted for fingerprints by a compassionate officer who takes time to talk to my younger daughter (age three), who is still awake and who is confused about why mommy and daddy are so upset. We make an itemized list of about 20 things that are missing, including my wedding ring, an iPod, and some of my daughters' jewelry. As the officers walk out the door, I ask, "What could I have done to prevent this?"

"Not much," they say. "If they want in, they'll just break down the door."

I say goodnight, close the door, and go back inside.

- *What is justice?*
- *Has your answer from Part 1 been confirmed, or has it changed?*

Case Story: Part 3

About a week later, much to our surprise, we get a call from the B&E (Break & Enter) Unit of the Waterloo Regional Police Service. They've caught the person, they think, but we need to come and identify our stuff. I imagine picking my computer out of a lineup. Unfortunately, it isn't among the items recovered—only my iPod, my wedding ring, and one of my daughter's necklaces.

The officers speak openly about the individual whom they caught. He's well known to police—a crack addict who supports his addiction through B&Es. They followed him, caught him breaking into another house, and found some of our items on his person.

I think back to a conversation I had a few years ago with a local Crown attorney. He explained that if we could take 10 individuals off the street, we would reduce B&Es in the Waterloo Region by 90 percent.

I ask the officers what they think the outcome will be in court. They suspect he'll get provincial time. I pause. "Can I do a victim impact statement?" I ask. They provide me with the forms. "What about restorative justice?" I ask.

"You mean meeting the offender?" the officer says.

"Sort of," I respond. "I'd like to ask him some questions and tell him how I was affected by this situation."

"You don't wanna do that," they say. "He's a bad dude!"

I think of the many "bad dudes" I've met in my time working in the federal prison system. Some of them are, indeed, scary, but most are like you and me. The only difference is that they've made some really "bad" choices. Often these choices arise from a context of their own hurts, or traumas, mental health issues, or addictions.

"What will jail do for him?" I ask the officers.

"Nothing," one replies. "The drugs are just as rampant in Maplehurst, and the place is even more violent than the streets. He'll do drugs in there then he'll do drugs again back on the streets."

- *What is justice?*
- *Has your definition or have your thoughts about it changed at all based on this new information?*

Case Story: Part 4

It's been a few months, and the police have told me the offender would likely be going to trial in June. I contact the Crown attorney assigned to my case, letting them know I'd like to attend and do a victim impact statement at sentencing. The Crown assures me that I can and says a trial date is set for June.

June comes around and I don't hear anything. I phone the Crown's office. The case has been assigned to a new Crown attorney. I leave a message for this person. I don't hear anything back. I follow up again. And again, nothing.

Finally, a few weeks later, I get through to someone. Apparently the man pleaded guilty and sentencing is already complete. They forgot to let me know, ignoring my right to give a victim impact statement. The offender was given one year in prison and six months probation.

Case closed.

- *What is justice?*
- *Has your definition or have your thoughts about it changed at all based on this new information?*

The overall outcome of the event I've just described left me largely unsatisfied. When we got home the day of the crime, initially, my partner and I were pretty shaken up. Many people who have experienced this type of crime report it as a significant violation. The sacredness of home feels shattered. For me, it wasn't that extreme. I was upset and I felt quite vulnerable; however, what I really needed was an opportunity to understand something about the offender: Who was he? How did he come to start breaking into homes? What did he need in order to do something different with his life? I felt an odd sense of connection; almost an obligation toward him. I knew that the break-and-enter had little to do with me, and that it was more a crime of opportunity related to fueling an addiction. At the time, this perspective helped me not to take it so personally. My partner had a more difficult time with it. She'd lost an entire collection of photography on our computer and was sickened by it. Everyone experiences crime differently.

In an attempt to make contact with the offender, I later found his probation and parole officer (PPO), phoned this person, and asked to be able to have some contact or to send a gift card to the offender. Once again, I never heard back. I don't blame the PPO. It's well outside the scope of their role to facilitate this type of contact. In fact, the PPO might have thought that it was in the best interests of community safety (my safety) not to create this type of contact. Given his history of addiction, perhaps the PPO thought that the offender would take advantage of my generosity. However, again, I was left feeling unsatisfied. It was my house. It was my stuff that was taken. Yet, I was at the mercy of the system to get any of the justice that I was looking for.

Of course, some victims would respond differently than I did. Some would want their pound of flesh, or revenge—and that's okay. But, even in cases where people do long for retribution, the criminal justice system often leaves them wanting. **Victimology**—the scientific study of victims and their needs—has been examining the issue of victim satisfaction since the 1970s. A comprehensive review of the literature reveals that victim satisfaction hinges both on the procedural and on the outcome aspects of criminal justice. Procedurally, voice (opportunity to participate to the degree they would like), respect (interest, friendliness, and receptiveness of criminal justice professionals), information (regular updates on their case), and compensation (adequate resources, including financial resources to pay for whatever was damaged) are all important.[12] From an outcomes perspective, victims are looking for a range of things, and it can vary widely from person to person. However, research reveals three overall themes: retribution, behavioural change, and restorative justice. The first refers to the offender receiving a punishment proportionate to how the victim views the crime, the second to punishment functioning as a vehicle of change—helping to ensure that what happened to them never happens to anyone else—and the third refers to the victim receiving some type of restitution, whether it be symbolic, like an apology, or some other type of compensation from the offender.[13]

Analyses of criminal justice processes reveal that the satisfaction of victims is largely mixed. Apparently, satisfaction is too dependent on individual needs for it to be determined, at this point, how generally satisfied victims are with criminal justice. What's more, even when an offender gets the harsh punishment a victim thinks they deserve, the passage of time often leaves the victim feeling hollow.[14] Victims sometimes want punishment because it validates their pain, however, as researcher Susan L. Miller says:

> The passage of time changed victims' feelings about punitiveness, tempering their initial support for severe penalties ... many felt hollow, as though the satisfaction they were supposed to feel by participating in the formal criminal justice process or knowing their offenders were behind bars was not enough. Over time, victims' desires for retribution were eclipsed, but not completely replaced, by the need to find answers and be heard.[15]

Both the victim who wants a pound of flesh and the one who's curious about the lived experience of the offender want some ownership of their healing. The crime was their experience; the Crown attorney (or the Queen) did not experience it. Danish criminologist Nils Christie talks about **conflict as property**—as something that's owned by victims, but taken away when the state intervenes: "Material compensation is not what I have in mind with the formulation of 'conflicts as property.' It is the conflict itself that represents the most interesting property taken away, not the goods originally taken away from the victim or given back to him. In our types of society, conflicts are more scarce than property. And they are immensely more valuable."[16] What do we give up when the state takes away our property, our conflict? Christie cites a number of things, most of which impact the victim:

- Victims lose the opportunity to participate meaningfully in justice.
- Society loses the opportunity to define what is most important about the resolution of conflict. For example, in my case, the court narrowly defined that punishment resolved the issue. I was looking for something more—a process that looked at deeper causes. Really, I didn't want anyone else's house to be broken into again, let alone my own. Plus, I'm interested in all people, especially those with addiction issues, being able to live meaningful lives. If I hadn't lost ownership of my conflict—or if it hadn't have been taken away—a process might have considered some of these aspects.
- Offenders lose an opportunity to meaningfully engage with what they've done. Christie says that once the property of their conflict is taken, offenders only focus on the punishment aspect. He suggests that this allows offenders to avoid truly facing what they've done. I, for one, would have liked to have had contact with the offender to communicate to him the effects his crime had.[17]

Has any progress been made over the past 1,000 years of criminal justice? The writings of Zehr, Johnstone, and Ward all question whether progress is always natural, always in the direction of positive change. We might ask what was gained and what was lost for victims when the state began to control the outcomes of conflicts. On one hand, victims have gained the ability to save face where honour might have otherwise required victims to seek revenge. There have also been some protections built in for victims. The state became "victim" to protect the actual victims of a crime so that victims wouldn't be responsible for deciding what should happen to offenders.[18] On the other hand, what's been lost seems to have more dramatically affected victims. Victims have lost control over process and outcomes—the opportunity to participate in the ways that they wish.

All of this indicates a need for restorative justice, for frameworks that are victim-centred.

Significantly, in comparative analyses, satisfaction has been much higher for victims who have participated in restorative justice than for those who participated in criminal justice processes. Examining why this is the case, researchers Tinneke Van Camp and Jo-Anne Wemmers suggest four factors:

1. Flexibility—victims have more power, including being able to decide whether or not to participate.
2. Care for victims—the need for dignified contacts with professionals that are both informal and professional. Plus, process is focused on emotional reparation.
3. Opportunity for dialogue—a chance to be heard.
4. Contributes to a better society—victims felt like they were contributing to the greater good by participating in restorative justice.[19]

Because restorative justice scores so well in evaluative analyses, but isn't suitable in certain cases—where an offender isn't caught or isn't willing to take responsibility, or where a victim doesn't need or want it— some have suggested a dual-track approach to justice, whereby criminal justice and restorative justice run parallel to each other.[20] Perhaps there's a middle road to be found as a way to meet the needs of victims.

A BRIEF HISTORY OF THE VICTIM MOVEMENT

In the late 1960s and early 1970s, in light of concerns with criminal justice, the victim movement emerged. According to criminologist Heather Strang, the victim movement is a social movement concerned with the continued injustice experienced by victims of crime even after a crime has been committed.[21] The movement emerged in Europe and North America after a period of significantly high crime rates in the 1960s.[22] Those who have studied the beginnings of the victim movement suggest that an increase in crime rates led to an increase in people dissatisfied by criminal justice. Others claim that the victim movement, in the United States at least, arose in conjunction with the development of the field of study of victimology, and with the emergence of the women's movement.[23] The victim movement shares some commonalities with other social movements.

Sociologists Macionis and Gerber define a **social movement** as any "organized activity that encourages or discourages social change."[24] Social movements are different from other forms of social activity in that they're deliberate and consequential, containing three defining characteristics: they're well-organized internally, long-term, and their aim is to either reorganize or preserve some part of society.[25] This is true of the victim movement. Indeed, it is a well-organized, long-term, deliberate movement supporting and advocating for victims and for change within the social system of justice.

Three Theoretical Explanations for Social Movements

1. **Deprivation theory**, as described by Macionis and Gerber: "Social movements arise as a response to a perception of being deprived of what is deemed fair."[26] As victims are unable to meet or are deprived of their needs, they respond by bonding together against injustice.
2. **Mass-society theory**, as fashioned by sociologist William Kornhauser, suggests that people who are isolated and feel insignificant will bond together in order to gain a sense of belonging and participation within society.[27] Strang identifies this very situation within the victim movement; it is both a response to injustice and a place where victims reaffirm their identity and legitimize their concerns.[28] Undeniably, it is a common experience of victimization to feel disconnected and isolated[29] and, as such, victims need others with whom to belong.
3. **Structural-strain theory** suggests that social movements emerge as people deem that society is unable to operate as it should.[30] The very existence of a victim movement is a clear indication that the criminal justice system is unable to meet the expectations of the victims it is supposed to be serving. As researcher Diane Whitely says, "The rise of the victims' rights movement is a signal that the justice system has missed something."[31] These theories draw attention to what Strang calls the neglected role of the victim within the criminal justice system.[32]

The victim movement is primarily expressed in two ways: advocacy and support. Strang refers to these two ways of supporting victims based on region and dominant expression. The "United States model" is rights-focused and the "European model" is support-focused.[33] Her suggestion (a generalization) is that the victim movement in the United States has been largely about tipping the balance of rights away from offenders toward victims, while in Europe, the victim movement is primarily about helping to alleviate the suffering of victims.[34]

Indeed, a central push of the victim movement in the United States, and North America, has been for the rights of victims to be respected and for their voices to be heard at critical moments during prosecution.[35] Some argue that this push for rights has been largely punitive.[36] Demands for change often come from angry victims and from a disturbed community who are, understandably, upset with offenders and with the criminal justice system. As Strang notes, "The precipitating condition for victim advocacy is usually an especially horrifying or aberrant crime which stirs moral panic in the community and the atmosphere generated by these events, as well as the attitudes of the victims concerned, is likely to be overwhelmingly punitive."[37] It's possible that this punitive response is not a result of vengeful victims but of the co-optation of their cause. As with many other social movements, those in the political sphere have in significant ways co-opted the agenda of the victim movement and made it their own. Politicians have been elected into office brandishing such media savvy slogans as "Get tough on crime" and "The war on crime." Yet, as feminist scholars have known since the early 1980s, this co-optation and its punitive results have done very little, if anything, to help meet victim needs.[38] In fact, it may even have exacerbated the entire problem.[39]

However, saying that the victim movement has gone awry (or been completely co-opted) would ignore the positive steps the movement has allowed for victims. Certainly, the victim movement has raised the profile of victims and has helped to offer many services and supports to victims to help in meeting their needs post-crime.

In Canada, the victim movement has made significant strides since the early 1980s. Some of its accomplishments include:

1. Organizations that advocate for victim needs and rights:
   - Research Centres
   - Child Advocacy Centres
   - Issue-Specific Organizations
   - Violence against Women Provincial Steering Groups
2. Organizations that support victims:
   - Womens' Shelters
   - Non-profit Groups
   - Police and Court-Based Victim Services
   - Restorative Justice Programs
3. Changes in policy and legislation:
   - Changes in law regarding sexual assault and domestic violence
   - National Sex Offender Registry
   - Victim Impact Statements
   - Victim Input at Parole Hearings
   - Victim Registration for Information about an Offender Serving Federal Time
   - Establishment of a Federal Ombudsperson for Victims of Crime
   - Canadian Victim Bill of Rights[40]

The Canadian Victims Bill of Rights[41]

This enactment enacts the Canadian Victims Bill of Rights, which specifies that victims of crime have the following rights:

(a) the right to information about the criminal justice system, the programs and services that are available to victims of crime and the complaint procedures that are available to them when their rights have been infringed or denied;

(b) the right to information about the status of the investigation and the criminal proceedings, as well as information about reviews while the offender is subject to the corrections process, or about hearings after the accused is found not criminally responsible on account of mental disorder or unfit to stand trial, and information about the decisions made at those reviews and hearings;
(c) the right to have their security and privacy considered by the appropriate authorities in the criminal justice system;
(d) the right to protection from intimidation and retaliation;
(e) the right to request testimonial aids;
(f) the right to convey their views about decisions to be made by authorities in the criminal justice system that affect the victim's rights under this Act and to have those views considered;
(g) the right to present a victim impact statement and to have it considered;
(h) the right to have the courts consider making, in all cases, a restitution order against the offender; and
(i) the right to have a restitution order entered as a civil court judgment that is enforceable against the offender if the amount owing under the restitution order is not paid.

The Canadian Victims Bill of Rights also specifies

(a) the periods during which the rights apply;
(b) the individuals who may exercise the rights;
(c) the complaint mechanism for victims and the requirements for federal departments to create complaint mechanisms; and
(d) how the Canadian Victims Bill of Rights is to be interpreted.

This enactment amends the Criminal Code to

(a) align the definition of "victim" with the definition of "victim" in the Canadian Victims Bill of Rights;
(b) protect the privacy and security interests of complainants and witnesses in proceedings involving certain sexual offences and ensure that they are informed of their right to be represented by legal counsel;
(c) broaden the conduct to which the offence of intimidation of justice system participants applies;
(d) expand the list of factors that a court may take into consideration when determining whether an exclusion order is in the interest of the proper administration of justice;
(e) make testimonial aids more accessible to vulnerable witnesses;
(f) enable witnesses to testify using a pseudonym in appropriate cases;
(g) make publication bans for victims under the age of 18 mandatory on application;

(h) provide that an order for judicial interim release must indicate that the safety and security of every victim was taken into consideration;
(i) require the court to inquire of the prosecutor if reasonable steps have been taken to inform the victims of any plea agreement entered into by the accused and the prosecutor in certain circumstances;
(j) add victim impact statement forms to assist victims to convey their views at sentencing proceedings and at hearings held by Review Boards;
(k) provide that the acknowledgment of the harm done to the victims and to the community is a sentencing objective;
(l) clarify the provisions relating to victim impact statements;
(m) allow for community impact statements to be considered for all offences;
(n) provide that victims may request a copy of a judicial interim release order, probation order or a conditional sentence order;
(o) specify that the victim surcharge must be paid within the reasonable time established by the lieutenant governor of the province in which it is imposed;
(p) provide a form for requesting a restitution order; and
(q) provide that courts must consider the making of a restitution order in all cases, and that, in multiple victim cases, a restitution order may specify the amounts owed to each victim and designate the priority of payment among the victims.

The enactment amends the Canada Evidence Act to provide that no person is incompetent, or uncompellable, to testify for the prosecution by reason only that they are married to the accused. It also amends that Act to add a new subsection to govern the questioning of witnesses over the age of 14 years in certain circumstances.

This enactment amends the Corrections and Conditional Release Act to

(a) align the definition of "victim" with the definition of "victim" in the Canadian Victims Bill of Rights;
(b) permit victims to have access to information about the offender's progress in relation to the offender's correctional plan;
(c) permit victims to be shown a current photograph of the offender at the time of the offender's conditional release or the expiration of the offender's sentence;
(d) permit the disclosure of information to victims concerning an offender's deportation before the expiration of the offender's sentence;
(e) permit the disclosure to victims of an offender's release date, destination and conditions of release, unless the disclosure would have a negative impact on public safety;
(f) allow victims to designate a representative to receive information under the Act and to waive their right to information under the Act;
(g) require that the Correctional Service of Canada inform victims about its victim-offender mediation services;

> (h) permit victims who do not attend a parole hearing to listen to an audio recording of the hearing;
> (i) provide for the provision to victims of decisions of the Parole Board of Canada regarding the offender; and
> (j) require, when victims have provided a statement describing the harm, property damage or loss suffered by them as the result of the commission of an offence, that the Parole Board of Canada impose victim non-contact or geographic restrictions as conditions of release, where reasonable and necessary, to protect the victims in relation to an offender who is the subject of a long-term supervision order.

TRAUMA-INFORMED YOUTH JUSTICE AS VICTIM-CENTRED

Being the victim of crime is often a traumatic experience. Trauma expert Nancy Good Sider compares "ordinary stress" with "traumatic stress." "Ordinary stress" is a slow or gradual change. It diminishes over time and people are still able to plan and problem-solve throughout. "Traumatic stress," on the other hand, is brought about by a sudden, significant loss. It has a piercing intensity and gives a shock to the system, causing the individual to feel overwhelmingly helpless.[42] In fact, a traumatic event is one that's so intense that it typically terrifies and renders helpless anyone who faces it.[43] Many sorts of crime are experienced as traumatic. The most obviously traumatic (violent) crimes, as Zehr writes, devastate "all areas of one's life."[44] But what is often overlooked is that crimes that aren't physically violent can also be experienced as traumatic, although usually in a less intense way.[45] As a matter of fact, I recall observing a Family Group Conference about 10 years ago where the victim, whose car had been stolen, told the offender that the victimization "felt like rape." At the time, I silently questioned this drastic comparison (and in some ways I still do), especially in the context of some of the violence that I have heard about in my working life, yet as Zehr explains, at its core, crime is a violation of people and relationships.[46]

Evolutionary biologist Mary Clark argues that human beings have three fundamental needs or, as she terms them, propensities: bonding, autonomy, and meaning.[47] Clark uses the term propensities to describe our fundamental human needs because the term connotes a powerful innate tendency that is flexible in being satisfied, unlike terms like *instinct* or *drives* that are often used to describe needs.[48] Bonding, in her view, is essential to human survival; humans would not be able to survive without relationships.[49] Crime damages bonding, our ability to relate to others. This is because in order to be able to relate to others, we first need to be able to trust others.[50] Healthy relationships with others make us feel whole and help with identity formation.[51] By interfering with our ability to trust, crime also confuses our identity. Judith Herman describes trauma: "Traumatic events have primary effects not only on the psychological structures of self but also on the systems of attachment and meaning that link individual and community."[52] Compounded with distrust, victims of trauma also experience overwhelming feelings of doubt, shame, and guilt that alienate them from the community.[53]

Autonomy, the second propensity identified by Clark, is also necessary in order for humans to learn to survive.[54] Crime estranges us from others, but at the same time damages our autonomy—our ability to act independently. Fundamentally, a crime dehumanizes us by seizing control from us.[55] Zehr offers that this "loss of control is deeply demoralizing and affects one's sense of safety, identity and well-being."[56] This demoralizing effect is so profound that there can be permanent changes in arousal, emotions, cognition, and memory, and even in how these functions integrate together.[57] This confusion and disintegration of the connections in the mind produces a feeling of utter helplessness, which Herman calls "the essential insult of trauma."[58] As such, the ability to act autonomously is wounded.

Finally, humans are meaning-making creatures. We act based on our explanations and interpretations of our environments—we have values and reasons for doing things.[59] Crime damages a victim's sense of meaning because it's often an event that they cannot fit into their sense of order.[60] Meaninglessness and fear arise in victims if the world feels void of discernable order.[61] Often, victimization makes someone feel totally abandoned and, as such, meaning is lost. Herman argues that a traumatic event causes a person to think and feel that they've been cast outside of human and divine systems of care and protection.[62] Crime also damages how a person sees the world, causing them to discard basic assumptions about life and human nature.

One of the primary tasks of trauma-informed youth justice is to be victim-centred. Recognizing that crime is harmful, in many cases traumatic, justice must consider the rehabilitation of victims. Victim-centred justice means putting the needs of rehabilitation of the victim at the forefront. In an article titled "What Does Victim Rehabilitation Look Like?" the Canadian Resource Centre for Victims of Crime suggests:

> Victims in Canada need rehabilitation to ensure their physical, emotional, financial & legal recovery. A very wise client of ours reminded me of this simple idea this week. It is a wonderful thought. Imagine if our social services and health care systems focused on victim rehabilitation in the aftermath of crime? Canadian communities and families would be so much better off. If we provided the same level of consideration for victims as is granted to the offender in his/her rehabilitation, victims could concentrate on their healing, return to work when they are ready, retain supportive relationships, and move forward positively. Rebuilding the lives of victims/survivors should be viewed as equally significant to charging, trying, and convicting the perpetrator.
>
> 1. Physical: Concentrate on victim safety—keep victims safe from further acts of violence and secure safe/affordable housing for them when their living situation is compromised.
> 2. Emotional: Address victims' mental health needs in the aftermath of violence which means allowing them to access professional counselling

services when they need them, not when the government says they can have them.

3. **Financial & Legal:** Provide free legal assistance for victims to help them enforce civil and criminal court restitution orders when they have been defrauded. Provide financial assistance or compensation in a less bureaucratic way by offering standardized access to funds across Canada to help victims pay expenses that are a result of the crime such as counselling, medical/treatment expenses, funeral costs, rehabilitation, relocation, crime scene clean up, etc.[63]

The task of victim rehabilitation, then, is about creating opportunity for safety and choice (autonomy), connection (bonding), and making sense of their past and present (meaning-making). One organization, the Sexual Assault Centre for Quinte and District, has put efforts into creating a unique healing environment for victims. This example signals the type of resources needed for victim healing.

"Healing Centre Opens," from the *Belleville Intelligencer*, September 5, 2013

BIG ISLAND - Let the healing begin.

Survivors of sexual abuse have a new place in which to recover: a picturesque Prince Edward County property near the Bay of Quinte.

It's called Paths of Courage Healing and Retreat Centre, a creation of the Sexual Assault Centre for Quinte and District.

Unique in Ontario, it's the home of a pioneering program developed by staff.

Groups of 10 survivors, divided by gender, spend a week undergoing therapy, physical activity and more. Some of the challenges were borrowed from the Outward Bound outdoor education program....

Counsellor Gaye Feller said it's a relief to know some of the people she helps on a weekly basis at the centre's Belleville headquarters may also recover further if they participate in the healing program. It's the perfect setting, she said.

"This is gorgeous," Feller said.

"There's privacy. There's peace. There's water. There's comfort."

She said she's witnessed a "tremendous transformation" in clients.

"It's like night and day.... It makes me cry." [...]

"We're very proud to have you here," said county Councillor Bev Campbell. She said its "creative" program is "very much needed."

Ontario Coalition of Rape Crisis Centres co-ordinator Nicole Pietsch said the centre's ability to reach sex-crime victims in a more intensive way may even be "life-saving" and the facility is the envy of crisis centres across Ontario.[64]

IN THE WORDS OF SURVIVORS

In order to put victim/survivor voices at the forefront of this discussion, I connected with my local sexual assault support centre. Having volunteered for a number of years in the Male Allies Against Sexual Violence program, I knew a number of the staff members at the centre. They eagerly agreed to see if any survivors would be willing to talk about their experiences of the justice system with me. The narrative below is the outcome of my meeting with a focus group of five survivors (one male, four female), and one staff member from the Waterloo Region Sexual Assault Support Centre.

On July 8, 2014, I arrived at the meeting location to find a full room. Everyone seemed eager—yet nervous—to talk and share. After a round of introductions, I explained my intent and told the group a little bit about my book project. We would spend two hours together, and there would be two questions:

1. What was your experience of the criminal justice system, particularly court?
2. What would you have liked, or what did you need, from the justice system? In other words, what does "justice" mean to you?

The voices of survivors are centrally important to understanding what's wrong with our justice system so that we can work to improve it. One person said, "It's people like us who can help."

1. Experience of Criminal Justice

A number of themes emerged from the initial question. Survivors are blamed, doubted, made to feel unsafe, and harmed by criminal justice proceedings. Furthermore, they're told how to act, and the scales of justice are tipped in favour of the offender.

Blamed: Survivors spoke about many instances in court where they were made to feel like the sexual assault was their fault. Much of this had to do with questioning by defence lawyers: "Why did you dress the way you did?" "Why were you there?" and so on. Before arriving in court, survivors have already given detailed statements to police, yet the group told me that they were constantly asked to revisit each part of the experience. This blame often extended beyond the courtroom, into the community. Family members, too, were guilty of ostracizing survivors, as if the survivor had broken the veneer of the idyllic family by going to the police (where offenders were also family members). Many victims spoke about family members standing by the offender, rather than supporting them.

> "I actually stood up and did something about it—many don't because they are apprehensive. Because of what I've experienced, I often wonder if I should have walked the other way." (focus group participant)

Doubted: Survivors spoke about constantly feeling doubted. The male survivor was unable to convince the justice system to press charges. He was convinced that because a female had sexually assaulted him, his story had not been believed. Survivors also talked about the strength and courage it took just to come forward to the police, and reported that their experiences with the police had been mixed. Some felt interrogated, others supported. Some felt triggered and panicky, while constantly having to prove their story. The experience of court was talked about as the most traumatic part, however. Victims were doubted and were forced to relive the experience, while it was assumed that they'd made it all up.

> "If the accused is innocent until proven guilty, it is as if I am lying until proven truthful." (focus group participant)

Unsafe: Each of the survivors talked about feeling terror after going to the police—not knowing when or if the offender would be arrested; not knowing if the offender would come and find them to retaliate; not knowing if they would be believed in court; waiting for court dates; not knowing if the offender would be found guilty. By going to the criminal justice system, the survivor is handing significant control of their life over to a system that's oriented toward dealing with the offender. Some survivors talked about using drugs to survive, because no one would listen to them.

> "I lost a year of my life in terror, waiting for the court date." (focus group participant)

Harmed: The topic most discussed was defence lawyers and the harmful tactics they'd used in an open, public court setting. Not only does the survivor have to share the most painful parts of her or his life in a public court, they're also cross-examined by a defence lawyer, who typically displays no compassion for their circumstances. A number of survivors spoke about being blamed by defence lawyers for their sexual abuse even though they were children at the time. The defence would say things like, "Well, you must have been flirting with him," or "You were kind of like his girlfriend." The defence would pick apart aspects of their lives, making them feel like garbage, like they were being bullied. After court, the survivors wondered why they were hurting so badly.

> "Defence victimizes victims in the worst kind of way, they verbally rape you in court." (focus group participant)

Loss of control: When survivors disclosed their sexual assault to police they felt a loss of control. Police, together with a Crown attorney, would decide whether charges should be laid. Furthermore, survivors were told by criminal justice professionals how to act on the stand, to maintain composure even when they were angry or upset—essentially, to present themselves in a way that they might not be feeling. This "acting" was supposed to help with their credibility. A composed victim is one who is believable. An angry victim is not.

> "I knew I couldn't say certain things on the stand, I have limitations. Either I fall apart or I come across cold. If you react aggressively, they are not going

to listen to you. If you're cold, they're not going to listen to you." (focus group participant)

Scales of justice tipped in favour of the offender: Survivors struggled with how courts seemed to favour offenders—focusing on protecting their rights, often at the expense of the rights of survivors. Survivors also struggled with not being able to be present for much of the trial (because they are witnesses and testifying), while offenders could sit through all of it. All of the survivors mentioned that they felt this gave the offender an advantage.

"Court seems to protect offenders, rather than victims." (focus group participant)

2. Justice Needs

When I asked the survivors what could have helped—or what they needed from justice, they shared the following:

Information: Many times survivors felt that they didn't have adequate information about their cases. They would show up to court only to find out it was adjourned or postponed. The stress and anxiety of preparing to testify and then having dates change was very difficult to bear. Survivors were also concerned that there weren't enough resources for court-driven programs (like victim services) to provide adequate support.

Equality: Survivors want to be treated the same as offenders. Resources appear skewed in the direction of the offender, as is the overall procedure. One survivor suggested that similar to how an offender is read their rights, victims should be read the victim bill of rights when disclosing a crime to a police officer.

Safety: Survivors were unanimous in their desire (or need) to feel more secure and to have more of a voice in the criminal justice process. Part of this is about education, helping the public to understand more about sexual abuse so that survivors are not blamed by friends and family. Part is providing adequate support and information. Many feared backlash from offenders and wondered what could be done about this.

Compassion: Survivors spoke about the need for compassionate justice system professionals. Many were able to give examples of professionals who had listened and who had been respectful, and articulated the difference this made for them. All of the survivors wished that everyone in the system understood trauma better. They also said that a compassionate justice system would move faster (cases wouldn't take so long to proceed through the court), would have less people in the court room when a survivor is testifying (or only those who matter to the case), and would only use a major case unit for interviewing survivors (or only those with specialized expertise in the area). A compassionate justice system would also give standing to sexual assault centre staff to be expert witnesses. This would counteract the many ways that defence attorneys discount survivor testimony.

Proportional laws: Survivors scoffed at how many offenders are actually convicted. (The numbers are very low.) Furthermore, where a conviction happens, survivors were often disappointed with the punishment, suggesting that sexual abuse isn't taken seriously when punishments don't match the harm done.

To be believed: This theme came up over and over again. The suggestion was made to start from a place of belief rather than doubt. Why would a person make something like this up? Why would they put themselves through the public humiliation and torture? If the system started from a place of belief, survivors were convinced that their cases would have been properly investigated, and that they wouldn't have been humiliated in court.

> "There is a need to believe the victim until proven otherwise." (focus group participant)

I'm very grateful to the courageous survivors who willingly shared parts of their stories, as well as their valuable ideas, with me. There's much to be learned when we listen to those most affected by crime and harm.

CONCLUSION: RESTORATIVE JUSTICE AND VICTIMS

A restorative justice framework for trauma-informed youth justice takes victims off the sidelines of criminal justice and gives them a decision-making role. While not all victims will want control of justice processes and outcomes, it's important to give victims choice. As a restorative justice mediator with the Restorative Opportunities program of Correctional Service of Canada (CSC) I have yet to meet a victim who didn't at least want choice about whether to participate in a process. Some will say things like, "I don't want anything to do with the program or with meeting with an offender," but this is always followed by, "but I can understand why some people might." The point is to empower victims. This is central to the task of healing.

It shouldn't stop with individual cases, either. Victims should be involved in designing justice programs. Victim advocate Mary Achilles, along with Howard Zehr, has put together a list of 10 ways that restorative justice programs and organizations can work toward appropriate victim involvement:

1. ... victims and their advocates are represented on governing bodies and initial planning committees.
2. ... efforts to involve victims grows out of a desire to assist them, not offenders. Victims are not responsible to rehabilitate the offender unless they choose to do so.
3. ... victim's safety is a fundamental element of program design.

4. ... victims clearly understand their roles in the program including potential benefits and risks to themselves and offenders.
5. ... confidentiality is provided within clear guidelines.
6. ... victims have as much information as possible about their case, the offense and the offender.
7. ... victims can identify and articulate their needs and are given choices.
8. ... victims opportunity for involvement are maximized.
9. ... program design provides referrals for additional support and assistance.
10. ... services are available to victims even when their offender(s) have not been arrested or are unwilling or unable to participate.[65]

In this chapter, I've traced how victims have surrendered control of the conflict of crime to the state. Some scholars have suggested that the state is now actually more vengeful, more retributive, than victims typically used to be. This doesn't mean that some victims don't want an offender to suffer for what they've done. However, victims are often looking for something more, or at least something different from justice. For example, the group of survivors of sexual abuse that I met with expressed a desire for information, safety, compassion, and to be believed. This chapter puts forward one of the most significant principles of trauma-informed youth justice—that justice processes must be victim-centred. From a restorative justice perspective, crime is something that affects people and relationships. The first task of trauma-informed youth justice is to help people who have been hurt work toward healing.

GLOSSARY OF TERMS

Conflict as property is an idea proposed by criminologist Nils Christie that conflict is something that's owned by individuals or communities. When we professionalize justice, as we do in the criminal justice system, we give this property away. Christie argues that communities should retain ownership of their conflicts.

A **social movement** is a group of people banding together to advocate or work toward a particular cause.

Victimology is the study of victims and their experiences with the criminal justice system.

QUESTIONS FOR REFLECTION

1. Based on your reading of this chapter, if you could change one thing about how the criminal justice system treats sexual assault survivors, what would it be?
2. What do you think about Nils Christie's idea about conflict as property? Do you think the state should be less involved than it is in resolving issues related to crime, or is there a more appropriate way for communities to share power with the state?
3. Would you feel more comfortable working with victims or offenders? Why? What draws you toward one population over the other?

RECOMMENDED READING

Bloom, Sandra L. *Creating Sanctuary: Toward the Evolution of Sane Societies.* New York: Routledge, 1997.

Dr. Sandra L. Bloom writes about trauma and how to create sanctuary, or safe spaces, for healing for victims.

Moroney, Shannon. *Through the Glass.* Doubleday Canada, 2011.

The cover eloquently describes what this book is about, "One month into our marriage, my husband committed horrific violent crimes. In that instant, the life I knew was destroyed. I vowed that one day I would be whole again. This is my story."

Conclusion: Principles of Trauma-Informed Youth Justice

"Peace comes from being able to contribute the best that we have, and all that we are, toward creating a world that supports everyone. But it is also securing the space for others to contribute the best that they have and all that they are."
—Hafsat Abiola, Nigerian Human Rights Activist

The world is full of suffering. Why add to it? I believe in harm reduction, in reducing pain wherever possible. Harm reduction is often talked about in relation to drug addiction. Instead of punishing addicts through criminalization, some have advocated for an approach that recognizes addiction as an illness. This means providing methadone treatments and clean needle exchanges to help people manage addictions in safer ways. Why add more harm?

I believe criminal justice should also adopt a harm reduction mentality. At this stage in Canadian history we've become addicted to punishment. It gives us a high, a feeling of superiority. The "bad" people get what they deserve. The "good" people can continue to feel good because they aren't one of "them." But when we look at who is "bad"—who our young offenders are—we discover that they're people with childhood traumas, with mental health challenges, and with addictions. We discover that they're Indigenous peoples, and people struggling in poverty—essentially, people who are often acting out because others have already punished them. Whether it was a dad who beat his son, or colonialism that beat down Indigenous peoples, there is pain. As I have written, based on the quote of Franciscan Richard Rohr, pain that is not transformed is often transferred. It gets passed along from one person to the next, and from one generation to another. Then along comes the justice system, which is addicted to punishment, to add to the violence.

I wish I could eradicate this addiction. Prison abolitionists would like to throw out the whole justice system. They're probably right. We should. Those who work in the justice system would probably say that it just needs reforming; that there are broken elements, but we need to retain other parts and ways of controlling—perhaps even punishing—people who are bent on (criminally) hurting others. They're probably right, too. We should.

I'm not going to propose that there's a happy middle ground between these two positions. There isn't. There's no bridge between abolition and social control. There are only human beings caught up in what human beings do, sometimes loving, sometimes hurting each other.

Justice is complicated. Part of it involves figuring out your own identity, your own role in it. I'm still working on mine. I'd like to share a quick story about a visit I made to a prison. The story highlights some of the challenges of finding my own identity in this work.

> *June 9, 2014:* I arrive at the prison. I'm a guest speaker for a university class that brings together people who are inmates with people who are university students. It's called Inside Out. The inmates are Inside students, the university students, Outside students. When I arrive at security, I check in as I normally do. I'm a part-time correctional staff member—doing some restorative justice work in the system—so the process is familiar to me. A correctional officer walks with me to the program room where the class is taking place. We talk about air conditioning. When I arrive a staff member notices that I'm wearing institutional identification. "Oh," he says, "You're one of us."
>
> The class begins. There is a lot of meaningful conversation about masculinity and male violence—the topics I've been asked to facilitate discussion around. There's some conflict during discussions: Outside students trying to tell it "like it is"—at least intellectually. Inside students calmly but defensively reacting, sharing their truths. All of it is healthy. Mostly the Insiders and Outsiders banter back and forth in agreement about the toxicity of a masculinity that pursues dominance, power, control, and ultimately violence. At the end, the students, who are sitting in a circle, check out by sharing a few words about how they're doing at the end of the session. Some are tired, some excited, others less satisfied; all have been impacted in some way by the topics, by being in relationship.
>
> I'm packing up my things. An Inside student walks up to me. She looks at me, at my identification. She says, "At first I saw your ID when you arrived, and thought 'Oh, great,' but I think, really, you're one of us."

As I've said, justice is complicated. I don't have all the answers—but I do know that what we're doing isn't working well, and that better ways exist. In this chapter, I want to start to map a way forward. I've created a list of principles for trauma-informed youth justice that builds on the shared values articulated in chapter 1. It isn't a complete list, but my hope is that it will function like a compass, pointing us in the direction of safer, more livable communities for people affected by youth crime. Sullivan and Tifft, two criminologists I cited earlier, suggest that it isn't enough to be critical, that a critical philosophy must also be a liberating force.[1] That is, it should also map the development of a new consciousness, and a new way of living.[2] Anyone can be a critic. It takes another level of imagination and commitment to articulate, and to try to live, a new set of principles and values. Below, I identify five principles, as a starting point. Following each, I list several subprinciples, with recommendations for implementation.

We are working toward trauma-informed youth justice when:

- Principle 1: A set of shared values gives shape to practices.
- Principle 2: Indigenous peoples and women are in leadership roles in order to decolonize and dismantle patriarchy.
- Principle 3: Restorative justice is the framework.
- Principle 4: Trauma-informed care and prevention guides practices.
- Principle 5: Justice processes are victim-centred.

PRINCIPLE 1: WE NEED A SET OF SHARED VALUES TO GIVE SHAPE TO PRACTICES

1.1   *The foundation is respect for all people and treating everyone with human dignity.*
1.1.1   Trauma-informed youth justice practices must have integrity: people and processes that are accountable to these shared values.
1.1.2   It should be understood that working in this area requires a tremendous amount of kindness, compassion, and patience.

1.2   *Crime should be considered an issue of peace: the goal is safe, livable communities for all people.*
1.2.1   Crime must be looked at holistically, considering harms (individually and structurally) as well as root causes.
1.2.2   Crime control practices committed to "do no harm" should be based on principles of non-violence.
1.2.3   It should be understood that trauma-informed youth justice requires collaboration, listening, and democracy.
1.2.4   Although violence is considered harmful, conflict should be viewed as an opportunity for growth.
1.2.5   The relationship of the individual to the environment must also be considered: How are we creating sustainable communities through our justice practices?

1.3   *Imagination and creative approaches are honoured.*
1.3.1   Arts-based approaches to trauma healing should be more widely used.
1.3.2   The healing practices of theatre and yoga can be a part of this.

PRINCIPLE 2: INDIGENOUS PEOPLES AND WOMEN SHOULD BE IN LEADERSHIP ROLES IN ORDER TO DECOLONIZE AND DISMANTLE PATRIARCHY

2.1   *Indigenous peoples should be leading the way in decolonizing Canada.*
2.1.1   A process of decolonization should be begun, allowing Indigenous societies to live with self-determination and self-governance.

2.1.2 Land should be returned. Canada must acknowledge the illegitimacy of its sovereignty over Indigenous peoples.
2.1.3 Resources should be provided for support in a transition from assimilation to decolonization.
2.1.4 The recommendations of the Royal Commission on Aboriginal Peoples should be implemented.
2.1.5 Treaty relationships should be revisted and reaffirmed. Canada needs to honour treaty obligations.
2.1.6 A pluralistic legal framework for dealing with criminal cases where the offender is Indigenous and the victim is settler Canadian should be implemented.

2.2 *Women lead the way in dismantling patriarchy.*
2.2.1 Laws and policies should be systematically analyzed for ways that patriarchy remains embedded within social systems including, but not limited to, law, government, education, and so forth.
2.2.2 Widespread programs similar to Male Allies Against Sexual Violence and Draw the Line should be implemented as part of elementary school curriculum in order to raise men and boys who better understand respectful relationships.

PRINCIPLE 3: RESTORATIVE JUSTICE SHOULD BE THE FRAMEWORK

3.1 *Commit to a "do no (further) harm" model of justice.*
3.1.1 The incarceration of young people should be further reduced, if not eliminated.
3.1.2 Community-based justice models should be further advanced.
3.1.3 Restorative justice opportunities for young people—as a framework and as a practice—should be further advanced.

3.2 *Accountability should happen within a context of support.*
3.2.1 Meaningful consequences should occur so that young offenders understand how their choices have hurt others and themselves.
3.2.2 Accountability should promote empathy.
3.2.3 Accountability should promote reparation and, where possible, restitution and amends.
3.2.4 Where a young person fails to fulfill their obligations, failure should be understood as part of the progression toward healing/change. We should not give up, even when young people give up on themselves by perpetrating further harm.
3.2.5 It should be recognized that accountability happens best within a context of care for the individual.

PRINCIPLE 4: TRAUMA-INFORMED CARE AND PREVENTION SHOULD GUIDE PRACTICES

4.1 *The trauma of victims and young offenders must be acknowledged.*
4.1.1 This means understanding the connection between the behaviour of young people and their traumatic experiences.
4.1.2 Justice officials should be trained in trauma and its impacts in order to help create a society and a justice culture that is trauma-informed.
4.1.3 Young people need to be believed. Victims need to be believed.
4.1.4 The experiences of victims and offenders need to be validated. Both groups should be treated not as their labels, "victim" and "offender," but as brother, sister, daughter, son, or person.
4.1.5 We must also acknowledge the collective traumas of colonialism, patriarchy, and other issues not discussed much in this book (e.g., poverty).

4.2 *The focus of youth justice should be on healing, not punishment.*
4.2.1 Youth justice should shift from a risk focus to a resilience focus.
4.2.2 Instead of allowing victims to suffer in isolation, and offenders to be separated from society, we should consider how to include people from both categories as part of our communities.
4.2.3 The goal should be to create meaningful relationships, a secure base. Attachment, hope, and belonging must be considered.
4.2.4 The safety of the individual must be considered alongside the safety of the community.
4.2.5 Focus should be placed on healing (e.g., remembrance, normalizing, educating, integration, and mourning).
4.2.6 Survivors should be given control and autonomy to allow for informed decision-making.
4.2.7 Addiction and mental health supports must be adequately available.
4.2.8 We must acknowledge the damage caused by incarceration, risk-based justice, and punishment.

4.3 *Individual accountability needs to be nested within community accountability.*
4.3.1 Communities, including governments, need to take responsibility for harms done to young people.
4.3.2 It should be recognized that resources are better used toward prevention than intervention.
- Parents need more support.
- Children need to be better educated about Canada's history of colonialism.
- Children need to be better educated about male violence and healthy relationships.

4.4 *Legislation needs to further embed notions of trauma.*
4.4.1 Deterrence needs to be removed from legislation, unless society is committed to practices (e.g., restorative justice) that actually deter.
4.4.2 An examination of rule of law should be undertaken. Who does it benefit? Who does it hurt? Who has input into making change? How are youth voices, especially the voices of those on the margins, included?
4.4.3 Decriminalization of drugs needs to be considered. Addiction should be considered a health issue, not an issue of justice.
4.4.4 We should continue to more clearly delineate consequences for non-violent versus violent crimes.
4.4.5 We should continue the implementation of specialized drug treatment and mental health courts.

PRINCIPLE 5: JUSTICE PROCESSES NEED TO BE VICTIM-CENTRED

5.1 *The youth justice system needs to be victim-centred.*
5.1.1 Crime needs to be understood as more than laws broken, but as something that affects people, relationships, and communities.
5.1.2 We must recognize that punishment does little to meet the needs of victims.
5.1.3 It must be understood that victims need safe space to heal both inside and apart from justice systems.
5.1.4 Victim services need to be more adequately resourced—in a comparable amount to the money spent on offenders.

LIMITATIONS OF THIS BOOK

As my mentor Howard Zehr, one of the forerunners in the restorative justice movement, often says, every social movement has unintended consequences. It isn't difficult to imagine that a shift toward trauma-informed youth justice as I have articulated it here will have unintended consequences as well. As a privileged, white male it's likely that I'm making some errors in the presentation of this text and that my privilege gets in the way of me seeing some of these issues as clearly as I should.

Furthermore, there are a number of topics beyond the scope of this text that must be incorporated into further discussions of trauma-informed youth justice. One such topic is the war on drugs, which includes mandatory minimum sentences for drug possession (especially in the United States, but now Canada too). This has placed many individual drug users behind bars (especially people of colour), but has done nothing to stem the flow of drugs in communities. Another issue that has not been fully addressed here is a clearer articulation of socio-economic status and criminal justice marginalization. In this text, I have focused on male violence and colonialism, but the war on drugs and the number of impoverished people behind bars are just as troubling. There are movements afoot globally, and in the United States, to decriminalize certain drugs. Canada is late to this discussion. It's time for drug use, particularly addictions, to be considered more of a health issue than a criminal issue.

As to poverty and its correlation to crime, as Jeffrey Reiman says in *The Rich Get Richer and the Poor Get Prison: Ideology, Class, and Criminal Justice*, the criminal justice system is failing because it overemphasizes individual crimes without attention to structures of inequality that create a criminal social order.[3]

Another significant challenge is the potential for trauma-informed youth justice to oversimplify complex issues. There are some paradigms at work in criminal justice that are clearly in opposition to each other. A **paradigm** is a distinct pattern of thought. One paradigm at work in criminal justice is the idea that offenders should be punished for crimes. Another is the belief that offenders should receive treatment to help them change. Yet another is the principle of deterrence that believes in just enough punishment to scare away future offenders. Another paradigm I've proposed is a restorative justice framework that believes in trying to make things right by focusing on healing in the aftermath of crime. These are very different, competing outlooks. As Thomas Kuhn, famous for articulating how paradigm shift happens in the sciences, says, "the proponents of competing paradigms practice their trades in different worlds."[4] Educator Paul Joseph Wendel, talking about the work of Kuhn and others who have tried to explain how different paradigms have no common basis, argues that it isn't possible for theorists from different paradigms to see the world in the same way.[5] This might explain part of why criminal justice cannot seem to reconcile punishment with rehabilitation, or, perhaps, why punishing a young person by sending them to prison means they're more likely to reoffend in the future than to be rehabilitated. Each paradigm makes different assumptions about reality and about what constitutes appropriate intervention.

What does this mean for the criminal justice practitioner? Practitioners grapple with paradoxes. The resolution of difficult issues is often not an either/or proposition, but a matter of both/and. In her timely paper "Experiences in Reconciling Risk Management and Restorative Justice: How Circles of Support and Accountability Work Restoratively in the Risk Society" in the *International Journal of Offender Therapy and Comparative Criminology*, criminologist Stacey Hannem speaks to the strategic nature of practising in one paradigm, while being dominated by another.[6] As you may recall, Circles of Support and Accountability (CoSA), as explained in chapter 8, is a restorative justice program that works with high-risk sex offenders reintegrating back into the community after imprisonment. Hannem claims that the restorative perspective of CoSA gets "obscured by the instrumental function of community protection", but not to the detriment of the program.[7] The Government of Canada is a primary funder of CoSA because it desires public safety. Of course, CoSA also wants no further harm, but it accomplishes this by creating a community where everyone can belong as safely as possible. Hannem argues that CoSA strikes a precarious balance between risk management and community-building, "… and demonstrates that the concerns of the risk society can be addressed in a restorative way that builds communities, rather than fracturing them, and embraces offenders, rather than shaming and isolating them."[8] As restorative justice advocates seek to understand how their work might or might not fit with a punishment paradigm, some argue that what is shared by the two approaches is a sense that wrongdoing has happened. Where the difference lies is in how to deal with it.[9] Perhaps this common starting point—of harm done—demonstrates how two seemingly opposed paradigms can still coexist, at least from the vantage point of the practitioner.

Another challenge of *Trauma-Informed Youth Justice in Canada* is the background of the author. I have been educated and raised in white, Eurocentric, male-dominated institutions. My work here, as much as it rejects some of this, also builds on it. The educational system in Canada has effectively silenced certain traditions, while privileging others. In *Southern Theory*, sociologist Raewyn Connell describes how this has happened in the academic realm of social theory. Traditional theorists have erased theorizing that occurs in marginalized communities. She calls this an exclusion by the Global North of the Global South.[10] One of the consequences of this is that systemic violence is often ignored in sociological theory.[11] No wonder Western theories of crime have focused primarily on offenders' choices, individualizing responsibility, often to the exclusion of the contexts in which crimes take place. Otherwise the contexts, too, would be implicated. Of course, this pertains to Indigenous experiences in Canada.

Anishinaabe researcher Kathleen Absolon explains how, during her doctoral research, she struggled to fit in at the academy because her Indigenous worldview did not fit within the theories taught.[12] Absolon, in her book *Kaandossiwin: How We Come to Know*, beautifully critiques academia for the ways it shuts out or belittles some people of academia. She also describes an Indigenous worldview that sees an academic person as part of a web of relationships; her perspective is that knowledge is relational.[13] Furthermore, she suggests that the jargon of academia is confusing: "Academics tend to use words like ontology, epistemology, methodology and axiology. I find them confusing and would rather speak without jargon. I wonder what words in Anishinaabe would [explain] our understanding of our existence and how we come to know about our reality and existence?"[14] If I'm reading her correctly, Absolon is not only critiquing Western academia for its colonization of Indigenous knowledge, but also how it tends to disguise its intents and purposes through the use of language—big words to smother those who would resist. Of course, academia is often oppressive. It has been a part of colonial and patriarchal violence, lacking direct accountability to the lived experience of people, especially those on the margins of society.

CONCLUSION: VIOLENCE RIPPLES, KINDNESS MAKES WAVES

> "The purpose of life is not to be happy. It is to be useful, to be honorable, to be compassionate, to have it make some difference that you have lived and lived well."
>
> —Ralph Waldo Emerson

I've never considered myself much of a writer. (I'm sure my editors can attest to why.) I consider myself more of an artist, a painter. I'm better with images than with words. I have a fairly vivid, visual imagination. Not necessarily for creating new things, but for seeing objects—trees, rivers, places, people—in new ways. When I paint, I first imagine in my mind the end product, but as it unfolds, I'll pause to see what's happening along the way. The painting I've included in this chapter is titled "Still." It was painted in honour of a friend's mom who passed away from cancer. It reminds me that life is fragile. Yet, even as I work to support people in the aftermath of serious crime, life is also beautiful.

Figure 12.1: "Still"—Judah Oudshoorn, acrylic on canvas

The problem with writing a book, and having it published, is that there's only minimal pause involved. Once the ink is dry, there's some finality. However, as a way of concluding, let me articulate how I pictured the words of this book coming together.

I imagined this book being held together by relationships. I wanted to be accountable to the victims, offenders, practitioners, students, and researchers I've met. I also wanted to articulate the effects of trauma on young offenders and victims, and to describe how the justice system exacerbates this pain. I imagined saying that it doesn't have to be this way, and proposing some viable alternatives.

For the past decade, I've been teaching and working in various arenas of criminal justice. Sometimes this involves going into federal penitentiaries to meet adult offenders. Behind prison doors, I listen as people share stories about their crimes. The more I listen, the more I discover that many offenders carry histories of victimization, having endured traumatic childhoods. I often ask myself: If I had walked in their shoes, or lived what they had lived, would I have done similar things? Would I be in jail, too? Quite likely. As I continue listening to their stories, I hear that many first came into conflict with the law as young people. I ask myself: Why are they still here in prison, many decades later? Are we exacerbating some of the very behaviours we're trying to eliminate? After a visit, the prison gates close behind me. I walk out with memories of stories and faces, with questions, and with a desire for something else, something more just. I know we can do better.

Other times, my work has taken me to the homes of victims, to hear their stories and to see their faces. I hear their pain and I feel grief (sorrow is palpable). Sadly, criminal justice systems fail to touch victims in a way that helps. Instead, their pain, grief, and sorrow are compounded by a system that pushes them aside. Always, I am amazed by their courage and by their capacity to survive. Would I be able to do that? I'm not sure. I walk out of their homes determined to make things better.

These days my work mostly brings me into the college classroom, working with students who are hoping to be the next criminal justice professionals. Their creativity and enthusiasm excites me. I feel compelled to bring stories of victims, offenders, and a broken criminal justice system to them, so that they can emerge with passion and with the ability to think critically. However, most importantly, my goal is to see them develop empathy and kindness that they can carry into their work and their lives. After all, this, above all else, is what will lead to change. This is what will create a safer, more livable society. I have similar hopes for you, the reader of this book. I've said it before, but it bears repeating and deserves a place as the concluding thought in this text: violence ripples, but kindness makes waves.

GLOSSARY OF TERMS

A **paradigm** is a distinct pattern of thought.

QUESTIONS FOR REFLECTION

1. Which of the five principles cited in this chapter resonates most with you? Why? Do you think it is possible to implement it in youth justice?
2. After finishing this book, what is one leftover question that you have? How will you try to find answers to this question?
3. For me, art (painting) is a really important part of how I understand my role in being a part of trauma-informed youth justice processes. Is there something (e.g., a song, a band, a book, an author, etc.) that inspires you to work in this field? What is it about that "something" that helps you understand better who you are—and how you want to carry yourself in contributing to the work of justice?

RECOMMENDED READING

Christie, Nils. *Limits to Pain: The Role of Punishment in Penal Policy.* Eugene: Wipf & Stock, 1981.

In this provocative essay, Danish criminologist Nils Christie argues that pain will likely always be a part of doing the work of criminal justice, but humanity should try to limit it as much as possible.

Notes

DEDICATION

1. Excerpted from song lyrics by Bob Dylan, "Forever Young," *Planet Waves* (Asylum, 1974).

FOREWORD

1. The photos and stories here come from three of my books: *Doing Life: Reflections of Men and Women Serving Life Sentences*; *Transcending: Reflections of Crime Victims*; and (with Lorraine Stutzman Amstutz), *What Will Happen to Me?* Used by permission of the publisher, Good Books.

INTRODUCTION

1. Carly B. Dierkhising et al., "Trauma Histories among Justice-Involved Youth: Findings from the National Child Traumatic Stress Network," *European Journal of Psychotraumatology* 4 (2013): 1–12.
2. Lesley McAra and Susan McVie, "Youth Justice? The Impact of System Contact on Patterns of Desistance from Offending," *European Journal of Criminology* 4 (2007): 315-345.
3. Howard Zehr, *The Little Book of Restorative Justice* (Intercourse: Good Books, 2002).
4. Zehr, *The Little Book of Restorative Justice*.
5. bell hooks, "Eros, Eroticism and the Pedagogical Process," *Cultural Studies* 7 (1993): 59.

CHAPTER 1

1. Derrick Jensen, *Endgame: Volume 1 The Problem of Civilization* (New York: Seven Stories Press, 2006), 17.
2. Christine Courtois, *Recollections of Sexual Abuse: Treatment Principles & Guidelines* (New York: W. W. Norton & Co., 1999).
3. Shawn Wilson, *Research Is Ceremony: Indigenous Research Methods* (Halifax: Fernwood Publishing, 2008), 22.

4. Wilson, *Research Is Ceremony*.
5. Wilson, *Research Is Ceremony*.
6. Kathleen E. Absolon, *Kaandossiwin: How We Come to Know* (Halifax: Fernwood Publishing, 2011), 28–29.
7. Jeff Karabanow, "Street Kids as Delinquents, Menaces and Criminals: Another Example of the Criminalization of Poverty," in *Poverty, Regulation and Social Exclusion. Readings on the Criminalization of Poverty*, eds. Diane Crocker and Val Marie Johnson (Halifax: Fernwood, 2010): 146.
8. Karabanow, "Street Kids as Delinquents, Menaces and Criminals," 146.
9. Bernard Schissel, *Still Blaming Children: Youth Conduct and the Politics of Child Hating* (Halifax: Fernwood, 2006), 26.
10. Robert C. Bogden and Sari Knopp Biklen, *Qualitative Research for Education: An Introduction to Theory and Method* (Boston: Allyn & Bacon, 1998): 204, as cited in Christine Ashby, "Whose 'Voice' Is It Anyway? Giving Voice and Qualitative Research Involving Individuals That Type to Communicate," *Disability Studies Quarterly* (2009): 2.
11. Beth B. Hess and Myra Marx Ferree, *Analyzing Gender: A Handbook of Social Science Research* (New York: Sage Publications, 1987), 13.
12. Sandra L. Kirby, Lorraine Greaves, and Colleen Reid, *Experience. Research. Social Change: Methods Beyond the Mainstream*, 2nd Edition (Toronto: University of Toronto Press, 2010), 13.
13. Sandra L. Kirby and Kate McKenna, *Experience. Research. Social Change. Methods from the Margins* (Toronto: Garamond Press, 1989), 13.
14. Vincent Lyon-Callo, *Inequality, Poverty and Neoliberal Governance: Activist Ethnography in the Homeless Sheltering Industry* (Peterborough: Broadview Press, 2004).
15. Rachel Pain and Peter Frances, "Reflections on Participatory Research," *Area* 35 (2003): 46–54.
16. Kirby and McKenna, *Experience. Research. Social Change. Methods from the Margins*.
17. Kirby and McKenna, *Experience. Research. Social Change. Methods from the Margins*, 15.
18. Howard S. Becker, "Whose Side Are We On?," *Social Problems* 14 (1967): 241.
19. Becker, "Whose Side Are We On?," 241.
20. Kirby, Greaves, and Reid, *Experience. Research. Social Change: Methods Beyond the Mainstream*, 39.
21. Kirby, Greaves, and Reid, *Experience. Research. Social Change: Methods Beyond the Mainstream*, 40.
22. Kirby, Greaves, and Reid, *Experience. Research. Social Change: Methods Beyond the Mainstream*, 40.
23. Mike Kesby, "Retheorizing Empowerment through Participation as a Performance in Space: Beyond Tyranny to Transformation," *Signs* 30 (2005): 2037–2065.
24. Todd Parr, *The Peace Book* (New York: Megan Tingly Books. Little, Brown and Company, 2004).

25. Parr, *The Peace Book.*
26. United Nations, *What Is Peacebuilding?* (Geneva: http://www.unpbf.org/application-guidelines/what-is-peacebuilding, 1992), accessed August 9, 2014.
27. Hal Pepinsky, "Peacemaking Criminology," *Critical Criminology* 21 (2013): 319–339.
28. Pepinsky, "Peacemaking Criminology," 319–339.
29. Pepinsky, "Peacemaking Criminology," 337.
30. John Paul Lederach, *The Moral Imagination: The Art and Soul of Building Peace* (New York: Oxford University Press, 2005), 5.
31. Lederach, *The Moral Imagination*, 63.
32. Lederach, *The Moral Imagination*, 27.
33. M. Scott Peck, *The Road Less Traveled* (New York: Simon and Schuster, 1978), 32.
34. Robert Beaglehole et al., "Public Health in the New Era: Improving Health through Collective Action," *Lancet* 363 (2004): 2084.
35. Tomris Turmen, "The Health Dimension," *UN Chronicle* 5 (1998): 18.
36. Turmen, "The Health Dimension," 18.
37. James Gilligan, "Violence in Public Health and Preventative Medicine," *The Lancet* 355 (2000): 1804.
38. Gilligan, "Violence in Public Health and Preventative Medicine," 1804.
39. Paulo Freire, *Pedagogy of the Oppressed* (New York: Continuum, 1970), 91.
40. This paragraph is based on Freire, *Pedagogy of the Oppressed*, 89–93.
41. Craig Proulx, *Reclaiming Aboriginal Justice, Identity, and Community* (Saskatoon: Purich, 2003), 39.
42. As cited in Rupert Ross, *Returning to the Teachings: Exploring Aboriginal Justice* (Toronto: Penguin Canada, 1996), 123.
43. Glen Sean Coulthard, *Red Skin White Masks: Rejecting the Colonial Politics of Recognition* (Minneapolis: University of Minnesota Press, 2014), 63–64.
44. Howard Zehr, *The Little Book of Restorative Justice* (Intercourse: Good Books, 2002), 21.
45. Zehr, *The Little Book of Restorative Justice*, 21.
46. Zehr, *The Little Book of Restorative Justice*, 37.
47. Michelle Brown, *The Culture of Punishment: Prison, Society, and Spectacle* (New York: New York University Press, 2009), 202–203.
48. Jennifer J. Llewellyn, "Restorative Justice: Thinking Relationally about Justice," in *Being Relational: Reflections on Relational Theory and Health Law*, eds. Jocelyn Downie and Jennifer J. Llewellyn (Vancouver: UBC Press, 2012): 89–108.
49. Llewellyn, "Restorative Justice: Thinking Relationally about Justice," 90.
50. Llewellyn, "Restorative Justice: Thinking Relationally about Justice," 89–108.
51. Elizabeth M. Elliott, *Security With Care: Restorative Justice & Healthy Societies* (Halifax: Fernwood Publishing, 2011), 69.
52. Melanie Randall and Lori Haskell, "Trauma-Informed Approaches to Law: Why Restorative Justice Must Understand Trauma and Psychological Coping," *Dalhousie Law Journal* 36 (2013): 501–533.
53. Elliott, *Security With Care: Restorative Justice & Healthy Societies*, 140.

CHAPTER 2

1. John S. Milloy, *A National Crime: The Canadian Government and the Residential School System, 1879 to 1986* (Winnipeg: University of Manitoba Press, 1999), 33.
2. Eugene A. Forsey, *How Canadians Govern Themselves* (Ottawa: Library of Parliament, 1980), 30.
3. Harry Glasbeek, *Wealth by Stealth: Corporate Crime, Corporate Law, and the Perversion of Democracy* (Toronto: Between the Lines, 2002), 267.
4. Department of Justice Canada, *The Evolution of Juvenile Justice in Canada* (Ottawa, 2004), 1.
5. Russell Smandych, "From 'Misguided Children' to 'Criminal Youth,'" in *Youth at Risk and Youth Justice: A Canadian Overview*, eds. John Winterdyk and Russell Smandych (Don Mills: Oxford University Press, 2012): 8–9.
6. Smandych, "From 'Misguided Children' to 'Criminal Youth,'" 8–9.
7. Smandych, "From 'Misguided Children' to 'Criminal Youth,'" 14.
8. *Appendix to the Journals of the Legislative Assembly of the Province of Canada* (Canada, 1849), page numbers not indicated.
9. *Appendix to the Journals of the Legislative Assembly of the Province of Canada* (Canada, 1849), page numbers not indicated.
10. Simon Devereux, "The Making of the Penitentiary Act, 1775–1779," *The Historical Journal* 42 (1999): 408.
11. Randall McGowan, "The Well-Ordered Prison: England, 1780–1865," in *The Oxford History of the Prison: The Practice of Punishment in Western Society*, eds Norval Morris and David J. Rothman (Oxford: Oxford University Press, 1995): 77.
12. Anthony J. Draper, "Cesare Beccaria's Influence on English Discussions of Punishment, 1764–1789," *History of European Ideas* 26 (2000): 180
13. Draper, "Cesare Beccaria's Influence on English Discussions of Punishment, 1764–1789," 181.
14. *Appendix to the Journals of the Legislative Assembly of the Province of Canada* (Canada, 1849), page numbers not indicated.
15. *Appendix to the Journals of the Legislative Assembly of the Province of Canada* (Canada, 1849), page numbers not indicated.
16. *Appendix to the Journals of the Legislative Assembly of the Province of Canada* (Canada, 1849), page numbers not indicated.
17. *Appendix to the Journals of the Legislative Assembly of the Province of Canada* (Canada, 1849), page numbers not indicated.
18. Smandych, "From 'Misguided Children' to 'Criminal Youth,'" 16.
19. Smandych, "From 'Misguided Children' to 'Criminal Youth,'" 17.
20. Aboriginal Affairs and Northern Development Canada, *Royal Commission Report on Aboriginal Peoples* (Canada, 1996), 312.
21. As quoted in John S. Milloy, *A National Crime: The Canadian Government and the Residential School System, 1879 to 1986* (Winnipeg: University of Manitoba Press, 1999), xiii.

22. Truth and Reconciliation Commission of Canada, *They Came for the Children* (Winnipeg: Truth and Reconciliation Commission of Canada, 2012), 2.
23. Truth and Reconciliation Commission of Canada, *They Came for the Children*, 2.
24. Truth and Reconciliation Commission of Canada, *They Came for the Children*, 22.
25. 38th Parliament, 1st session, Standing Committee on Aboriginal Affairs and Northern Development (http://www.parl.gc.ca/HousePublications/Publication.aspx?DocId=1648068&Language=E&Mode=1, February 17, 2005), accessed April 24, 2014.
26. Jon Parmenter, "The Meaning of *Kaswentha* and the Two Row Wampum Belt in Haudenosaunee (Iroquois) History: Can Indigenous Oral Tradition Be Reconciled with the Documentary Record?," *Journal of Early American History* 3 (2013): 85.
27. Parmenter, "The Meaning of *Kaswentha* and the Two Row Wampum Belt in Haudenosaunee (Iroquois) History: Can Indigenous Oral Tradition Be Reconciled with the Documentary Record?," 85.
28. Parmenter, "The Meaning of *Kaswentha* and the Two Row Wampum Belt in Haudenosaunee (Iroquois) History: Can Indigenous Oral Tradition Be Reconciled with the Documentary Record?," 82.
29. Milloy, *A National Crime*, 22–25.
30. Milloy, *A National Crime*, 22–25.
31. Truth and Reconciliation Commission of Canada, *They Came for the Children*, 10.
32. CBC News, "A History of Residential Schools in Canada" (www.cbc.ca/news/canada/a-history-of-residential-schools-in-canada-1.702280, May 16, 2008), accessed May 19, 2014.
33. Milloy, *A National Crime*, 37.
34. "Making Citizens of the Indians," *Toronto Daily Star*, March 19, 1920: 6.
35. John Borrows, "Wampum at Niagara: The Royal Proclamation, Canadian Legal History, and Self-Government," in *Aboriginal Treaty Rights in Canada*, ed. Michael Asch (Vancouver: UBC Press, 1997).
36. *Toronto Daily Star*, September 3, 1902.
37. Milloy, *A National Crime*, 55.
38. Dr. P. H. Bryce, *The Report on the Indian Schools of Manitoba and the North-West Territories* (Canada: Department of Indian Affairs, 1907), 14.
39. Juvenile Delinquents Act., R.S., c. 160, s. 2(1).
40. Prisoners' Aid Society (1894): 3.
41. Sandra J. Bell, *Young Offenders and Youth Justice: A Century After the Fact* (Toronto: Nelson Education Ltd, 2012), 33.
42. Bell, *Young Offenders and Youth Justice*, 34.
43. Juvenile Delinquents Act, R.S., c. 160, s. 38.
44. Department of Justice Canada, *Juvenile Delinquency in Canada: The Report of the Committee on Juvenile Delinquency, 1965* (Ottawa: Public Works and Government Services Canada, 1965), 7.
45. Department of Justice Canada, *Juvenile Delinquency in Canada*, 13.

46. Department of Justice Canada, *Juvenile Delinquency in Canada*, 26.
47. Department of Justice Canada, *Juvenile Delinquency in Canada*, 105.
48. Solicitor General Canada, *Young Persons in Conflict with the Law* (Ottawa: Ministry of the Solicitor General Committee on Legislation on Young Persons in Conflict with the Law, 1975), 3.
49. Solicitor General Canada, *Young Persons in Conflict with the Law*, 3.
50. Solicitor General Canada, *Young Persons in Conflict with the Law*, 4.
51. Jeffrey S. Leon, "The Development of Canadian Juvenile Justice: A Background for Reform," *Osgoode Hall Law Journal* 15.1 (1977): 72.
52. Solicitor General of Canada, *Young Persons in Conflict with the Law*.
53. Truth and Reconciliation Commission of Canada, *They Came for the Children*, 22.
54. Truth and Reconciliation Commission of Canada, *They Came for the Children*, 18.
55. Dr. P. H. Bryce, *The Story of a National Crime: Being an Appeal for Justice to the Indians of Canada* (1922), 8–9.
56. Bryce, *The Story of a National Crime*, 11.
57. Bryce, *The Story of a National Crime*, 11.
58. Bryce, *The Story of a National Crime*, 11.
59. Milloy, *A National Crime*, 77.
60. Milloy, *A National Crime*, 83–84.
61. Milloy, *A National Crime*, 189–210.
62. Milloy, *A National Crime*, 67.
63. Milloy, *A National Crime*, 67.
64. 1968, R. F. Davey, as cited in Milloy, *A National Crime*, 170.
65. Milloy, *A National Crime*, 154.
66. Truth and Reconciliation Commission of Canada, *They Came for the Children*, 41.
67. PatrickWolfe, "Settler Colonialism and the Elimination of the Native," *Journal of Genocide Research* 8 (2006): 387–409.

CHAPTER 3

1. Bernard Schissel, *Still Blaming Children: Youth Conduct and the Politics of Child Hating* (Halifax: Fernwood Publishing, 2006), 53.
2. Statistics Canada, "Admission to Youth Correctional Services in Canada, 2011/2012" (http://www.statcan.gc.ca/pub/85-002-x/2014001/article/11917-eng.htm?fpv=2693), accessed July 4, 2014.
3. Bryan Hogeveen and Joanne C. Minaker, "Critical Criminology and Youth Justice in the Risk Society: Issues of Power and Justice," in *Youth at Risk and Youth Justice: A Canadian Overview*, eds. John Winterdyk and Russell Smandych (Don Mills: Oxford University Press, 2012): 182.
4. Gary Oakes, "Teen Gets 20 Months for 7 Week Spree of Office Burglaries," *Toronto Star*, December 24, 1985.
5. Young Offenders Act, 1980-81-82-83, c. 110, s. 1.

6. Schissel, *Still Blaming Children*, 7–24.
7. Schissel, *Still Blaming Children*, 7–24.
8. Schissel, *Still Blaming Children*, 47.
9. Schissel, *Still Blaming Children*, 39–44.
10. Schissel, *Still Blaming Children*, 53.
11. Felipe Estrada, "Juvenile Violence as a Social Problem: Trends, Media Attention and Societal Response," *British Journal of Criminology* 41 (2001): 653.
12. Schissel, *Still Blaming Children*, 53.
13. Nicholas Bala, "What's Wrong with YOA Bashing? What's Wrong with the YOA?—Recognizing the Limits of Law," *Canadian Journal of Criminology* 36 (1994): 247–250.
14. Bala, "What's Wrong with YOA Bashing? What's Wrong with the YOA?," 247–250.
15. Julian Tanner, *Teenage Troubles: Youth and Deviance in Canada* (Don Mills: Oxford University Press, 2010), 9.
16. Tanner, *Teenage Troubles*, 4–5.
17. Bala, "What's Wrong with YOA Bashing? What's Wrong with the YOA?," 247–250.
18. Alan W. Leschied and Paul Gendreau, "Doing Justice in Canada: YOA Policies That Can Promote Community Safety," *Canadian Journal of Criminology* 36 (1994).
19. Jim Hackler, "How Should We Respond to Youth Crime?," *Canadian Journal of Law and Society* 20 (2005): 204.
20. Tanner, *Teenage Troubles*, 10.
21. Indigenous Foundations, *Sixties Scoop* (Vancouver: UBC, http://indigenousfoundations.arts.ubc.ca/home/government-policy/sixties-scoop.html, 2009), accessed May 1, 2014.
22. Indigenous Foundations, Sixties Scoop (Vancouver: UBC, http://indigenousfoundations.arts.ubc.ca/home/government-policy/sixties-scoop.html, 2009), accessed May 1, 2014.
23. 38th Parliament, 1st session, Standing Committee on Aboriginal Affairs and Northern Development (http://www.parl.gc.ca/HousePublications/Publication.aspx?DocId=1648068&Language=E&Mode=1, February 17, 2005), accessed April 24, 2014.
24. Prime Minister of Canada, Right Honourable Stephen Harper, Statement of Apology—to Former Students of Indian Residential Schools (http://www.aadnc-aandc.gc.ca/eng/1100100015644/1100100015649, June 11, 2008), accessed May 31, 2014.
25. Paulette Regan, *Unsettling the Settler Within: Indian Residential Schools, Truth Telling, and Reconciliation in Canada* (Vancouver: UBC Press, 2010), 177.
26. Regan, *Unsettling the Settler Within*, 178.
27. Regan, *Unsettling the Settler Within*, 178.
28. Melissa L. Walls et al., "'Rebuilding Our Community': Hearing Silenced Voices on Aboriginal Youth Suicide," *Transcultural Psychiatry* 51 (2014): 48.
29. Walls et al., "'Rebuilding Our Community,'" 48.

30. Brenda Elias et al., "Trauma and Suicide Behaviour Histories among a Canadian Indigenous Population: An Empirical Exploration of the Role of Canada's Residential School System," *Social Science & Medicine* 74 (2012).
31. Rita Daly, "Kids Who Hurt Can also Heal; Offenders, Victims Meet in Mediation Attempt to Reduce Courtroom Trials," *Toronto Star*, March 28, 2004.
32. Department of Justice Canada, *The Youth Criminal Justice Act: Summary and Background* (Ottawa: Minister of Justice and Attorney General of Canada, 2013), 1.
33. John Winterdyk and Nicholas Jones, "The Shifting Visage of Youth Justice in Canada: Moving Towards a More Responsive Regulatory Model within a Human Rights Framework," in *Rights and Restoration within Youth Justice*, ed. Theo Gavrielides (Whitby: de Sitter Publications, 2012): 228.
34. Youth Criminal Justice Act, S.C. 2002, c. 1, s. 3(1).
35. Youth Criminal Justice Act, S.C. 2002, c. 1, s. 3(1).
36. Youth Criminal Justice Act, S.C. 2002, c. 1, s. 3(1).
37. Department of Justice Canada, *The Youth Criminal Justice Act*, 4.
38. Peter J. Carrington and Jennifer L. Schulenberg, *The Impact of the Youth Criminal Justice Act on Police Charging Practices with Young Persons: A Preliminary Statistical Assessment* (Ottawa: Department of Justice Canada, 2005).
39. Youth Criminal Justice Act, S.C. 2002, c. 1, s. 6(1).
40. Youth Criminal Justice Act, S.C. 2002, c. 1, s. 6(1).
41. Daly, "Kids Who Hurt Can also Heal; Offenders, Victims Meet in Mediation Attempt to Reduce Courtroom Trials," *Toronto Star*, March 28, 2004.
42. Statistics Canada, "Police-Reported Crime Severity Indexes, Canada, 2002 to 2012," (http://www.statcan.gc.ca/pub/85-002-x/2013001/article/11854/tbl/tbl08b-eng.htm), accessed July 4, 2014.
43. Statistics Canada, "Ten Most Common Cases Completed in Youth Court, Canada, 2011/2012" (http://www.statcan.gc.ca/pub/85-002-x/2013001/article/11803-eng.htm?fpv=2693), accessed July 4, 2014.
44. Statistics Canada, "Admission to Youth Correctional Services in Canada, 2011/2012."
45. Statistics Canada, "Admission to Youth Correctional Services in Canada, 2011/2012."
46. Statistics Canada, "Probation Most Common Type of Youth Court Sentence," (http://www.statcan.gc.ca/pub/85-002-x/2013001/article/11803-eng.htm?fpv=2693#a5), accessed July 4, 2014.
47. Auditor General of Ontario, *Chapter 3, Section 3.13, Youth Justice Services Program* (Toronto: Auditor General of Ontario, 2012), 311.
48. Auditor General of Ontario, *Chapter 3, Section 3.13, Youth Justice Services Program*, 306.
49. Jeffrey S. Leon, "The Development of Canadian Juvenile Justice: A Background for Reform," *Osgoode Hall Law Journal* 15.1 (1977): 72
50. Leon, "The Development of Canadian Juvenile Justice," 93.
51. Leon, "The Development of Canadian Juvenile Justice," 93.

52. Janani Umamaheswar, "Bringing Hope and Change: A Study of Youth Probation Officers in Toronto," *International Journal of Offender Therapy and Comparative Criminology* 57 (2012): 1166–1167.
53. Raymond R. Corrado, Karla Gronsdahl, David MacAlister, and Irwin M. Cohen, "Youth Justice in Canada: Theoretical Perspectives of Youth Probation Officers," *Canadian Journal of Criminology and Criminal Justice* 52 (2010): 415–417.
54. Fergus McNeill, "What Works and What's Just?," *European Journal of Probation* 1 (2009): 22.
55. Rob Nicholson, Speech to Canadian Parliament (https://openparliament.ca/debates/2010/3/19/rob-nicholson-1/only/, March 10, 2010), accessed September 15, 2010.
56. Youth Criminal Justice Act, S.C. 2002, c. 1, s. 3(1).
57. D. Merlin Nunn, *Spiralling Out of Control: Lessons Learned from a Boy in Trouble, Report of the Nunn Commission of Inquiry* (Nova Scotia: Province of Nova Scotia, 2006), 23.
58. Nunn, *Spiralling Out of Control*, 24–25.
59. Nunn, *Spiralling Out of Control*, 236–248.
60. Ed Fast, Speech to Canadian Parliament (http://openparliament.ca/politicians/ed-fast/?page=32, March 17, 2010), accessed September 15, 2010.
61. Nicholson, Speech to Canadian Parliament.
62. Nunn, *Spiralling Out of Control*.
63. Don Sabo, Terry A. Kupers, and Willie London, *Prison Masculinities* (Philadelphia: Temple University Press, 2001), 15.
64. CTV News, "Justice Minister Defends Unreported Crimes Claim" (www.ctvnews.ca/justice-minister-defends-day-s-unreported-crimes-claim-1.539083, 2010), accessed September 15, 2010.
65. Regan, *Unsettling the Settler Within*, 180.

CHAPTER 4

1. Larry Tifft and Dennis Sullivan, *The Struggle to Be Human: Crime, Criminology & Anarchism* (Orkney, UK: Cienfuegos Press, 1980), 23.
2. Tifft and Sullivan, *The Struggle to Be Human*, 6–11.
3. John Galliher, "The Life and Death of Liberal Criminology," *Contemporary Crises* 2 (1978).
4. Galliher, "The Life and Death of Liberal Criminology."
5. Galliher, "The Life and Death of Liberal Criminology."
6. Michael J. Sandel, *Justice: What's the Right Thing to Do?* (New York: Farrar, Straus and Giroux, 2009).
7. Sandel, *Justice*.
8. Sandel, *Justice*.
9. Philip Jenkins, "Varieties of Enlightenment Criminology," *British Journal of Criminology* 24 (1984): 114–116.
10. Tullo Caputo and Rick Linden, "Early Theories of Criminology," in *Criminology: A Canadian Perspective*, ed. Rick Linden (Toronto: Nelson Education Ltd, 2012): 257–283.

11. Galliher, "The Life and Death of Liberal Criminology."
12. Galliher, "The Life and Death of Liberal Criminology."
13. Galliher, "The Life and Death of Liberal Criminology."
14. Galliher, "The Life and Death of Liberal Criminology."
15. Galliher, "The Life and Death of Liberal Criminology."
16. Katherine Ramsland, "The Measure of a Man: Cesare Lombroso and the Criminal Type," *The Forensic Examiner* 18 (2009).
17. Ramsland, "The Measure of a Man: Cesare Lombroso and the Criminal Type."
18. Ramsland, "The Measure of a Man: Cesare Lombroso and the Criminal Type."
19. Paolo Mazzarello, "Lombroso and Tolstoy," *Nature* 409 (2001).
20. Mazzarello, "Lombroso and Tolstoy."
21. "Twin Studies," *Acta Psychiatrica Scandinavica* 33 (1958): 12–15.
22. James H. Satterfield and Anne Schell, "A Prospective Study of Hyperactive Boys with Conduct Problems and Normal Boys: Adolescent and Adult Criminality," *Journal of the American Academy of Child & Adolescent Psychiatry* 36 (1997): 1726-1735.
23. Daniel Glaser, "Criminality Theories and Behavioral Images," *American Journal of Sociology* 61 (1956).
24. Michael T. Neitzel, *Crime and Its Modification: A Social Learning Perspective* (New York: Pergamon, 1979).
25. Glaser, "Criminality Theories and Behavioral Images."
26. James E. Cote and Charles Levine, "A Formulation of Erikson's Theory of Ego Identity Formation," *Developmental Review* 7 (1987): 273–325.
27. Erik H. Erikson as cited in James E. Cote and Charles Levine, "A Formulation of Erikson's Theory of Ego Identity Formation," *Developmental Review* 7 (1987): 273–325
28. O. L. Zangwill, "Early Days of Behaviourism," *Nature* 282 (1979): 148–149.
29. T. M. Bloomfield, "About Skinner: Notes on the Theory and Practice of 'Radical Behaviourism,'" *Philosophy of the Social Sciences* 6 (1976): 75–82.
30. Bloomfield, "About Skinner."
31. Bloomfield, "About Skinner."
32. Bloomfield, "About Skinner."
33. S. Sutherland, "Skinnerian Behaviour," *Nature* 282 (1979): 149–150.
34. Patricia Zapf, Nathalie C. Gagnon, David N. Cox, and Ronald Roesch, "Psychological Perspective on Criminality," in *Criminology: A Canadian Perspective*, ed. Rick Linden (Toronto: Nelson Education Ltd, 2012): 296.
35. Albert Bandura, "Social Learning Theory of Aggression," *Journal of Communication* 28 (1978): 12–29.
36. Bandura, "Social Learning Theory of Aggression," 12–29.
37. Zapf et al., "Psychological Perspective on Criminality," 294–296.
38. Christine Olson, "The Deep Roots of the Fairness Committee in Kohlberg's Moral Development Theory," *Schools: Studies in Education* 8 (2011): 125–135.
39. Olson, "The Deep Roots of the Fairness Committee in Kohlberg's Moral Development Theory," 125–135.
40. Zapf et al., "Psychological Perspective on Criminality," 289–292.

41. S. K. Wong, "Youth Crime and Family Disruption in Canadian Municipalities: An Adaptation of Shaw and McKay's Social Disorganization Theory," *International Journal of Law, Crime and Justice* 40 (2012): 100–114.
42. Wong, "Youth Crime and Family Disruption in Canadian Municipalities," 100–114.
43. James C. Hackler, "Strain Theories" in *Criminology: A Canadian Perspective*, ed. Rick Linden (Toronto: Nelson Education Ltd, 2012): 324.
44. P. Johnson and J. Duberley, "Anomie and Culture Management: Reappraising Durkheim," *Organization* 18 (2011): 563–584.
45. Johnson and Duberley, "Anomie and Culture Management: Reappraising Durkheim," 563–584.
46. Robert K. Merton, "Social Structure and Anomie," *American Sociological Review* 3 (1938): 672–682.
47. Lloyd E. Ohlin, "Delinquent Boys: The Culture of the Gang by Albert K. Cohen, Review by: Lloyd E. Ohlin," *Social Science Review* 30 (1956): 379–380.
48. Richard A. Cloward, and Lloyd Ohlin as cited in Cesare J. Rebellon, Michelle E. Manasse, Karen T. Van Gundy, and Ellen S. Cohn, "Perceived Injustice and Delinquency: A Test of General Strain Theory," *Journal of Criminal Justice* 40 (2012): 230–237.
49. Robert Agnew, "Foundation for a General Strain Theory of Crime and Delinquency," *Criminology* 30 (1992): 47–88.
50. Agnew, "Foundation for a General Strain Theory of Crime and Delinquency," 47–88.
51. Sandra J. Ball-Rokeach, "Values and Violence: A Test of the Subculture of Violence Thesis," *American Sociological Review* 38 (1973): 736–749.
52. Richard B. Felson, Allen E. Liska, Scott J. South, and Thomas L. McNulty, "The Subculture of Violence and Delinquency: Individual vs. School Context Effects," *Social Forces* 73 (1994): 155–173.
53. This paragraph based on the work of Felson et al., "The Subculture of Violence and Delinquency," 155–173.
54. S. Kobrin, "Review of Delinquency and Drift by David Matza," *American Journal of Sociology* 72 (1966): 322–324.
55. Gresham M. Sykes and David Matza, "Techniques of Neutralization: A Theory of Delinquency," *American Sociological Review* 22 (1957): 664–670.
56. This section based on the work of Sykes and Matza, "Techniques of Neutralization," 664–670.
57. Julian D. Ford, John Chapman, Daniel F. Connor, and Keith R. Cruise, "Complex Trauma and Aggression in Secure Juvenile Justice Settings," *Criminal Justice and Behaviour* 39 (2012): 694–724; Carly B. Dierkhising, Susan J. Ko, Briana Woods-Jaeger, Ernstine C. Briggs, Robert Lee, and Robert S. Pynoos, "Trauma Histories among Justice-Involved Youth," *European Journal of Psychotraumatology* 4 (2013): 1–12.
58. Ford et al., "Complex Trauma and Aggression in Secure Juvenile Justice Settings," 694–724; Dierkhising et al., "Trauma Histories among Justice-Involved Youth," 1–12.

59. Sonya G. Wanklyn, David M. Day, Trevor A. Hart, and Todd A. Girard, "Cumulative Childhood Maltreatment and Depression among Incarcerated Youth: Impulsivity and Hopelessness as Potential Intervening Variables," *Child Maltreatment* 17 (2012): 306–317.
60. Karen M. Abram et al., "PTSD, Trauma, and Comorbid Psychiatric Disorders in Detained Youth," *Juvenile Justice Bulletin* (2013): 1–16.
61. Zachary W. Adams et al., "Psychiatric Problems and Trauma Exposure in Nondetained and Nondelinquent Adolescents," *Journal of Clinical Child & Adolescent Psychology* 42 (2013): 323–331.
62. Prison Reform Trust, *Bromley Briefings Prison Fact File* (London: Prison Reform Trust, 2013), 41–44.
63. Fatos Kaba et al., "Traumatic Brain Injury among Newly Admitted Adolescents in the New York Jail System," *Journal of Adolescent Health* 54 (2014): 615–617.
64. Martin Brokenleg, "Transforming Cultural Trauma into Resilience," *Reclaiming Children and Youth* 21 (2012): 9–13.
65. James Anaya, *Report of the Special Rapporteur on the Rights of Indigenous Peoples: The Situation of Indigenous Peoples in Canada* (Geneva: United Nations General Assembly, 2014).
66. Anaya, *Report of the Special Rapporteur on the Rights of Indigenous Peoples*, 7.
67. Brokenleg, "Transforming Cultural Trauma into Resilience," 9–13.
68. Anaya, *Report of the Special Rapporteur on the Rights of Indigenous Peoples*, 11.
69. Melissa L. Walls et al., "'Rebuilding Our Community': Hearing Silenced Voices on Aboriginal Youth Suicide," *Transcultural Psychiatry* 51 (2014): 48; Brenda Elias et al., "Trauma and Suicide Behaviour Histories among a Canadian Indigenous Population: An Empirical Exploration of the Role of Canada's Residential School System," *Social Science & Medicine* 74 (2012).
70. Raymond R. Corrado, Sarah Kuehn, and Irina Margaritescu, "Policy Issues Regarding Overrepresentation of Incarcerated Aboriginal Young Offenders in a Canadian Context," *Youth Justice* 14 (2014): 43.
71. Elizabeth Comack, *Out There, In Here: Masculinity, Violence and Prisoning* (Winnipeg: Fernwood Publishing, 2008), 57–64.
72. Erin M. Espinosa, Jon R. Sorensen, and Molly A. Lopez, "Youth Pathways to Placement: The Influence of Gender, Mental Health Need and Trauma on Confinement in the Juvenile Justice System," *Journal of Youth Adolescence* 42 (2013): 1824–1836.
73. Elizabeth Moore, Claire Gaskin, and Devon Indig, "Childhood Maltreatment and Post-traumatic Stress Disorder among Incarcerated Young Offenders," *Child Abuse & Neglect* 37 (2013): 862.
74. Roger Grimshaw, Joseph Schwartz, and Rachel Wingfield, *My Story: Young People Talk About the Trauma and Violence in their Lives* (London: Centre for Crime and Justice Studies, 2011), 16.
75. Grimshaw, Schwartz, and Wingfield, *My Story*, 23.
76. James Gilligan, *Preventing Violence* (New York: Thames & Hudson Inc, 2001), 29.
77. Gilligan, *Preventing Violence*, 30.

78. Carolyn Yoder, *The Little Book of Trauma Healing: When Violence Strikes and Community Security Is Threatened* (Intercourse: Good Books, 2005), 18.
79. Yoder, *The Little Book of Trauma Healing*, 38.
80. Yoder, *The Little Book of Trauma Healing*, 33.
81. Yoder, *The Little Book of Trauma Healing*, 33.
82. Cathy Spatz Widom, "The Cycle of Violence," *Science* 244 (1989): 160–166.
83. Widom, "The Cycle of Violence," 163.
84. Valentina Nikulina, Cathy Spatz Widom, and Sally Czaja, "The Role of Childhood Neglect and Childhood Poverty in Predicting Mental Health, Academic Achievement and Crime in Adulthood," *American Journal of Community Psychology* 48 (2011): 310.
85. Nikulina, Widom, and Czaja, "The Role of Childhood Neglect and Childhood Poverty in Predicting Mental Health, Academic Achievement and Crime in Adulthood," 309–321.
86. James Topitzes, Joshua P. Mersky, and Arthur J. Reynolds, "From Child Maltreatment to Violent Offending: An Examination of Mixed-Gender and Gender-Specific Models," *Journal of Interpersonal Violence* 27 (2012): 2322–2347.
87. Thomas Frisell, P. Lichtenstein, and N. Langstrom, "Violent Crime Runs in Families: A Total Population Study of 12.5 Million Individuals," *Psychological Medicine* 41 (2011): 97–105.
88. Frisell, Lichtenstein, and Langstrom, "Violent Crime Runs in Families," 97–105.
89. Robin M. Hartinger-Saunders et al., "Victimization, Psychological Distress and Subsequent Offending among Youth," *Children and Youth Services Review* 33 (2011): 2375–2385.
90. Kenneth Corvo, "Violence, Separation, and Loss in Families of Origin of Domestically Violent Men," *Journal of Interpersonal Violence* 21 (2006): 117–125.
91. Anne McGillivray and Brenda Comaskey, *Black Eyes All of the Time: Intimate Violence, Aboriginal Women, and the Justice System* (Toronto: University of Toronto Press, 1999).
92. Matthew R. Durose et al., *Family Violence Statistics: Including Statistics on Strangers and Acquaintances* (Washington: U.S. Department of Justice, 2005).
93. Durose et al., *Family Violence Statistics*.
94. Durose et al., *Family Violence Statistics*.
95. Durose et al., *Family Violence Statistics*.
96. bell hooks, "Feminism: Crying for Our Souls," *Women & Therapy* 17 (1995): 265–271.
97. hooks, "Feminism: Crying for Our Souls," 266.
98. bell hooks, "Out of the Academy and into the Streets," *Ms* 3 (1992): 80–82.
99. hooks "Out of the Academy and into the Streets," 80.
100. Comack, *Out There/In Here*, 15.
101. Comack, *Out There/In Here*, 15.
102. Comack, *Out There/In Here*, 14–18.
103. Kimberle W. Crenshaw, "Demarginalizing the Intersection of Race and Sex," *University of Chicago Legal Forum* (1989): 139–167.
104. Crenshaw, "Demarginalizing the Intersection of Race and Sex," 149.

105. Kimberle W. Crenshaw, "Mapping the Margins: Intersectionality, Identity Politics, and Violence Against Women of Color," *Stanford Law Review* 43 (1991): 1241–1299.
106. Tifft and Sullivan, *The Struggle to Be Human*.

CHAPTER 5

1. Judith Herman, *Trauma and Recovery: The Aftermath of Violence—From Domestic Abuse to Political Terror* (New York: Basic Books, 1997), 33.
2. Bessel A. van der Kolk, "Trauma and Memory," *Psychiatry and Clinical Neurosciences* 52 (1998): 52–64.
3. Sandra L. Bloom, "Bridging the Black Hole of Trauma: The Evolutionary Significance of the Arts," *Psychotherapy and Politics International* 8 (2010): 200.
4. Lori Haskell and Melanie Randall, "Disrupted Attachments: A Social Context Complex Trauma Framework and the Lives of Aboriginal Peoples in Canada," *Journal of Aboriginal Health* (2009): 49.
5. Brene Brown, "The Power of Vulnerability" (TEDxHouston: http://www.ted.com/talks/brene_brown_on_vulnerability.html), accessed January 15, 2014.
6. Phyllis T. Stien and Joshua Kendall, *Psychological Trauma and the Developing Brain: Neurologically Based Interventions for Troubled Children* (New York: Routledge, 2004), 97.
7. Stien and Kendall, *Psychological Trauma and the Developing Brain*, 97.
8. Headings in this section are similar to those used by Stien and Kendall, *Psychological Trauma and the Developing Brain*, chapter 4.
9. Stien and Kendall, *Psychological Trauma and the Developing Brain*, 101.
10. Herman, *Trauma and Recovery*, 36.
11. Eamon J. McCrory et al., "Heightened Neural Reactivity to Threat in Child Victims of Family Violence," *Current Biology* 21 (2011): R947–R948.
12. McCrory et al., "Heightened Neural Reactivity to Threat in Child Victims of Family Violence," R947–R948.
13. McCrory et al., "Heightened Neural Reactivity to Threat in Child Victims of Family Violence," R947.
14. Bessel van der Kolk and Alexander C. McFarlane, "The Black Hole of Trauma," in *Traumatic Stress: The Effects of Overwhelming Experience on Mind, Body, and Society*, eds. Bessel A. van der Kolk, Alexander C. McFarlane, and Lars Weisaeth (New York: Guildford Press, 2007): 13.
15. Van der Kolk and McFarlane, "The Black Hole of Trauma," 13.
16. Van der Kolk and McFarlane, "The Black Hole of Trauma," 12.
17. Stien and Kendall, *Psychological Trauma and the Developing Brain*, 104.
18. Stien and Kendall, *Psychological Trauma and the Developing Brain*, 103.
19. Stien and Kendall, *Psychological Trauma and the Developing Brain*, 104.
20. Van der Kolk and McFarlane, "The Black Hole of Trauma," 9.
21. Sandra L. Bloom, *Creating Sanctuary: Toward the Evolution of Sane Societies* (New York: Routledge, 1997), 26.
22. Bloom, *Creating Sanctuary*, 26.
23. Herman, *Trauma and Recovery*, 38.

24. Stien and Kendall, *Psychological Trauma and the Developing Brain*, 107.
25. Stien and Kendall, *Psychological Trauma and the Developing Brain*, 108.
26. Stien and Kendall, *Psychological Trauma and the Developing Brain*, 109.
27. Van der Kolk and McFarlane, "The Black Hole of Trauma," 13.
28. Vincent Felitti and Ruth Buczynski, *Why the Most Significant Factor in Predicting Chronic Disease May Be Childhood Trauma* (The National Institute for the Clinical Application of Behavioral Medicine, 2011).
29. Shanta R. Dube, Michelle L. Cook, and Valerie J. Edwards, "Health-Related Outcomes of Adverse Childhood Experiences in Texas, 2002," *Preventing Chronic Disease Public Health Research, Practice, and Policy* 7 (2010): 1–9.
30. Markus H. Schafer and Kenneth F. Ferraro, "Childhood Misfortune as a Threat to Successful Aging: Avoiding Disease," *The Gerontologist* 52 (2012): 111–120.
31. Divya Mehta et al., "Childhood Maltreatment Is Associated with Distinct Genomic and Epigenetic Profiles in Posttraumatic Stress Disorder," *Proceedings of the National Academy of Sciences* 110 (2013): 8302.
32. Wendy D'Andrea et al., "Understanding Interpersonal Trauma in the Context in Children: Why We Need a Developmentally Appropriate Trauma Diagnosis," *American Journal of Orthopsychiatry* 82 (2012): 187–200.
33. Bessel A. van der Kolk, "The Compulsion to Repeat Trauma: Re-enactment, Revictimization, and Masochism," *Psychiatric Clinics of North America* 12 (1989): 389–411.
34. Van der Kolk, "The Compulsion to Repeat Trauma," 389–411.
35. Van der Kolk, "The Compulsion to Repeat Trauma," 389–411.
36. Mary E. Vandergoot, *Justice for Young Offenders: Their Needs, Our Responses* (Saskatoon: Purich Publishing Inc, 2006), 48.
37. Bloom, *Creating Sanctuary*, 26.
38. Bloom, *Creating Sanctuary*, 45.
39. Bloom, *Creating Sanctuary*, 45.
40. Bloom, *Creating Sanctuary*, 32.
41. Bloom, *Creating Sanctuary*, 36.
42. As quoted on (http://www.brainpickings.org/), accessed July 13, 2014.
43. Summarized from (http://www.ptsd.va.gov/professional/PTSD-overview/dsm5_criteria_ptsd.asp), accessed July 3, 2014.
44. J. Christopher Fowler et al., "Exposure to Interpersonal Trauma, Attachment Insecurity, and Depression Severity," *Journal of Affective Disorders* 149 (2013): 313–318.
45. Fowler et al., "Exposure to Interpersonal Trauma, Attachment Insecurity, and Depression Severity," 316.
46. Barry J. Gibb, *The Rough Guide to the Brain* (New York: Rough Guides Ltd, 2007), 148.
47. This paragraph based on the work of Falk Leichsenring et al., "Borderline Personality Disorder," *Lancet* 377 (2011): 74–84.
48. Bessel A. van der Kolk, "The Complexity of Adaptation to Trauma: Self-Regulation, Stimulus Discrimination, and Characterological Development" in *Traumatic Stress: The Effects of Overwhelming Experience on Mind, Body, and Society*,

eds. Bessel A. van der Kolk, Alexander C. McFarlane, and Lars Weisaeth (New York: Guildford Press, 2007).
49. Van der Kolk, "The Complexity of Adaptation to Trauma," 201.
50. Van der Kolk, "The Complexity of Adaptation to Trauma," 201.
51. Van der Kolk, "The Complexity of Adaptation to Trauma," 203.
52. Van der Kolk, "The Complexity of Adaptation to Trauma," 201.
53. Van der Kolk, "The Complexity of Adaptation to Trauma," 201.
54. Martin J. Dorahy et al., "Dissociative Identity Disorder: An Empirical Overview," *Australian and New Zealand Journal of Psychiatry* 48 (2014): 404 and 408.
55. Vandergoot, *Justice for Young Offenders*, 45.
56. Vandergoot, *Justice for Young Offenders*, 48.
57. Vandergoot, *Justice for Young Offenders*, 48.
58. Vandergoot, *Justice for Young Offenders*, 48.
59. Gabor Maté, *In the Realm of Hungry Ghosts: Close Encounters with Addiction* (Toronto: Alfred A. Knopf Canada, 2008), 128–129.
60. Maté, *In the Realm of Hungry Ghosts*.
61. Maté, *In the Realm of Hungry Ghosts*, 174.
62. Maté, *In the Realm of Hungry Ghosts*, 139.
63. Maté, *In the Realm of Hungry Ghosts*, 139.
64. Maté, *In the Realm of Hungry Ghosts*, 139.
65. Maté, *In the Realm of Hungry Ghosts*, 193.
66. Joyce Fowler, "Psychoneurobiology of Co-Occurring Trauma and Addictions," *Journal of Chemical Dependency Treatment* 8 (2006): 145.
67. Fowler, "Psychoneurobiology of Co-Occurring Trauma and Addictions," 145.
68. Nora LaFond Padykula and Philip Conklin, "The Self Regulation Model of Attachment Trauma and Addiction," *Clinical Social Work Journal* 38 (2010): 351.
69. Padykula and Conklin, "The Self Regulation Model of Attachment Trauma and Addiction," 352.
70. David Marjot, "An Attachment Theory of Addiction," *Addiction* 103 (2014): 2065.
71. Howard Zehr, *Transcending: Reflections of Crime Victims* (Intercourse: Good Books, 2001), 9.
72. Zehr, *Transcending: Reflections of Crime Victims*, 130.
73. Zehr, *Transcending: Reflections of Crime Victims*, 31.
74. Herman, *Trauma and Recovery*, 51.
75. Herman, *Trauma and Recovery*, 52.
76. Colby Pearce, *A Short Introduction to Attachment and Attachment Disorder* (London: Jessica Kingsley Publishers, 2009), 13.
77. Pearce, *A Short Introduction to Attachment and Attachment Disorder*, 13.
78. John Bowlby, *Attachment* (London: Random House, 1969).
79. Bowlby, *Attachment*, xi.
80. Bowlby, *Attachment*, 179.
81. Bowlby, *Attachment*.
82. Mario Mikulincer and Phillip R. Shaver, *Attachment in Adulthood: Structure, Dynamics, and Change* (London: The Guildford Press, 2007).
83. Bowlby as quoted in Mikulincer and Shaver, *Attachment in Adulthood*, 7.

84. Bowlby as quoted in Mikulincer and Shaver, *Attachment in Adulthood*, 7.
85. Bowlby as quoted in Mikulincer and Shaver, *Attachment in Adulthood*, 27.
86. John Bowlby, *A Secure Base: Parent-Child Attachment and Healthy Human Development* (London: Routledge, 1988), 9.
87. Bowlby, *A Secure Base*, 11.
88. Bowlby, *A Secure Base*, 9.
89. Herman, *Trauma and Recovery*, 53.
90. Herman, *Trauma and Recovery*, 54.
91. Herman, *Trauma and Recovery*, 53.
92. Bloom, *Creating Sanctuary*, 37.
93. C. R. Brewin, R. Garnett, and B. Andrews, "Trauma, Identity and Mental Health in UK Military Veterans," *Psychological Medicine* 41 (2011): 1736.
94. Brewin, Garnett, and Andrews, "Trauma, Identity and Mental Health in UK Military Veterans," 1736.
95. Zehr, *Transcending: Reflections of Crime Victims*, 127.
96. Maté, *In the Realm of Hungry Ghosts*, 128–129.

CHAPTER 6

1. Maya Angelou, excerpt from poem, "A Brave & Startling Truth," 50th Anniversary Commemoration of the United Nations (June 1995).
2. Maria Yellow Horse Brave Heart, "The Return to the Sacred Path: Healing the Historical Trauma and Historical Unresolved Grief Response among the Lakota through Psychoeducational Group Intervention," *Smith College Studies in Social Work* 68 (1998): 288.
3. Maria Yellow Horse Brave Heart, "The Historical Trauma Response among Natives and Its Relationship with Substance Abuse: A Lakota Illustration," *Journal of Psychoactive Drugs* 35 (2003): 7.
4. Gabriele Schwab, *Haunting Legacies: Violent Histories and Transgenerational Trauma* (New York: Columbia University Press, 2010), 1 and 3.
5. Amy Desjarlais, "Emptying the Cup – Healing Fragmented Identity: An Anishinawbekwe Perspective on Historical Trauma and Culturally Appropriate Consultation," *Fourth World Journal* 11 (2012): 45.
6. Eduardo Duran, Judith Firehammer, and John Gonzalez, "Liberation Psychology as the Path Toward Healing Cultural Soul Wounds," *Journal of Counselling and Development* 86 (2008): 288.
7. Lori Haskell and Melanie Randall, "Disrupted Attachments: A Social Context Complex Trauma Framework and the Lives of Aboriginal Peoples in Canada," *Journal of Aboriginal Health* (2009): 52.
8. Cynthia C. Wesley-Esquimaux and Magdalena Smolewski, *Historic Trauma and Aboriginal Healing* (Ottawa: Aboriginal Healing Foundation, 2004), iv.
9. Schwab, *Haunting Legacies*, 49.
10. Aboriginal Healing Foundation, *Program Handbook, 2nd Edition* (Ottawa: Aboriginal Healing Foundation, 1999), A5.
11. Schwab, *Haunting Legacies*.

12. Sir John A. MacDonald as quoted in Indigenous Foundations, *Origins of the Indian Act* (Vancouver: UBC, http://indigenousfoundations.arts.ubc.ca/home/government-policy/the-indian-act.html, 2009), accessed May 1, 2014.
13. James Anaya, *Report of the Special Rapporteur on the Rights of Indigenous Peoples: The Situation of Indigenous Peoples in Canada* (Geneva: United Nations General Assembly, 2014), 11.
14. Raymond R. Corrado, Sarah Kuehn, and Irina Margaritescu, "Policy Issues Regarding Overrepresentation of Incarcerated Aboriginal Young Offenders in a Canadian Context," *Youth Justice* 14 (2014): 43.
15. James Daschuk, *Clearing the Plains: Disease, Politics of Starvation, and the Loss of Aboriginal Life* (Regina: University of Regina Press, 2013), 100.
16. Derek Summerfield, "Addressing Human Response to War and Atrocity: Major Challenges in Research and Practices and the Limitations of Western Psychiatric Models," in *Beyond Trauma: Cultural and Societal Dynamics*, eds. Rolf J. Kleber, Charles R. Figley, and Berthold P. R. Gersons (New York: Plenum Press, 1995): 19.
17. Summerfield, "Addressing Human Response to War and Atrocity," 20.
18. David Becker, "The Deficiency of the Concept of Posttraumatic Stress Disorder When Dealing with Victims of Human Rights Violations," in *Beyond Trauma: Cultural and Societal Dynamics*, eds. Rolf J. Kleber, Charles R. Figley, and Berthold P. R. Gersons (New York: Plenum Press, 1995): 106.
19. Becker, "The Deficiency of the Concept of Posttraumatic Stress Disorder When Dealing with Victims of Human Rights Violations," 104.
20. These four points from Becker, "The Deficiency of the Concept of Posttraumatic Stress Disorder When Dealing with Victims of Human Rights Violations."
21. Klinic Community Health Centre, *The Trauma-Informed Toolkit* (Winnipeg: 2008), 34.
22. Chantelle A. M. Richmond, "Narratives of Social Support and Health in Aboriginal Communities," *Canadian Journal of Public Health* 98 (2007): 348.
23. Kathleen Wilson and Mark Rosenberg, "Exploring the Determinants of Health for First Nations Peoples in Canada: Can Existing Frameworks Accommodate Traditional Activities?," *Social Science & Medicine* 55 (2002): 2017–2031.
24. The preceding point(s) from Chantelle A. M. Richmond and Nancy Ross, "The Determinants of First Nation and Inuit Health: A Critical Population Health Approach," *Health & Place* 15 (2009): 403–411.
25. Vern Neufeld Redekop, *From Violence to Blessing: How an Understanding of Deep-Rooted Conflict Can Open Paths to Reconciliation* (Ottawa: Novalis, 2002), 31–46.
26. Redekop, *From Violence to Blessing*, 31–46.
27. Redekop, *From Violence to Blessing*, 31–46.
28. Redekop, *From Violence to Blessing*, 31–46.
29. Redekop, *From Violence to Blessing*, 31–46.
30. Redekop, *From Violence to Blessing*, 31–46.
31. Redekop, *From Violence to Blessing*, 56.
32. Glen Sean Coulthard, *Red Skin White Masks: Rejecting the Colonial Politics of Recognition* (Minneapolis: University of Minnesota, 2014), 62.

33. Coulthard, *Red Skin White Masks*, 96.
34. The United Nations Convention on the Prevention and Punishment of the Crime of Genocide (Geneva: United Nations), Article II.
35. Richmond, "Narratives of Social Support and Health in Aboriginal Communities."
36. M. C. Black et al., *The National Intimate Partner and Sexual Violence Survey (NISVS): 2010 Summary Report* (Atlanta, GA: National Center for Injury Prevention and Control, Centers for Disease Control and Prevention, 2011), 49.
37. Rick Linden, *Criminology: A Canadian Perspective* (Toronto: Nelson, 2012), 191.
38. Linden, *Criminology*.
39. Linden, *Criminology*, 194, quoting Dobash and Dobash (1979).
40. Statistics Canada, *Measuring Violence Against Women: Statistical Trends — Key Findings* (Ottawa: www.statcan.gc.ca/pub/85-002-x/2013001/article/11766-eng.pdf, 2013), accessed June 21, 2014.
41. Information from www.conferenceboard.ca, accessed July 12, 2014.
42. Erin M. Espinosa, Jon R. Sorensen, and Molly A. Lopez, "Youth Pathways to Placement: The Influence of Gender, Mental Health Need and Trauma on Confinement in the Juvenile Justice System," *Journal of Youth Adolescence* 42 (2013): 1824–1836.
43. Jackson Katz, *The Macho Paradox: Why Some Men Hurt Women and How All Men Can Help* (Naperville: Sourcebooks, 2006), 25.
44. Maire Sinha, *Measuring Violence Against Women: Statistical Trends* (Ottawa: Statistics Canada, 2013).
45. Sinha, *Measuring Violence Against Women*.
46. Matthew R. Durose et al., *Family Violence Statistics: Including Statistics on Strangers and Acquaintances* (Washington: U.S. Department of Justice, 2005).
47. Durose et al., *Family Violence Statistics*.
48. Durose et al., *Family Violence Statistics*.
49. Futures Without Violence, *Perpetrator Risk Factors for Violence Against Women*.
50. Black et al., *The National Intimate Partner and Sexual Violence Survey (NISVS): 2010*, 49.
51. Black et al., *The National Intimate Partner and Sexual Violence Survey (NISVS)*, 49.
52. Black et al., *The National Intimate Partner and Sexual Violence Survey (NISVS)*, 49.
53. Black et al., *The National Intimate Partner and Sexual Violence Survey (NISVS)*, 49.
54. Chris Wood, "Why Do Men Do It?" *Maclean's* 113 (2000): 34.
55. Linden, *Criminology*, 294.
56. Raewyn Connell, *Masculinities* (Sydney: Allen & Unwin, 1995).
57. Douglas Litowitz, "Gramsci, Hegemony, and the Law," *Brigham Young University Law Review* (2000): 515–551.
58. Connell, *Masculinities*, 832.
59. Jackson Katz, *Tough Guise: Violence, Media, and the Crisis in Masculinity* (Mediaed: 1999).

60. Tony Coles, "Negotiating the Field of Masculinity," *Men and Masculinities* 12 (2009): 30–44.
61. Coles, "Negotiating the Field of Masculinity," 30–44.
62. Coles, "Negotiating the Field of Masculinity," 30–44.
63. Connell, *Masculinities*.
64. Neil Malamuth et al., "Testing Hypotheses Regarding Rape: Exposure to Sexual Violence, Sex Differences, and the 'Normality' of Rapists," *Journal of Research in Personality* 14 (1980): 121–137.
65. R. G. Stille, N. M. Malamuth, and J. R. Schallow, *Prediction of Rape Proclivity by Rape Myth Attitudes and Hostility Toward Women* (New York: Paper presented at the American Psychological Association meeting, 1987).
66. Julie A. Osland, Marguerite Fitch, and Edmond E. Willis, "Likelihood to Rape in College Males," *Sex Roles* 35 (1996): 179.
67. This list is a collection of quotes from: Timothy Beneke, *Men on Rape: What They Have to Say about Sexual Violence* (New York: St. Martin's Press, 1982): 13–14.
68. David M. Fergusson and Paul E. Mullen, *Child Sexual Abuse: An Evidence Based Perspective* (London, UK: Sage Publications Inc., 1999).
69. Centers for Disease Control and Prevention, *Sexual Violence* (http://www.cdc.gov/violenceprevention/pdf/sv-datasheet-a.pdf, 2012), accessed August 6, 2014.
70. Lundy Bancroft, *Why Does He Do That?: Inside the Minds of Angry and Controlling Men* (New York: Berkeley Books, 2002), 54.
71. Bancroft, *Why Does He Do That?*, 70.
72. Angela J. Narayan, Michelle M. Englund, and Byron Egeland, "Developmental Timing and Continuity of Exposure to Interparental Violence and Externalizing Behavior as Prospective Predictors of Dating Violence," *Development and Psychopathology* 25 (2013): 973–990.
73. Narayan, Englund, and Egeland, "Developmental Timing and Continuity of Exposure to Interparental Violence and Externalizing Behavior as Prospective Predictors of Dating Violence," 973.
74. Alison Cunningham and Linda Baker, *Little Eyes, Little Ears: How Violence Against a Mother Shapes Children as They Grow* (London: The Centre for Children and Families in the Justice System, 2007).
75. Narayan, Englund, and Egeland, "Developmental Timing and Continuity of Exposure to Interparental Violence and Externalizing Behavior as Prospective Predictors of Dating Violence," 973–990.
76. Donald G. Dutton and Katherine R. White, "Attachment Insecurity and Intimate Partner Violence," *Aggression and Violent Behavior* 17 (2012): 475–481.
77. Dutton and White, "Attachment Insecurity and Intimate Partner Violence," 475–481.
78. Dutton and White, "Attachment Insecurity and Intimate Partner Violence," 476.
79. Crawford et al., "Self-Reported Attachment, Interpersonal Aggression, and Personality Disorder in a Prospective Community Sample of Adolescents and Adults," *Journal of Personality Disorders* 20 (2006): 331–351; Dutton and White, "Attachment Insecurity and Intimate Partner Violence."

80. Judith Herman, *Trauma and Recovery: The Aftermath of Violence—From Domestic Abuse to Political Terror* (New York: Basic Books, 1997).
81. Herman, *Trauma and Recovery*, 9.
82. Herman, *Trauma and Recovery*, 14.
83. Herman, *Trauma and Recovery*, 14.
84. Herman, *Trauma and Recovery*, 14.
85. Herman, *Trauma and Recovery*, 9.
86. Nicole M. Else-Quest and Shelley Grabe, "The Political Is Personal: Measurement and Application of Nation-Level Indicators of Gender Equity in Psychological Research," *Psychology of Women Quarterly* 36 (2012): 131–144.
87. This paragraph based on the work of Else-Quest and Grabe, "The Political Is Personal: Measurement and Application of Nation-Level Indicators of Gender Equity in Psychological Research," 131–144.
88. Judith Butler, *Undoing Gender* (New York: Routlege, 2004), 24.
89. bell hooks, "Tearing Out the Root of Self-Hatred," *The Other Side* (2003): 10.
90. Kai Erikson as quoted in Simona L. Perry, "Development, Land Use, and Collective Trauma: The Marcellus Shale Gas Boom in Rural Pennsylvania," *The Journal of Culture & Agriculture* 34 (2012): 89.
91. Kai T. Erikson, "Trauma at Buffalo Creek," *Society* 13 (1976): 58.
92. Erikson, "Trauma at Buffalo Creek," 58.
93. Erikson, "Trauma at Buffalo Creek," 63–64.

CHAPTER 7

1. T. Richard Snyder, *The Protestant Ethic and the Spirit of Punishment* (Grand Rapids: Wm. B. Eerdmans Publishing Co, 2001), 3.
2. Youth Criminal Justice Act, S.C. 2002, c. 1, s. 38(1), 2(f), 83(1).
3. Social Distortion, "Prison Bound" (Fullerton: Restless Records, 1988).
4. Uberto Gatti, Richard E. Tremblay, and Frank Vitaro, "Iatrogenic Effect of Juvenile Justice," *The Journal of Child Psychology and Psychiatry* 50 (2009): 991–998.
5. Gatti, Tremblay, and Vitaro, "Iatrogenic Effect of Juvenile Justice," 995.
6. William D. Bales and Alex R. Piquero, "Assessing the Impact of Prison on Recidivism," *Journal of Experimental Criminology* 8 (2012): 71–101.
7. Bales and Piquero, "Assessing the Impact of Prison on Recidivism," 71–101.
8. Francesco Drago, "Prison Conditions and Recidivism," *American Law and Economics Review* 13 (2011): 103–130.
9. David M. Bierie, "Is Tougher Better?: The Impact of Prison Conditions on Inmate Violence," *International Journal of Offender Therapy and Comparative Criminology* 56 (2012): 351.
10. W. Kondro, "Canada Lags in Preventing Hospital Infections," *Canadian Medical Association Journal* 183 (2011): E160.
11. Public Health Agency of Canada, *The Chief Public Health Officer's Report on the State of Public Health in Canada, 2013: Infectious Disease—The Never-Ending Threat* (Canada: Public Health Agency of Canada, 2013).

12. Public Health Agency of Canada, *The Chief Public Health Officer's Report on the State of Public Health in Canada*, 2013.
13. Public Health Agency of Canada, *The Chief Public Health Officer's Report on the State of Public Health in Canada*, 2013.
14. Hans Toch, "Punitiveness as 'Behavior Management,'" *Criminal Justice and Behavior* 35 (2008): 388.
15. Dennis A. Challeen, *Making It Right: A Common Sense Approach to Criminal Justice* (Melius Peterson Publishing Co, 1986).
16. Richard A. Mendel, *No Place for Kids: The Case for Reducing Juvenile Incarceration* (Baltimore: The Annie E. Casey Foundation, 2011), 6–7.
17. Barry Holman and Jason Zeidenberg, *The Dangers of Detention: The Impact of Incarcerating Youth in Detention and Other Secure Facilities* (Washington: Justice Policy Institute, 2006).
18. Holman and Zeidenberg, *The Dangers of Detention*.
19. Mendel, *No Place for Kids*, 9.
20. Mendel, *No Place for Kids*, 10.
21. Mendel, *No Place for Kids*, 11.
22. Mendel, *No Place for Kids*, 12.
23. Ian Lambie and Isabel Randell, "The Impact of Incarceration on Juvenile Offenders," *Clinical Psychology Review* 33 (2013): 448–469.
24. Holman and Zeidenberg, *The Dangers of Detention*.
25. Patrick Smith, *Illinois Counting on Cook County Program to Fix Juvenile Parole* (Peoria Public Radio, June 2014).
26. Rod Morgan, "Children and Young People in Custody, Quoting a Young Offender" in *The Prisoner*, eds. Ben Crewe and Jamie Bennett (New York: Routledge, 2012): 79.
27. Statistics Canada, "Admission to Youth Correctional Services in Canada, 2011/2012" (http://www.statcan.gc.ca/pub/85-002-x/2014001/article/11917-eng.htm?fpv=2693), accessed July 4, 2014.
28. Mendel, *No Place for Kids*, 16.
29. Mendel, *No Place for Kids*, 16.
30. Mendel, *No Place for Kids*, 19.
31. Waterloo Region Crime Prevention Council, *Youth Crime Fact Sheet Canada* (Waterloo: 2007).
32. Terry A. Kupers, "How to Create Madness in Prisons," in *Humane Prisons*, ed. D. Jones (Oxford: Radcliffe Publishing, 2006): 4–5.
33. Kupers, "How to Create Madness in Prisons," 8.
34. Lambie and Randell, "The Impact of Incarceration on Juvenile Offenders," 448–469.
35. J. Mendez, *Torture and Other Cruel, Inhuman or Degrading Treatment or Punishment* (Geneva: United Nations General Assembly, 2011), 2.
36. Mendez, *Torture and Other Cruel, Inhuman or Degrading Treatment or Punishment*, 17.
37. Mendez, *Torture and Other Cruel, Inhuman or Degrading Treatment or Punishment*, 18.

38. Mendez, *Torture and Other Cruel, Inhuman or Degrading Treatment or Punishment*, 18.
39. Mendez, *Torture and Other Cruel, Inhuman or Degrading Treatment or Punishment*, 18.
40. United Nations, UN Standard Minimum Rules for the Administration of Juvenile Justice (http://www.un.org/documents/ga/res/40/a40r033.htm, 1985) accessed July 3, 2014.
41. Hans Toch, "Warehouses for People?," *Annals of the American Academy of Political and Social Sciences* 478 (1985): 58–72.
42. Toch, "Warehouses for People?," 58–72.
43. Holly M. Harner and Suzanne Riley, "The Impact of Incarceration on Women's Mental Health: Responses from Women in a Maximum-Security Prison," *Qualitative Health Research* 23 (2013): 26–42.
44. Harner and Riley, "The Impact of Incarceration on Women's Mental Health," 26–42.
45. Harner and Riley, "The Impact of Incarceration on Women's Mental Health," 33.
46. Daniel S. Murphy, *Corrections and Post-traumatic Stress Symptoms* (Durham: Carolina Academic Press, 2012), 10.
47. Bierie, "Is Tougher Better?"
48. Neil Boyd, *The Work of Correctional Officers in British Columbia, 2008: Changing Working Conditions, Changing Inmate Populations and the Challenges Ahead*, Paper (2008): 1–31.
49. Boyd, *The Work of Correctional Officers in British Columbia, 2008*, 1–31.
50. Elizabeth Comack, *Out There, In Here: Masculinity, Violence and Prisoning* (Winnipeg: Fernwood Publishing, 2008).
51. Comack, *Out There, In Here*, 71.
52. Comack, *Out There, In Here*, 84.
53. Don Sabo, Terry A. Kupers, and Willie London, *Prison Masculinities* (Philadelphia: Temple University Press, 2001).
54. Sabo, Kupers, and London, *Prison Masculinities*, 12.
55. Rudy Chato Paul Sr., "Night Crier," in *Prison Masculinities*, eds. Don Sabo, Terry A. Kupers, and Willie London, (Philadelphia: Temple University Press, 2001): 198.
56. Bob Dylan, "Dignity," *Bob Dylan's Greatest Hits Volume 3* (Columbia, 1994).
57. Mark E. Olver, Keira C. Stockdale, and J. Stephen Wormith, "Risk Assessment with Young Offenders: A Meta-Analysis of Three Assessment Measures," *Criminal Justice and Behavior* 36 (2009): 329–353.
58. This list taken from "Box 3" in Mairead Dolan, "Psychopathic Personality in Young People," *Advances in Psychiatric Treatment* 10 (2004): 470.
59. Dolan, "Psychopathic Personality in Young People," 470.
60. Olver, Stockdale, and Wormith, "Risk Assessment with Young Offenders," 329–353.
61. Mary E. Vandergoot, *Justice for Young Offenders: Their Needs, Our Responses* (Saskatoon: Purich Publishing Inc, 2006).

62. Vandergoot, *Justice for Young Offenders*.
63. Olver, Stockdale, and Wormith, "Risk Assessment with Young Offenders," 329–353.
64. Olver, Stockdale, and Wormith, "Risk Assessment with Young Offenders," 329–353.
65. Olver, Stockdale, and Wormith, "Risk Assessment with Young Offenders," 329–353.
66. Daniel J. Ozer, "Correlation and the Coefficient of Determination," *Quantitative Methods in Psychology* 97 (1985): 307–315.
67. Paula Maurutto and Kelly Hannah-Moffat, "Understanding Risk in the Context of the Youth Criminal Justice Act," *Canadian Journal of Criminology and Criminal Justice* 49 (2007): 465–491.
68. Maurutto and Hannah-Moffat, "Understanding Risk in the Context of the Youth Criminal Justice Act," 465–491.
69. Department of Justice Canada, "Youth Risk/Need Assessment: An Overview of Issues and Practices" (http://www.justice.gc.ca/eng/rp-pr/cj-jp/yj-jj/rr03_yj4-rr03_jj4/p4b.html#fn21), accessed January 16, 2015.
70. New World Encyclopedia, *Psychologists* (http://www.newworldencyclopedia.org/entry/Psychologists), accessed August 1, 2014.
71. Ulrich Orth, "Does Perpetrator Punishment Satisfy Victims' Feelings of Revenge?," *Aggressive Behavior* 30 (2004): 62–70.
72. Orth, "Does Perpetrator Punishment Satisfy Victims' Feelings of Revenge?," 62–70.
73. Ulrich Orth, "Secondary Victimization of Crime Victims by Criminal Proceedings," *Social Justice Research* 15 (2002): 313–325.
74. Rebecca Campbell et al., "Preventing the 'Second Rape': Rape Survivors Experiences with Community Service Providers," *Journal of Interpersonal Violence* 16 (2001): 1239–1259.
75. Bob Dylan, "Blowin' in the Wind," *The Freewheelin' Bob Dylan* (New York: Columbia, 1963).
76. Michel Foucault, *Discipline & Punish: The Birth of the Prison* (New York: Vintage Books, 1975).
77. Nils Christie, *Limits to Pain: The Role of Punishment in Penal Policy* (Eugene: Wipf & Stock, 1981), 16.
78. Elizabeth M. Elliott, *Security With Care: Restorative Justice & Healthy Societies* (Winnipeg: Fernwood Publishing, 2011), 33.
79. Sabo, Kupers, and London, *Prison Masculinities*, 15.
80. John Pratt and Anna Eriksson, *Contrasts in Punishment: An Explanation of Anglophone Excess and Nordic Exceptionalism* (New York: Routledge, 2013), 27.
81. Pratt and Eriksson, *Contrasts in Punishment*, 28.
82. Pratt and Eriksson, *Contrasts in Punishment*, 29.
83. Pratt and Eriksson, *Contrasts in Punishment*, 27.
84. Robert Wilson, "Fear vs. Power" (http://www.psychologytoday.com/blog/the-main-ingredient/201303/fear-vs-power, 2013), accessed August 1, 2014.

CHAPTER 8

1. Howard Zehr, *The Little Book of Restorative Justice* (Intercourse: Good Books, 2002), 37.
2. Zehr, *The Little Book of Restorative Justice*, 21.
3. Correctional Service of Canada, *Let's Talk*, March 2014.
4. Larry Tifft and Dennis Sullivan, "Needs-Based Justice as Restorative," in *A Restorative Justice Reader*, ed. Gerry Johnstone (New York: Routledge, 2013).
5. Tifft and Sullivan, "Needs-Based Justice as Restorative," 212.
6. Tifft and Sullivan, "Needs-Based Justice as Restorative," 212.
7. Allan Weaver, *So You Think You Know Me?* (Sheffield: Waterside Press, 2008).
8. Weaver, *So You Think You Know Me?*, 96. Emphasis in original.
9. Weaver, *So You Think You Know Me?*, 63. Emphasis in original.
10. Rupert Ross, *Returning to the Teachings: Exploring Aboriginal Justice* (Toronto: Penguin Canada, 1996), 67.
11. Craig Proulx, *Reclaiming Aboriginal Justice, Identity, and Community* (Saskatoon: Purich Publishing Ltd, 2003).
12. Proulx, *Reclaiming Aboriginal Justice, Identity, and Community*, 35.
13. Proulx, *Reclaiming Aboriginal Justice, Identity, and Community*.
14. Proulx, *Reclaiming Aboriginal Justice, Identity, and Community*, 39.
15. David Milward, *Aboriginal Justice and the Charter: Realizing a Culturally Sensitive Interpretation of Legal Rights* (Vancouver: UBC Press, 2012).
16. Milward, *Aboriginal Justice and the Charter*.
17. Elizabeth M. Elliott, *Security With Care: Restorative Justice & Healthy Societies* (Winnipeg: Fernwood Publishing, 2011).
18. Ottawa Citizen, "How a Drunken Rampage Changed Legal History," March 2, 2007 (Originally published Saturday, September 11, 2004).
19. Howard Zehr, *Changing Lenses: A New Focus for Crime and Justice* (Scottdale: Herald Press, 1990), 131.
20. Susan L. Miller, *After the Crime: The Power of Restorative Justice Dialogues Between Victims and Violent Offenders* (New York: New York University Press, 2011).
21. Kay Pranis, Barry Stuart, and Mark Wedge, *Peacemaking Circles: From Crime to Community* (St. Paul: Living Justice Press, 2003), 31, 83; Judge Barry Stuart, *Building Community Justice Partnerships: Community Peacemaking Circles* (Ottawa: Department of Justice Canada, 1997), 13.
22. Stuart, *Building Community Justice Partnerships*, 9.
23. Antone Grafton and The Toronto Pine Tree Healing Circle, *Restoring Right Relations* (Toronto, 2003) quoting Eva Bald Eagle, 26.
24. Grafton, *Restoring Right Relations*, 52.
25. Pranis, Stuart, and Wedge, *Peacemaking Circles*, 70.
26. Pranis, Stuart, and Wedge, *Peacemaking Circles*, 70.
27. Pranis, Stuart, and Wedge, *Peacemaking Circles*, 68.
28. Pranis, Stuart, and Wedge, *Peacemaking Circles*, 31.
29. Pranis, Stuart, and Wedge, *Peacemaking Circles*, 33.

30. Pranis, Stuart, and Wedge, *Peacemaking Circles*, 34, 47.
31. Pranis, Stuart, and Wedge, *Peacemaking Circles*, 34.
32. Pranis, Stuart, and Wedge, *Peacemaking Circles*, 34.
33. Pranis, Stuart, and Wedge, *Peacemaking Circles*, 82.
34. Pranis, Stuart, and Wedge, *Peacemaking Circles*, 82.
35. Pranis, Stuart, and Wedge, *Peacemaking Circles*, 82.
36. Pranis, Stuart, and Wedge, *Peacemaking Circles*, 85.
37. This paragraph based on the work of Pranis, Stuart, and Wedge, *Peacemaking Circles*, 85–93.
38. Grafton, *Restoring Right Relations*, 58.
39. Pranis, Stuart, and Wedge, *Peacemaking Circles*, 98.
40. Pranis, Stuart, and Wedge, *Peacemaking Circles*, 104.
41. Pranis, Stuart, and Wedge, *Peacemaking Circles*, 106–111.
42. Allan MacRae and Howard Zehr, *The Little Book of Family Group Conferences New Zealand Style: A Hopeful Approach When Youth Cause Harm* (Intercourse: Good Books, 2004), 11.
43. MacRae and Zehr, *The Little Book of Family Group Conferences New Zealand Style*, 19–20.
44. Quoted verbatim from MacRae and Zehr, *The Little Book of Family Group Conferences New Zealand Style*, 20–23.
45. Judge Fred W. M. McElrea, "The New Zealand Model of Family Group Conferences," *European Journal on Criminal Policy and Research* 6 (1998): 527.
46. McElrea, "The New Zealand Model of Family Group Conferences," 527.
47. Lily Trimboli, *An Evaluation of the NSW Youth Justice Conferencing Scheme* (Report) (Sydney: New South Wales Bureau of Justice Statistics and Research, 2000).
48. Lawrence W. Sherman et al., *Recidivism Patterns in the Canberra Reintegrative Shaming Experiments* (RISE) (Report) (Canberra: Centre for Restorative Justice, Research School of Social Sciences, Australian National University, 2000).
49. Garth Luke and Bronwyn Lind, "Reducing Juvenile Crime: Conferencing Versus Court," *Contemporary Issues in Crime and Justice* 69 (2002): 1–20.
50. Hennessey Hayes and Kathleen Daly, "Conferencing and Re-offending in Queensland," *The Australian and New Zealand Journal of Criminology* 37 (2004): 170.
51. Hayes and Daly, "Conferencing and Re-offending in Queensland."
52. Hayes and Daly, "Conferencing and Re-offending in Queensland," 187.
53. Miller, *After the Crime*, 110, 115–116.
54. Correctional Service of Canada, *Circles of Support & Accountability: A Guide to Training Potential Volunteers* (Ottawa: 2002), no page numbers given.
55. Robin J. Wilson, Janice E. Picheca, and Michelle Prinzo, *Circles of Support & Accountability: An Evaluation of the Pilot Project in South-Central Ontario* (Ottawa: Correctional Service of Canada, 2005).
56. Lois Presser and Emily Gaarder, "Can Restorative Justice Reduce Battering? Some Preliminary Considerations," *Social Justice* 27 (2000): 175-195; Stephanie Coward, *Restorative Justice in Cases of Domestic and Sexual Violence: Healing Justice?* (Unpublished paper, 2000), 14.

57. Presser and Gaarder, "Can Restorative Justice Reduce Battering?"
58. Mary Achilles and Howard Zehr, "Restorative Justice for Crime Victims: The Promise and the Challenge," in *Restorative Community Justice: Repairing Harm & Transforming Communities*, eds. Gordon Bazemore and Maria Schiff (Cincinatti: Anderson Publishing Co., 2001): 93; Coward, *Restorative Justice in Cases of Domestic and Sexual Violence*, 20.
59. Presser and Gaarder, "Can Restorative Justice Reduce Battering?"
60. Coward, *Restorative Justice in Cases of Domestic and Sexual Violence*, 12.
61. Judith Herman, "Justice from the Victim's Perspective," Paper for Special Issue on *Feminism, Restorative Justice, and Violence Against Women* (Final Draft, 2003): 20, 36.
62. Waterloo Region Community Safety and Crime Prevention Council. *Reducing Violence by Enhancing Human and Social Development—A 40-Year Plan for Waterloo Region* (Waterloo, Ontario: Ginsler & Associates Inc, Draft January 2006), 17.
63. Allison Morris, "Re-visioning Men's Violence Against Female Partners," *The Howard Journal of Criminal Justice* 39 (2000): 412–428.
64. Mika et al., *Taking Victims and their Advocates Seriously: A Listening Project* (2002), 5.
65. Herman, "Justice from the Victim's Perspective," 12.
66. Mika et al., *Taking Victims and their Advocates Seriously*, 7.
67. Susan Herman, "Is Restorative Justice Possible without a Parallel System for Victims?," in *Critical Issues in Restorative Justice*, eds. Howard Zehr and Barb Toews (New York: Willan Publishing, 2004): 77.
68. Coward, *Restorative Justice in Cases of Domestic and Sexual Violence*, 15; Presser and Gaarder, "Can Restorative Justice Reduce Battering?"
69. Coward, *Restorative Justice in Cases of Domestic and Sexual Violence*, 22; Mika et al., *Taking Victims and their Advocates Seriously*, 9.
70. Howard Zehr, "Evaluation and Restorative Justice Principles," in *A Restorative Justice Reader*, ed. Gerry Johnstone (New York: Routledge, 2013).
71. Kathleen J. Bergseth and Jeffrey A. Bouffard, "The Long-Term Impact of Restorative Justice Programs for Juvenile Offenders," *Journal of Criminal Justice* 35 (2007): 433–451.
72. Daly et al., "Youth Sex Offending, Recidivism and Restorative Justice: Comparing Court and Conference Cases," *Australian and New Zealand Journal of Criminology* 46 (2013): 241–267.
73. Deborah Kirby Forgays and Lisa DeMilio, "Is Teen Court Effective for Repeat Offenders? A Test of the Restorative Justice Approach," *International Journal of Offender Therapy and Comparative Criminology* 49 (2005): 107–118.
74. John Braithwaite, "Does Restorative Justice Work," in *A Restorative Justice Reader*, ed. Gerry Johnstone (New York: Routledge, 2013): 265.
75. Braithwaite, "Does Restorative Justice Work."
76. Daniel Reisel, "The Neuroscience of Restorative Justice" (TED: http://www.ted.com/talks/daniel_reisel_the_neuroscience_of_restorative_justice, 2013), accessed August 3, 2014.

77. Reisel, "The Neuroscience of Restorative Justice."
78. Reisel, "The Neuroscience of Restorative Justice."
79. Zehr, *The Little Book of Restorative Justice*, 37.

CHAPTER 9

1. Niki A. Miller and Lisa M. Najavits, "Creating Trauma-Informed Correctional Care: A Balance of Goals and Environment," *European Journal of Psychotraumatology* 3 (2012): 1–8.
2. Miller and Najavits, "Creating Trauma-Informed Correctional Care," 1–8.
3. Shannon Moroney, *Through the Glass* (Canada: Doubleday Canada, 2011).
4. Catherine Panter-Brick and James F. Leckman, "Editorial Commentary: Resilience in Child Development—Interconnected Pathways to Wellbeing," *Journal of Child Psychology and Psychiatry* 54 (2013): 333.
5. Panter-Brick and Leckman, "Editorial Commentary," 333.
6. Linda Liebenberg, Michael Ungar, and Fons Van de Vijver, "Validation of the Child and Youth Resilience Measure-28 (CYRM-28) among Canadian Youth," *Research on Social Work Practice* 22 (2012): 219.
7. Michael Ungar, "Resilience, Trauma, Context, and Culture," *Trauma, Violence, & Abuse* 14 (2013): 255.
8. Liebenberg, Ungar, and Van de Vijver, "Validation of the Child and Youth Resilience Measure-28 (CYRM-28) among Canadian Youth," 222.
9. Ungar, "Resilience, Trauma, Context, and Culture," 222.
10. Ungar, "Resilience, Trauma, Context, and Culture," 260.
11. Sandra L. Bloom, *Creating Sanctuary: Toward the Evolution of Sane Societies* (New York: Routledge, 1997), 115.
12. Judith Herman, *Trauma and Recovery: The Aftermath of Violence—From Domestic Abuse to Political Terror* (New York: Basic Books, 1997), 159.
13. Susan L. McCammon, "Systems of Care as Asset-Building Communities: Implementing Strengths-Based Planning and Positive Youth Development," *American Journal of Community Psychology* 49 (2012): 556–565.
14. Catherine A. Simmons and Peter Lehmann, "Strengths-Based Batterer Intervention: A New Direction with a Different Paradigm" in *Strengths-Based Batterer Intervention: A New Paradigm in Ending Family Violence*, eds. Peter Lehmann, & Catherine A. Simmons (New York: Springer Publishing Company, 2009): 41
15. Angie Hart et al., *Mental Health and the Resilient Therapy Toolkit* (Sussex: Experience in Mind, 2011).
16. Hart et al., *Mental Health and the Resilient Therapy Toolkit*, 12–14.
17. This Box taken from www.resilienceresearch.org, accessed July 15, 2014.
18. Avril Bellinger and Tish Elliott, "What Are You Looking At?: The Potential of Appreciative Inquiry as a Research Approach for Social Work," *British Journal of Social Work* 41 (2011): 708–725.

19. Bellinger and Elliott, "What Are You Looking At?," 708–725.
20. Bellinger and Elliott, "What Are You Looking At?," 711–712.
21. Kansas Coalition Against Sexual and Domestic Violence, *Appreciative Inquiry: Asking Powerful Questions* (http://design.umn.edu/about/intranet/documents/AppreciativeInquiry-Asking%20Powerful%20Questions.pdf), accessed July 22, 2014.
22. Klinic Community Health Centre, *The Trauma-Informed Toolkit* (Winnipeg: 2008), 22–23.
23. Herman, *Trauma and Recovery*, 140.
24. Howard Zehr, *Transcending: Reflections of Crime Victims* (Intercourse: Good Books, 2001), 155.
25. Bloom, *Creating Sanctuary*, 119–120.
26. Zehr, *Transcending*, 188.
27. Zehr, *Transcending*, 188.
28. Zehr, *Transcending*, 189.
29. Zehr, *Transcending*, 190.
30. Zehr, *Transcending*, 191.
31. Zehr, *Transcending*, 9.
32. Zehr, *Transcending*, 9.
33. Zehr, *Transcending*, 9.
34. Zehr, *Transcending*, 193.
35. Box taken from Hart et al., *Mental Health and the Resilient Therapy Toolkit*, 18–19.
36. Herman, *Trauma and Recovery*, 133.
37. Conrad G. Brunk, "Restorative Justice and the Philosophical Theories of Criminal Punishment," in *The Spiritual Roots of Restorative Justice*, ed. Michael L. Hadley (New York: State University of New York Press, 2001): 35.
38. Howard Zehr, *Changing Lenses: A New Focus for Crime and Justice* (Scottdale: Herald Press, 1990), 202.
39. Howard Zehr, *The Little Book of Restorative Justice* (Intercourse: Good Books, 2002), 28–32.
40. Zehr, *The Little Book of Restorative Justice*, 17.
41. Miller and Najavits, "Creating Trauma-Informed Correctional Care," 1.
42. Miller and Najavits, "Creating Trauma-Informed Correctional Care," 1.
43. Miller and Najavits, "Creating Trauma-Informed Correctional Care," 1.
44. Barb Toews and Deanna Van Buren, PACS690 *Peace by Design Syllabus* (Harrisonburg: Summer Peacebuilding Institute, 2014).
45. Tania Petrellis, *The Restorative Justice Living Unit at Grande Cache Institution: Exploring the Application of Restorative Justice in a Correctional Environment*, (Ottawa: Correctional Service of Canada, 2007).
46. Tania Petrellis, *The Restorative Justice Living Unit at Grande Cache Institution*.
47. Tania Petrellis, *The Restorative Justice Living Unit at Grande Cache Institution*.
48. See http://www.csc-scc.gc.ca/002/007/002007-0004-eng.shtml, accessed June 12, 2014.

49. Tania Petrellis, *The Restorative Justice Living Unit at Grande Cache Institution.*
50. Carolyn Yoder, *The Little Book of Trauma Healing: When Violence Strikes and Community Security Is Threatened* (Intercourse: Good Books, 2005), 61.
51. Yoder, *The Little Book of Trauma Healing.*
52. Howard B. Levine, "Large-Group Dynamics and World Conflict: The Contributions of Vamik Volkan," *japa* 54 (2006): 274–280.
53. Vamik Volkan, "Trauma, Identity and Search for a Solution in Cyprus," *Insight Turkey* 10 (2008): 95–110.
54. Volkan, "Trauma, Identity and Search for a Solution in Cyprus," 101.
55. Barbara Ann Baker, "Art Speaks in Healing Survivors of War: The Use of Art Therapy in Treating Trauma Survivors," *Journal of Aggression Maltreatment & Trauma* 12 (2006): 184.
56. Nigel C. Hunt, *Memory, War and Trauma* (Cambridge: Cambridge University Press, 2010), 57.
57. Hunt, *Memory, War and Trauma.*
58. Hunt, *Memory, War and Trauma.*

CHAPTER 10

1. Leanne Simpson, *Dancing on Our Turtle's Back: Stories of Nishnaabeg Re-Creation, Resurgence and a New Emergence* (Winnipeg: Arbeiter Ring Publishing, 2011), 15.
2. Frantz Fanon, *The Wretched of the Earth* (New York: Grove Press, 1963), 23.
3. Fanon, *The Wretched of the Earth,* 3.
4. Eve Tuck and K. Wayne Yang, "Decolonization Is Not a Metaphor," *Decolonization: Indigeneity, Education & Society* 1 (2012): 1.
5. Jeff Corntassel, "Re-envisioning Resurgence: Indigenous Pathways to Decolonization and Sustainable Self-Determination," *Decolonization: Indigeneity, Education & Society* 1 (2012): 89.
6. Wei-he Guo and Ming-sum Tsui, "From Resilience to Resistance: A Reconstruction of the Strengths Perspective in Social Work Practice," *International Social Work* 53 (2010): 233–245.
7. Guo and Tsui, "From Resilience to Resistance," 238.
8. Guo and Tsui, "From Resilience to Resistance," 240.
9. See http://www.cbc.ca/strombo/news/aboriginal-youth-on-a-1500km-walk-to-parliament-hill-expected-to-arrive-in-
10. Derrick Jensen, *Endgame: Volume 1 The Problem of Civilization* (New York: Seven Stories Press, 2006), 49.
11. Jensen, *Endgame,* 17.
12. Aboriginal Affairs and Northern Development Canada, *Royal Commission Report on Aboriginal Peoples* (Canada, 1996).
13. Aboriginal Affairs and Northern Development Canada, *Royal Commission Report on Aboriginal Peoples.*
14. Aboriginal Affairs and Northern Development Canada, *Royal Commission Report on Aboriginal Peoples.*

15. James Anaya, *Report of the Special Rapporteur on the Rights of Indigenous Peoples: The Situation of Indigenous Peoples in Canada* (Geneva: United Nations General Assembly, 2014).
16. Taiaiake Alfred, *Wasase: Indigenous Pathways of Action and Freedom* (Toronto: University of Toronto Press, 2009).
17. John Borrows, *Recovering Canada: The Resurgence of Indigenous Law* (North York: University of Toronto Press, 2002), 117.
18. Borrows, *Recovering Canada*.
19. John Borrows, *Canada's Indigenous Constitution* (Toronto: University of Toronto Press, 2010).
20. A case study I wrote for "The Basic Resource Kit" for Restorative Justice Week 2013 in Canada, printed by Correctional Service of Canada. Reprinted with permission.
21. Michael E. McCullough, *Beyond Revenge: The Evolution of the Forgiveness Instinct* (Jossey-Bass, 2008).
22. Aboriginal Affairs and Northern Development Canada, *Royal Commission Report on Aboriginal Peoples*, 312.
23. Judah Oudshoorn, "Returning Conflict and Justice to Aboriginal Peoples: Restorative Justice Reconsidered," in *Reconstructing Restorative Justice Philosophy*, eds. Theo Gavrielides and Vasso Artinopoulou (Surrey: Ashgate, 2013): 257.
24. Christine Sivell-Ferri, *The Four Circles of Hollow Water* (Public Works & Government Services Canada, Aboriginal Peoples Collection: APC 15 CA, 1997), 14.
25. Sivell-Ferri, *The Four Circles of Hollow Water*.
26. Rupert Ross, *Returning to the Teachings: Exploring Aboriginal Justice* (Toronto: Penguin Canada, 1996), 29.
27. Ross, *Returning to the Teachings*, 29.
28. Ross, *Returning to the Teachings*, 30.
29. Sivell-Ferri, *The Four Circles of Hollow Water*, 14.
30. Sivell-Ferri, *The Four Circles of Hollow Water*, 90.
31. Sivell-Ferri, *The Four Circles of Hollow Water*, 100.
32. Sivell-Ferri, *The Four Circles of Hollow Water*, 116.
33. Ross, *Returning to the Teachings*, 30–32.
34. Community Holistic Circle Healing Program, *Community Holistic Circle Healing Position on Incarceration* (Hollow Water, Manitoba: CHCH files, 1993): as cited in Sivell-Ferri, *The Four Circles of Hollow Water*, 95–96.
35. Ross, *Returning to the Teachings*, 37.
36. Ross, *Returning to the Teachings*, 37.
37. Sivell-Ferri, *The Four Circles of Hollow Water*, 15.
38. Sivell-Ferri, *The Four Circles of Hollow Water*, 15.
39. Sivell-Ferri, *The Four Circles of Hollow Water*, 38.
40. Sivell-Ferri, *The Four Circles of Hollow Water*, 42.
41. Sivell-Ferri, *The Four Circles of Hollow Water*, 39.
42. Sivell-Ferri, *The Four Circles of Hollow Water*, 117.

43. Sivell-Ferri, *The Four Circles of Hollow Water*, 118.
44. Sivell-Ferri, *The Four Circles of Hollow Water*, 118.
45. Sivell-Ferri, *The Four Circles of Hollow Water*, 118.
46. Sivell-Ferri, *The Four Circles of Hollow Water*, 120.
47. Peter Menzies, "Developing an Aboriginal Healing Model for Intergenerational Trauma," *International Journal of Health Promotion & Education* 46 (2006): 41–48.
48. Patti Laboucane-Benson, *Reconciliation, Repatriation and Reconnection: A Framework for Building Resilience in Canadian Indigenous Families* (University of Alberta: Doctoral Thesis, 2009), 125.
49. Laboucane-Benson, *Reconciliation, Repatriation and Reconnection*, 134.
50. Laboucane-Benson, *Reconciliation, Repatriation and Reconnection*, 134.
51. Laboucane-Benson, *Reconciliation, Repatriation and Reconnection*, 135.
52. Linda Archibald, *Decolonization and Healing: Experiences in the United States, New Zealand, Australia and Greenland* (Ottawa: Aboriginal Healing Foundation, 2006), 28.
53. Waterloo Region Community Safety and Crime Prevention Council, *Reducing Violence by Enhancing Human and Social Development — A 40-Year Plan for Waterloo Region* (Waterloo, Ontario: Ginsler & Associates Inc, Draft January 2006), 17.
54. Waterloo Region Community Safety and Crime Prevention Council, *Reducing Violence by Enhancing Human and Social Development*, 17.
55. Waterloo Region Community Safety and Crime Prevention Council, *Reducing Violence by Enhancing Human and Social Development*, 17.
56. Waterloo Region Community Safety and Crime Prevention Council, *Reducing Violence by Enhancing Human and Social Development*, 24–26.
57. Lois Presser and Emily Gaarder, "Can Restorative Justice Reduce Battering? Some Preliminary Considerations," *Social Justice* 27 (2000): 175–195; Stephanie Coward, *Restorative Justice in Cases of Domestic and Sexual Violence: Healing Justice?* (Unpublished paper, 2000), 14; Allison Morris, "Re-visioning Men's Violence Against Female Partners," *The Howard Journal of Criminal Justice* 39 (2000): 412–428.
58. Presser and Gaarder, "Can Restorative Justice Reduce Battering?"
59. Waterloo Region Community Safety and Crime Prevention Council, *Reducing Violence by Enhancing Human and Social Development*, 17.
60. Waterloo Region Community Safety and Crime Prevention Council, *Reducing Violence by Enhancing Human and Social Development*, 17.
61. D. Garin, "Report No. #5702c" (Washington, DC: Peter D. Hart Research Associates, Inc, 2000).
62. Rus Ervin Funk, "Men's Work: Men's Voices and Actions against Sexism and Violence," *Journal of Prevention & Intervention in the Community* 36 (2008): 155–171.
63. Funk, "Men's Work: Men's Voices and Actions against Sexism and Violence," 155–171.
64. Mark Yantzi, *Sexual Offending and Restoration* (Waterloo: Herald Press, 1998), 21.
65. Inter-Ministerial Provincial Advisory Committee, *Service Issues for Adolescents Who Sexually Offend* (2005), 19.

CHAPTER 11

1. Shannon Moroney, *Through the Glass* (Canada: Doubleday Canada, 2011).
2. Howard Zehr, *Changing Lenses: A New Focus for Crime and Justice* (Scottdale: Herald Press, 1990).
3. Gerry Johnstone and Tony Ward, *Law & Crime: Key Approaches to Criminology* (Los Angeles: Sage, 2010).
4. Johnstone and Ward, *Law & Crime*, 28.
5. Johnstone and Ward, *Law & Crime*.
6. Zehr, *Changing Lenses*.
7. Zehr, *Changing Lenses*, 99.
8. Zehr, *Changing Lenses*, 99.
9. Johnstone and Ward, *Law & Crime*, 26–28.
10. Johnstone and Ward, *Law & Crime*, 26–28.
11. Jane Doe, *The Story of Jane Doe: A Book About Rape* (Toronto: Random House of Canada Ltd, 2003), 63.
12. Malini Laxminarayan and Mark Bosmans, "Victim Satisfaction with Criminal Justice: A Systematic Review," *Victims and Offenders* 8 (2013): 119–147.
13. Laxminarayan and Bosmans, "Victim Satisfaction with Criminal Justice," 119–147.
14. Miller, *After the Crime: The Power of Restorative Justice Dialogues Between Victims and Violent Offenders* (New York: New York University Press, 2011).
15. Susan L. Miller, *After the Crime*, 160.
16. Nils Christie, "Conflicts as property" in *A Restorative Justice Reader*, ed. Gerry Johnstone (New York: Routledge, 2013): 39.
17. Christie, "Conflicts as property."
18. Adam Crawford, "Salient Themes towards a Victim Perspective and the Limitations of Restorative Justice: Some Concluding Comments," in *Integrating a Victim Perspective with Criminal Justice*, eds. Adam Crawford and Jo Goodey (Burlington: Ashgate Publishing Co, 2000): 291.
19. Tinneke Van Camp and Jo-Anne Wemers, "Victim Satisfaction with Restorative Justice: More than Simply Procedural Justice," *International Review of Victimology* 19 (2013), 117–143.
20. Van Camp and Wemers, "Victim Satisfaction with Restorative Justice," 117–143.
21. Heather Strang, *Repair or Revenge: Victims & Restorative Justice* (Oxford: Clarendon Press, 2002), 26.
22. Strang, *Repair or Revenge*, 27.
23. Marlene Young and John Stein, *The History of the Crime Victim's Movement in the United States* (www.ojp.usdoj.gov/ovc), accessed September 8, 2013.
24. John J. Macionis and Linda M. Gerber, *Sociology* (Toronto: Pearson Education Canada, 1994), 619.
25. Macionis and Gerber, *Sociology*, 628.
26. Macionis and Gerber, *Sociology*, 629–630.
27. Macionis and Gerber, *Sociology*, 631, 635.
28. Strang, *Repair or Revenge*, 26.

29. Judith Herman, *Trauma and Recovery: The Aftermath of Violence—From Domestic Abuse to Political Terror* (New York: Basic Books, 1997), 51; Howard Zehr, *Transcending: Reflections of Crime Victims* (Intercourse: Good Books, 2001), 188.
30. Macionis and Gerber, *Sociology*, 635.
31. Diane Whiteley, "The Victim and the Justification of Punishment," *Criminal Justice Ethics* 17 (1998): 42.
32. Strang, *Repair or Revenge*.
33. Strang, *Repair or Revenge*, 29–34.
34. Strang, *Repair or Revenge*, 29–34.
35. Young and Stein, *The History of the Crime Victim's Movement in the United States*.
36. Strang, *Repair or Revenge*, 29.
37. Strang, *Repair or Revenge*, 31.
38. Lois Presser and Emily Gaarder, "Can Restorative Justice Reduce Battering? Some Preliminary Considerations," *Social Justice* 27 (2000): 177.
39. Presser and Gaarder, "Can Restorative Justice Reduce Battering?," 177.
40. Victims of Violence, *An Exploration of the Victims' Movement in Canada* (Ottawa: Canadian Centre for Missing Children, 2014).
41. Bill C-32, *An Act to Enact the Canadian Victims Bill of Rights and to Amend Certain Acts*, 2d sess., 41st Parliament, 2015. http://www.parl.gc.ca/HousePublications/Publication.aspx?Language=E&Mode=1&DocId=7850450. As of publication this is still before Parliament. Check the Government of Canada website for final wording.
42. Nancy Good Sider, "At the Fork in the Road: Trauma Healing," *Conciliation Quarterly* (Akron: Mennonite Central Committee, 2001).
43. Herman, *Trauma and Recovery*, 57.
44. Zehr, *Changing Lenses*, 186.
45. Zehr, *Changing Lenses*, 24.
46. Zehr, *Changing Lenses*, 24.
47. Mary E. Clark, *In Search of Human Nature* (New York: Routledge, 2002).
48. Clark, *In Search of Human Nature*.
49. Clark, *In Search of Human Nature*.
50. Zehr, *Transcending*, 188.
51. Zehr, *Transcending*, 188.
52. Herman, *Trauma and Recovery*, 51.
53. Herman, *Trauma and Recovery*, 53.
54. Clark, *In Search of Human Nature*.
55. Zehr, *Transcending*, 188.
56. Zehr, *Transcending*, 188.
57. Herman, *Trauma and Recovery*, 34.
58. Herman, *Trauma and Recovery*, 41.
59. Clark, *In Search of Human Nature*.
60. Zehr, *Transcending*, 188.
61. Zehr, *Transcending*, 188.
62. Herman, *Trauma and Recovery*, 52.

63. Canadian Resource Centre for Victims of Crime, *National Justice Network Update* 21(5) (2014).
64. Luke Hendry, "Healing Centre Opens," *The Belleville Intelligencer*, September 5, 2013 (http://www.intelligencer.ca/2013/09/05/healing-centre-opens), accessed October 10, 2013.
65. Mary Achilles and Howard Zehr, "Restorative Justice Signposts for Victim Involvement," bookmark.

CONCLUSION

1. Larry Tifft and Dennis Sullivan, *The Struggle to Be Human: Crime, Criminology & Anarchism* (Orkney, UK: Cienfuegos Press, 1980).
2. Tifft and Sullivan, *The Struggle to Be Human*.
3. Jeffrey Reiman, *The Rich Get Richer and the Poor Get Prison: Ideology, Class, and Criminal Justice* (Boston: Allyn and Bacon, 1998), 156–162.
4. Thomas Kuhn, *The Structure of Scientific Revolutions* (Chicago: University of Chicago Press, 1970), 150.
5. Paul J. Wendel, "Models and Paradigms in Kuhn and Halloun," *Science and Education* 17 (2008): 131–141.
6. Stacey Hannem, "Experiences in Reconciling Risk Management and Restorative Justice: How Circles of Support and Accountability Work Restoratively in the Risk Society," *International Journal of Offender Therapy and Comparative Criminology* 57 (2013): 269–288.
7. Hannem, "Experiences in Reconciling Risk Management and Restorative Justice," 279.
8. Hannem, "Experiences in Reconciling Risk Management and Restorative Justice," 284.
9. Howard Zehr, *The Little Book of Restorative Justice* (Intercourse: Good Books, 2002).
10. Raewyn Connell, *Southern Theory* (Cambridge: Polity, 2007), 63.
11. Connell, *Southern Theory*.
12. Kathleen E. Absolon, *Kaandossiwin: How We Come to Know* (Halifax: Fernwood Publishing, 2011).
13. Absolon, *Kaandossiwin*, 28–29.
14. Absolon, *Kaandossiwin*, 53.

Selected References

Aboriginal Affairs and Northern Development Canada. *Royal Commission Report on Aboriginal Peoples.* Canada, 1996.

Aboriginal Healing Foundation. *Program Handbook, 2nd Edition.* Ottawa: Aboriginal Healing Foundation, 1999.

Abram, Karen M., Teplin, Linda A., King, Devon C., Longworth, Sandra L., Emanuel, Kristin M., Romero, Erin G., McClelland, Gary M., Dulcan, Mina K., Washburn, Jason J., Welty, Leah J., and Olson, Nichole D. "PTSD, Trauma, and Comorbid Psychiatric Disorders in Detained Youth." *Juvenile Justice Bulletin* (2013): 1–16.

Absolon, Kathleen E. *Kaandossiwin: How We Come to Know.* Halifax: Fernwood Publishing, 2011.

Abu-Nimer, Mohammed. *Reconciliation, Justice, and Coexistence: Theory and Practice.* Lanham: Lexington Books, 2001.

Adams, Zachary W., McCart, Michael R., Zajac, Krisyn, Danielson, Carla K., Sawyer, Genelle K., Saunders, Benjamin E., and Kilpatrick, Dean G. "Psychiatric Problems and Trauma Exposure in Nondetained and Nondelinquent Adolescents." *Journal of Clinical Child & Adolescent Psychology* 42 (2013): 323–331.

Agnew, Robert. "Foundation for a General Strain Theory of Crime and Delinquency." *Criminology* 30 (1992): 47–88.

Alfred, Taiaiake. *Wasase: Indigenous Pathways of Action and Freedom.* North York: University of Toronto Press, 2009.

Anaya, James. *Report of the Special Rapporteur on the Rights of Indigenous Peoples: The Situation of Indigenous Peoples in Canada.* Geneva: United Nations General Assembly, 2014.

Archibald, Linda. *Decolonization and Healing: Experiences in the United States, New Zealand, Australia and Greenland.* Ottawa: Aboriginal Healing Foundation, 2006.

Ardino, Vittoria. "Offending Behaviour: The Role of Trauma and PTSD." *European Journal of Psychotraumatology* 3 (2012): 1–4.

Arya, Neil. "Peace through Health I: Development and Use of a Working Model." *Medicine, Conflict and Survival* 20 (2004): 242–257.

Asch, Michael. *Aboriginal Treaty Rights in Canada.* Vancouver: UBC Press, 1997.

Ashby, Christine. "Whose 'Voice' Is It Anyway? Giving Voice and Qualitative Research Involving Individuals That Type to Communicate." *Disability Studies Quarterly* (2009): 1–21.

Auditor General of Ontario. *Chapter 3, Section 3.13, Youth Justice Services Program.* Toronto: Auditor General of Ontario, 2012.

Baker, Barbara A. "Art Speaks in Healing Survivors of War: The Use of Art Therapy in Treating Trauma Survivors." *Journal of Aggression Maltreatment & Trauma* (2006): 183–198.

Bala, Nicholas. "What's Wrong with YOA Bashing? What's Wrong with the YOA? – Recognizing the Limits of Law." *Canadian Journal of Criminology* (1994): 247–270.

Bales, William D., and Piquero, Alex R. "Assessing the Impact of Prison on Recidivism." *Journal of Experimental Criminology* 8 (2012): 71–101.

Ball-Rokeach, S. J. "Values and Violence: A Test of the Subculture of Violence Thesis." *American Sociological Review* 38 (1973): 736–749.

Bancroft, Lundy. *Why Does He Do That?: Inside the Minds of Angry and Controlling Men.* New York: Berkeley Books, 2002.

Bandura, Albert. "Social Learning Theory of Aggression." *Journal of Communication* 28 (1978): 12–29.

Bath, Howard. "The Three Pillars of Trauma-Informed Care." *Reclaiming Children and Youth* 17 (2008): 17–21.

Bazemore, Gordon, and Schiff, Mara. *Restorative Community Justice: Repairing Harm & Transforming Communities.* Cincinatti: Anderson Publishing Co., 2001.

Beaglehole, Robert, Bonita, Ruth, Horton, Richard, Adams, Orvill, and McKee, Martin. "Public Health in the New Era: Improving Health through Collective Action." *Lancet* 363 (2004): 2084–2086.

Beaver, Kevin M., Rowland, Meghan W., Schwartz, Joseph A., and Nedelec, Joseph L. "The Genetic Origins of Psychopathic Personality Traits in Adult Males and Females: Results from an Adoption-Based Study." *Journal of Criminal Justice* 39 (2011): 426–432.

Becker, Howard S. "Whose Side Are We On?" *Social Problems* 14 (1967): 239–247.

Bell, Sandra J. *Young Offenders and Youth Justice: A Century After the Fact.* Toronto: Nelson Education Ltd, 2012.

Bellinger, Avril, and Elliott, Tish. "What Are You Looking At? The Potential of Appreciative Inquiry as a Research Approach for Social Work." *British Journal of Social Work* 41 (2011): 708–725.

Beneke, Timothy. *Men on Rape: What They Have to Say about Sexual Violence.* New York: St. Martin's Press, 1982.

Bergseth, Kathleen J., and Bouffard, Jeffrey A. "The Long-Term Impact of Restorative Justice Programs for Juvenile Offenders." *Journal of Criminal Justice* 35 (2007): 433–451.

Bierie, David M. "Is Tougher Better?: The Impact of Prison Conditions on Inmate Violence." *International Journal of Offender Therapy and Comparative Criminology* 56 (2012): 338–355.

———. "The Impact of Prison Conditions on Staff Well-Being." *International Journal of Offender Therapy and Comparative Criminology* 56 (2012): 81–95.

Black, M. C., Basile, K. C., Breiding, M. J., Smith, S. G., Walters, M. L., Merrick, M. T., Chen, J., and Stevens, M. R. *The National Intimate Partner and Sexual Violence*

Survey (NISVS): 2010 Summary Report. Atlanta, GA: National Center for Injury Prevention and Control, Centers for Disease Control and Prevention, 2011.

Bloom, Sandra L. *Creating Sanctuary: Toward the Evolution of Sane Societies.* New York: Routledge, 1997.

———. "Bridging the Black Hole of Trauma: The Evolutionary Significance of the Arts." *Psychotherapy and Politics International* 8 (2010): 198–212.

Bloom, Sandra L., and Sreedhar, Sarah Y. "The Sanctuary Model of Trauma-Informed Organizational Change." *Reclaiming Children and Youth* 17 (2008): 48–53.

Bloomfield, T. M. "About Skinner: Notes on the Theory and Practice of 'Radical Behaviourism.'" *Philosophy of the Social Sciences* 6 (1976): 75–82.

Borrows, John. *Recovering Canada: The Resurgence of Indigenous Law.* Toronto: University of Toronto Press, 2002.

———. *Canada's Indigenous Constitution.* Toronto: University of Toronto Press, 2010.

Bowlby, John. *Attachment.* London: Random House, 1969.

———. *A Secure Base: Parent-Child Attachment and Healthy Human Development.* London: Routledge, 1988.

Boyd, Neil. *The Work of Correctional Officers in British Columbia, 2008: Changing Working Conditions, Changing Inmate Populations and the Challenges Ahead.* Paper (2008) 1–31.

Brave Heart, Maria, Y. H. "The Return to the Sacred Path: Healing the Historical Trauma and Historical Unresolved Grief Response among the Lakota through Psychoeducational Group Intervention." *Smith College Studies in Social Work* 68 (1998): 287–305.

———. "The Historical Trauma Response among Natives and Its Relationship with Substance Abuse: A Lakota Illustration." *Journal of Psychoactive Drugs* 35 (2003): 7–13.

Brennan, P. A., and Mednick, S. A. "Genetic Perspectives on Crime." *Acta Psychiatrica Scandinavica* 87 (1993): 19–26.

Brewin, Chris R., Garnett, R., and Andrews, Bernice. "Trauma, Identity and Mental Health in UK Military Veterans." *Psychological Medicine* 41 (2011): 1733–1740.

Brokenleg, Martin. "Transforming Cultural Trauma into Resilience." *Reclaiming Children and Youth* 21 (2012): 9–13.

Brosi, George, and hooks, bell. "The Beloved Community: A Conversation Between bell hooks and George Brosi." *Appalachian Heritage* 40 (2012): 76–86.

Brown, Brene. "The Power of Vulnerability." TEDxHouston. Retrieved from http://www.ted.com/talks/brene_brown_on_vulnerability.html, 2010.

Brown, Michelle. *The Culture of Punishment: Prison, Society, and Spectacle.* New York: New York University Press, 2009.

Bryce, Peter H. *The Report on the Indian Schools of Manitoba and the North-West Territories.* Canada: Department of Indian Affairs, 1907.

———. *The Story of a National Crime: Being an Appeal for Justice to the Indians of Canada,* 1922.

Burrell, Gibson, and Morgan, Gareth. *Sociological Paradigms and Organisational Analysis.* Ashgate Publishing, 1979.

Butler, Judith. *Undoing Gender*. New York: Routledge, 2004.
Cadoret, Remi J., and Stewart, Mark A. "An Adoption Study of Attention Deficit/Hyperactivity/Aggression and Their Relationship to Adult Antisocial Personality." *Comprehensive Psychiatry* 32 (1991): 73–82.
Campbell, Rebecca, Wasco, Sharon M., Ahrens, Courtney E., Sefl, Tracy, and Barnes, Holly E. "Preventing the 'Second Rape': Rape Survivors Experiences with Community Service Providers." *Journal of Interpersonal Violence* 16 (2001): 1239–1259.
Canada. Parliament. House of Commons. Standing Committee on Aboriginal Affairs and Northern Development. Minutes of Proceedings. 38th Parliament, 1st session, meeting no. 19. Retrieved from the Parliament Canada website: www.parl.gc.ca/HousePublications/Publication.aspx?DocId=1648068&Language=E&Mode=1, 2005.
Carrington, Peter J. "Trends in the Seriousness of Youth Justice in Canada, 1984–2011." *Canadian Journal of Criminology and Criminal Justice* 55 (2013): 293–314.
Carrington, Peter J., and Moyer, Sharon. "Trends in Youth Crime and Police Response, Pre- and Post-YOA." *Canadian Journal of Criminology* 36 (1994): 1–28.
Carrington, Peter J., and Schulenberg, Jennifer L. *The Impact of the Youth Criminal Justice Act on Police Charging Practices with Young Persons: A Preliminary Statistical Assessment*. Canada: Department of Justice, 2005.
Catton, Katherine, and Leon, Jeffrey S. "Legal Representation and the Proposed Young Persons in Conflict with the Law Act." *Osgoode Hall Law Journal* 15 (1977): 107–135.
CBC News. "A History of Residential Schools in Canada." Retrieved from www.cbc.ca/news/canada/a-history-of-residential-schools-in-canada-1.702280, May 16, 2008.
Centers for Disease Control and Prevention. *Sexual Violence*. Retrieved from http://www.cdc.gov/violenceprevention/pdf/sv-datasheet-a.pdf, 2012.
Challeen, Dennis A. *Making It Right: A Common Sense Approach to Criminal Justice*. Melius Peterson Publishing Co, 1986.
Cheely, Catherine A., Carpenter, Laura A., Letourneau, Elizabeth J., Nicholas, Joyce S., Charles, Jane, and King, Lydia B. "The Prevalence of Youth with Autism Spectrum Disorders in the Criminal Justice System." *Journal of Autism and Developmental Disorders* 42 (2012): 1856–1862.
Christie, Nils. *Limits to Pain: The Role of Punishment in Penal Policy*. Eugene: Wipf & Stock, 1981.
Clark, Mary E. *In Search of Human Nature*. New York: Routledge, 2002.
Cloward, Richard A., and Ohlin, Lloyd. *Delinquency and Opportunity*. New York: Free Press, 1960.
Codato, Mike. "Hunger Pains in a Cold Forest: A Reexamination of the Disappearance of the Beothuk." *Totem: The University of Western Ontario Journal of Anthropology* 1 (1994): 50–56.
Coles, Tony. "Negotiating the Field of Masculinity." *Men and Masculinities* 12 (2009): 30–44.
Comack, Elizabeth. *Out There/In Here: Masculinity, Violence and Prisoning*. Winnipeg: Fernwood Publishing, 2008.

Community Holistic Circle Healing Program. *Community Holistic Circle Healing Position on Incarceration*. Hollow Water, Manitoba: CHCH files, 1993.

Connell, Raewyn W. *Masculinities*. Sydney: Allen & Unwin, 1995.

———. *Southern Theory*. Cambridge: Polity, 2007.

Corntassel, Jeff. "Re-envisioning Resurgence: Indigenous Pathways to Decolonization and Sustainable Self-Determination." *Decolonization: Indigeneity, Education & Society* 1 (2012): 86–101.

Corrado, Raymond R., Gronsdahl, Karla, MacAlister, David, and Cohen, Irwin M. "Youth Justice in Canada: Theoretical Perspectives of Youth Probation Officers." *Canadian Journal of Criminology and Criminal Justice* 52 (2010): 397–426.

Corrado, Raymond R., Kuehn, Sarah, and Margaritescu, Irina. "Policy Issues Regarding Overrepresentation of Incarcerated Aboriginal Young Offenders in a Canadian Context." *Youth Justice* 14 (2014): 40–62.

Correctional Service of Canada. *Circles of Support & Accountability: A Guide to Training Potential Volunteers*. Ottawa: 2002.

Corvo, Kenneth. "Violence, Separation, and Loss in the Families of Origin of Domestically Violent Men. *Journal of Interpersonal Violence* 21 (2006): 117–125.

Cote, James E., and Levine, Charles. "A Formulation of Erikson's Theory of Ego Identity Formation. *Developmental Review* 7 (1987): 273–325.

Coulthard, Glen S. *Red Skin White Masks: Rejecting the Colonial Politics of Recognition*. Minneapolis: University of Minnesota, 2014.

Courtois, Christine A. *Recollections of Sexual Abuse: Treatment Principles & Guidelines*. New York: W. W. Norton & Co., 1999.

Coward, Stephanie. *Restorative Justice in Cases of Domestic and Sexual Violence: Healing Justice?* Unpublished paper, 2000.

Crawford, Adam, and Goodey, Jo. *Integrating a Victim Perspective within Criminal Justice*. Burlington: Ashgate Publishing Co, 2000.

Crawford, Thomas N., Shaver, Phillip R., Cohen, Patricia, Pilkonis, Paul A., Gillath, Omri, and Kasen, Stephanie. "Self-Reported Attachment, Interpersonal Aggression, and Personality Disorder in a Prospective Community Sample of Adolescents and Adults." *Journal of Personality Disorders* 20 (2006): 331–351.

Crenshaw, Kimberle W. "Demarginalizing the Intersection of Race and Sex." *University of Chicago Legal Forum* (1989): 139–167.

———. "Mapping the Margins: Intersectionality, Identity Politics, and Violence Against Women of Color." *Stanford Law Review* 43 (1991): 1241–1299.

Crewe, Ben, and Bennett, Jamie. *The Prisoner*. New York: Routledge, 2012.

Cunningham, Alison, and Baker, Linda. *Little Eyes, Little Ears: How Violence Against a Mother Shapes Children as They Grow*. London: The Centre for Children and Families in the Justice System, 2007.

Daly, Kathleen, Bouhours, Brigitte, Broadhurst, Roderic, and Loh, Nini. "Youth Sex Offending, Recidivism and Restorative Justice: Comparing Court and Conference Cases." *Australian and New Zealand Journal of Criminology* 46 (2013): 241–267.

D'Andrea, Wendy, Ford, Julian, Stolbach, Bradley, Spinazzola, Joseph, and van der Kolk, Bessel A. "Understanding Interpersonal Trauma in the Context in

Children: Why We Need a Developmentally Appropriate Trauma Diagnosis." *American Journal of Orthopsychiatry* 82 (2012): 187–200.
Daschuk, James. *Clearing the Plains: Disease, Politics of Starvation, and the Loss of Aboriginal Life.* Regina: University of Regina Press, 2013.
Deetz, Stanley. "Describing Differences in Approaches to Organization Science: Rethinking Burrell and Morgan and Their Legacy." *Organization Science* 7 (1996): 191–207.
DeGroot, Jennifer. *Peace Is … Women Imagine a Peaceful World.* Winnipeg: Mennonite Central Committee Canada, 2001.
Department of Justice Canada. *Juvenile Delinquency in Canada: The Report of the Committee on Juvenile Delinquency, 1965.* Ottawa: Public Works and Government Services Canada, 1965.
⸺. *The Evolution of Juvenile Justice in Canada.* Ottawa: 2004.
⸺. *Extrajudicial Measures.* Ottawa: Youth Justice, 2013.
⸺. *Recent Changes to Canada's Youth Justice System.* Ottawa: Youth Justice, 2013.
⸺. *The Youth Criminal Justice Act: Summary and Background.* Ottawa: Minister of Justice and Attorney General of Canada, 2013.
Desjarlais, S. A. "Emptying the Cup – Healing Fragmented Identity: An Anishinawbekwe Perspective on Historical Trauma and Culturally Appropriate Consultation." *Fourth World Journal* 11 (2012): 43–70.
Devereux, Simon. "The Making of the Penitentiary Act, 1775–1779." *The Historical Journal* 42 (1999): 405–433.
Dierkhising, Carly B., Ko, Susan J., Woods-Jaeger, Briana, Briggs, Ernestine C., Lee, Robert, and Pynoos, Robert S. "Trauma Histories among Justice-Involved Youth: Findings from the National Child Traumatic Stress Network." *European Journal of Psychotraumatology* 4 (2013): 1–12.
Doe, Jane. *The Story of Jane Doe: A Book About Rape.* Toronto: Random House of Canada Ltd, 2003.
Dolan, Mairead. "Psychopathic Personality in Young People." *Advances in Psychiatric Treatment* 10 (2004): 466–473.
Doob, Anthony N. "Youth Justice Research in Canada: An Assessment." *Canadian Journal of Criminology* 41 (2004): 217–222.
Doob, Anthony N., and Sprott, Jane B. "Youth Justice in Canada." *Crime and Justice* 31 (2004): 185–242.
Dorahy, Martin J., Brand, Bethany L., Sar, Vedat, Kruger, Christa, Stravopoulos, Pam, Martinez-Taboas, Alfonso, Lewis-Fernandez, Roberto, and Middleton, Warwick. "Dissociative Identity Disorder: An Empirical Overview." *Australian and New Zealand Journal of Psychiatry* 48 (2014): 402–417.
Downie, Jocelyn, and Llewellyn, Jennifer J. *Being Relational: Reflections on Relational Theory and Health Law.* Vancouver: UBC Press, 2012.
Drago, Francesco. "Prison Conditions and Recidivism." *American Law and Economics Review* 13 (2011): 103–130.
Draper, Anthony J. "Cesare Beccaria's Influence on English Discussions of Punishment, 1764–1789." *History of European Ideas* 26 (2000): 177–199.
Dube, Shanta R., Cook, Michelle L., and Edwards, Valerie J. "Health-Related Outcomes of Adverse Childhood Experiences in Texas, 2002." *Preventing Chronic Disease Public Health Research, Practice, and Policy* 7 (2010): 1–9.

Duran, Eduardo, Firehammer, Judith, and Gonzalez, John. "Liberation Psychology as the Path Toward Healing Cultural Soul Wounds." *Journal of Counselling and Development* 86 (2008): 288–295.

Durose, Matthew R., Harlow, Caroline W., Langan, Patrick A., Motivans, Mark, Rantala, Ramona, and Smith, Erica L. *Family Violence Statistics: Including Statistics on Strangers and Acquaintances*. Washington: U.S. Department of Justice, 2005.

Dutton, Donald G., and White, Katherine R. "Attachment Insecurity and Intimate Partner Violence." *Aggression and Violent Behavior* 17 (2012): 475–481.

Elias, Brenda, Mignone, Javier, Hall, Madelyn, Hong, Say P., Hart, Lyna, and Sareen, Jitender. "Trauma and Suicide Behaviour Histories among a Canadian Indigenous Population: An Empirical Exploration of the Role of Canada's Residential School System." *Social Science & Medicine* 74 (2012): 1560–1569.

Elliott, Elizabeth M. *Security With Care: Restorative Justice & Healthy Societies*. Winnipeg: Fernwood Publishing, 2011.

Else-Quest, Nicole M., and Grabe, Shelly. "The Political Is Personal: Measurement and Application of Nation-Level Indicators of Gender Equity in Psychological Research." *Psychology of Women Quarterly* 36 (2012): 131–144.

Erikson, Erik H. *Identity: Youth and Crisis*. New York: Norton, 1968.

———. *Life History and the Historical Moment*. New York: Norton, 1975.

Erikson, Kai T. "Trauma at Buffalo Creek." *Society* 13 (1976): 58–65.

Espinosa, Erin M., Sorensen, Jon R., and Lopez, Molly A. "Youth Pathways to Placement: The Influence of Gender, Mental Health Need and Trauma on Confinement in the Juvenile Justice System." *Journal of Youth Adolescence* 42 (2013): 1824–1836.

Estrada, Felipe. "Juvenile Violence as a Social Problem: Trends, Media Attention and Societal Response." *British Journal of Criminology* 41 (2001): 639–655.

Fanon, Frantz. *The Wretched of the Earth*. New York: Grove Press, 1963.

Fast, Elizabeth, and Collin-Vezina, Delphine. "Historical Trauma, Race-Based Trauma and Resilience of Indigenous Peoples: A Literature Review." *First Peoples Child & Family Review* 5 (2010): 126–136.

Felitti, Vincent, and Buczynski, Ruth. *Why the Most Significant Factor in Predicting Chronic Disease May Be Childhood Trauma*. The National Institute for the Clinical Application of Behavioral Medicine: Teleseminar, 2011.

Felson, Richard B., Liska, Allen E., South, Scott J., and McNulty, Thomas L. "The Subculture of Violence and Delinquency: Individual vs. School Context Effects." *Social Forces* 73 (1994): 155–173.

Fitzgerald, Robin T., and Carrington, Peter J. "Disproportionate Minority Contact in Canada: Police and Visible Minority Youth." *Canadian Journal of Criminology and Criminal Justice* 53 (2011): 449–487.

Ford, Julian D., and Blaustein, Margaret E. "Systemic Self-Regulation: A Framework for Trauma-Informed Services in Residential Juvenile Justice Programs." *Journal of Family Violence* 28 (2013): 665–677.

Ford, Julian D., Chapman, John, Connor, Daniel F., and Cruise, Keith R. "Complex Trauma and Aggression in Secure Juvenile Justice Settings." *Criminal Justice and Behaviour* 39 (2012): 694–724.

Forgays, Deborah K., and DeMilio, Lisa. "Is Teen Court Effective for Repeat Offenders? A Test of the Restorative Justice Approach." *International Journal of Offender Therapy and Comparative Criminology* 49 (2005): 107–118.

Forsey, Eugene A. *How Canadians Govern Themselves*. Ottawa: Library of Parliament, 1980.

Foucault, Michel. *Discipline & Punish: The Birth of the Prison*. New York: Vintage Books, 1975.

Fowler, J. Christopher, Allen, Jon G., Oldham, John M., and Frueh, B. Christopher. "Exposure to Interpersonal Trauma, Attachment Insecurity, and Depression Severity." *Journal of Affective Disorders* 149 (2013): 313–318.

Fowler, Joyce. "Psychoneurobiology of Co-Occurring Trauma and Addictions." *Journal of Chemical Dependency Treatment* 8 (2006): 129–152.

Freire, Paulo. *Pedagogy of the Oppressed*. New York: Continuum, 1970.

Frisell, Thomas, Lichtenstein, Paul, and Langstrom, Niklas. "Violent Crime Runs in Families: A Total Population Study of 12.5 Million Individuals." *Psychological Medicine* 41 (2011): 97–105.

Funk, Rus E. "Men's Work: Men's Voices and Actions against Sexism and Violence." *Journal of Prevention & Intervention in the Community* 36 (2008): 155–171.

Futures Without Violence. *Perpetrator Risk Factors for Violence Against Women*. Washington, DC: Fact Sheet, no date given.

Galliher, John F. "The Life and Death of Liberal Criminology." *Contemporary Crises* 2 (1978): 245–263.

Garin, G. D. Report No. #5702c. Washington, DC: Peter D. Hart Research Associates, Inc, 2000.

Gatti, Uberto, Tremblay, Richard E., and Vitaro, Frank. "Iatrogenic Effect of Juvenile Justice." *The Journal of Child Psychology and Psychiatry* 50 (2009): 991–998.

Gavrielides, Theo. *Rights and Restoration within Youth Justice*. Whitby: de Sitter Publications, 2012.

Gavrielides, Theo, and Artinopoulou, Vasso. *Reconstructing Restorative Justice Philosophy*. Surrey: Ashgate, 2013.

Gendreau, Paul, Goggin, Claire, and Cullen, Francis T. *The Effects of Prison Sentences on Recidivism*. Ottawa: Public Services and Government Works, 1999.

Gibb, Barry J. *The Rough Guide to the Brain*. New York: Rough Guides Ltd, 2007.

Gilligan, James. "Violence in Public Health and Preventative Medicine." *The Lancet* 355 (2000): 1802–1804.

———. *Preventing Violence*. New York: Thames & Hudson Inc, 2001.

Glasbeek, Harry. *Wealth by Stealth: Corporate Crime, Corporate Law, and the Perversion of Democracy*. Toronto: Between the Lines, 2002.

Glaser, Daniel. "Criminality Theories and Behavioral Images." *American Journal of Sociology* 61 (1956): 433–444.

Gone, Joseph P. "Redressing First Nations Historical Trauma: Theorizing Mechanisms for Indigenous Culture as Mental Health Treatment." *Transcultural Psychiatry* 50 (2013): 683–706.

Good Sider, Nancy. "At the Fork in the Road: Trauma Healing." *Conciliation Quarterly* 20 (2001).

Goodwin, Rick, and Patton, Mark. *Survivors Helping Survivors: A Practical Guide to Understanding Peer-Support Services for Survivors of Sexual Violence*. Ottawa: Cornwall Public Inquiry, 2009.

Gottfredson, Michael R., and Hirschi, Travis. *A General Theory of Crime*. Stanford, CA: Stanford University Press, 1990.

Grafton, Antone, and The Toronto Pine Tree Healing Circle. *Restorating Right Relations*. Toronto, 2003.

Greer, Allan. "Commons and Enclosure in the Colonization of North America." *American Historical Review* (2012): 365–386.

Grimshaw, Roger. *My Story: Young People Talk About the Trauma and Violence in Their Lives*. London, Centre for Crime and Justice Studies, 2011.

Guo, Wei-he, and Tsui, Ming-sum. "From Resilience to Resistance: A Reconstruction of the Strengths Perspective in Social Work Practice." *International Social Work* 53 (2010): 233–245.

Hackler, Jim. "How Should We Respond to Youth Crime?" *Canadian Journal of Law and Society* 20 (2005): 193–208.

Hadley, Michael L. *The Spiritual Roots of Restorative Justice*. New York: State University of New York Press, 2001.

Hannah-Moffat, Kelly, and Maurutto, Paula. *Youth Risk/Need Assessment: An Overview of Issues and Practices*. Ottawa: Department of Justice, Research and Statistics Division, 2003.

Hannem, Stacey. "Experiences in Reconciling Risk Management and Restorative Justice: How Circles of Support and Accountability Work Restoratively in the Risk Society." *International Journal of Offender Therapy and Comparative Criminology* 57 (2013): 269–288.

Harner, Holly, and Burgess, Ann W. "Using a Trauma-Informed Framework to Care for Incarcerated Women." *Journal of Obstetric, Gynecologic, & Neonatal Nursing* 40 (2011): 469–476.

Harner, Holly M., and Riley, Suzanne. "The Impact of Incarceration on Women's Mental Health: Responses from Women in a Maximum-Security Prison." *Qualitative Health Research* 23 (2013): 26–42.

Harris, Maxine, and Fallot, Roger D. "Envisioning a Trauma-Informed Service System: A Vital Paradigm Shift." *New Directions for Mental Health Services* 89 (2001): 3–22.

Hart, Angie, and Taylor, S. *Mental Health and the Resilient Therapy Toolkit*. Sussex: Experience in Mind, 2011.

Hartinger-Saunders, R. M., Rittner, B., Wieczorek, W., Nochajski, T., Rine, C. M., and Welte, J. "Victimization, Psychological Distress and Subsequent Offending among Youth." *Children and Youth Services Review* 33 (2011): 2375–2385.

Hartnagel, Timothy F. "The Rhetoric of Youth Justice in Canada." *Criminal Justice* 4 (2004): 355–374.

Haskell, Lori, and Randall, Melanie. "Disrupted Attachments: A Social Context Complex Trauma Framework and the Lives of Aboriginal Peoples in Canada." *Journal of Aboriginal Health* (2009): 48–99.

Hayes, Hennessey, and Daly, Kathleen. "Conferencing and Re-offending in Queensland." *The Australian and New Zealand Journal of Criminology* 37 (2004): 167–191.

Heide, Kathleen M., and Solomon, Eldra P. "Biology, Childhood Trauma, and Murder: Rethinking Justice." *International Journal of Law and Psychiatry* 29 (2006): 220–233.

Herman, Judith L. *Trauma and Recovery: The Aftermath of Violence—From Domestic Abuse to Political Terror*. New York: Basic Books, 1997.

_____. "Justice from the Victim's Perspective." Paper for Special Issue on *Feminism, Restorative Justice, and Violence Against Women*. Final Draft, 2003.

Hess, Beth B., and Ferree, Myra M. *Analyzing Gender: A Handbook of Social Science Research*. New York: Sage Publications, 1987.

Hill, Susan M. "Conducting Haudenosaunee Historical Research from Home: In the Shadow of the Six Nations—Caledonia Reclamation." *American Indian Quarterly* 33 (2009): 479–498.

Hodgdon, Hilary B., Kinniburgh, Kristine, Gabowitz, Dawna, Blaustein, Margaret E., and Spinazzola, Joseph. "Development and Implementation of Trauma-Informed Programming in Youth Residential Centers Using the ARC Framework." *Journal of Family Violence* 28 (2013): 679–692.

Holman, Barry, and Zeidenberg, Jason. *The Dangers of Detention: The Impact of Incarcerating Youth in Detention and Other Secure Facilities*. Washington: Justice Policy Institute, 2006.

Holt, Stephanie, Buckley, Helen, and Whelan, Sadhbh. "The Impact of Exposure to Domestic Violence on Children and Young People: A Review of the Literature." *Child Abuse & Neglect* 32 (2008): 797–810.

hooks, bell. "Out of the Academy and into the Streets." *Ms* 3 (1992): 80–82.

_____. "Eros, Eroticism and the Pedagogical Process." *Cultural Studies* 7 (1993): 58–63.

_____. "Feminism: Crying for Our Souls." *Women & Therapy* 17 (1995): 265–271.

_____. "Tearing Out the Root of Self-Hatred." *The Other Side* (2003): 10–15.

Hunt, Nigel C. *Memory, War and Trauma*. Cambridge: Cambridge University Press, 2010.

Hylton, John H. "Get Tough or Get Smart? Options for Canada's Youth Justice System in the Twenty-First Century." *Canadian Journal of Criminology* 36 (1994): 229–246.

Indigenous Foundations. *Origins of the Indian Act*. Retrieved from http://indigenous foundations.arts.ubc.ca/home/government-policy/the-indian-act.html, 2009.

Jenkins, Philip. "Varieties of Enlightenment Criminology." *British Journal of Criminology* 24 (1984): 112–130.

Jensen, Derrick. *Endgame: Volume 1 The Problem of Civilization*. New York: Seven Stories Press, 2006.

Johnson, Phil, and Duberley, Joanne. "Anomie and Culture Management: Reappraising Durkheim." *Organization* 18 (2011): 563–584.

Johnstone, Gerry. *A Restorative Justice Reader*. New York: Routledge, 2013.

Johnstone, Gerry, and Ward, Tony. *Law & Crime: Key Approaches to Criminology*. Los Angeles: Sage, 2010.

Juvenile Delinquents Act, R.S., c. 160.

Kaba, Fatos, Diamond, Pamela, Haque, Alpha, MacDonald, Ross, and Venters, Homer. "Traumatic Brain Injury among Newly Admitted Adolescents in the New York Jail System." *Journal of Adolescent Health* 54 (2014): 615–617.

Karabanow, Jeff. "Street Kids as Delinquents, Menaces and Criminals: Another Example of the Criminalization of Poverty." Pp. 138–147 in eds. D. Crocker and V. M. Johnson. *Poverty, Regulation and Social Exclusion. Readings on the Criminalization of Poverty*. Halifax: Fernwood, 2010.

Katz, Jackson. *Tough Guise: Violence, Media, and the Crisis in Masculinity*. Mediaed, 1999.

———. *The Macho Paradox: Why Some Men Hurt Women and How All Men Can Help*. Naperville: Sourcebooks, 2006.

Kenny, Lorraine. *Workbook For Residential School Survivors: To Recognize, Create and Share Their Own Resiliency Stories*. Nishnawbe Aski Nation: Sunset Women's Aboriginal Circle, 2003.

Kesby, Mike. "Retheorizing Empowerment through Participation as a Performance in Space: Beyond Tyranny to Transformation." *Signs* 30 (2005): 2037–2065.

Kessler, Seymour, and Moos, Rudolf H. "The XYY Karyotype and Criminality: A Review." *Journal of Psychiatric Research* 7 (1970): 153–170.

Kirby, Sandra, Greaves, Lorraine, and Reid, Colleen. *Experience. Research. Social Change: Methods Beyond the Mainstream*, 2nd Edition. Toronto: University of Toronto Press, 2010.

Kirby, Sandra, and McKenna, Kate. *Experience. Research. Social Change. Methods from the Margins*. Toronto: Garamond Press, 1989.

Kirmayer, Laurence J., Dandeneau, Stephane, Marshall, Elizabeth, Phillips, Morgan K., and Williamson, Karla J. "Rethinking Resilience From Indigenous Perspectives." *Canadian Journal of Psychiatry* 56 (2011): 84–91.

Kleber, Rolf J., Figley, Charles R., and Gersons, Berthold P. R. *Beyond Trauma: Cultural and Societal Dynamics*. New York: Plenum Press, 1995.

Klinic Community Health Centre. *The Trauma-Informed Toolkit*. Winnipeg, 2008.

Kobrin, S. "Review of Delinquency and Drift by David Matza." *American Journal of Sociology* 72 (1966): 322–324.

Kondro, W. "Canada Lags in Preventing Hospital Infections." *Canadian Medical Association Journal* 183 (2011): E160.

Kraft, Dina. "By Talking, Inmates and Victims Making Things 'More Right.'" *New York Times*, July 5, 2014.

Kuhn, Thomas S. *The Structure of Scientific Revolutions*. Chicago: University of Chicago Press, 1970.

Kupers, Terry A. "How to Create Madness in Prisons." In ed. D. Jones. *Humane Prisons*. Oxford: Radcliffe Publishing, 2006.

———. "Trauma and Its Sequelae in Male Prisoners: Effects of Confinement, Overcrowding, and Diminished Services." *American Journal of Orthopsychiatry* 66 (1966): 189–196.

Laboucane-Benson, Patricia. *Reconciliation, Repatriation and Reconnection: A Framework for Building Resilience in Canadian Indigenous Families*. University of Alberta: Doctoral Thesis, 2009.

Lambie, Ian, and Randell, Isabel. "The Impact of Incarceration on Juvenile Offenders." *Clinical Psychology Review* 33 (2013): 448–469.

Latimer, Jeff, Dowden, Craig, and Muise, Danielle. "The Effectiveness of Restorative Justice Practices: A Meta-Analysis." *The Prison Journal* 85 (2005): 127–144.

Latimer, Jeff, and Foss, Laura C. *A One-Day Snapshot of Aboriginal Youth in Custody Across Canada: Phase II*. Ottawa: Department of Justice, 2004.

Laxminarayan, Malini, and Bosmans, Mark. "Victim Satisfaction with Criminal Justice: A Systematic Review." *Victims and Offenders* 8 (2013): 119–147.

Lebowitz, Leslie, Harvey, Marie R., and Herman, Judith L. "A Stage-by-Dimension Model of Recovery from Sexual Trauma." *Journal of Interpersonal Violence* 8 (1993): 378–391.

Lederach, John P. *The Moral Imagination: The Art and Soul of Building Peace*. New York: Oxford University Press, 2005.

Lehmann, Peter, and Simmons, Catherine A. *Strengths-Based Batterer Intervention: A New paradigm in ending family violence*. New York: Springer Publishing Company, 2009.

Leichsenring, Falk, Leibing, Eric, Kruse, Johannes, New, Antonia S., and Leweke, Frank. "Borderline Personality Disorder." *Lancet* 377 (2011): 74–84.

Leon, Jeffrey S. "The Development of Canadian Juvenile Justice: A Background for Reform." *Osgoode Hall Law Journal* 15.1 (1977): 71–106.

Leschied, Alan W., and Gendreau, Paul. "Doing Justice in Canada: YOA Policies That Can Promote Community Safety." *Canadian Journal of Criminology* 36 (1994): 291–303.

Levine, Howard B. "Large-Group Dynamics and World Conflict: The Contributions of Vamik Volkan." *japa* 54 (2006): 274–280.

Levine, Stephen Z. "Elaboration on the Association between IQ and Parental SES with Subsequent Crime." *Personality and Individual Differences* 50 (2011): 1233–1237.

Liebenberg, Linda, Ungar, Michael, and Van de Vijver, Fons. "Validation of the Child and Youth Resilience Measure-28 (CYRM-28) among Canadian Youth." *Research on Social Work Practice* 22 (2012): 219–226.

Linden, Rick. *Criminology: A Canadian Perspective*. Toronto: Nelson Education Ltd, 2012.

Linden, Sidney B. *Report of the Ipperwash Inquiry*. Ontario, 2007.

Litowitz, Douglas. "Gramsci, Hegemony, and the Law." *Brigham Young University Law Review* (2000): 515–551.

Lonsway, Kimberly A., and Archambault, Joanne. "The 'Justice Gap' for Sexual Assault Cases: Future Directions for Research and Reform." *Violence Against Women* 18 (2012): 145–168.

Luke, Garth, and Lind, Bronwyn. "Reducing Juvenile Crime: Conferencing Versus Court." Crime and Justice Bulletin: *Contemporary Issues in Crime and Justice* 69 (2002): 1–20.

Lyon-Callo, Vincent. *Inequality, Poverty and Neoliberal Governance: Activist Ethnography in the Homeless Sheltering Industry*. Peterborough: Broadview Press, 2004.

Macionis, John J., and Gerber, Linda M. *Sociology*. Toronto: Pearson Education Canada, 1994.

MacRae, Allan, and Zehr, Howard. *The Little Book of Family Group Conferences New Zealand Style: A Hopeful Approach When Youth Cause Harm*. Intercourse: Good Books, 2004.

Maddan, Sean, Walker, Jeffrey T., and Miller, J. Mitchell. "Does Size Really Matter?" *The Social Science Journal* 45 (2008): 330–344.

Malamuth, Neil M., Haber, Scott, and Feshbach, Seymour. "Testing Hypotheses Regarding Rape: Exposure to Sexual Violence, Sex Differences, and the 'Normality' of Rapists." *Journal of Research in Personality* 14 (1980): 21–137.

Marjot, David. "An Attachment Theory of Addiction." *Addiction* 103 (2014): 2065.

Maté, Gabor. *In the Realm of Hungry Ghosts: Close Encounters with Addiction*. Toronto: Alfred A. Knopf Canada, 2008.

Matza, David. *Delinquency and Drift*. New York, NY: Wiley, 1964.

Maurutto, Paula, and Hannah-Moffat, Kelly. "Understanding Risk in the Context of the Youth Criminal Justice Act." *Canadian Journal of Criminology and Criminal Justice* 49 (2007): 465–491.

Mayes, Thomas A. "Persons with Autism and Criminal Justice." *Journal of Positive Behavior Interventions* 5 (2003): 92–100.

Mazzarello, Paolo. "Lombroso and Tolstoy." *Nature* 409 (2001): 983.

McAra, Lesley, and McVie, Susan. "Youth Justice? The Impact of System Contact on Patterns of Desistance from Offending." *European Journal of Criminology* 4 (2007): 315–345.

McCammon, Susan L. "Systems of Care as Asset-Building Communities: Implementing Strengths-Based Planning and Positive Youth Development." *American Journal of Community Psychology* 49 (2012): 556–565.

McCrory, Eamon J., De Brito, Stephane A., Sebastien, Catherine L., Mechelli, Andrea, Bird, Geoffrey, Kelly, Phillip A., and Viding, Essi. "Heightened Neural Reactivity to Threat in Child Victims of Family Violence." *Current Biology* 21 (2011): R947–R948.

McCullough, Michael E. *Beyond Revenge: The Evolution of the Forgiveness Instinct*. Jossey-Bass, 2008.

McDonald, R. Michael, and Towberman, Donna. "Psychosocial Correlates of Adolescent Drug Involvement." *Adolescence* 28 (1993): 925.

McElrea, Fred W. M. "The New Zealand Model of Family Group Conferences." *European Journal on Criminal Policy and Research* 6 (1998): 527–543.

McGillivray, Anne, and Comaskey, Brenda. *Black Eyes All of the Time: Intimate Violence, Aboriginal Women, and the Justice System*. Toronto: University of Toronto Press, 1999.

McMillin, Patrick N. "From Pioneer to Punisher: America's Quest to Find Its Juvenile Justice Identity." *Houston Law Review* 51 (2014): 1485–1517.

McNeill, Fergus. "What Works and What's Just?" *European Journal of Probation* 1 (2009): 21–40.

Mehta, Divya, Klengel, Torsten, Conneely, Karen N., Smith, Alicia K., Altmann, Andre, Pace, Thaddeus W., Rex-Haffner, Monika, Loeschner, Anne, Gonik, Mariya, Mercer, Kristina B., Bradley, Bekh, Muller-Myhsok, Bertram, Ressler, Kerry J., and Binder, Elisabeth B. "Childhood Maltreatment Is Associated with Distinct Genomic and Epigenetic Profiles in Posttraumatic Stress Disorder." *Proceedings of the National Academy of Sciences* 110 (2013): 8302–8307.

Mendel, Richard A. *No Place for Kids: The Case for Reducing Juvenile Incarceration*. Baltimore: The Annie E. Casey Foundation, 2011.

Mendez, Juan E. *Torture and Other Cruel, Inhuman or Degrading Treatment or Punishment.* Geneva: United Nations General Assembly, 2011.

Menzies, Peter. "Developing an Aboriginal Healing Model for Intergenerational Trauma." *International Journal of Health Promotion & Education* 46 (2008): 41–48.

Merton, Robert K. "Social Structure and Anomie." *American Sociological Review* 3 (1938): 672–682.

Metfessel, Milton, and Lovell, Constance. "Recent Literature on Individual Correlates of Crime." *Psychological Bulletin* 39 (1942): 133–164.

Mikulincer, Mario, and Shaver, Phillip R. *Attachment in Adulthood: Structure, Dynamics, and Change.* London, The Guildford Press, 2007.

Miller, Niki A., and Najavits, Lisa M. "Creating Trauma-Informed Correctional Care: A Balance of Goals and Environment." *European Journal of Psychotraumatology* 3 (2012): 1–8.

Miller, Susan L. *After the Crime: The Power of Restorative Justice Dialogues Between Victims and Violent Offenders.* New York: New York University Press, 2011.

Milloy, John S. *A National Crime: The Canadian Government and the Residential School System, 1879 to 1986.* Winnipeg: University of Manitoba Press, 1999.

Milward, David. *Aboriginal Justice and the Charter: Realizing a Culturally Sensitive Interpretation of Legal Rights.* Vancouver: UBC Press, 2012.

Mika, Harry, Achilles, Mary, Stutzman Amstutz, Lorraine, and Zehr, Howard. *Taking Victims and Their Advocates Seriously: A Listening Project.* 2002.

Moore, Elizabeth, Gaskin, Claire, and Indig, Devon. "Childhood Maltreatment and Post-traumatic Stress Disorder among Incarcerated Young Offenders." *Child Abuse & Neglect* 37 (2013): 861–870.

Moroney, Shannon. *Through the Glass.* Canada: Doubleday Canada, 2011.

Morris, Allison, and Gelsthorpe, Loraine. "Re-visioning Men's Violence Against Female Partners." *The Howard Journal of Criminal Justice* 39 (2000): 412–428.

Morris, Norval, and Rothman, David J. *The Oxford History of the Prison: The Practice of Punishment in Western Society.* Oxford: Oxford University Press, 1995.

Murphy, Daniel S. *Corrections and Post-traumatic Stress Symptoms.* Durham: Carolina Academic Press, 2012.

Narayan, Angela J., Englund, Michelle M., and Egeland, Byron. "Developmental Timing and Continuity of Exposure to Interparental Violence and Externalizing Behavior as Prospective Predictors of Dating Violence." *Development and Psychopathology* 25 (2013): 973–990.

National Research Council. *Crime Victims with Developmental Disabilities: Report of a Workshop.* Washington, DC: National Academy Press, 2001.

Neisser, Ulric, Boodoo, Gwyneth, Bouchard Jr., Thomas J., Boykin, A. Wade, Brody, Nathan, Ceci, Stephen J., Halpern, Diane F., Loelhin, John C., Perloff, Robert, Sternberg, Robert J., and Urbina, Susana. "Intelligence: Knowns and Unknowns." *American Psychologist* 51 (1996): 77–102.

Neitzel, Michael T. *Crime and Its Modification: A Social Learning Perspective.* New York: Pergamon, 1979.

Neufeld, Roger. "Cabals, Quarrels, Strikes, Impudence: Kingston Penitentiary, 1890–1914." *Social History* 31 (1998): 95–125.

Nikulina, Valentina, Widom, Cathy S., and Czaja, Sally. "The Role of Childhood Neglect and Childhood Poverty in Predicting Mental Health, Academic Achievement and Crime in Adulthood." *American Journal of Community Psychology* 48 (2011): 309–321.

Nunn, D. Merlin. *Spiralling Out of Control: Lessons Learned from a Boy in Trouble, Report of the Nunn Commission of Inquiry*. Nova Scotia: Province of Nova Scotia, 2006.

Ohlin, Lloyd E. "Delinquent Boys: The Culture of the Gang by Albert K. Cohen." *Social Science Review* 30 (1956): 379–380.

Olson, Christine. "The Deep Roots of the Fairness Committee in Kohlberg's Moral Development Theory." *Schools: Studies in Education* 8 (2011): 125–135.

Olver, Mark E., Stockdale, Keira C., and Wormith, J. Stephen. "Risk Assessment with Young Offenders: A Meta-Analysis of Three Assessment Measures." *Criminal Justice and Behavior* 36 (2009): 329–353.

Orth, Ulrich. "Secondary Victimization of Crime Victims by Criminal Proceedings." *Social Justice Research* 15 (2002): 313–325.

———. "Does Perpetrator Punishment Satisfy Victims' Feelings of Revenge?" *Aggressive Behavior* 30 (2004): 62–70.

Osland, Julie A., Fitch, Marguerite, and Willis, Edmond E. "Likelihood to Rape in College Males." *Sex Roles* 35 (1996): 171–183.

Ozer, Daniel J. "Correlation and the Coefficient of Determination." *Quantitative Methods in Psychology* 97 (1985): 307–315.

Padykula, Nora L., and Conklin, Philip. "The Self Regulation Model of Attachment Trauma and Addiction." *Clinical Social Work Journal* 38 (2010): 351–360.

Pain, Rachel, and Frances, Peter. "Reflections on Participatory Research." *Area* 35 (2003): 46–54.

Panter-Brick, Catherine, and Leckman, James F. "Editorial Commentary: Resilience in Child Development—Interconnected Pathways to Wellbeing." *Journal of Child Psychology and Psychiatry* 54 (2013): 333–336.

Parmenter, Jon. "The Meaning of *Kaswentha* and the Two Row Wampum Belt in Haudenosaunee (Iroquois) History: Can Indigenous Oral Tradition Be Reconciled with the Documentary Record?" *Journal of Early American History* 3 (2013): 82–109.

Pearce, Colby. *A Short Introduction to Attachment and Attachment Disorder*. London: Jessica Kingsley Publishers, 2009.

Peck, M. Scott. *The Road Less Traveled*. New York: Simon and Schuster, 1978.

Pepinsky, Hal. "Peacemaking Criminology." *Critical Criminology* 21 (2013): 319–339.

Perry, Simona L. "Development, Land Use, and Collective Trauma: The Marcellus Shale Gas Boom in Rural Pennsylvania." *The Journal of Culture & Agriculture* 34 (2012): 81–92.

Petrellis, Tania. *The Restorative Justice Living Unit at Grande Cache Institution: Exploring the Application of Restorative Justice in a Correctional Environment*. Ottawa: Correctional Service of Canada, 2007.

Pranis, Kay, Stuart, Barry, and Wedge, Mark. *Peacemaking Circles: From Crime to Community*. St. Paul: Living Justice Press, 2003.

Pratt, Jon, and Eriksson, Anna. *Contrasts in Punishment: An Explanation of Anglophone Excess and Nordic Exceptionalism.* New York: Routledge, 2013.

Presser, Lois, and Gaarder, Emily. "Can Restorative Justice Reduce Battering? Some Preliminary Considerations." *Social Justice* 27 (2000): 175–195.

Prison Reform Trust. *Bromley Briefings Prison Fact File.* London: Prison Reform Trust, 2013.

Proulx, Craig. *Reclaiming Aboriginal Justice, Identity, and Community.* Saskatoon: Purich Publishing Ltd, 2003.

Public Health Agency of Canada. *The Chief Public Health Officer's Report on the State of Public Health in Canada, 2013: Infectious Disease–The Never-Ending Threat.* Canada: Public Health Agency of Canada, 2013.

Pullen, Mary, and Matthews, Sheila. "Creating Art and Social Change in Vancouver's Downtown Eastside." *Women & Environments International Magazine,* Fall (2006): 72–73.

Ramsland, Katherine. "The Measure of a Man: Cesare Lombroso and the Criminal Type." *The Forensic Examiner* 18 (2009): 70.

Randall, Melanie, and Haskell, Lori. "Trauma-Informed Approaches to Law: Why Restorative Justice Must Understand Trauma and Psychological Coping." *Dalhousie Law Journal* 36 (2013): 501–533.

Rebellon, Cesare J., Manasse, Michelle E., Van Gundy, Karen T., and Cohn, Ellen S. "Perceived Injustice and Delinquency: A Test of General Strain Theory." *Journal of Criminal Justice* 40 (2012): 230–237.

Redekop, Vern N. *From Violence to Blessing: How an Understanding of Deep-Rooted Conflict Can Open Paths to Reconciliation.* Ottawa: Novalis, 2002.

Regan, Paulette. *Unsettling the Settler Within: Indian Residential Schools, Truth Telling, and Reconciliation in Canada.* Vancouver: UBC Press, 2010.

Reiman, Jeffrey S. *The Rich Get Richer and the Poor Get Prison: Ideology, Class, and Criminal Justice.* Boston: Allyn and Bacon, 1998.

Reitano, Julie. "Youth Custody and Community Services in Canada, 2002/2003." *Juristat Canadian Centre for Justice Statistics* 24 (2004).

Richardson, Glenn E. "The Metatheory of Resilience and Resiliency." *Journal of Clinical Psychology* 58 (2002): 307–321.

Richmond, C. A. M. "Narratives of Social Support and Health in Aboriginal Communities." *Canadian Journal of Public Health* 98(2007): 347–351.

Richmond, Chantelle A. M., and Ross, Nancy A. "The Determinants of First Nation and Inuit Health: A Critical Population Health Approach." *Health & Place* 15 (2009): 403–411.

Rivard, Jeanne C., McCorkle, David, Duncan, Mariama E., Pasquale, Lina E., Bloom, Sandra L., and Abramovitz, Robert. "Implementing a Trauma Recovery Framework for Youths in Residential Treatment." *Child and Adolescent Social Work Journal* 21 (2004): 529–550.

Rosen, Philip. *The Young Offenders Act.* Ottawa: Parliamentary Research Branch, 2000.

Ross, Rupert. *Returning to the Teachings: Exploring Aboriginal Justice.* Toronto: Penguin Canada, 1996.

Sabo, Don, Kupers, Terry A., and London, Willie. *Prison Masculinities.* Philadelphia: Temple University, 2001.

Sandel, Michael J. *Justice: What's the Right Thing to Do?* New York: Farrar, Straus and Giroux, 2009.

Satterfield, James H., and Schell, Anne. "A Prospective Study of Hyperactive Boys with Conduct Problems and Normal Boys: Adolescent and Adult Criminality." *Journal of the American Academy of Child & Adolescent Psychiatry* 36 (1997): 1726–1735.

Savignac, Julie. *Tools to Identify and Assess the Risk of Offending among Youth.* Public Safety Canada, National Crime Prevention Centre, 2010.

Schafer, Markus H., and Ferraro, Kenneth F. "Childhood Misfortune as a Threat to Successful Aging: Avoiding Disease." *The Gerontologist* 52 (2012): 111–120.

Schissel, Bernard. *Still Blaming Children: Youth Conduct and the Politics of Child Hating.* Halifax: Fernwood Publishing, 2006.

Schwab, Gabriele. *Haunting Legacies: Violent Histories and Transgenerational Trauma.* New York: Columbia University Press, 2010.

Sherman, Lawrence W., Strang, Heather, and Woods, Daniel J. *Recidivism Patterns in the Canberra Reintegrative Shaming Experiments* (RISE) (Report). Canberra: Centre for Restorative Justice, Research School of Social Sciences, Australian National University, 2000.

Simpson, Leanne. *Dancing on Our Turtle's Back: Stories of Nishnaabeg Re-Creation, Resurgence and a New Emergence.* Winnipeg: Arbeiter Ring Publishing, 2011.

Sinha, Maire. *Measuring Violence Against Women: Statistical Trends.* Ottawa: Statistics Canada, 2013.

Sivell-Ferri, Christine. *The Four Circles of Hollow Water.* Public Works & Government Services Canada, Aboriginal Peoples Collection: APC 15 CA, 1997.

Smith, Andrea. "Indigeneity, Settler Colonialism, White Supremacy." *Global Dialogue* 12 (2010): 1–15.

Snyder, T. Richard. *The Protestant Ethic and the Spirit of Punishment.* Grand Rapids: Wm. B. Eerdmans Publishing Co, 2001.

Solicitor General Canada. *Young Persons in Conflict with the Law.* Ottawa: Ministry of the Solicitor General Committee on Legislation on Young Persons in Conflict with the Law, 1975.

Solomon, Robert C. *The Big Questions: A Short Introduction to Philosophy.* Fort Worth: Harcourt Brace College Publishers, 1994.

SpearIt. "Gender Violence in Prison & Hyper-masculinities in the 'Hood': Cycles of Destructive Masculinity." *Journal of Law & Policy* 37 (2011): 89–147.

Sprott, Jane B., and Doob, Anthony N. "Youth Crime Rates and the Youth Justice System." *Canadian Journal of Criminology and Criminal Justice* 50 (2008): 621–639.

Statistics Canada. *Youth Custody and Community Services.* Retrieved from http://www.statcan.gc.ca/pub/85-002-x/2010001/article/11147-eng.htm#a9, 2011.

———. *Measuring Violence Against Women: Statistical Trends — Key Findings.* Retrieved from www.statcan.gc.ca/pub/85-002-x/2013001/article/11766-eng.pdf, 2013.

———. "Admission to Youth Correctional Services in Canada, 2011/2012." Retrieved from http://www.statcan.gc.ca/pub/85-002-x/2014001/article/11917-eng.htm?fpv=2693, 2014.

Steele, William, and Kuban, Caelan. "Trauma-Informed Resilience and Posttraumatic Growth." *Reclaiming Children and Youth* 20 (2011): 44–46.

Stewart, V. Lorne. "Three and a Half Steps Toward Juvenile Justice in Canada." *Interchange* 8 (1977–1978): 203–209.

Stien, Phyllis T., and Kendall, Joshua. *Psychological Trauma and the Developing Brain: Neurologically Based Interventions for Troubled Children*. New York: Routledge, 2004.

Stille, R. G., Malamuth, Neil, and Schallow, J. R. *Prediction of Rape Proclivity by Rape Myth Attitudes and Hostility Toward Women*. New York: Paper presented at the American Psychological Association meeting, 1987.

Stimmel, Matthew A., Cruise, Keith R., Ford, Julian D., and Weiss, Rebecca A. "Trauma Exposure, Posttraumatic Stress Disorder Symptomatology, and Aggression in Male Juvenile Offenders." *Psychological Trauma: Theory, Research, Practice, and Policy* 6 (2013): 184–191.

Strang, Heather. *Repair or Revenge: Victims & Restorative Justice*. Oxford: Clarendon Press, 2002.

Stuart, Barry. *Building Community Justice Partnerships: Community Peacemaking Circles*. Ottawa: Department of Justice Canada, 1997.

Sutherland, Stuart. "Skinnerian Behaviour." *Nature* 282 (1979): 149–150.

Sykes, Gresham M., and Matza, David. "Techniques of Neutralization: A Theory of Delinquency." *American Sociological Review* 22 (1957): 664–670.

Tanner, Julian. *Teenage Troubles: Youth and Deviance in Canada*. Don Mills: Oxford University Press, 2010.

Tifft, Larry, and Sullivan, Dennis. *The Struggle to Be Human: Crime, Criminology & Anarchism*. Orkney: Cienfuegos Press, 1980.

Toch, Hans. "Warehouses for People?" *Annals of the American Academy of Political and Social Sciences* 478 (1985): 58–72.

———. "Punitiveness as 'Behavior Management.'" *Criminal Justice and Behavior* 35 (2008): 388–397.

Topitzes, James, Mersky, Joshua P., and Reynolds, Arthur J. "From Child Maltreatment to Violent Offending: An Examination of Mixed-Gender and Gender-Specific Models." *Journal of Interpersonal Violence* 27 (2012): 2322–2347.

Trimboli, Lily. *An Evaluation of the NSW Youth Justice Conferencing Scheme* (Report). Sydney: New South Wales Bureau of Justice Statistics and Research, 2000.

Truth and Reconciliation Commission of Canada. *They Came for the Children*. Winnipeg: Truth and Reconciliation Commission of Canada, 2012.

Tuck, Eve, and Yang, K. Wayne. "Decolonization Is Not a Metaphor." *Decolonization: Indigeneity, Education & Society* 1 (2012): 1–40.

Turmen, T. "The Health Dimension." *UN Chronicle* 5 (1998): 18–19.

Twenge, Jean M., Catanese, Kathleen R., and Baumeister, Roy F. "Social Exclusion Causes Self-Defeating Behavior." *Journal of Personality and Social Psychology* 83 (2002): 606–615.

"Twin studies." *Acta Psychiatrica Scandinavica* 33 (1958): 12–15.

Umamaheswar, Janani. "Bringing Hope and Change: A Study of Youth Probation Officers in Toronto." *International Journal of Offender Therapy and Comparative Criminology* 57 (2012): 1158–1182.

Ungar, Michael. "Resilience among Children in Child Welfare, Corrections, Mental Health and Educational Settings: Recommendations for Service." *Child & Youth Care Forum* 34 (2005): 445–464.

———. "Resilience, Trauma, Context, and Culture." *Trauma, Violence, & Abuse* 14 (2013): 255–266.

United Nations. *What Is Peacebuilding?* Retrieved from http://www.unpbf.org/application-guidelines/what-is-peacebuilding, 1992.

Van Camp, Tinneke, and Wemers, Jo-Anne. "Victim Satisfaction with Restorative Justice: More than Simply Procedural Justice." *International Review of Victimology* 19 (2013): 117–143.

Vancouver Status of Women. *History in Our Faces on Occupied Land: A Race Relations Timeline.* Vancouver: Vancouver Status of Women, Feminist Working Group, 2008.

Vandergoot, Mary E. *Justice for Young Offenders: Their Needs, Our Responses.* Saskatoon: Purich Publishing Inc, 2006.

Van der Kolk, Bessel A. "The Compulsion to Repeat Trauma: Re-enactment, Revictimization, and Masochism." *Psychiatric Clinics of North America* 12 (1989): 389–411.

———. "Trauma and Memory." *Psychiatry and Clinical Neurosciences* 52 (1998): 52–64.

Van der Kolk, Bessel A., McFarlane, Alexander C., and Weisaeth, Lars. *Traumatic Stress: The Effects of Overwhelming Experience on Mind, Body, and Society.* New York: Guildford Press, 2007.

Vermeiren, Robert, Jespers, Ine, and Moffitt, Terrie. "Mental Health Problems in Juvenile Justice Populations." *Child and Adolescent Psychiatry Clinics of North America* 15 (2006): 333–351.

Victims of Violence. *An Exploration of the Victims' Movement in Canada.* Ottawa: Canadian Centre for Missing Children, 2014.

Vold, George B. *Theoretical Criminology.* New York: Oxford University Press, 1958.

Volkan, Vamik. "Trauma, Identity and Search for a Solution in Cyprus." *Insight Turkey* 10 (2008): 95–110.

Waid, Courtney A., and Clements, Carl B. "Correctional Facility Design: Past, Present and Future." *Journal of the American Correctional Association* 26 (2001): 2–5, 25–29.

Walls, Melissa L., Hautala, Dane, and Hurley, Jenna. "'Rebuilding Our Community': Hearing Silenced Voices on Aboriginal Youth Suicide." *Transcultural Psychiatry* 51 (2014): 57–72.

Wanklyn, Sonya G., Day, David M., Hart, Trevor A., and Girard, Todd A. "Cumulative Childhood Maltreatment and Depression among Incarcerated Youth: Impulsivity and Hopelessness as Potential Intervening Variables." *Child Maltreatment* 17 (2012): 306–317.

Waterloo Region Community Safety and Crime Prevention Council. *Reducing Violence by Enhancing Human and Social Development — A 40-Year Plan for Waterloo Region.* Waterloo, Ontario: Ginsler & Associates Inc, Draft January 2006.

Weaver, Allan. *So You Think You Know Me?* Sheffield: Waterside Press, 2008.

Wendel, Paul J. "Models and Paradigms in Kuhn and Halloun." *Science and Education* 17 (2008): 131–141.

Wesley-Esquimaux, Cynthia C., and Smolewski, Magdalena. *Historic Trauma and Aboriginal Healing*. Ottawa: Aboriginal Healing Foundation, 2004.

Whiteley, Diane. "The Victim and the Justification of Punishment." *Criminal Justice Ethics* 17 (1998): 42–54.

Widom, Cathy S. "The Cycle of Violence." *Science* 244 (1989): 160–166.

Wilson, Kathleen, and Rosenberg, Mark W. "Exploring the Determinants of Health for First Nations Peoples in Canada: Can Existing Frameworks Accommodate Traditional Activities?" *Social Science & Medicine* 55 (2002): 2017–2031.

Wilson, Kathleen, Rosenberg, Mark W., and Abonyi, Sylvia. "Aboriginal Peoples, Health and Healing Approaches: The Effects of Age and Place on Health." Social *Sciences & Medicine* 72 (2011): 355–364.

Wilson, Robin J., Picheca, Janice E., and Prinzo, Michelle. *Circles of Support & Accountability: An Evaluation of the Pilot Project in South-Central Ontario*. Ottawa: Correctional Service of Canada, 2005.

Wilson, Shawn. *Research Is Ceremony: Indigenous Research Methods*. Halifax: Fernwood Publishing, 2008.

Winterdyk, John, and Smandych, Russell. *Youth at Risk and Youth Justice: A Canadian Overview*. Don Mills: Oxford University Press, 2012.

Wolfe, Patrick. "Settler Colonialism and the Elimination of the Native." *Journal of Genocide Research* 8 (2006): 387–409.

Wolfgang, Marvin E., and Ferracuti, Franco. *The Subculture of Violence: Towards an Integrated Theory in Criminology*. London: Social Science Paperbacks in association with Tavistock Publications, 1967.

Wong, Siu K. "Youth Crime and Family Disruption in Canadian Municipalities: An Adaptation of Shaw and McKay's Social Disorganization Theory." *International Journal of Law, Crime and Justice* 40 (2012): 100–114.

Wood, Chris. "Why Do Men Do It? *Maclean's* 113 (2000): 34.

Wood, Jane, and Alleyne, Emma. "Street Gang Theory and Research: Where Are We Now and Where Do We Go from Here?" *Aggression and Violent Behavior* 15 (2010): 100–111.

Woodbury-Smith, Marc R., Clare, Isabel. C. H., Holland, Anthony J., Kearns, Anthony, Staufenberg, Ekkehart, and Watson, Peter. "A Case-Control Study of Offenders with High Functioning Autistic Spectrum Disorders." *Journal of Forensic Psychiatry & Psychology* 16 (2005): 747–763.

Yantzi, Mark. *Sexual Offending and Restoration*. Waterloo: Herald Press, 1998.

Yates, Horatio. *Statement of the Accounts and Affairs of the Provincial Penitentiary for the Year 1848*. Toronto: Legislative Assembly of the Province of Canada, 1849.

Yoder, Carolyn. *The Little Book of Trauma Healing: When Violence Strikes and Community Security Is Threatened*. Intercourse: Good Books, 2005.

Young, Marlene, and Stein, John. *The History of the Crime Victim's Movement in the United States*. Retrieved from www.ojp.usdoj.gov/ovc, 2004.

Young Offenders Act, 1980-81-82-83, c. 110.

Youth Criminal Justice Act, S.C. 2002, c. 1.

Zangwill, O. L. "Early Days of Behaviourism." *Nature* 282 (1979): 148–149.

Zehr, Howard. *Changing Lenses: A New Focus for Crime and Justice.* Scottdale: Herald Press, 1990.

———. *Transcending: Reflections of Crime Victims.* Intercourse: Good Books, 2001.

———. *The Little Book of Restorative Justice.* Intercourse: Good Books, 2002.

Zehr, Howard, and Toews, Barb. *Critical Issues in Restorative Justice.* New York: Willan Publishing, 2004.

Copyright Acknowledgements

DEDICATION

Lyrics from "Forever Young" by Robert Dylan. Copyright © 1973 Robert Dylan, Rams Horn Music (SESAC). Reprinted by permission. International copyright secured. All rights reserved.

FOREWORD

Photos from Howard Zehr's books *Doing Life: Reflections of Men and Women Serving Life Sentences*; *Transcending: Reflections of Crime Victims*; and *What Will Happen to Me?* Reprinted by permission. Copyright © 1996, 2001, and 2010 Good Books.

CHAPTER 2

Testimony by Ruth Roulette and Flora Merrick to 38th Parliament, 1st session, Standing Committee on Aboriginal Affairs and Northern Development, available at http://www.parl.gc.ca/HousePublications/Publication.aspx?DocId=1648068&Language=E&Mode=1. Reprinted by permission. Copyright © 2005 Office of the Speaker of the House of Commons.

CHAPTER 3

Text Box 3.1 adapted from Oakes, Gary. "Teen gets 20 months for 7 week spree of office burglaries," *Toronto Star*, December 24, 1985. Reprinted by permission. Copyright © 1985 Toronto Star Newspapers.

Text Box 3.2 adapted from Daly, Rita. "Kids who hurt can also heal; Offenders, victims meet in mediation; Attempt to reduce courtroom trials," *Toronto Star*, March 28, 2004. Reprinted by permission. Copyright © 2004 Toronto Star Newspapers.

CHAPTER 4

Excerpt from hooks, bell. "Out of the academy and into the streets." *Ms Magazine* 3(1), 80-82. Copyright © 1992 bell hooks.

CHAPTER 6

Excerpt from "A Brave and Startling Truth" from *A Brave and Startling Truth* by Maya Angelou, copyright © 1995 by Maya Angelou. Used by permission of Random House, an imprint and division of Penguin Random House LLC. All rights reserved. Any third party use of this material, outside of this publication, is prohibited. Interested parties must apply directly to Penguin Random House LLC for permission.

Lyrics from "Coming Back to Life." David Jon Gilmour. Copyright © 2014 Pink Floyd Music Publishers Inc. All Rights Reserved. Used By Permission

CHAPTER 7

Lyrics from "Prison Bound." Words and Music by Michael Ness. Copyright © 1988 Goodbye Cruel World Music. All Rights Administered Worldwide by Downtown DLJ Songs. All Rights Reserved. Used by Permission. *Reprinted by Permission of Hal Leonard Corporation.*

Poem from Challeen, Dennis A. *Making it Right: A Common Sense Approach to Criminal Justice.* Reprinted by permission. Copyright © 1986 Melius Peterson Publishing Co, Dennis A. Challeen.

Lyrics from "Blowin' in the Wind" by Robert Dylan. Copyright © 1962 by Warner Bros. Inc; renewed 1990 by Robert Dylan, Special Rider Music (SESAC). Reprinted by permission. International copyright secured. All rights reserved.

CHAPTER 8

Quotation from Heather White © Source: "Through a Terrible Crime," *Let's Talk Express*, Correctional Service Canada, March 2014. Reproduced with the permission of the Minister of Public Works and Government Services Canada, 2015.

Figure 8.1 and Figure 8.2 from Pranis, Kay, Barry Stuart, and Mark Wedge. *Peacemaking Circles: From Crime to Community.* Reprinted by permission. Copyright © 2003 Living Justice Press.

CHAPTER 9

The Child and Youth Resilience Measure-28 from Liebenberg, Linda, Michael Ungar, and Fons Van Vijver. "Validation of the Child and Youth Resilience Measure-28 (CYRM-28) Among Canadian Youth" originally published in *Research on Social Work Practice* 22 (2012): 222, now available at http://resilienceresearch.org/research/resources/tools/33-the-child-and-youth-resilience-measure-cyrm. Reprinted by permission. Copyright © 2013 Resilience Research Centre, Dalhousie University.

Resilience Tree guidelines from *Youth Resilience: Resilience Tree Handout*, available at http://resilienceresearch.org/research/projects/pathways-to-resilience Reprinted by permission. Copyright © 2013 Resilience Research Centre, Dalhousie University.

CHAPTER 10

Excerpt from Oudshoorn, Judah. "Restorative Justice: It's Complex" from *Restorative Justice Week 2013 in Canada: The Basic Resource Kit*. Reprinted by permission. Copyright © 2013 Correctional Service Canada.

Figure 10.1: "CHCH Process" from Sivell-Ferri, Christine. *The Four Circles of Hollow Water*. Public Works &
Government Services Canada, Aboriginal Peoples Collection: APC 15 CA, 1997. Copyright © 1997 Christine Sivell-Ferri.

CHAPTER 11

Excerpt from "What Does Victim Rehabilitation Look Like?" *National Justice Network Update* 21(5) June 2014, available at http://crcvc.ca/njn/NJN-June-2014.pdf. Reprinted by permission. Copyright © 2014 Canadian Resource Centre for Victims of Crime.

Excerpt from Hendry, Luke. "Healing Centre Opens," *The Belleville Intelligencer*, September 5, 2013, available at http://www.intelligencer.ca/2013/09/05/healing-centre-opens. Copyright © 2013 Belleville Intelligencer.

Index

Abiola, Hafsat, 249
Aboriginal Affairs Parliamentary Committee, 28–29
Aboriginal Healing Foundation, 110
Aboriginal Justice and the Charter: Realizing a Culturally Sensitive Interpretation of Legal Rights (Milward), 164
Aboriginal peoples. *See* Indigenous peoples of Turtle Island (North America)
Aboriginal Peoples' Television Network, 37
Absolon, Kathleen E., 5, 256
academia, and theory, 5
accountability, 3, 16, 158, 159, 194–196, 206, 220
Achilles, Mary, 246
acknowledgement, 185
Act for Establishing Prisons for Young Offenders (1857), 33
Act Respecting Arrest, Trial and Imprisonment of Youthful Offenders (1894), 33
Action ontarienne contre la violence faite aux femmes (AOcVF), 223
acts in, 78
acts out, 78
addiction, 100–101, 106
adopted children, 68
adult corrections, 132
adult criminal behaviour, 78
adverse childhood experiences, 93–94
advocacy, 236
After the Crime: The Power of Restorative Justice Dialogues Between Victims and Violent Offenders (Miller), 172
aggression, 120
Agnew, Robert, 71
AI. *See* Appreciative Inquiry (AI)
Ainsworth, Mary, 103
Alfred, Taiaiake, 210
Algeria, 206
Allen, Jon, 98

alternative measures, 51
American Journal of Orthopsychiatry, 94
amygdala, 91, 178
anarchist criminology, 81–82
Andrews, B., 105
Angelou, Maya, 107, 126
Anglican Church, 18, 36
Anishinaabe, 14, 164, 211
Annie E. Casey Foundation, 134
anomie, 71
anterior insula, 91
anti-racist perspective, 81
apology, 48–49
appeal to higher loyalties rationalization, 72
Appreciative Inquiry (AI), 188–189
Archibald, Linda, 216
architecture for peacebuilding, 197
Artinopoulou, Vasso, 210
arts-based community dialogue, 202
Asian Canadians, 22
Assembly of First Nations, 209
Assembly of Manitoba Chiefs, 37
assimilation, 18, 28, 37, 201
attachment, 101–104, 106, 124
attachment insecurity, 124
attachment insecurity spectrum, 124
attachment theory, 17, 101–104
attention deficit hyperactive disorder (ADHD), 68, 99–100
Atwood, Margaret, 77
Auburn Correctional Facility, 26
Australia, 171
autobiographical sketch (Oudshoorn), 117–118
autonomy, 3, 241
avoidance, 95
Ayers, Pam and Robert, 101

Baker, Barbara Ann, 202
Baker, Linda, 123
Bala, Nicholas, 46

Bancroft, Lundy, 122–123
Bandura, Albert, 69, 120
Beauche, Antoine, 27
Beccaria, Cesare, 26, 67
Becker, David, 112
The Behaviour of Organisms (Skinner), 69
behavioural impacts of trauma, 90
behaviourism, 69
Bell, Sandra J., 33
Belleville Intelligencer, 242
Bellinger, Avril, 188
belonging, 3
Beneke, Timothy, 122
Bennett, Jamie, 135
Bentham, Jeremy, 67
Beyond Trauma: Cultural and Societal Dynamics (Summerfield), 112
Bierie, David M., 132, 139
biological perspective, 17, 68
Black Canadians, 152
Blake, S. H., 36
Bloom, Sandra, 87, 93, 96, 97, 105, 184, 190, 191
"Blowin' in the Wind" (Dylan), 149
body, and impacts of trauma, 90–94
body types, 68
bonding, 240
borderline personality disorder, 98–99, 124
Borrows, John, 210–211
Bouhours, Brigitte, 177
Bourdieu, Pierre, 208
Bowlby, John, 102–103, 104
Boyd, Neil, 140
brain, and impacts of trauma, 90–94
brain hemispheres, 93
Braithwaite, John, 178
Brave Heart, Maria Yellow Horse, 108–109
breach of probation orders, 52
Brewin, C. R., 105
Broadhurst, Roderic, 177
broken youth justice system, 1–2
Brown, George, 27
Brown, Michelle, 16
Bryce, P. H., 31, 36
Building on Youth Strengths (BOYS) Club, 221
Butler, Judith, 115, 125

Canada's Indigenous Constitution (Borrows), 211
Canadian Charter of Rights and Freedoms. *See* Charter of Rights and Freedoms
Canadian Department of Justice, 52
Canadian Journal of Criminology, 46
Canadian Medical Association, 132
Canadian Resource Centre for Victims of Crime, 241

Canadian Royal Commission on Aboriginal Peoples (RCAP), 209–210
Canadian Victims Bill of Rights, 237–240
Canadian youth justice system. *See* youth justice system
capitalism, dark side of, 6
Carrier, 211
case development, 166
"A Case Study of Victim-Offender Conferencing" (Irvine), 173
Catholic Church, 28
Cayuga, 18, 29
Center for Justice and Peacebuilding, 197
Centers for Disease Control and Prevention, 79, 120
Centre for Addiction and Mental Health, 215
Centre for Children and Families in the Justice System, 123
Centre for Crime and Justice Studies, 74
Challeen, Dennis A., 133–134
Changing Lenses: A New Focus for Crime and Justice (Zehr), 15, 165
Charter of Rights and Freedoms, 23, 45, 50
Child and Youth Resilience Measure-28, 183–184
"Child Maltreatment Is Associated with Distinct Genomic and Epigenetic Profiles in Posttraumatic Stress Disorder," 94
child offender, 34
child-savers movement, 27, 55
choice, 3
Christie, Nils, 150, 234
chronic trauma, 112
Churchill, Winston, 21
Circle guidelines, 169, 170
Circle processes, 166, 167–169
Circle values, 168
Circles of Support and Accountability (CoSA), 174–175, 255
Clallams, 164
Clark, Mary, 240, 241
class, 38
classical criminology, 66–67
Clearing the Plains: Disease, Politics of Starvation, and the Loss of Aboriginal Life (Daschuk), 111
Cloward, Richard, 71
Coast Salish, 164
coefficient of determination, 144–145
coerced participation, 186
Cohen, Stanley, 44, 71
Coles, Tony, 121
collective trauma, 87, 88, 107, 126
   colonialism, 49, 73, 110
   community health, well-being, and care, effect on, 125–126

Index 325

described, 108–110
historical trauma response, 109
individual and group identity, effect on, 113–114
limits of medical model, 112
patriarchy. *See* patriarchy
political nature of, 124–125
structural trauma, 109
colonialism, 49, 73, 110
colonization, 18, 25, 205
Comack, Elizabeth, 80, 140
communication in safe way, 185
communities
    arts-based community dialogue, 202
    collective trauma, effect of, 125–126
    in need of repair, 1
    needs of, and restorative justice, 159–161
    responsibility of community, 160
    safer, more livable communities, 2, 129–130
    trauma-informed care, 200–202
Community Holistic Circle Healing (CHCH) program, 214–215
Community Justice Initiatives (CJI), 217
community outreach, 218–219, 220
condemnation of the condemners, 72
conduct disorder (CD), 100
Confederation, 25
Conference Board of Canada, 116
conflict as property, 234, 247
Conklin, Philip, 100–101
connection, 3
Connell, Raewyn, 121, 256
consortium, 116
constructionists, 45
contact-based restorative justice practices, 165–167, 177, 196
conventional stage, 70
coping strategies, 95
core values. *See* values of trauma-informed youth justice
Corntassel, Jeff, 207
Corrado, Raymond R., 73, 111
correctional institutions. *See* prison
Correctional Service of Canada (CSC), 157, 175, 198, 246
Corrections and Post-traumatic Stress Symptoms (Murphy), 139
correlation coefficient, 144
cortisol, 92
CoSA. *See* Circles of Support and Accountability (CoSA)
Coulthard, Glen Sean, 15, 114
court case titles, 16

court system, 229–230
Courtois, Christine, 3
"Creating Trauma-Informed Correctional Care: A Balance of Goals and Environments" (Miller and Najavits), 196
Cree, 164, 211, 216
Crenshaw, Kimberle Williams, 81
Crewe, Ben, 135
crime
    common protective factors, 217
    common risk factors, 217, 219–222
    damage to bonding, 240
    damage to people and relationships, 16
    holistic approach, 11–13
    individualization of crime, 177
    as issue of peace, 9
    politicization of crime, 60–61
    violent crime, 60
    war on crime as "war against youth," 44
    why youth commit crimes. *See* theoretical explanations of youth crimes
crime statistics, 21
Criminal Code of Canada, 50
criminal justice
    criminal justice philosophies, 149
    traditional criminal justice, *vs.* restorative justice, 15–16, 156
The Criminal Man (Lombroso), 68
"criminal other," 47
criminogenic, 46, 62
criminology, 66
    anarchist criminology, 81–82
    classical criminology, 66–67
    and feminism, 80
    and history of Canadian youth justice, 21
    peacemaking criminology, 10
    positivist criminology, 67–68
    and scientific neutrality, 66
Criminology: A Canadian Perspective (Linden), 116
critical scholarship, 42
critical thinking, 5
cultural genocide, 114, 126
The Culture of Punishment: Prison, Society, and Spectacle (Brown), 16
culture of violence, 220
Cunningham, Alison, 123
current youth justice practices
    conclusion, 152–153
    prison, 133–141
    punishment, problems of, 149–152
    risk assessment, 141–148
    and trauma-informed approach, 131–133
    victims, and satisfaction with criminal justice, 148

current youth justice system
    conclusion, 61
    power in, 41–42
    Young Offenders Act, 42–47
    Youth Criminal Justice Act. *See* Youth Criminal Justice Act (YCJA)
cycle of violence, 66, 82
    see also trauma-informed theory
    anti-racist perspective, 81
    components of, 77
    moral imagination, 10
    research on cycle of violence theory, 78–79
    steps to explain, 77
    theoretical explanation for, 75–78
Daly, Kathleen, 171–172, 177
D'Andrea, Wendy, 94
The Dangers of Detention: The Impact of Incarcerating Youth in Detention and Other Secure Facilities, 135
dark side of capitalism, 6
Daschuk, James, 111
Davin Report, 30
decision-making in court system, 229
declarative memory, 92–93
decolonization, 205, 206–217, 224, 251–252
    honouring treaties, 209–210
    learning from Indigenous peoples, 213–217
    pluralism in youth criminal justice, 210–213
Decolonization: Indigeneity, Education & Society, 207
"Decolonization Is Not a Metaphor" (Tuck and Yang), 207
Dene, 164
denial of injury, 72
denial of responsibility, 72
denial of the victim, 72
denunciation, 60
Department of Indian Affairs, 37
depression, 98
deprivation theory, 236
Desjarlais, S. Amy, 109
deterrence, 60
Devereux, Simon, 26
Diagnostic and Statistical Manual-5, 97–98
dialogue
    arts-based community dialogue, 202
    that leads to change, 13–14
differential treatment of young people, 25
"Dignity" (Dylan), 141
Director of Educational Services, 37
Discipline and Punish: The Birth of the Prison (Foucault), 150

disconnection, 102, 221–222
disruptive behaviour disorders, 99–100
dissociation, 97
dissociative identity disorder, 99
diversity, 186
Dixon, Charles, 211–212, 213
Doe, Jane, 230
domestic violence, 79, 102, 108, 175–176
Dorahy, Martin J., 99
Dostoyevsky, Fyodor, 133
"Draw the Line" (Lalonde), 223
drug possession, 254
due process, 43
Duran, Eduardo, 109
Durkheim, Emile, 71, 152
Dutton, Donald G., 123
Dylan, Bob, 141, 149

Eastern Mennonite University, 197, 200
effect size, 145
Egeland, Bryon, 123
EJM. *See* extrajudicial measures (EJM)
EJS. *See* extrajudicial sanctions (EJS)
Elders, 162, 163
Elliott, Elizabeth M., 17, 151
Elliott, Tish, 188
Else-Quest, Nicole M., 125
Emerson, Ralph Waldo, 256
emotional impacts of trauma, 90
empathy, 185
encounter-based restorative justice programs. *See* contact-based restorative justice practices
Endgame: Volume 1 The Problem of Civilization (Jensen), 208
Englund, Michelle M., 123
Ensler, Eve, 97
episodic trauma, 87, 88
equality, 150
equity, 150
Erasmus, George, 209
Erikson, Erik, 68
Erikson, Kai, 126
Eriksson, Anna, 152
Espinosa, Erin M., 116
Estrada, Felipe, 44
etiology, 109, 126
Euro-Canadian philosophies of criminal justice, 149
European Journal of Psychotraumatology, 196
European model, 236
Evans, Marion, 198–200, 203
The Evening Star, 24
expense of youth incarceration, 136

Index

"Experiences in Reconciling Risk Management and Restorative Justice: How Circles of Support and Accountability Work Restoratively in the Risk Society" (Hannem), 255
extrajudicial, 62
extrajudicial measures (EJM), 51, 52
extrajudicial sanctions (EJS), 51, 52

face-to-face meetings, 157, 158, 164–165
fairness, 150
family group conferencing, 166, 167, 170–172
family violence, 79, 102, 108, 117–118
Fanon, Frantz, 206–207
Fast, Ed, 60
fear, 152
fearful attachment, 124
feminisms, 79–80
fetal alcohol spectrum disorder, 99–100
fight or flight, 91, 95
Firehammer, Judith, 109
First Nations. *See* Indigenous peoples of Turtle Island (North America)
flashbacks, 92, 106
folk devils, 44
Fontaine, Phil, 37
Ford, Julian, 94
forgiveness, 201
Forsey, Eugene E., 23
Fort Alexander residential school, 37
Foucault, Michel, 150
The Four Circles of Hollow Water, 214
Fowler, J. Christopher, 98
Fowler, Joyce, 100
framework for trauma-informed youth justice
    broken youth justice system, 1–2
    finding hope, 18–19
    healing relationships, 18–19
    restorative justice worldview, 14–18
    safer, more livable communities, 2
    values of trauma-informed youth justice, 4–14
    vision for trauma-informed youth justice system, 3–4
Freire, Paulo, 13–14
Freud, Sigmund, 125
Freudians, 68
"From Child Maltreatment to Violent Offending: An Examination of Mixed-Gender and Gender-Specific Models" (Topitzes, Mersky, and Reynolds), 78
"From Resilience to Resistance: A Reconstruction of the Strengths Perspective in Social Work Practice" (Guo and Tsui), 207–208

From Violence to Blessing: How an Understanding of Deep-Rooted Conflict Can Open Paths to Reconciliation (Redekop), 113–114
Frueh, B. Christopher, 98
future victimization, 95

Gaarder, Emily, 176
Garnett, R., 105
Gatti, Uberto, 132
Gavrielides, Theo, 210
gender
    see also patriarchy
    and family violence, 79
    and history of Canadian youth justice, 22, 38
    income inequality, 116
    male violence, 108
Gendreau, Paul, 46
general strain theory (GST), 71
genocide, 114
Gerber, Linda M., 236
Germany, 109, 213
Gilligan, James, 11, 76, 77
Gladue principle, 210, 211–212
Glassbeek, Harry, 23
Godwin, William, 14
Golding, Emma, 21
Goldman, Emma, 160
Gonzalez, John, 109
government role, 176
Grabe, Shelley, 125
Gradual Civilization Act, 25
Grafton, Antone, 167
Gramsci, Antonio, 121
Grand Valley Institution for Women, 198, 203
group identity, 201
Guo, Wei-he, 207–208

Hannah-Moffat, Kelly, 147
Hannem, Stacey, 255
harm reduction mentality, 249
Harper, Elijah, 209
Harper, Stephen, 48
Hart, Angie, 187, 190, 192
Haskell, Lori, 17, 87, 110, 178
Haudenosaunee/Iroquois, 29–31, 211
Haunting Legacies: Violent Histories and Transgenerational Trauma (Schwab), 110
Hayes, Hennessey, 171–172
healing, 3
    and Indigenous communities, 14, 18
    and justice, 17–18
    relationships, 18–19
    restorative justice, and healing trauma, 178

three-phase model of healing, 216
trauma-healing principles, 3
victims, and ownership of healing, 234
"Healing Centre Opens" (*Belleville Intelligencer*), 242
healing circles, 18, 111
healthy dialogue, 13–14
healthy practitioner, 189–190
hegemonic masculinity, 120–123, 126–127
hegemony, 121
hemispheres of the brain, 93
Henry, Myeengun, 162, 206
Herchmer, W. M., 26
hereditary explanations, 68
Herman, Judith, 87, 98, 102, 124–125, 176, 177, 185, 190, 194, 227–228, 240, 241
hierarchical power, 229–230
hippocampus, 92–93
historical trauma, 87, 88
  see also collective trauma
historical trauma response, 109
history of Canadian youth justice
  from Confederation to 1907, 24–31
  considerations of power, race, gender, and class, 38–39
  and criminology, 21
  current youth justice system. *See* current youth justice system
  differential treatment of young people, 25
  gender, 22
  legislation, 21
  from 1908 to 1984, 31–36
  the penitentiary, 25–27
  race, 22
  rule of law, 22–24
Hogeveen, Bryan, 42
holistic approach
  to addressing crime, 11–13
  and determinants of health, 12–13
  and peace, 10
Hollow Water, MB, 213–215
Holocaust, 126
homelessness, 6–9, 12
homicide rates, 45
honour, 192
hooks, bell, 79–80, 125
hope, 3, 13, 18–19, 224
hospital-acquired infections, 132–133
"How a Drunken Rampage Changed Legal History" (*Ottawa Citizen*), 164–165
How Canadians Govern Themselves (Forsey), 23
human dignity, 5–6
Hunt, Nigel, 202
hurting others, 95

hyperarousal, 91, 106
hypothesis, 66

iatrogenic, 46, 62
iatrogenic issues, 132, 133
identity, 104–105, 113–114, 192, 201
immorality, 24
immune system dysfunction, 93–94
impacts of trauma, 88–94
  behavioural impacts, 90
  on the brain and the body, 90–94
  brain hemispheres, effects on, 93
  emotional impacts, 90
  hippocampal volume, decrease in, 92–93
  immune system dysfunction, 93–94
  neuroendocrine dysfunction, 93–94
  physical impacts, 89–90
  stress response, damaged or dysregulated, 91–92
  worldview impacts, 90
impartiality, 150
In the Realm of Hungry Ghosts: Close Encounters with Addiction (Maté), 100
incapacitation, 158
incarceration. *See* prison
income inequality, 116
Indian Act, 30, 205
Indigenous legal traditions, 210–211
Indigenous peoples of Turtle Island (North America), 14, 22, 25, 39
  Aboriginal offenders and social transformation, 212
  assimilation, 18, 28, 37, 201
  child welfare system, Indigenous children in, 47
  colonialism, 49, 110
  colonization, 18, 25
  cultural genocide, 114
  focus on healing, 14, 18
  focus on traditional ways, 216
  gift-giving, 164
  healing circles, 18
  Indigenous legal traditions, 210–211
  Indigenous women, as victims of violence, 23, 73–74
  infant mortality, 113
  interdependency of relationships, 15
  intergenerational trauma, 47, 49, 73
  in leadership roles, 251–252
  learning from, 213–217
  life expectancy, 113
  needs of Indigenous youth, 41
  overrepresentation in youth justice system, 18, 22, 54, 110–114, 135, 151–152, 162

Index 329

physical and sexual abuse, 110
residential schools. *See* residential schools and restorative justice, 14
right to vote, 22
roots of restorative justice in Indigenous traditions, 161–164
self-determination, 29, 31
self-governance, 29, 31
settler colonialism, 28, 73, 108, 110–114
settler relationships, 22
sixties scoop, 47, 205
suicide rates, 49
trauma, effects of, 73
treaties, 29–30, 36, 209–210
individual responsibility, 43
individual trauma
and addictions, 100–101
generally, 86–87
identity, 104–105
impacts of trauma, 88–94
meaning of trauma, 87
mental health, 94–100
and relationships, 101–104
individualization of crime, 177
industrial schools, 22
infant mortality, 113
informed consent, 186
insecure attachment, 124
interconnectedness, 168
interdependency of relationships, 15
intergenerational trauma, 47, 49, 73, 87, 88
see also collective trauma
International Journal of Offender Therapy and Comparative Criminology, 255
International Social Work, 207
interpersonal violence, 108
intimate partner violence (IPV), 88, 115, 119–120, 123–124
Inuit, 211
see also Indigenous peoples of Turtle Island (North America)
Irvine, Arley, 173
Italy, 132

Jacques, Stephen, 26
JDA. *See* Juvenile Delinquents Act
Jensen, Derrick, 1, 208
John Howard Society, 33
Johnston, Patrick, 47
Johnstone, Gerry, 228, 229, 235
Jones, Nicholas, 50
Journal of Child Psychology and Psychiatry, 182
Journal of Interpersonal Violence, 78
Journal of Youth Adolescence, 116

justice, 150, 192
Justice for Young Offenders: Their Needs, Our Responses (Vandergoot), 99
Justice Policy Institute, 135
"Juvenile Court Cases" (*Toronto Daily Star*), 31–32
juvenile delinquency, 25, 32–33, 34
juvenile delinquents, 32, 34
Juvenile Delinquents Act (JDA), 21, 22, 25, 27, 32, 33–35, 43

Kaandossiwin: How We Come to Know (Absolon), 5, 256
Kansas Coalition Against Sexual and Domestic Violence, 188
Kaswentha, 30
Katz, Jackson, 119, 121
Kelso, J.J., 27, 55
Kendall, Joshua C., 90–91
"Kids Who Hurt Can also Heal; Offenders, Victims Meet in Mediation Attempt to Reduce Courtroom Trials" (*Toronto Star*), 49
Kingston Penitentiary, 25–27, 33, 139
Klinic Community Health Centre, 189
Kohlberg, Lawrence, 70
Kornhauser, William, 236
Kuehn, Sarah, 73, 111
Kuhn, Thomas, 255
Kupers, Terry A., 61, 136–137, 140, 151

Laboucane-Benson, Patti, 216
Lafleur, Alexis, 27
Lalonde, Julie S., 223, 224
land, dispossession of, 113
Lashley, Karl, 69
learned helplessness, 96
learning disabilities, 68
Leckman, James F., 182–183
Lederach, John Paul, 10
legal pluralism, 210–213, 224
legislation, 21
Lehmann, Peter, 186
Leon, Jeffrey S., 35, 55
Leschied, Alan, 46
Let's Talk, 157
Level of Service Inventory models (LSI), 142, 143, 144
life expectancy, 113
limits of a trauma-informed lens, 82
Linden, Rick, 116
listening, 185
Litowitz, Douglas, 121
The Little Book of Family Group Conferences New Zealand Style (MacRae and Zehr), 170

The Little Book of Trauma Healing: When Violence Strikes and Community Security Is Threatened (Yoder), 77, 200
Little Eyes, Little Ears: How Violence Against a Mother Shapes Children as They Grow (Cunningham and Baker), 123
livable communities, 130
Llewellyn, Jennifer J., 16, 178
Loh, Nini, 177
Lombroso, Cesare, 67–68
London, Willie, 61, 140, 151
Lopez, Molly A., 116
loss, 98
Louie, Del, 211–212
LSI. *See* Level of Service Inventory models (LSI)

MacDonald, John A., 110, 124
Macionis, John J., 236
MacLean's, 120
MacRae, Allan, 170
Magnuson, Diane, 101
major depressive episodes (MDD), 78
Male Allies Against Sexual Violence program, 220, 221, 224, 243
male violence, 108, 115
    cycles of trauma, influence of, 123–124
    hegemonic masculinity, 120–123
    impact of, 175–176
    men, and ending male violence, 220–221
    permission, 120–123
    statistics, 119–120
mandatory minimum sentences, 254
manipulative offenders, 176
manslaughter, 159
Maori, 14, 170
Margaritescu, Irina, 73, 111
Marjot, David, 101
Marxist feminism, 80
masculinity, hegemonic, 120–123, 126–127
Mason, Raymond, 47–48
mass-society theory, 236
Maté, Gabor, 86, 100
Matza, David, 72
Maurutto, Paula, 147
McConnell, Gordon, 164–165
McCrory, Eamon J., 91
McCullough, Michael, 211
McElrea, Fred, 171
McEvoy, Theresa, 58, 59
McFarlane, Alexander, 91, 93
McKinney, Flora, 28
McLeod Report, 34, 35
McLuhan, Marshall, 44

McNeill, Fergus, 57
MDD. *See* major depressive episodes (MDD)
meaning, 192, 241
meaningful accountability, 3, 16
Measuring Violence Against Women, 116
media, role of, 44–47, 61, 120
mediation, as term, 176
medical trauma, 86–87
Meech Lake Accord, 209
memory, 92–93
Memory, War and Trauma (Hunt), 202
"Men Engaged in the Work of Ending Male Violence" (Tuchlinsky), 220–221
Men on Rape: What They Have to Say about Sexual Violence (Beneke), 122
Mendel, Richard, 135, 136
Mennonite peace tradition, 164–165
mental disabilities, 22
mental health, 68
    borderline personality disorder, 98–99, 124
    depression, 98
    disruptive behaviour disorders, 99–100
    dissociative identity disorder, 99
    fetal alcohol spectrum disorder, 99–100
    and overrepresentation in prisons, 152
    post-traumatic stress disorder (PTSD), 78, 94–98
    and trauma, 94–100
Menzies, Peter, 215
Merrick, Angus, 28
Merrick, Flora, 28–29
Merton, Robert K., 71
"methods from the margins" approach, 6–9
Métis, 211
    see also Indigenous peoples of Turtle Island (North America)
Mi'kmaq, 14, 164, 211
Mikulincer, Mario, 103
Miller, Niki A., 196–197
Miller, Susan L., 166, 172, 234
Milloy, John S., 22, 28, 30, 36–37
Milward, David, 164
Minaker, Joanne C., 42
Minister of Aboriginal Affairs, 36
Ministry of Children and Youth Services, 54
mino-pimatisiwin, 216, 224
Mohawk, 18, 29, 209
Mohawk Institute, 37
money, 23
moral development theory, 69–70
moral imagination, 10
The Moral Imagination: The Art and Soul of Building Peace (Lederach), 10

moral reasoning, 70
Moroney, Shannon, 182, 227, 228
Mother-Child program, 198–200, 203
mourning, 185
multiple regression analysis, 145–146
Murphy, Daniel S., 139
Murphy, Sandra, 190
Mush Hole, 37
My Story: Young People Talk about the Trauma and Violence in Their Lives, 74
Myron, Archie, 28

Najavits, Lisa M., 196–197
Narayan, Angela J., 123
A National Crime: The Canadian Government and the Residential School System, 1879 to 1986 (Milloy), 22
National Intimate Partner and Sexual Survivor Survey, 120
Native Children and the Child Welfare System (Johnston), 47
Native Women's Association of Canada, 74
Navajo, 164
Nazis, 126, 213
needs principle, 144
Ness, Mike, 131
neuroendocrine dysfunction, 93–94
neurogenesis, 178
"The Neuroscience of Restorative Justice" (Reisel), 178
neutralization, techniques of, 72
New South Wales, 171
New World Encyclopedia, 147
New Zealand, 170–171
    see also Maori
Nicholson, Rob, 58, 60
"Night Crier" (Paul Sr.), 141
Nisga'a, 211
Nisquallys, 164
No Place for Kids: The Case for Reducing Juvenile Incarceration, 134, 136
noble truths, 187
nonjudgment, 186
normalize, 185
normative, 129–130, 153
numbing, 95
Nunn Inquiry, 58–60, 61

offenders
    Aboriginal offenders and social transformation, 212
    denial of guilt, 158–159
    manipulative offenders, 176
    needs of, and restorative justice, 158–159
    trauma-informed accountability, 194–196
    trauma-informed care, 194
    trauma-informed incapacitation, 196–200
"Offenders Found Guilty To-day" (*Evening Star*), 24
Office of Child and Family Services Advocacy, 222
Ohlin, Lloyd, 71
Oji-Cree Sandy Lake First Nation, 15
Ojibway, 162–163, 214
Oka crisis, 209
Oldham, John, 98
Omnibus Crime bill, 57–58
On Crimes and Punishments (Beccaria), 67
Oneida, 18, 29
Onondaga, 18, 29
Ontario Coalition of Rape Crisis Centres (OCRCC), 223, 242
oppositional defiant disorder (ODD), 100
ordinary memory, 92–93
ordinary stress, 240
Original peoples, 25, 151
    see also Indigenous peoples of Turtle Island (North America)
Osland, Julie A., 122
Ottawa Citizen, 164–165
Oudshoorn, Abe, 11–13
Oudshoorn, Judah, 66, 115–116, 117–118, 211–212, 257
Out There, In Here: Masculinity, Violence and Prisoning (Comack), 140
overgeneralization, 59–60
overrepresentation in youth justice system, 18, 22, 23, 54, 110–114, 135, 151–152, 162

PACT, 49, 52
Padykula, Nora LaFond, 100–101
Panter-Brick, Catherine, 182–183
paradigm, 255, 258
parens patriae, 32, 33
"Parenting Behind Bars" (Evans), 198–200
Parmenter, Jon, 30
Parr, Todd, 9
participation, 6–9
Paths of Courage Healing and Retreat Centre, 242
patriarchal dividend, 121
patriarchy, 38, 39, 108, 114–124
    cycles of trauma, influence of, 123–124
    definitions of, 116
    dismantling patriarchy, 217–224, 251–252
    hegemonic masculinity, 120–123
    male violence, 119–124
    permission, 120–123

privilege from, 119–120
purpose of identifying men (masculinity) as a problem, 119–120
and young offenders, 116
Paul, Rudy Chato, Sr., 141
PCL-YV. *See* Psychopathy Checklist-Youth Version (PCL-YV)
peace, 9–11
The Peace Book (Parr), 9
peacebuilding, 9, 10–11, 197
peacemaking Circles, 51, 167–169, 215
Peacemaking Circles: From Crime to Community, 168
peacemaking criminology, 10
Pearce, Colby, 102
Peck, M. Scott, 11
Pedagogy of the Oppressed (Freire), 13
penitentiary, 25–27
Pepinksy, Hal, 10
permission, 120–123
Perry, Christopher, 98
persistent trauma, 87, 88
Petrellis, Tania, 198
philosophies of criminal justice, 149
physical abuse, 37, 110
physical impacts of trauma, 89–90
physiological characteristics, 68
Piaget, Jean, 69–70
pluralism, 210–213
p'madaziwin, 214–215, 224
police officers, 51–52
"The Political is Personal" (Else-Quest and Grabe), 125
political nature of collective trauma, 124–125
politicization of crime, 60–61, 62
position of respect, 186
positionality, 117, 127
positivist criminology, 67–68
post-trauma, 104
post-traumatic stress disorder (PTSD), 78, 94–98, 112
post-traumatic stress reaction, 97
postconventional stage, 70
poverty, 152
power
    in current youth justice system, 41–42
    and fear, correlation between, 152
    hierarchical power and decision-making in court system, 229–230
    and history of Canadian youth justice, 24, 38
    unequal power, and peacemaking, 10
    and youth justice, 22
Pranis, Kay, 168

Pratt, John, 152
pre-sentence reports, 55, 147
pre-trauma, 104
pre-trial detention, 58, 59
preconventional stage, 70
predictor (x) variables, 146
prenatal development, 100
Presser, Lois, 176
prevention. *See* trauma-informed prevention
"Prevention of Violence: A Public Health Priority," 11
prevention through intervention, 222
primary prevention, 222
principles of trauma-informed youth justice, 249–254
    Indigenous peoples, and leadership roles, 251–252
    restorative justice framework, 252
    shared values to give shape to practices, 251
    trauma-informed care and prevention, 253–254
    victim-centred justice processes, 254
    women, and leadership roles, 251–252
prison, 133–141
    criminogenic effect, 132
    dangerous, 134–135
    hostile environment, 137
    hypermasculine, in toxic way, 140–141
    inadequacy, 136
    ineffective outcomes, 135
    obsolete, 136
    prison environment, 137, 197–198
    prison reform, 26–27
    psychological damage, 139
    rules of the prison code, 140–141
    solitary confinement, 137
    traumatic nature of incarceration, 136–140
    unnecessary, 136
    wasteful, 136
    youth incarceration rates, 41, 52, 54, 136
"Prison Bound" (Social Distortion), 131, 140
Prison Masculinities (Sabo, Kupers, and London), 61, 140
The Prisoner (Crewe and Bennett), 135
prisoners, 22
Prisoners' Aid Society, 33
private vengeance, 228
privilege, 24, 119–120, 224
probation officer, 54–57, 147
procedural justice, 43
procedural memory, 92–93
Prochnow, Herbert V., 208

protection of society, 43–44, 58
Protestant Church, 28
Proulx, Craig, 14, 164
psychoanalysis, 124–125
psychoanalytic theory, 68
psychological theories, 68–70
Psychology Today, 152
Psychopathy Checklist-Youth Version (PCL-YV), 142–143, 144
PTSD. *See* post-traumatic stress disorder (PTSD)
public consultation, 219
public education, 219, 220
public health, 11
punishment, 133
    definition of, 150, 153
    effect of, 2
    questioning usefulness of, 149
    vs. rehabilitation, 34
    vs. restorative justice, 3
"pure" prevention, 222
Puyallups, 164

Quebec, 209

racism
    anti-racist perspective, 81
    race, and history of Canadian youth justice, 22, 38
    racist media portrayals, 46–47
    residential schools, 28, 31
radical feminism, 80
Randall, Melanie, 17, 87, 110, 178
rational thinking, 67
Reagan, Ronald, 45
recidivism, 4, 19, 60, 132, 144–147, 177, 214
recognition of humanity, 158
reconciliation, 176, 207
Reconciliation, Repatriation and Reconnection: A Framework for Building Resilience in Canadian Indigenous Families (Laboucane-Benson), 216
Reconstructing Restorative Justice Philosophy (ed. Gavrielides and Artinopoulou), 210, 213
Red Skin White Masks: Rejecting the Colonial Politics of Recognition (Coulthard), 114
Redekop, Vern Neufeld, 113–114
re-enactment of trauma, 95
reform, 24, 26–27, 33, 149
reformatories, 22
Regan, Paulette, 48
rehabilitation, 33, 34–35, 43, 56, 149, 151, 241–242
Reiman, Jeffrey, 255

reintegration policy, 60
Reisel, Daniel, 178
relational damage, 192
relational theory of justice, 16, 178
relationships
    resilience through relationships, 182–184
    and trauma, 101–104
remorse, 159
The Report of the Department of Justice Committee on Juvenile Delinquency, 34
The Report on the Indian Schools of Manitoba and the North-West Territories, 31
Research Is Ceremony: Indigenous Research Methods (Wilson), 5
residential schools, 18, 22, 107–108
    apology, 48–49
    Bryce report, 31, 36
    closure of, 47–49
    deplorable conditions, 31, 38
    effects of, 73
    from 1879 to 1907, 27–31
    health, 37
    intergenerational impact, 111
    from 1908 to 1983, 36–38
    physical and sexual abuse, 37
    racist attitudes, 28, 31
    structural inequality, 110
    treaties, 30
    tuberculosis, 36–37
resilience, 182–184, 186–187, 190, 192, 203, 207
Resilience Research Centre, 183, 187
Resilience Tree guidelines, 187
resistance, 207
respect, 186
responsivity principle, 144
restitution, 149
restorative justice, 2, 19, 155, 178
    case development, 166
    central tasks of, 156
    Circle guidelines, 169, 170
    Circle processes, 166, 167–169
    Circle values, 168
    community needs, 159–161
    contact-based restorative justice practices, 165–167, 177, 196
    critiques of, 175–177
    domestic and sexual violence, 175–176
    as effective intervention for youth, 177–178
    face-to-face meetings, 157, 158
    family group conferencing, 166, 167, 170–172
    as framework, 252
    guiding questions for, 156

healing trauma, 178
history of, 161–165
and Indigenous communities, 14
individualization of crime, 177
justice as healing, 17
limited programming, 177
living unit (RJU), 198
manipulative offenders, 176
as means of crime prevention, 218
multiple levels of focus, 17–18
offender needs, 158–159
offender-oriented, 176–177
peacemaking Circles, 167–169
as philosophy, 51
as practice, 51
in practice, 165–175
prison environment, 198
problematic definitions, terms, and goals, 176
vs. punishment, 3
questions asked by, 15–16
as relational theory of justice, 16
repair of attachment, 17
restoration of relationships, 17
and role of government, 176
roots of, in Indigenous traditions, 161–164
roots of, in Mennonite peace tradition, 164–165
support-based restorative justice programs, 167, 174–175
vs. traditional criminal justice, 15–16, 156
victim needs, 16, 156–158, 176, 177
victim-offender mediation, 166, 167, 172–174
and victim satisfaction, 235
and victims, 246–247
where offender denies guilt, 158
worldview, 14–18
"Restorative Justice: It's Complex" (Oudshoorn), 211–212
Restorative Opportunities program, 157, 246
re-storying, 192
retribution, 149
Returning to the Teachings: Exploring Aboriginal Justice (Ross), 14–15
revenge, 192
Revive program, 217–220, 222
The Rich Get Richer and the Poor Get Prison: Ideology, Class, and Criminal Justice (Reiman), 255
Richmond, Chantelle, 113
rights-based justice model, 43
risk assessment, 141–142, 153

effectiveness of risk assessment tools, 144–148
Level of Service Inventory models (LSI), 143, 144
Psychopathy Checklist-Youth Version (PCL-YV), 142–143, 144
statistical models, and prediction of recidivism, 144–147
Structured Assessment of Violence Risk in Youth (SAVRY), 142, 143, 144
tools, 142–144
risk factors for crime, 217, 219–222
Risk Needs Assessment—Case Management Review (RNA), 143
risk principle, 143–144
The Road Less Traveled (Peck), 11
Robinson, Jennifer, 6
Rohr, Richard, 65, 66
root causes, 160–161
Ross, Rupert, 14–15, 163–164, 214
Royal Proclamation of 1763, 31
rule of law, 22–24

Sabo, Don, 61, 140, 151
Saechao, Kao, 56–57
safer communities, 129–130
safety, 3
Sanctuary Model, 190, 191
SAVRY. *See* Structured Assessment of Violence Risk in Youth (SAVRY)
Schissel, Bernard, 41, 44, 47
Schwab, Gabriele, 109, 110
scientific neutrality, 66
Scott, Duncan, 36
Scott, W. L., 27
Sebastien's Law, 58–60
secondary prevention, 222
Security With Care: Restorative Justice and Healthy Societies (Elliott), 17, 151
self-care, 190
self-determination, 29, 31
self-doubt, 104
self-governance, 29, 31
self-harming, 95
self-help theory, 229
Seneca, 18, 29
sensory memory, 92
sentencing
    mandatory minimum sentences, 254
    Sebastien's Law, 60
    under Young Offenders Act, 47
    under Youth Criminal Justice Act, 53
settlement, 228–229
settler colonialism, 28, 39, 73, 108, 110–114

Index   335

sexual abuse, 37, 88–90, 102, 108, 110, 175–176, 218–219
sexual assault, 119, 120, 122, 175–176, 243–246
Sexual Assault Centre for Quinte and District, 242
Sexual Assault Support Centre (Waterloo Region), 221, 243
sexual violence. *See* sexual abuse; sexual assault
Sexual Violence Action Plan (Ontario), 223
Shakespeare, William, 114–115
shame, 104
Shaver, Phillip R., 103
Shiner, Lynn, 101
Sider, Nancy Good, 240
Simmons, Catherine A., 186
Simpson, Leanne, 205, 224
Sivell-Ferri, Christine, 214
Six Nations, 18
Sixth Canadian Conference of Charities and Corrections, 55
sixties scoop, 47
Skinner, B. F., 69
"Skinner box," 69
Smandych, Russell, 25, 27
Snyder, T. Richard, 129, 153
So You Think You Know Me? (Weaver), 160
social causes, 32
social change, 13–14
social constructionist perspective, 45
social contract theory, 229
"Social Determinants of Health" (Oudshoorn), 11–13
social disorganization theory, 70
Social Distortion, 131
social learning theory, 69, 120, 124
social movement, 236, 247
social welfare model, 33, 43
socio-economic status, 22
sociological theories, 70–72
solitary confinement, 137
Sorensen, Jon R., 116
Southern Theory (Connell), 256
Sparling, Diane, 52
Special Rapporteur on the Rights of Indigenous Peoples, 73, 210
Spinazzola, Joseph, 94
Spiralling Out of Control: Lessons Learned from a Boy in Trouble (Nunn), 58–60
stalking, 120
statistical models, and prediction of recidivism, 144–147
Statistics Canada, 54, 110, 116, 120
statutory release, 174

Stevenson, Bryan, 213
Stien, Phyllis, 90–91
Still Blaming Children: Youth Conduct and the Politics of Child Hating (Schissel), 44
"Still" (Oudshoorn), 257
Stolbach, Bradley, 94
The Story of a National Crime: Being an Appeal for Justice to the Indians of Canada (Bryce), 36
The Story of Jane Doe: A Book About Rape (Doe), 230
storytelling, 192
strain theory, 71
Strang, Heather, 177–178, 235, 236
Strategies for Trauma Awareness and Recovery (STAR) program, 200
strengths-based approach, 186–189
stress
    ordinary, 240
    post-traumatic stress disorder (PTSD), 78, 94–98, 112
    post-traumatic stress reaction, 97
    vs. trauma, 3, 87
    trauma, and impact on stress response, 91–92
    traumatic, 240
stress response, 91–92
structural inequality, 110
structural-strain theory, 236
structural trauma, 109
Structured Assessment of Violence Risk in Youth (SAVRY), 142, 143, 144
The Struggle to Be Human: Crime, Criminology and Anarchism (Tifft and Sullivan), 81
Stuart, Barry, 168
"Studying Youth Homelessness: Methods from the Margins" (Robinson), 6–9
subculture of violence theory, 71–72
substance abuse, 57
suicide rates, 49
Sullivan, Dennis, 66, 81, 158, 250
Summerfield, Derek, 112
superpredators, 61
support-based restorative justice programs, 167, 174–175, 236
survivors, 104–105, 202, 243–246
    see also victims
    believed, need to be, 246
    blamed, 243
    compassion, need for, 245–246
    doubted, 243–244
    equality, need for, 245
    harmed by criminal justice proceedings, 244
    information, need for, 245

justice needs, 245–246
    loss of control, 244–245
    made to feel unsafe, 244
    proportional laws, need for, 246
    safety, need for, 245
    scales of justice tipped in favour of offender, 245
Sykes, Gresham, 72

Tanner, Julian, 45, 46
techniques of neutralization, 72
Teen Courts, 177
"Teen Gets 20 Months for 7 Week Spree of Office Burglaries" (*Toronto Star*), 42–43
theoretical explanations of youth crimes
    behaviourism, 69
    biological perspective, 17, 68
    classical criminology, 66–67
    general strain theory (GST), 71
    generally, 65–66
    history of, 66–72
    moral development theory, 69–70
    positivist criminology, 67–68
    psychoanalytic theory, 68
    psychological theories, 68–70
    social disorganization theory, 70
    social learning theory, 69
    sociological theories, 70–72
    strain theory, 71
    subculture of violence theory, 71–72
    techniques of neutralization, 72
    trauma-informed theory. *See* trauma-informed theory
theory, 5, 66, 82
    see also theoretical explanations of youth crimes
They Came for the Children, 37
Thorogood, Josiah, 66
three-phase model of healing, 216
Through the Glass (Moroney), 182
Tifft, Larry, 66, 81, 158, 250
Toch, Hans, 133, 138
Toews, Barb, 197
Toronto Daily Star, 30, 31
Toronto Humane Society, 27
Toronto Pine Tree Healing Circle, 18
Toronto Star, 24, 42–43, 49
torture, 137, 150
Torture and Other Cruel, Inhuman or Degrading Treatment or Punishment, 137
Tough Guise (Katz), 121
tough-on-crime politics, 61
traditional criminal justice, *vs.* restorative justice, 15–16

Transcending: Reflections of Crime Victims (Zehr), 101, 192
transformation, 158
transformative leadership, 201–202
transgenerational trauma, 109
trauma, 3, 19
    and addictions, 100–101
    chronic, 112
    as collective experience, 3
    collective. *See* collective trauma
    episodic, 87, 88
    expansive definition, 112
    historical, 87, 88
    and identity, 104–105
    impacts of, 88–94
    influence on violent crime, 123–124
    intergenerational, 47, 49, 73, 87, 88
    as limiting experience, 3
    meaning of, 87
    and mental health, 94–100
    persistent, 87, 88
    and prenatal development, 100
    psychological *vs.* medical trauma, 86–87
    re-enactment of, 95
    and relationships, 101–104
    vs. stress, 3, 87
    structural, 109
    transgenerational, 109
    types, 87, 88
trauma-healing principles, 3
trauma-informed, 3, 19, 189–190
trauma-informed accountability, 194–196
trauma-informed care, 181
    communication in safe way, 185
    with communities, 200–202
    definition, 203
    guidance for practices, 253–254
    healthy practitioner, 189–190
    model for, 184–190
    moving toward new understanding of, 202–203
    with offenders, 194
    resilience through relationships, 182–184
    take position of respect, 186
    trauma-informed accountability with offenders, 194–196
    trauma-informed incapacitation with offenders, 196–200
    use of strengths-based approach, 186–189
    with victims, 190–193
trauma-informed incapacitation, 196–200
trauma-informed prevention
    decolonization, 206–217
    from despair to hope, 224

dismantling patriarchy, 217–224
guidance for practices, 253–254
prevention through intervention, 222
"pure" or primary prevention, 222
secondary prevention, 222
trauma-informed theory
anti-racist perspective, 81
cycle of violence theory, theoretical explanation for, 75–78
described, 73–75
feminist, 79–80
limits of a trauma-informed lens, 82
research on cycle of violence theory, 78–79
trauma, as common denominator, 74
The Trauma-Informed Toolkit, 113, 189
trauma-informed youth justice framework
see also framework for trauma-informed youth justice
principles of, 249–254
restorative justice worldview, 14–18
safer, more livable communities, 2
values of, 4–14
as victim-centred, 240–242
traumatic memory, 92–93
traumatic stress, 240
treaties, 29–30, 36, 209–210
Trepenier, Jean, 25
trigger, 91, 106
trustworthiness, 186
Truth and Reconciliation Commission (TRC), 48, 207
Tsui, Ming-sum, 207–208
tuberculosis, 36–37
Tuchlinsky, Joan, 220, 224
Tuck, Eve, 207
Turtle Island. *See* Indigenous peoples of Turtle Island (North America)
Tuscarora, 18, 29
Twanas, 164
twins, 68
Two Row Wampum treaty, 29–30

Ungar, Michael, 183–184
United Church, 18
United Nations, 9, 73, 137–138, 139
United Nations Convention on the Prevention and Punishment of the Crime of Genocide, 114
United Nations Convention on the Rights of the Child, 50
United States, 61, 132, 135–137, 177, 254
United States model, 236

UN Standard Minimum Rules for the Administration of Juvenile Justice, 137–138
utilitarianism, 67, 149

validation, 185
values of trauma-informed youth justice, 4–14
critical thinking, 5
holistic approach to addressing crime, 11–13
human dignity, 5–6
participation, 6–9
peace, 9–11
social change, 13–14
Van Buren, Deanna, 197
Van Camp, Tinneke, 235
Vandergoot, Mary E., 96, 99
van der Kolk, Bessel, 87, 91, 93, 94, 98–99
vengeance, 228
victim-centred justice
see also victims
Canadian Victims Bill of Rights, 237–240
case story: victim in a break-and-enter, 230–235
historical sidelining of victims, 228–230
rehabilitation of the victim, 241–242
restorative justice, and victims, 246–247
trauma-informed youth justice as victim-centred, 240–242
victim-centred justice processes, 254
victim movement, 235–240
in the words of the survivors, 243–246
victim impact statement, 232–233
victim movement, 235–240
victim-offender mediation, 166, 167, 172–174
Victim Offender Mediation (VOM) program, 176
Victim Offender Reconciliation Program, 165, 176
victim rehabilitation, 241–242
victimology, 233, 235, 247
victims
see also survivors; victim-centred justice
appropriate victim involvement, 246–247
denial of the victim, 72
disempowerment, 227
dissatisfaction of, 1, 148
experience of criminal justice, 243–245
face-to-face meetings with offenders, 157
future victimization, 95
needs of, and restorative justice, 16, 156–158, 176, 177
ownership of healing, 234
PACT program, 49, 52
pathways to resilience, 192

rehabilitation, 241–242
relational damage, 192
and restorative justice, 246–247
restorative justice, and satisfaction, 235
restorative justice term, discomfort with, 176
satisfaction of, 234–235
trauma-informed care, 190–193
vindication, 211–212
in the words of the survivors, 243–246
working with young youth and children, 192–193
young people as victims, 227
vindication, 192, 211–212
violence, 74, 82
    basic psychological motive, 76
    culture of, 220
    cycle of. *See* cycle of violence
    directed inward and outward, 78
    domestic, 79, 102, 108, 175–176
    family, 79, 102, 108, 117–118
    interpersonal, 108
    intimate partner violence (IPV), 123–124
    male, 108, 115, 119–124, 175–176
    as public health issue, 11
    subculture of violence theory, 71–72
    against women, 116
"Violence in Public Health and Preventative Medicine" (Gilligan), 11
violent crime, 60
Virchow, Rudolph, 11
vision for trauma-informed youth justice system, 3–4
Vogt, Joanne, 105
Volkan, Vamik, 201, 202
voluntary participation, 186

"war against youth," 44
war on drugs, 45, 254
Ward, Tony, 228, 229, 235
warriors, 162–163
Waterloo Region Community Safety and Crime Prevention Council, 217, 220
Weaver, Allan, 160
Wedge, Mark, 168
Wemmers, Jo-Anne, 235
Wendel, Paul Joseph, 255
We Were Children, 37
Whapmagoostui, 208
"What Does Victim Rehabilitation Look Like?", 241–242
"what if" questions, 95
"What Is a Man?" (Oudshoorn), 115–116
"What Makes a Good Youth Probation Officer?" (Saechao), 56–57

"What's Wrong with YOA Bashing? What's Wrong with the YOA?—Recognizing the Limits of Law" (Bala), 46
Wheeler, Paley, 26
White, Heather, 157, 158
White, Katherine, 123
white, male privilege, 224
WHO. *See* World Health Organization (WHO)
Why Does He Do That?: Inside the Minds of Angry and Controlling Men (Bancroft), 122–123
why youth commit crimes. *See* theoretical explanations of youth crimes
Widom, Cathy Spatz, 78
Wilson, Robert, 152
Wilson, Robin, 175
Wilson, Shawn, 5
Winterdyk, John, 50
women
    Indigenous, as victims of violence, 23, 73–74
    in leadership roles, 251–252
    Mother-Child program, 198–200, 203
    and patriarchy. *See* patriarchy
    right to vote, 22
    as second-class citizens, 38
    sexual assault. *See* sexual assault
    and stalking, 120
    violence against, 116
Wood, Chris, 120
World Health Assembly, 11
World Health Organization (WHO), 11, 103
worldview impacts of trauma, 90
The Wretched of the Earth (Fanon), 206

Yang, K. Wayne, 207
Yantzi, Mark, 161, 164–165, 222
YCJA. *See* Youth Criminal Justice Act (YCJA)
YOA. *See* Young Offenders Act
Yoder, Carolyn, 77–78, 200–201
Young Offender Level of Service Inventory/Case Management Inventory (YO-LSI/CMI), 143
Young Offenders Act, 21, 35, 42–47
Young Persons in Conflict with the Law Act, 35
Youth at Risk and Youth Justice: A Canadian Overview (ed. Winterdyk and Smandych), 25, 42
youth courts, 25
youth crime rates, 53
Youth Criminal Justice Act (YCJA), 21, 41
    alternative measures, 51–52
    change in principles, 57–58

Index

conflicting agendas, 55–56
Declaration of Principle, 51
decrease in youth incarceration, 52, 54
described, 50–54
and restorative justice, 155
risk assessment tools, 147
sanctions, purposes of, 130
Sebastien's Law, 58–60
sentencing principles, 53
tracking changes to, 57–61
youth incarceration rate, 136
youth probation officer, 54–57
youth gangs, 45
youth incarceration rates, 41, 52, 54, 136
youth justice system
broken justice system, 1–2
current practices. *See* current youth justice practices
current system. *See* current youth justice system
history of in Canada. *See* history of Canadian youth justice
justice system, purposes of, 129–130
and needs of Indigenous youth, 41
overrepresentation of marginalized populations, 18, 22, 54, 110–114, 135, 151–152, 162
and patriarchy, 38
vision for trauma-informed, 3–4
youth incarceration rates, 41
youth offender, 34
"Youth Pathways to Placement: The Influence of Gender, Mental Health Need and Trauma on Confinement in the Juvenile Justice System" (Espinosa, Sorensen, and Lopez), 116
youth probation officer, 54–57, 147
"Youth Sex Offending, Recidivism and Restorative Justice: Comparing Court and Conference Cases" (Daly, Bouhours, Broadhurst, and Loh), 177

Zehr, Howard, 15, 101, 105, 155, 165, 170, 190, 195, 211, 228–229, 235, 240, 241, 246, 254